M000020512

INTRODUCTION

The language of the street is always strong . . . I confess to some pleasure from the stinging rhetoric of the rattling oath in the mouths of truckmen and teamsters . . . Moreover they who speak them have this elegancy, that they do not trip in their speech. It is a shower of bullets, whilst Cambridge men and Yale men correct themselves and begin again every half sentence.

Ralph Waldo Emerson

Right again! With irritating consistency, Ralph Waldo Emerson keeps coming up with correct answers, even when the questions aren't asked, and well over a century after his death. By what right did this nosy, individualistic Unitarian and Abolitionist rattle the cages of the established Ivy League grammarians, who had painstakingly and with assiduous scholarship set up unalterable paradigms for the English language?

Could it be that Mr. Know-it-all Emerson really *did* know something more about language than the linguists? Was he conscious of the fact that he himself was setting new standards of prose? Did he know, perhaps, that the language was changing daily? Changing in many ways: new words, new uses and variations of meanings of the old words, new spellings and truncations of established words. "Banjo" and "prairie schooner" appear; "pioneer" develops a new definition for itself.

The "telegraph" is patented, publicized and infused into the mainstream vocabulary, almost as fast as "xerography" will be a century later.

Yes, Emerson knew about America's volatile language and protean grammar, but it was Walt Whitman who would exult in it and alter it again; and H. L. Mencken who would boldly declare that "American" was a disjunctive and distinct language, ramified from English, yes, but newborn as an expanding energetic entity unto itself.

Since Americans tended more to be doers than theorists, many of these words came from the shops, factories, farms and forests. The lumberjack gave us "topper" and "logrolling," lifted by politicians and by the journalists who dogged the politicians, to refer to the ever-suspicious activities of that oratorical, legislative breed. Wall Street pre-yuppies presented us with "insider trading" and "crash," the cowboy with "corral" and "cayuse," jazz/swing musicians with "licorice stick" and "ivories," the builders with "skyscrapers" and "high rise." All the major trades added snippets of their argot into this great, simmering basic stew known as the American language. There is a brash and fresh spirit felt in these breezy new idioms and improvised neologisms. Their color, appropriateness and leanings toward terseness give these "trade" words an immediate, workable value, and set them firmly in our memory with a strong mnemonic fix.

Paradoxically, it is this of-the-moment relevancy that can also give them the tag of "faddish" and "in," with the fate of most such words—the fads fade and "in" is soon "out." Where is "hip," "hep," "groovy," "with it," "heavy"? Or the onetime everyday words "Victrola," "Pianola," "trolley car," "auto crank"? Where have all "beatniks" gone? Or "hippies"? Or "Yippies"?

Media terms in the performing arts face the threat of faddish fragility possibly more than any other trade lexicon. Why? Equipment for recording, transmitting or filming evolves rapidly; acting styles change with technology and input levels of a fickle public taste; newer, accelerating technology creates a demand to describe its hardware and procedures in succinct terminology. These working words are created on-the-spot by grips, gaffers, cameramen, carpenters, actors and makeup artists. Sometimes even by directors. Rarely by writers. The lexicographer simply collects them, jots them down and passes them on.

In my case, I do this knowing that language cannot be pinned onto a board like an etymological specimen; that words cannot be hermetically sealed off, or put into a monstrance and worshipped. For words, even at their most rhapsodic, elevated or spiritual levels, are still serving utilitarian purposes.

Many of today's new terms in media, mechanics, music, pop arts and applied technology will become tomorrow's standard speech. This may be upsetting to contemplate for those coming out of schools of higher learning where they still cling to the prejudice of an "exact" definition for every word. They will immediately find out that such exactitude is an illusion, like the search for the Holy Grail or the "perfect mate." A number of the words will have changed or even become obsolete since their dictionary was published; or the words may have lost pungency from overuse.

Using a workable dictionary properly can help alleviate and even dispel the above quandary. This dictionary, deliberately specialized, can help you make your way through the verbal undergrowth of the media jungle.

So, unsheath your machete, don your khaki fatigues and pith helmet, and start cutting your way through. It should be an adventure. Hopefully, an exhilarating one. I hesitate to use the terrible "e" word, but I must warn all readers, there is always a danger of the whole process becoming "educational."

—Edmund Penney
Hollywood, CA

HOW TO USE THIS BOOK

What this book is not

This is not a book for the more arcane technical terms nor the obviously evanescent ones that glisten for a moment in the spotlight of mass media publications. It is neither an etymological-historical root-finder nor an informal wanderer down memory lane.

What it is

This is a dictionary for those who, for whatever reason, have an active interest in the performing arts in mass media and the adjuncts of those arts: hardware, advertising, publicity, to give a few examples.

It is comprised of terms used most often by the people in the various creative, technical and marginal areas of the "business," as it is broadly categorized in "the trades."

How to use it

Words are listed alphabetically. When multiple definitions of a single word are required, they are given. The obsolescent or obsolete definitions are seldom given, unless interwoven with other working terms in constant use.

A definition will be set forth in its most reduced and essential form, sometimes followed by background or augmenting material. This latter part of the explication is for the reader who wants to know more about the word than the definition.

To delineate areas that require more detailed forms, the appendix has various tools-of-the-trade that will be useful to any filmmaker, from tyro to veteran—tools such as a summary budget sheet, a footage-to-time conversion chart, a script format section, among others.

You can extend your comprehension of these basic book terms by noting the nuances and variations in different physical and geographical settings, for media vocabulary has different shadings not only internationally, but from coast to coast, from soundstage to soundstage, or within a production facility itself. At what point does this jargon become "common usage"? Since lexicographers, linguists and semanticists seem to have various theories on this, some contradictory, I've arbitrarily made such decisions on a word-by-word basis.

Since this book is both a dictionary and a working manual for today, and for the immediate future, I have also included in the appendix some basic film forms and graphs that can be used internationally. This is because filmmaking is an increasingly global affair, with planet Earth our soundstage.

The Facts On File
DICTIONARY
OF
FILM AND
BROADCAST
TERMS

A

A and B roll printing   Printing that is done with two or more rolls of film, conformed and matching, with alternate scenes intercut with opaque leaders. Rolls "A" and "B" have a common starting point. When Roll A presents the picture to be duplicated during printing, Roll B presents the OPAQUE LEADER, and vice-versa. This process permits single or double exposures, multiple exposures, and hands-on re-editing by the frame. It also allows for CHECKERBOARD cutting, which eliminates visual film splices on the screen. See A AND B ROLL EDITING.

A and B roll editing   A post-production term used by editor and lab. It refers to two rolls of film, arbitrarily A and B, which contain alternating segments of the original film and overlap each other when DISSOLVES are needed. The A and B technique permits dissolves and FADES to be made without going through another processing generation. Aside from this overlapping footage for dissolves, when one roll is running picture, the alternate roll is running LEADER and vice-versa. Each roll runs the full length of the film. If another roll is added, for TITLES and/or BURN INS, the first additional roll is designated "C". If one more roll is required for any reason, this roll becomes "D" and so forth. These are arbitrary letters, used for clarity in differentiating rolls. All rolls are separated in the editor's log sheets and given to the lab as are instructions for spotting the position and determining the length of dissolves, fades, miscellaneous burn-ins, graphics, titles and CREDITS. See A AND B ROLL PRINTING.

AATON   See CAMERA.

ABC   See AMERICAN BROADCASTING COMPANY.

aberration   The observable and measurable deviation from the ideal in the performance of lenses which impairs the quality of the images formed by the lenses.

abnormal propagation   The interference of atmospheric or ionospheric disturbances with radio waves as they move through space. The result is a degeneration of signals, and sometimes the total eradication of signals by noise.

AB power pack   Dual batteries—A and B—in a self-contained pack that provide requisite voltage power from an ALTERNATING CURRENT source. They are used for location shooting, particularly when out of reach of a plug-in AC or DC source.

abrasions   Unintentional marks and scratches on the surface of the film that are caused by contact with a sharp object. Sometimes deliberate abrasions are put onto film to give it the appearance of old news footage or to help reconstruct the look of black-and-white silent film. See SYNCH MARK.

absorption   To attain pre-selected light values, it is the process by which some transmitted light is retained within the lens system while some is sent on to make contact with the exposed film source or virgin tape.

absorption filter   A light filter which blocks specific wavelengths of light while transmitting others. This gives a color emphasis to the final image that is not naturally inherent in the perceived color balance.

1

abstract film A film that avoids "reality" in its dramatic unfolding, or one that creates a compressed or extreme close-up view of that reality. A film that takes the key elements of story or theme and rearranges them in a nonrepresentational form. Some examples of abstract films are: *Dogstar Man* (1959–1964) 16mm color/black and white—Stan Brakhage (78 minutes); *Chinese Fire Drill* (1968) 16mm color—Will Hindle (24 minutes); and *Andy Warhol's Exploding Plastic Inevitable* (1966) color/black and white—Ronald Nameth (30 minutes). Many of the abstract film techniques, which derive from MONTAGE and SPECIAL EFFECTS, were utilized by Stanley Kubrick in his *2001: A Space Odyssey*. These techniques—mixed with others—have been used extensively in music videos.

A/B switching A system in TV and electronics that allows two separate input sources to be routed through one input. It is used in the titling or BURN-INS of names, or in the mixing of other video or audio elements.

AC See ALTERNATING CURRENT or ASSISTANT CAMERAMAN.

Academy aperture See ACADEMY STANDARDS.

Academy awards Annual presentations of the OSCAR by the ACADEMY OF MOTION PICTURE ARTS AND SCIENCES. The Oscars recognize achievements in the following categories: acting, art direction, cinematography, costume design, directing, documentary, film editing, foreign language film, makeup, music, best picture, short films, sound, sound effects, visual effects and writing.

Academy Directory The directory of professional motion picture performers that is published biannually by the ACADEMY OF MOTION PICTURE ARTS AND SCIENCES. Each entry includes the performer's name, picture, and usually the talent agent or manager.

Academy leader A special industry-standardized film LEADER, which is placed at the HEAD and TAIL ends of RELEASE PRINTS. The Academy leader contains threading instructions and other information useful to the FILM EDITOR, NEGATIVE CUTTER and PROJECTIONIST, such as standby marks, sound-bleep placement, etc. The name is derived from ACADEMY OF MOTION PICTURE ARTS AND SCIENCES.

Academy of Motion Picture Arts and Sciences An internationally recognized academy for the motion picture industry, that is located in Beverly Hills, California. The Academy selects the nominees and final winners for the various Oscar categories. The Academy, in conjunction with the contracted television network, also supervises the production of the annual Awards Ceremony. See ACADEMY AWARDS.

Academy of Television Arts and Science (ATAS) The television counterpart to the ACADEMY OF MOTION PICTURE ARTS AND SCIENCES. ATAS gives out the EMMY awards, and sponsors publications and seminars.

Academy Standards Standards agreed upon by the Academy of Motion Picture Arts and Sciences setting specifications for projectors, film leaders and camera apertures and ratio-framing.

"A" camera ("B", "C" camera, etc.) The letter designation given to a specific camera in a multicamera situation. Each camera is slated and its camera reports recorded with this letter.

accelerated motion An effect of faster-than-normal motion that is achieved by running the camera at a slower frame rate than the 24 frames per second standard. This means that an interval is covered in less frames, resulting in apparent fast motion.

acceptance angle The two-dimensional angle that describes the particular area covered by a lens or a light meter.

access   Cable broadcasting production time that is accessible to the public. See PUBLIC ACCESS.

account executive   A member of the advertising agency staff who serves as business and creative mediator between the TV station or production company and the SPONSOR.

account group   Advertising agency cadre chosen to handle the creative and managerial responsibilities for one specific client.

accuracy   In news, documentary and general reportage, correct names, locations and dates are of the utmost importance not only to interviewees but to the general viewing audience, which tends to assume that media reports will be truthful. Such assumptions demand respect and imply responsibility on the part of the news-gathering and news-presenting team. Further, unverified accusations, misnaming of persons, or statements of personal disparagement can lead to lawsuits against the entire station or the specific reporter. Many newspaper and magazine editorials, as well as media classes, have become sharply critical of media distortion. On the other hand, the media has been critical of the increasing demands on reporters to reveal their sources, which both sources and reporters regard as an invasion of their constitutional and ethical rights.

ace   A spotlight powered by a 1000-watt bulb.

ACE   See AMERICAN CINEMA EDITORS.

AC erasing head   The head used on a MAGNETIC RECORDER to erase existing magnetic information and thereby clear the recording tape. It operates on ALTERNATING CURRENT (AC).

"A" certificate   ("A" stands for adult.) Rating certificate given by the British Board of Film Censors. It indicates a film that may be seen by children under sixteen only when accompanied by a parent or guardian.

ACES   See AUTOMATED CAMERA EFFECTS SYSTEM.

acetate base   Standard base for motion picture film that consists principally of cellulose acetate. Synonymous with SAFETY BASE.

acetate tape   Sound-tape with magnetically sensitive oxide coating on an acetate backing. Used for home and professional recording and duplication.

acetone   A clear, flammable liquid that is highly volatile and used to clean film print surfaces, SPLICERS, and various pieces of editing and camera gear.

Acey-Deucey   The original name for the peanut light, a small Fresnel lamp with a 200-watt quartz lamp, used for detail in close shots and close-ups; for example, a calendar insert detail where one day might fill the entire frame. The name came from the Hollywood company who developed it for multiple-camera filming of TV shows, the Acey-Deucey Co. The light is still used in professional TV and film production.

A-channel   Along with the B-channel, the two channels for stereo recording or general audio input/output. For use with speakers, microphones, recording decks, and other appropriate stereo equipment.

achromatic lens   A lens that has been corrected for distortions, such as longitudinal or chromatic aberration. All high quality lenses are achromatic.

AC noise   Noise generated in an alternating current system by overloading the response capability of the electrical receiving unit.

acoustic   The original vibrational, non-electronic method for recording sound cylinders and discs that was pioneered by Thomas A. Edison and others. Used as an adjective today to describe a group of instruments that are non-electronic, i.e., ones that are blown, struck, or bowed. Also used in the singular, as in, "It's an acoustic, not an electronic, flute."

acoustic filter   A selecting and absorbing sound unit that minimizes or virtually eradicates certain audio frequencies while simultaneously permitting preselected frequencies to pass through.

acoustical absorptivity   The differential between the sound-absorption capability of a surface and its ratio of sound reflectivity in relation to that absorption.

acoustical feedback   Partial return of sound output to the input in a speaker system. The cumulative interactive buildup between microphone and speaker usually results in a screeching sound.

acoustics   The science of transmission and reception of sound with particular emphasis on the effects of that reception. It also refers to the sound-receptive qualities of the enclosure itself: the sound stage, the TV studio, the auditorium, sound isolation booth or amphitheater. This science came to fruition in live theater in opera houses and theaters.

acquisition of rights   The finding, negotiating, contracting and optioning of the rights of a dramatic property. The contract has a date on which the agreement is considered in force as well as a date of expiration. It states all relevant names of the contracting parties and specifies the responsibilities of each.

AC receiver   Reception unit from an ALTERNATING CURRENT source only. The plug-in family radio of the '30s and '40s was an AC receiver. Alarm-radios that are powered by AC are other examples. A battery-operated unit would be a DC RECEIVER.

across the board   TV or radio programs regularly scheduled at the same time each week.

ACS   See ACTIVE COMMUNICATIONS SATELLITE.

acted delivery   In acting for commercials, a delivery of the lines "in character." The character may be a voice-over cockroach or an on-camera football coach. In opposition to the matter-of-fact AN-NOUNCER delivery.

acting   The performing work and studies of actors and actresses in the media performing arts and live theater, regarded as a discipline or profession. It is also used to describe the process in a performance situation, "The acting didn't seem uniformly polished throughout the teleplay."

acting out   In the new "reality" TV and in documentaries' restaging of events that happened, the particular incident or general event is often recreated by scripting scenes that are then "acted out" by the real persons involved in the story or by actors.

actinoelectricity   Electricity produced by the action of radiant energy upon crystals. It is the principle behind CORDLESS SYNCH; also called crystal synch and cableless synch. It is state-of-the-art for location and reality sound and allows for a wide range of uses for body mikes.

action   What is filmed or taped within camera range; the activity of a given scene. Term that differentiates PICTURE from SOUND on a reel of film or roll of tape for editorial purposes in post-production.

"Action!"   Cue given by the DIRECTOR or ASSISTANT DIRECTOR when the sound and picture cameras are up to speed to start the scene. This cue is sometimes given on a count, if it is a multiple-cue, or by a hand signal if it is a single cue that has to be given during the taping of the scene. In documentary, in order to informalize the proceedings and put the interviewee at ease, the director will sometimes cue the on-camera interviewee with his or her own name or by having interviewees respond directly to a question.

action field   See FIELD.

action outline   A written, structural form that delineates the physical dramatic progression of the film from sequence to sequence, or in a detailed action outline from SCENE to scene.

action properties or props   Used by on-camera performers in a filmed scene that are handled pointedly, to accent the dramaturgical content, or heighten the scenic reality. For example, a telephone, a gun, a car key or a book would be a prop. Also known as HAND PROPS.

action still   A photograph of a scene shot during rehearsal, or even while the scene is being filmed, to show the action essence of that scene. Also, a blow-up of a single frame from the actual filmed footage. Such frame blow-ups are used for publicity stills, to accompany releases, as bases for posters and lobby showcards, as well as for archival material about the film itself.

action viewer   VIEWFINDER used by the CAMERAMAN, sometimes attached to the camera, which approximates the FRAMING of the LENS. Used for spotting action, often in NEWS and DOCUMENTARY situations. The director often uses this type of meter for prespotting camera moves and setups. Often used for in-the-field SPECIAL EVENTS and sports COVERAGE.

active communications satellite (ACS)   A comsat with receivers and transmitters aboard for receiving beamed signals from a ground terminal, powerfully amplifying these signals, and retransmitting the enhanced signal to a different ground terminal. These interacting terminals and satellites have been meshed to give us the international scope of a worldwide "network," capable of many interlinking combinations.

active jamming   Deliberate tampering with electromagnetic waves by radiation or reradiation to interfere with the transmission and reception of electromagnetic signals, particularly in communications. Signals can be jammed for political, commercial or religious reasons, as well as accidentally through technical incompetence.

active lines   The 525 lines (in the NTSC system) that make up the TV images on our television sets. Inactive lines are made invisible by electronically blanking them out.

active voice   The best grammatical form for writing DIALOGUE, GENERAL DIRECTION, PERSONAL DIRECTION. The active voice brings a feeling of immediacy by using the ongoing present tense, thus avoiding a neutral sense of time, a passive sense with no strong action verbs, and an implied feeling of an event already past.

actor   Any person, animal, or product appearing in front of the camera as the subject or one of the subjects of the scene or shot. Any person on-camera in a DOCUMENTARY film, for example, although speaking for and appearing as himself or herself, is commonly referred to or utilized as the "actor." "Actor" is emerging as the generic term covering all these areas, including the category of ACTRESS. The more restricted use of the term "actor" applies to a person performing a role in any dramatic production in any medium. See HERO and HEROINE.

Actor's Equity Assocation (AEA)   Union for professional live theater actors. Singers and dancers who also act usually have dual "live" theater associations: AEA, AGVA (American Guild of Variety Artists) or AGMA (American Guild of Musical Artists).

Actor's Studio   School based on the Stanislavsky method, but adapted for American dramaturgy. Started by Lee Strasberg and his wife, Paula, in New

York City, it is now run by their daughter, Anna. The roll of students includes such names as Marlon Brando, Montgomery Clift, Jane Fonda, Marilyn Monroe, Maureen Stapleton, Eli Wallach, and Shelley Winters. It introduced, in the 1950s, a new, more "naturalistic" style into acting on stage and in front of the camera.

actress   The female counterpart of the word ACTOR.

actuality   The real sound ambience of an event, as opposed to added and mixed sound, foleying, additive music or narration. It is referred to as "sound bite" when you hear the off-camera as well as the on-camera reporter.

actuality programming   Programs that supposedly tackle stories "as they are," but often with a sensationalistic edge. Then too, much of the "actuality" is recreated in dramatized scenes.

acutance   The ability to reproduce sharp edges on an image in reference to film stocks or lenses.

adapt   To write a TREATMENT, i.e., a detailed outline or screenplay derived from material from another medium: novel, play, short story, stage musical, biography, autobiography, classic fiction, newspaper or magazine article.

adaptation   The noun for the above verb, ADAPT. The adaptation generally refers to the completed work, as a written entity.

adder   A color TV receiver circuit that amplifies the basic received signal.

additional dialogue replacement (ADR)   Additional words, phrases or scenes added to the script during filming or in post-production. In its abbreviated form it refers to the entire electro-mechanical process of adding new dialogue tracks by remixing, live recording or looping. It's a TV term analogous to film's ELECTRONIC LINE REPLACEMENT. See LOOPING.

additive color   An image system that utilizes two colored lights in combination to create a third.

additive primaries   Primary colors that can be blended to create a broad range of colors. The TV primaries are red, green, and blue.

addressable converter   TV set converters that allow the viewer special access to special cable, satellite or pay-per-view programs.

address code   The digital videotape system that employs control or cue track signals for retrieval.

ADI (area of dominant station influence)   Acronym used by the American Research Bureau. This market research tool is a classification that designates which areas watch their local TV channels most.

adjacent channel selectivity   The pinpointing of specific TV channels and cutting out of signals from contiguous channels to get a clear and clean reception.

ad-lib   Jokes, responses, introductory remarks or general commentaries that are improvised by performers; extemporized. However, much seeming-off-the-cuff humor and so-called spur-of-the-moment repartee is written-and-rehearsed material, performed in such a way as to make it look offhand. From the Latin *ad libitum*—"at one's pleasure."

ADR   See ADDITIONAL LINE REPLACEMENT.

Adult Film Association of America   An organization that promotes the distribution of soft-core and hard-core pornographic and sexually explicit films. It has a membership of producers, distributors and exhibitors of such films.

advance   The frames between picture and synchronous sound on composite film prints. This can be manually or mechanically adjusted to the pull-up requirements of the particular projector.

Advance can also mean money put into a project to be applied against its total production costs. A writer will sometimes receive an advance that secures and options the property, i.e., the screenplay, for the production company. This is seldom full payment with the balance to be paid in cash before filming begins as well as percentage payments from the producer's gross or net or residuals. For example, a composer sometimes gets an advance as a start-up fee to begin composing the score, or the art director to start sketching the sets.

advertisement   See COMMERCIAL.

advertising agency   A company that creates ads and ad campaigns in media for the sponsor or client.

advertising council   A group of member advertising agencies and others who sponsor public service announcements in all media.

advertising director   One who serves as a corporate liaison between the sponsor or client company and the advertising agency handling the client's account. The advertising director (also called ADVERTISING MANAGER) is often the person who represents the sponsor during the filming or taping of commercials and who is physically present on the set or location.

advertising-supported programming   Most commercial TV is advertising-supported with the exception of public service announcements and public service programming. See PUBLIC BROADCASTING SYSTEM.

AEA   See ACTOR'S EQUITY ASSOCIATION.

aerial, antenna   Equipment used to receive or transit broadcast signals. When it was used originally for radio it received, transmitted or relayed waves for local, regional or transcontinental broadcasts.

Now it is used in conjunction with cable and UHF stations for stereocasts.

aerial cinematography   Filming from planes, hot-air balloons, blimps and helicopters using special aerial mounts. It also includes plane-to-plane shooting, sky-diving filming with a helmet camera, shooting from a hang-glider or any other airborne manner.

aerial image   A true image formed at a given plane in space; this is done by a specialized device. A "floating" image is projected by this device within an optical system for developing purposes or for reprojection used in animation and for special effects.

aerial image animation stand   A customized animation stand that uses a projection system to generate an aerial image at the platen plane. This permits optical superimposition of cell animation over any other images—live, animated or computer-generated.

aerial mount   Special gear with high-precision locking systems to secure a camera to the particular airborne vehicle. Aerial mounts are required to have Federal Aviation Agency approval for filming in the United States. Other countries have their own systems of approval.

aerial shot   Any SHOT made from an airborne vehicle: film, tape or still.

AFC   See AUTOMATIC FREQUENCY CONTROL.

AFI   See AMERICAN FILM INSTITUTE.

AFM   See AMERICAN FEDERATION OF MUSICIANS.

AFTRA   See AMERICAN FEDERATION OF RADIO AND TELEVISION ARTISTS.

AGC   See AUTOMATIC GAIN CONTROL.

agency of record   The agency handling a specific corporate account which places that account's radio and TV ads.

agent   Person representing media acting talent, WRITERS, DIRECTORS, CAMERAMAN, and other crew members, including staff PRODUCERS and HYPHENATE producers. For services rendered by the agent for his clients—securing interviews, bargaining for fees and contractual advantages, and giving general career advice— the agent is paid 10 percent of the talent's gross earnings. Sometimes the agent will also serve as business manager for the talent for an additional negotiated percentage. This arrangement, however, has tended to decline because of the growing tendency toward bifurcation of functions between business manager and agent.

agitation   Deliberate turbulence created in film-processing to aerate the BATH to give a more even development of the negative.

AGS   See ANIMATED GRAPHICS SYSTEM.

aircheck   Originally a radio term from the 1930s, it was a disk recording made directly from a radio broadcast. When used for rebroadcast it was referred to as an "electrical transcription." Today the term refers to any recording of broadcast material, audio or video.

air column   Air volume within a speaker horn or acoustical chamber.

air date   Broadcast day, scheduled for date, time and channel of any given program.

air gap   Intermediate air space between magnetic or electrical points.

air quality   Technical broadcast requirements and standards for broadcast materials. Also referred to as BROADCAST QUALITY.

air squeegee or air squeeze   A part of the film developing process where a continuous jet of air blows on the motion picture film as it goes from the final wash to the dry box. This blows the water off the surface of the drying film.

air time   Segments of time allocated for programming during the broadcasting day. Air time can be as little as the time-purchase of a 10-second commercial spot to a multi-hour miniseries. Purchases are made by the ad agencies or time buyers for the client, or sometimes by the production companies directly.

air-to-air   Filming from one traveling aircraft to another. It is analogous to the PICTURE CAR being filmed by the CAMERA CAR. Air-to-air shots are often made using special AERIAL MOUNTS. See TYLER MOUNT and STEADICAM.

airwaves   An umbrella term covering the pathways of all transmitted broadcasting signals, radio or TV.

album-oriented rock   See AOR.

algol   A computer language that is used internationally. It was developed to handle logic problems. Used in presetting animation and animated camera movements in advanced animation systems. The term is derived from a blending of ALGOrithmic with Language.

align   To adjust the circuits of an electronic receiver or transmitter to achieve the proper reception of incoming signals.

alignment   The fine-tuning of pre-tuned circuits to achieve the desired frequency response in a receiver.

Alliance of Motion Picture and Television Producers (AMPTP)   Organization of the producers of major features and TV series. It was formed in 1982 as a negotiating force and as mediator in labor/management disputes within the film and TV industry. It has been a negotiator in various strikes in recent years.

alligator clamps   Metal spring clamps with serrated jaws—usually with shockproof, plastic-covered handles—that hold various objects in place during the production of a film. Alligator clamps have many uses: to clamp an improvised FLAG or CUTTER to a piece of furniture while lighting a room; to clamp a blanket between CENTURY STANDS for an on-the-spot sound baffle; to clamp a small tree branch to a century stand to use in front of the camera for a through-the-leaves shot, etc. Alligator clamps developed originally as hot-wiring clamps attached to the end of cables for going straight into electrical power sources, and are still so used.

all-metal tube   Vacuum tube that is enclosed in metal instead of glass. Forerunner of transistors, which bypass the vacuum clarify areas and replace that function with semiconductors.

allocation   The assignment of computer storage locations to main routines and subroutines. This sets the absolute values of symbolic addresses. It is used for pre-sets in on-line editing, and for programming animation moves.

alternate scenes   Cutaway and insert scenes, to work with the MASTER SHOT. The function of the alternate scene is to allow the editor a greater choice of elements with which to build the master. Alternate scenes also refers to special additional scenes, shot as possible replacements for existing scenes, and slated accordingly. In documentary filming and post-production, alternate scenes refer to a full complement of possible cutaway, MOS walking shots, graphics, scenic shots, stills, artifacts, etc. If the master shot is #27 and the close-up coverage shot is #27-A, the alternate scene could be slated #27-AA.

alternate voice copy   In commercials, the dialogue between Voice #1 and Voice #2. It is used on radio or in TV as VOICE OVER accompaniment to augmenting visuals.

alternating current (AC)   An electrical current that reaches maximum strength in one direction of flow, then reverses itself until it reaches maximum strength in the opposite direction. This cycle is continuously repeated; the number of cycles per second determines the frequency. AC is the standard wall-plug current. Standard United States' voltage is 110/120. For heavier-pull (industrial use or for washing machines, electrical ranges, etc.) 220 is generally used. These currents vary from country to country. The opposite of AC is DIRECT CURRENT.

alternative programming   Programs available on channels other than the big three networks (ABC, NBC and CBS) such as PBS, CABLE and PUBLIC ACCESS.

alternative television   TV fare, often on cable, with public access. Programming provided from sources other than the main networks or syndication makes up the bulk of this alternative scheduling and broadcasting.

AM   See AMPLITUDE MODULATION.

amateur   Performer or CREW member who is not paid and/or union-affiliated. Used derogatorily to refer to a person working in the performing media who has a nonprofessional attitude. Amateur also means someone who performs or serves on crew as a hobby or someone who is new to the professional scene.

amateur bands   Radio frequencies assigned by the FEDERAL COMMUNICATIONS COMMISSION to broadcasting amateurs only, the HAMS.

amateur station   A licensed transmitting station owned and operated by an amateur staff that is prohibited from receiving monetary gain for their services.

amateur station call letters   Easily differentiated from commercial call letters (three or four letters), e.g., KNX, WMKQ, WGN, KWKW; or network abbreviations—CBS, PBS, NBC, ABC, TBS, CNN, etc. The amateur call letters start with a prefix of one or two letters. This is followed by a numeral that indicates location, and then two or three additional letters, such as KZ910 or WR315. See AMATEUR STATION.

ambience   The general look, feeling or mood infusing the mise-en-scene. In sound, the term refers to the interior or exterior PRESENCE, the physical quality of the prevailing sound of an area, minus music, DIALOGUE or SOUND EFFECTS.

ambient light   Surrounding light of a particular scene that doesn't hit the performer(s) directly. It may come from the side, from above or below; when it comes from behind and the foreground figure is silhouetted, it is called BACKLIGHTING. It is used for low key effects, for a "natural" look, for "romantic mood," for suspenseful ambience, and in dramatic scenes more often than comedy.

ambient noise   In sound recording, the ambient sound level of the studio or location in relation to its impingement on the desired, received audio signals that are to be highlighted: dialogue, foreground synch-sound, or post-production foleying.

American Broadcasting Company (ABC)   One of the three major national TV networks in the United States of America. It was once an affiliate of NBC.

American Cinema Editors (ACE)   A TV and film professional society that originated with motion picture editors. It is in charge of presenting the annual Eddie Awards for best editing.

American Federation of Musicians (AFM)   The largest union for professional band and orchestra members who work live and in mass media.

American Federation of Television and Radio Artists (AFTRA)   A union representing radio performers that started with the American Federation of Radio Artists. With the advent of television, and after going through various forms with alternative affiliations, the union emerged as AFTRA. It is comprised of actors, singers, dancers and specialty performers (like magicians).

American Film Institute (AFI)   AFI was designed as an academy to stimulate and educate beginning writers, directors and technicians in high-level professional filmmaking. It approached this challenge by setting up a curriculum and a teaching and administrative staff. It was first located at the Greystone mansion in Beverly Hills, California, a large estate that was used not only for the school, but as a setting for many student film projects. AFI currently occupies the former home of Immaculate Heart, a Catholic school for girls. The academic program, augmented by filmmaking grants, continues. A monthly magazine is published by the Institute with an emphasis on Hollywood filmmaking as well as its own in-house activities. Its lifetime achievement awards are usually televised. In its caretaker capacity it has a growing archival library and works both independently and in conjunction with other film groups in film restoration efforts.

American National Standards Institute (ANSI)   The nonprofit organization that establishes and maintains technical criteria for film and television worldwide. Anything below these levels is considered technically substandard. ANSI was formerly known as ASA (the American Standards Association); veteran cameramen, among other technical crew personnel, still use the term "ASA rating." See also ASA SPEED.

American Society of Cinematographers (ASC)   An honorary organization of professional cinematographers that has its headquarters in Hollywood, California.

American Society of Composers, Authors and Publishers (ASCAP)   A national society that protects and polices the use of composers' and lyricists' works.

American Women in Radio and Television Professional group of women in creative and executive positions in TV stations or networks, radio and advertising agencies.

AM light Early-morning light, with heavily articulated shadows, that gives a person a different skin-tone quality than midday or late afternoon light. When accompanied by haze not yet burned off by the sun, a special soft, diffused look can be achieved. It is preferred by many cinematographers for its fresh, non-glare look. Along with twilight, AM light is often referred to as the "magic hours," or "golden hours." Flesh tones tend to go reddish at these times, though, and filming may require special camera filters.

amperage pull The total amperage required in a given shoot that is designated by the demand of the total number of lights and other units requiring electricity. In production, it is necessary to check with the head electrician at a studio and, more critically, when shooting in a "practical" location (the real factory, the real school, the real apartment). If the total "pull" is not properly determined, it is just a matter of precious time before an electrical overload and blowout will occur. Because of such oversight, many assembly lines have been shut down, cruise ships' electrical circuits shorted out and salesrooms' lighting short-circuited.

amplification Increase in an audio or video signal from one point to another, in whatever medium one is using. This increase may be measured in decibels or slated as a ratio.

amplification factor The stated amplification ratio and differential between output and input magnitudes. See AMPLIFICATION.

amplification noise Extraneous cracklings, hummings, whinings and generally unwanted sounds that are not part of the actual signal. Amplification noise should be regarded as one of the arch-enemies to anyone attempting to achieve clear, natural sound recording. See AMPLIFICATION.

amplifier A device that makes an electronic signal louder without decreasing its power; an electronic part that increases the power or voltage of incoming signals.

amplify To add to the strength of a current or signal; to increase the voltage.

amplitude modulation (AM) AM radio is the original standard for commercial broadcasting, the opposite of frequency modulation. AM modulates a carrier frequency current by varying its amplitude. See also FREQUENCY MODULATION.

AMPTP See ASSOCIATION OF MOTION PICTURE AND TELEVISION PRODUCERS.

AM tuner The electrical unit that converts amplitude-modulated signals into low-level audio frequencies. The standard tuner for the AM radio bands.

ANA See ASSOCIATION OF NATIONAL ADVERTISERS.

anaglyph Three-dimensional picture comprised of two images, one overlapping the other, viewed through 3-D "glasses" with two eyepieces of different but complementary colors. These colors are keyed to work with those on the screen for accurate coloration and apparent "depth."

analyzer An instrument used to test and check the working levels of electronic equipment.

anamorphic lens A lens designed and manufactured to deliberately distort an image to optical specifications. The lens compresses the image along one axis of the focal plane which results in a "squeezed" image. By projecting the resultant image through a correcting lens, the ultimate picture emerges as "normal." It is usually used in a wide-screen format.

anchor   The key on-camera person on a news broadcast. The news editor-presenter of that broadcast who, with the show's producer, allocates news assignments to newscasters and writes copy. The anchor sets the tone and style of the show and is the "headliner" that people watch to see.

ancillary rights   The additional, extended rights to distribute and merchandise a media product (film, tape, record, CD or disc). T-shirts, records, comic books, fictionalized novels derived from screenplays, spinoffs into TV specials or series, etc. are considered to be ancillary rights. Often, they produce more net income than the main work, i.e., the film or TV show. These rights should be negotiated separately and specifically, as they are all potential sources of income.

angel hair   The flaking slivers of film that are created when the film edges scrape against sharp edges or burrs, usually metallic, within the projector's drive mechanism or moving through the film gate. Angel hair, despite its poetic name, means immediate trouble. Also called skivings.

angle shots   Every shot is made from a specific angle, but as used in film and TV, the term refers to angles other than eye-level and HEAD-ON SHOTS. The angles referred to, for example, could be LOW ANGLE, DUTCH ANGLE, extreme close shot, HIGH SHOT, etc.

animal handler   A general term for all animal overseeing, and a specific term for a person working with smaller animals. It includes domestic animals working in scenes like cats, dogs, rabbits, or small, wild animals trained to work in front of a camera. The American Society for the Prevention of Cruelty to Animals

(ASPCA) is required to be on the set of any union-made film during the filming of sequences in which animals are used. For large animals, the animal trainer is often referred to as the wrangler.

Animated Graphics System (AGS)   A system that allows a video image to be electronically altered, diminished or augmented.

animation   Creation of apparent movement by sequential CEL animation or by moving objects in front of the camera and filming them in this articulated movement a frame at a time. Animation takes advantage of the brain's capacity to react to filmed or taped images in such a way as to fuse disparate images into a continuous flow. Objects set before the camera to be animated include cutouts, puppets and products to be featured in commercials. See TABLETOP PHOTOGRAPHY, CLAYMATION and TIME LAPSE.

In acting, animation is the level of liveliness and energy of an actor during filming or working live-on-stage.

animation camera   Camera used for filming animation. It is usually mounted on an animation stand, with its optical axis vertical so that it looks down on the objects being photographed. The camera-drive meter allows the film to move forward one frame at a time.

animation stand or crane   A precise, customized camera mount for animation usage. This mount is capable of accurate gradations of movement above the art work, pegboard or platen. The unit has various capabilities for subtle and complex moves.

animation table   A flat table with a circular rotary inset to allow the CEL to be turned to any angle for observation, matching, inking or painting. See ANIMATION, ANIMATION CAMERA.

animator   Person who draws, inks, paints or creates electronic images for animated pictures. It is sometimes the title for the person in charge of all aspects of animation, the animation director. Since much of today's animation has computer tie-ins, the animator must be able to work manually (for drawing) as well as mechanically and electronically. Some images are totally computer-generated while others have computerized tie-ins.

Annie Oakley   A free pass for a motion picture, live performance or a large-screen televised event. This name is derived from the famous markswoman's stunt of throwing a playing card into the air and shooting a hole through it. From this, an "Annie Oakley" came to mean any punched free theatrical ticket or complimentary pass.

announcement   A full COMMERCIAL or a SPOT announcement; an advertisement.

announcer   A voice-over or on-camera person who introduces and closes a radio or TV program, and gives informational and transitional announcements during the broadcast.

ANSI   See AMERICAN NATIONAL STANDARDS INSTITUTE.

answer print   First COMPOSITE print from the LAB with sound, music, picture, titles and FADES, DISSOLVES and OPTICAL EFFECTS. A print potentially ready for its release audience. (Also called a RELEASE PRINT.) However, there are nearly always visual corrections to be made, and even changes in sound, so that the first answer print generally serves as a guide to fine-tuning the prints that follow. There is then this gradation of difference: The answer print often precedes the first release print.

antenna coupler   Electronic junction unit designed to connect the receiver or transmitter to the antenna line that is used to determine the workable range of reception or transmission.

antenna effective area   A square of wavelength multiplied by the power gain in a given direction.

antenna lens   A configuration of vanes of metal or dielectric materials that focus microwave beams in a way that is analogous to the focusing function of an optical lens. Allows an electronic configuration to be focused in a similar manner as by an optical lens.

anthology series   One that has different stories with different characters, written by numerous writers over the span of the series; as opposed to a soap opera or sitcom where certain characters from the same group appear on each program. With PBS and cable, we have seen the re-emergence of documentary series, e.g., re-release of such series as "Victory at Sea," or the Frank Capra "Why We Fight" group, as well as new documentaries from various sources put under one particular series title that give a general description of all segments, e.g., "nature," "World War II and after," "science," etc. Also, new documentary series are now being produced for TV release.

antihero   See NONHERO.

AOR   A broadcasting format of album-oriented rock; specially selected rock programming built around an "old favorite" album or a newly released album. This can be a single-program or a general policy of the broadcasting station.

a-page   An inserted additional page in a treatment, teleplay or screenplay. An example of this insert pagination: a new page following page 12 and preceding page 13 becomes 12-a. If still another page needs to be added before page 13, this becomes 12-b, and so on. This system allows additions to script pages without renumbering.

aperture   Refers to the adjustable lens diaphragm that rises, with a wider or smaller opening, to regulate the amount of light that reaches the film. In a camcorder's lens openings, aperture is calibrated and marked in F NUMBERS. The lower the number, the greater amount of light that enters; conversely, the higher the number, the less the amount of light. In cameras, the aperture helps determine the effective speed of the lens. See EFFECTIVE APERTURE and FOCAL LENGTH.

In projectors, the aperture is set by the opening in the particular APERTURE PLATE.

aperture mask   The perforated plate interposed between three basic-color electron guns, red-green-blue, and a phosphor-dot screen all enclosed within a TV color-picture tube.

aperture plate   The plate in a camera or projector located close to where the photographic image is exposed or projected. For each gauge of film, the projector aperture is slightly smaller than the camera aperture in order to mask imperfections at the edges of the image and simplify correct FRAMING.

apochromatic lens   A LENS corrected for CHROMATIC ABERRATION and the consequent unclear focus, by bringing light of three wavelengths to a common focus. Lenses designed for accurate copy work are often apochromatic.

apple box   Single unit RISER that is usually made of wood and used to lift people and objects into camera range. Today's professional apple boxes are approximately $24'' \times 14'' \times 8''$; a half-apple is $4''$ high, a pancake $2''$ high. Often used to raise an actor to a higher level than the other person(s) working in the scene. Also used on irregular ground to provide a firm footing as well as additional height. The original apple box was just that, and the standard size reflects that origin.

approach   A writing style that determines the delivery of a story. The approach can be hard-hitting and attention-getting, it can be cool and lucid, heated and emotional, a frontal attack or a laid-back lead-in. The nature of the story should determine the approach. The trend in the '80s has been a drift toward frenetic sensationalism and so-called reality programming.

Approach can also refer to the movement of the camera toward the subject, in whatever manner, and with whatever gear.

appropriation   The budgeted and approved costs of a TV advertising campaign.

apron   Lip of a proscenium stage extending past the proscenium arch to the extreme downstage edge. "Playing it in one" refers to the apron area.

Arbitron Ratings Company   Along with competitor A. C. Nielsen Company, it is one of the two major rating organizations for television. A television rating percentile is based on all the potential viewers in a given area who are viewing the targeted program at the time the survey is made. This is done by direct phoning and questioning, checking logs of families selected to keep "viewing diaries," monitoring electronically pre-selected homes and by follow-up personal spot-surveys. Radio audience surveys are basically similar. Ratings are vital to broadcasting stations and networks because they determine the audience size which determines what the station can charge for its commercial time-slots which pay for their broadcasting. Program and personnel changes come directly from evaluations of these ratings, and alterations of program style or outright cancellation can be the end result. See NIELSEN TELEVISION INDEX.

arc gap   Space between negative and positive arcs in carbon-arc projectors, and the anode and cathode in the xenon arc projector. See ANODE.

arc lamp   See ARC LIGHT.

arc light   The illumination from an arc light comes from ionized, glowing gases generated by a burning arc between electrodes, different from the incandescent lamp, where the light is produced by a heated filament. The heat from arc lights is far more intense than in incandescent lamps. The arc lights work on DC, but some can work off DC as well. Arc generation of light is used for illuminating interior sets or exterior night scenes; also used in some theatrical motion picture projectors. Also called arc lamp.

area of dominant station influence. See ADI.

arranger (music)   The person who takes the composer's lead sheets or taped melody and orchestrates it for a specific musical group: combo, rock group, band, symphonic orchestra. Arrangements are often the critical difference between a song being a hit or a flop. Arrangers can take an indifferent melody and give it strength, clarity and style. A good classical example is the banal motif on which Beethoven built his powerful Symphony number 3 (the "Eroica"). A more recent and "popular" example would be the arrangement of the Beatles' songs for the film *Yellow Submarine*. For the film, the arrangements are calibrated to beats measured in tenths of seconds, when a click track is used. Often, the composer does his or her own arrangements. With the advent of the electronic, computerized scoring, the composer-arranger often works from a lead sheet, adding the harmony and actual "instrumentation," sometimes during the recording session itself.

Arri   The industry designation for an Arriflex camera. It was developed as a World War II combat camera by the Germans and it went on to become an important peacetime news and documentary camera in both 16 and 35mm formats. Its use became more widespread as it developed faster blimping capacity and, ultimately, self-blimping. The 16mm versions are used for news-gathering, industrials, commercials, and DOCUMENTARIES. 35mm models are also used for commercials, high-budget documentaries and industrials, as well as feature motion pictures. Conversely, features or parts of features are short on 16mm self-blimped models, and blown up into 35mm. The "Arri" in Arriflex comes from the inventors' names: "Ar" from Arnold and "ri" from Richter. See BLIMP and CAMERA, MOTION PICTURE TYPES.

art card   Special black cardboard on which to mount titles, credits or graphics for photography. The standard lettering consists of white letters or numbers hot-pressed onto the art card, but there are many color gradations in the art-card spectrum to allow for greater creative flexibility.

art department   The group in charge of designing and fabricating graphic concepts and materials for filming and taping who work within a studio or production house.

art director   The person in charge of the physical "look," the coordinated graphic visualization, of the film. The art director's duties consist in any or all of the following: making preliminary sketches, drawing STORY BOARDS, color-coordinating scenic PROPS with one another and with WARDROBE, sketching basic scenic designs, consulting with lighting GAFFER and director of photography on illumination CHROMA, working with or acting as graphics designer to give film a cohesive visual style, and, in some cases, actually selecting and making purchases of the scenic props.

art house   A term that is used less frequently now than in the 1950s and 1960s to refer to a theater that specializes in features by offbeat and independent American filmmakers, foreign films with subtitles, experimental and documentary films, and animation "festivals."

artist (animation)   One who does the basic drawing of the animation cels. These drawings are then turned over to the cel animators and inkers. Artists generally specialize in either foreground animation or background animation (scenery, animals, sky, water, etc.). Often the head animator will do the foregrounds based on characters he/she has developed.

Arts and Entertainment (A&E)   As one of the major cable networks A&E specializes in documentaries about performing artists and concerts by performing artists, sculptors, painters, and architects. It also presents plays, special concerts and many historical and biographical documentaries.

artsy-craftsy   A phrase said of both the artist and his work. It has a negative connotation, indicating "self-indulgent," "amateurish," "pompously self-conscious." Much conceptual art has been tagged "artsy-craftsy," as have the paintings of Sunday painters, "experimental" films by almost-talented neophytes, poetry by ladies and gentlemen in writing clubs and "performance art."

ASA speed (exposure index)   An alphanumerical gradation indicating the exposure capabilities of a film stock based on standards set by the AMERICAN NATIONAL STANDARDS INSTITUTE.

ASC   See AMERICAN SOCIETY OF CINEMATOGRAPHERS.

ASCAP   See AMERICAN SOCIETY OF COMPOSERS, AUTHORS AND PUBLISHERS.

ascertainment   Controversial FCC evaluation procedure that determines who in TV and radio broadcasting is to be licensed and who is not, and if existing licenses are to be extended. The evaluation is based on a station's sensitivity and resultant programming reflecting that sensitivity to the needs of local and regional requirements and to the needs of minorities.

aside   A comment made by an actor to the audience or to him or herself. In each case, the actor turns away from the scene of the action to express this feeling or idea. In films, these ideas are often handled as "thought" voice-overs. In Sir Laurence Olivier's film of Shakespeare's *Hamlet,* the soliloquies in part or whole utilized voice-over techniques to indicate their inner meanings. An extended use of asides was employed by Eugene O'Neill in his play *Strange Interlude,* wherein the actors would speak their regular dialogue, then follow it by an aside to the audience to express what they truly thought or felt.

aspect ratio   The relation of width to height in a motion picture frame. The original 35mm theatrical motion picture frame to screen ratio was $1 \times 1:33$. This ratio is approximated in TV screen images. Widescreen film formats in motion picture theaters range from 1.85 to 1 to 2.5 to 1.

aspheric mirror   A reflective mirror of high efficiency that is used in xenon arc projectors. Its special curvature and optical refinements give it its level of proficiency.

assembly   Editing the workprint shots of a film into approximately the right order. See ROUGH CUT and FINE CUT.

assignment pay   Money paid, often in the development and pre-production phase of a project, to a composer, writer or production manager to start work on a score, a script and a detailed budget and production board. Sometimes this pay is on a flat rate, subcontractual basis, sometimes on a week-to-week salary.

It also refers to filming duties, the performance of which are subcontracted at a pre-agreed rate. A movie helicopter pilot's fee would be an example as would a director of photography who supplies his own crew and who may subcontract its services to him or to the production company itself. Stunt pay is sometimes referred to as assignment pay.

assistant cameraman (AC)   The person who handles the camera duties assigned by the director of photography: zooming, following focus, rack-focusing, aperture changes, and other functions. In strictly union situations, the AC will not operate the camera, but will work with the operator. In less rigidly structured crew situations, the AC may actually operate the camera or work as operator on the second camera.

assistant director (AD)   In a small production unit, the AD takes over aspects of the PRODUCTION MANAGER's responsibilities, such as liaison with production authorities and with suppliers of services. In a larger production unit, the AD carries out the director's logistical instructions, a primary duty being to see that all cast and crew members are present at the right locale at the precise time designated.

Associated Press (AP)   A nonprofit newsgathering and distribution agency that serves newspapers, magazines, radio and TV broadcast outlets, and more recently business concerns (public relations groups, brokers, demographic-survey organizations) throughout the world. The AP puts out numerous publications, including the *Associated Press Broadcast News Handbook* and the *Associated Press Stylebook and Libel Manual.* The former is a guide for TV-newswriting style with the preferred spellings, grammatical structurings, and pronunciations. The latter covers some of the same materials, but with a broader approach, as well as including a considerable amount of material on invasion of privacy and libel. See REUTERS and UNITED PRESS INTERNATIONAL.

Association of Motion Picture and Television Producers (AMPTP)   An organization that grew out of the MOTION PICTURE ASSOCIATION OF AMERICA. It is an action arm of the MPAA set up to mediate labor disputes and serve as a unified voice for major studio and network TV producers. It has been involved in settling the Director's Guild, Writer's, SCREEN ACTORS GUILD and Teamster's strikes, among others.

Association of National Advertisers (ANA)   A national organization for the dissemination of data and general information to its members; it sets policies and standards for the advertising industry.

associate producer (AP)   Originally, in the old motion picture studio system, the AP was the person assigned by the producer to handle the logistical details of a particular film. In general current use, it simply means the direct assistant to the producer in an often undetermined or loosely defined capacity.

astigmatism   In optical lenses for filming, a lens in which the rays of light do not fully converge. In an electron-beam tube, astigmatism is a focus defect wherein electrons in various axial planes come into focus at different points. This unresolved focus causes blurred, soft-focus and out-of-focus images.

asynchronous sound   Sound related directly to the action but not synchronized to the exact frame. Laid in as MATCHING SOUND, background sound or off screen sound in postproduction. It is used as augmenting sound tracks to back up foreground action.

A-team   Common name for the on-camera actors or the STUNTPERSONS in a scene. It is regarded as a separate unit from the stand-ins who help the camera crew set up the shot, the A-team is also called the first-string.

atmosphere   A collective term meaning EXTRAS, or collectively "BACKGROUND."

The atmosphere also defines the mood or feeling of a scene. It is the physical or subtextual tone of a scene or the total film or videotape. Also the "smell," "taste," "temperature," and emotional ambience of the piece—in whole or part: suspense, sylvan calm, malaise, unresolved tension or incomplete unfolding of the plot.

atmospheric interference   Noise, such as electrical hissing, crackling and sputtering, as it comes over radio or TV channels and is received by individual sets. It is caused by electrical disturbances in the earth's atmosphere. It is also known as static interference.

ATS   See AUTOMATIC TRANSMISSION SYSTEM.

attention-getting   A common media term that is used mostly in commercial TV. It refers to the introduction of a TV film—special or series segment—which must catch the audience's interest within the first 20 to 30 seconds. Unless this introductory section "grabs the audience," they will switch to another channel.

attention span   It is the length of time an audience member's attention can be held. Today, because of commercials using rapid cuts, kinestatic films and subliminal cutting, the average film length of a "scene" is about 6 seconds, as opposed to 20 seconds in the 1960s. These time spans are based on American theatrical films. This truncated attention span has been strongly influenced by commercial TV, but is now apparent in public relations films, educational films, in-house training films and theatrical motion picture releases. This is true not only on a scene-by-scene basis, but on cumulative running time. For example, public relations films in the 1960s used to run 24 to 30 minutes. They now run 3 to 15 minutes. In-house training films have compressed both information and running times, as have educational and informational films.

attenuation loss   The diminution of the quantity of transmitted electrical energy via cable or wave. Attenuation can modify or distort the signal.

attribution   The crediting of a story's source on a news program or documentary. It is often incorporated into the story itself if not stated prior to the story.

audible   The sound level at which a signal or noise can be heard by the human ear.

audience   The people, as an aggregate, who watch or listen to performances, news or events. The human receptor of a film, TV program or live performance. There are different audience measurements, based on media survey: real audience of actual auditors, potential audience of maximum number that could tune in to a given program, as well as special audiences, demographically evaluated by such factors as age, income, geographical location, interest, sex, race, etc. Viewers are regarded as a mass entity, when viewing a film, program or event, or as the potential viewing matrix.

audience analysis   A breakdown of the total audience into sub-categories, such as: occupation, religion, education, social studies, age, affiliations, gender, economic level, cultural background, audience size, etc, for demographic input regarding possible marketing, or defining areas where audiences need to be expanded.

audience rating   The results of formal or informal surveys regarding an audience's opinion of a film or TV show. These surveys can be written or verbal and such appraisals are generally made with potential marketing in mind.

audience share   The percentage of a trial sampling of an audience who could be watching a given TV program. Those households with one or more TV sets who are viewing the program provide the data that determines the percentage.

audio   The sound part of film or TV that is made up of dialogue, music, sound effects, narration and electronic audio effects. It is the opposite side of a dual-columned script form, used for live TV, some commercials, industrials and documentaries; in TV one side is audio, the other VIDEO. (See SCRIPT FORMS in Appendix.) Basic equipment and augmenting gear are utilized to produce and/or reproduce sound. In a crew situation, audio is an inclusive term, taking in equipment, personnel and facilities. Audio is a term that stems from TV; SOUND is used in motion pictures.

audio amplifier Electronic device for amplifying audio impulses of signals within the approximate range of 15 to 20,000 hertz.

audioanimatronic Referring to AUDIOANIMATRONIC FIGURES; it is a portmanteau word coined by the Walt Disney organization.

audioanimatronic figures The fabricated human or animal figures, usually life-sized, that are seen in all the Disney theme parks (Disneyland, Disney World, EPCOT, etc.); figures such as Abraham Lincoln delivering the Gettysburg Address, the pirates in the Pirates of the Caribbean attraction, or the figures in the Small World ride at Disneyland, for example. They have since been copied by theme parks across the United States and throughout the world. The figures are electromechanically driven in sound synch to a master track or an audio-film loop in a separate loop-cabinet.

audioanimatronics The whole field of fabrication and programming for AUDIOANIMATRONIC FIGURES.

Audio Engineering Society Professional group that meets, publishes and functions to raise audio hardware to the highest standards in both the home unit and professional fields.

audio equalizer Device that raises or lowers the volume of pre-selected audible sound frequencies.

audio frequency Frequency range dealing with tones audible to the human ear, as well as guide-tones and informational pulses above and below that range, i.e., bass range (0–60 Hz), mid-bass range (60–240 Hz), mid-range (240–1000 Hz), mid-treble range (1000–3500 Hz) and treble range (3500–10,000 Hz).

audio frequency oscillator A transistor circuit, initially a simple electron tube, that generates audio signals.

audio inputs/outputs A routing device from one particular component to another: CD players, VCRs, monitors, turntables, etc.

audio mix The blending of multiple soundtracks into one while controlling the volume of each. See MIX.

audion The electronic amplifying tube for sound that makes modern radio and TV possible. It was invented in 1906 by Lee DeForest.

audiotape Plastic tape coated with magnetizable metallic oxide. Sound can be recorded on the magnetizable side of the tape. General widths are ⅛″ (used in nearly all commercial audio cassettes), ¼″ reel-to-reel (used now for basic single or multiple track recording, particularly for synchronous motion picture recording in the filming of a scene); all other widths are used primarily for professional assignments: ½″, 1″ and 2″, and sometimes ¾″.

audio/video input A group of electronic jacks with one for video, two for stereo audio. Integral units are on monitoring receivers and on VCRs.

audiovisual A total approach to the presentation of entertainment or information. Used for informational, commercial and entertainment purposes, an audiovisual presentation often blends any number of the following elements: film, video, film slides, music, effects, laser lighting, live performers and magical illusions among others. In a school situation, the term refers to an audiovisual section or department that handles video and TV presentations for classrooms or auditorium.

audiovisual script Specially designed scripts that indicate and separate live and mechanical sources. See SCRIPT FORMS in Appendix.

audition   A reading or tryout in which performers read dialogue, sing, dance, mime or display the particular talent required for the role.

audition channel   A closed channel within a production company or studio on which viewers can watch live on-camera auditions from a studio within the facility. Sometimes it is used for closed screening of taped dailies or completed films.

aural signal   The audible element of the signal for the sound part of a television show.

auteur theory   The theory that states by using lightweight and portable camera equipment, improvisation is encouraged in actors. By using these techniques to make a personal statement, the director becomes the "author" (auteur) of the film. Publicized in the French film magazine *Cahiers du Cinema* from 1951 and throughout the decade by writers Andre Bazin, Eric Rohmer, Francois Truffaut and others, it was "discovered" in America by Andrew Sarris, and used as terminology in some film history courses. This theory is repudiated by most writers; but hyphenates in the writer-director category often make a case for the auteur concept.

autofocus   In cameras and camcorders, it is the infrared sensors that activate the camera-focusing mechanism. The sensors are in the camera housing, contiguous to the lens. Some circuits are activated directly through the lens while other cameras use digital circuits with a micro-processor balancing the focus.

automated camera effects system (ACES)   A computer-operated system designed to film repeatable camera moves on separate exposures. It was developed by Disney Studios, followed by Lucasfilm, Apogee and other SPECIAL EFFECTS houses.

automatic exposure   An exposure device, that is self-activated and self-setting, based on the intensity of light entering the lens.

automatic frequency control (AFC)   A circuit that holds, maintains and monitors a frequency within specified limits.

automatic gain control (AGC)   A circuit utilized to stabilize the output volume of a receiver from any variations of the signal strength going into the receiver.

automatic image stabilizer   A compensating lens-movement device that smooths out the camera moves by utilizing a floating lens.

automatic sequencing   A computer's ability to perform sequential operations without additional human input or commands. It is useful in shooting animation images in sequence, as well as for performing simultaneous multiplex functions in audio, video or film.

automatic transmission system (ATS)   A sending system for any signal that requires minimal supervision because of its self-adjusting capabilities.

availability   The time a performer has open for bookings.

average brightness   The illumination of a television picture, averaged out by screen areas.

A wind   As single perf film, held in front of you, comes off a roll over the top, the sprockets determine the wind. If the sprockets are on your right it is an A wind, on the left it is a B WIND.

B

B   B is the symbol for PHOTOMETRIC BRIGHTNESS.

baby   A lighting unit that uses a 1000-watt bulb, next in size below a junior. A baby door is the BARN DOOR for this lamp.

baby legs   See BABY TRIPOD.

baby plate   A metal mount with a vertical shaft to hold a small spotlight.

baby spot   Studio spot for controlled light situations, interior or exterior. Its lamp is 500–750 watts.

baby tripod   A tripod with short legs for low angle shooting; it is used on tabletops or to maintain a low point-of-view level, as from the viewpoint of an animal or a child. Also called baby legs and sawed-offs.

backdrop   An artificial scene set up and lit to represent a realistic or stylistic setting. These painted background scenes can be on cycloramas, flats, photographer's paper or taut plastic on frames. Also called a DROP.

back focus   Distance from focal plane to the rear (back) of lens; a point set at infinity. This theoretical point is used to test and determine the FOCAL POINT of a lens.

background (BG)   That part of a framed scene that is farthest from the camera. Opposed to FOREGROUND where most of the primary action of the scene takes place. People, objects, set pieces and scenery that form the setting against which the foreground players and actions are set. An EXTRA is also referred to as part of the background, a background player.
   In news, information from various sources forms the research matrix (background) of a news story.

background action   The supporting action to what is happening in the foreground of the scene.

background music   Music not recorded in or visually part of a filmed scene. It is usually post-production-scored, timed and cued to action. Such music can be written and performed for the film, or can be selected from a music library and edited to fit the picture.

background noises   Additional sounds mixed with the foreground track to give a richer, more realistic sound texture to the scenic-image. See MATCHING, SYNCHRONOUS and FOLEY.

background plate   Photograph or artist's rendering on a glass plate that is used for rear screen projection to form a background image on which the live foreground image can be photographed.

background projection   See PROCESS PROJECTION.

backing   Coating on the back side of any film stock.

backlash   Equipment overslack, caused by loose mechanical connections, that creates spasmodic, abrupt pull-ups, damage or breakage. It is especially prevalent in take-up and rewind reels.

backlight   A light behind the subject with its illumination working within the camera's framing of the scene. It separates the subject from the background to enhance the feeling of depth and three-dimensionality.

backlighting   Illumination coming from sources visible or hidden behind the performers or subjects of a scene.

backlot   Exterior filming area of a studio that consists of standing sets and "streets," prop and scene storage areas, utility and generator sheds, and production backup units: trailers for cast, makeup, wardrobe; ponds or "lakes"; on-camera vehicles, etc. In the United States the backlots are diminishing rapidly, many of them sold completely or in part for real estate considerations, the profits of sales often put back into the operation of the studio or the financing of motion pictures. In the past a European scene would be filmed on the "European street" on the backlot. Today it is more likely that the European scenes are filmed in the actual locales, often shot by the SECOND UNIT, or taken from STOCK FOOTAGE.

back-up interlock system   A way of recording a multi-track mix with magnetic sound playbacks that can be reversed and erased, allowing technicians to go for another take. It is used in conjunction with basic recording and playback units.

back-up schedule   A schedule of alternative shots to be made in the event that the originally planned shooting is not feasible due to the inclement weather, absence of performers, or major technical or logistical problems.

baffle   An acoustically designed movable unit that can be placed where necessary in a recording studio or within a working TV or motion picture set to deflect and absorb sound, and to reduce reverberation. Baffle also refers to a loudspeaker element that is functionally built into the unit.

balance   The placement of musical instruments to achieve optimum acoustical blending while recording. Electronically, it is the tuning of the frequency response in an audio circuit to readjust for any shift in a signal's frequency response. This is done by the fine-tuning of high pass and low pass filters.

balance strip   A narrow band of magnetic coating on magnetic-coated film. It is placed opposite the magnetic sound track so that the film stock will stay flat and even as it moves over the magnetic heads in the projector, playback deck or recorder. The balance strip may be activated to hold and impart audio or magnetic cueing information.

ballyhoo   A term still used in Ireland and the United Kingdom, as in, "Hollywood ballyhoo." It refers to unrestrained and highly exaggerated publicity, over-extolling certain elements of a film or videotape that often have nothing to do with the piece being wildly lauded. In the United States it is occasionally used, but it is regarded as an outdated expression. See HYPE.

balun   See BAZOOKA.

bands   In satellite TV, the two basic frequency ranges. C-band is the most common and uses the familiar large-dish antenna to receive programming. The Ku-band is not used that often; it operates with a smaller dish antenna. In radio FCC-assigned and -rated channels are very low frequency (VLF) 10–30 Hz; low frequency (LF) 30–300 Hz; medium frequency (MF) 300–3,000 Hz; high frequency (HF) 3–30 MHz; very high frequency (VHF) 30–300 MHz; ultrahigh frequency (UHF) 300–3,000 MHz; superhigh frequency (SHF) 3,000–30,000 MHz; extremely high frequency (EHF) 3–300 GHz.

band selector   Switch that can be activated or adjusted for selection of desired bands in either transmitting or receiving units. The bands are selected by adjusting the variable resistances of the current.

bandwidth   The frequency range between a BAND's upper and lower levels.

bank   A cluster or a strip of lights. Bank is also used as a verb meaning to set up lights in a certain way. "The lighting crew had to bank the lights in such a way as to highlight the star."

barn door   Hinged door mounted on a studio LAMP which may be swung to block off light or pinpoint light in a given area.

Barney   A heavy, matted cloth covering for a sound camera. It is designed to deaden the sound of the camera when it is running. Apparently, the name derives from the comic strip "Barney Google," but whether it comes from Barney's horse with his blanket on, or from Barney's round eyes is conjectural.

barrel distortion   In camera images it is the apparent outward curving, like a barrel. In TV receivers this barreling distorts on all four sides of the RASTER.

barrel mount It is a special lens mount holding all lens elements, extending out from the camera. It is usually detachable.

bar sheets Charts used in ANIMATION that indicate the number of FRAMEs for each recorded syllable of dialogue as well as the pauses. See LEAD SHEETS.

base A preconditioner for face or body over which the full on-camera makeup is applied.

base, film See FILM BASE.

base down/base up These are self-explanatory positioning instructions for the threading of film in editing. Base in/base out are similar terms.

base film The transparent material onto which a photographic emulsion is coated. In itself it serves no photographic purpose, but it acts as a support for the thin light-sensitive emulsion layer. (NOTE: Since 1947 SAFETY FILM has phased out the flammable nitrate-base stock, and is now used universally.)

Base film also refers to the plastic backing on which magnetic recording materials are applied, thus producing magnetic tape.

base in/base out See BASE DOWN/BASE UP.

base light The general matrix light of a scene prior to any addition of detailing lights.

base side The protectively coated nonimage side. The obverse of the EMULSION side.

basic frequency The fundamental frequency, determined by function, e.g., it would be the driving frequency in a driven system. In a system of period wave frequencies, the dominant frequency would be regarded as "basic."

basic network A group of affiliated stations regarded as a unit for advertising placement or distribution purposes.

bass Those sounds in the low audio frequency range. In musical terms, all notes lower than middle C on the standard piano keyboard, i.e., 256 hertz.

bass control Manual tone control to change the level of bass frequencies emitted by an audio amplifier.

batch The quantity of photographic emulsion manufactured at any one time for the production of RAW STOCK is of essentially uniform quality. The stock on which the emulsion is coated is called a batch. Different batches of film may vary appreciably in their characteristics. For this reason, sensiometric tests are always made on a piece of film of the same batch as the film to be processed, since batch variations often necessitate the use of correction filters.

bath A liquid chemical solution of various formulas for the processing of all varieties of motion picture film. The water rinse of the processed film is also known as the bath.

batten The horizontal lengths of wood or pipe, rigged above the SET on ropes and pulleys, that are used for flying scenery or for mounting overhead lights. This device originated in live theater.

battery belt The direct power source of connected batteries in a leather, heavy cloth or plastic case. It is worn around the waist by the cameraman and plugged in directly to the camera's DC connection, allowing maximum mobility in hand-held shots; it is particularly useful in obtaining coverage in documentary news-gathering situations. It can be mounted in conjunction with other conformations: lying next to a low tripod on the ground; connected directly to a regular tripod; attached to a camera on a HIGH-HAT on the deck of a ship, a ledge of a building, or a playing field.

battery light   A high-powered, close-range light operated from a battery or battery belt. It is often used for news and documentary coverage.

baud   Rate of speed of a signaling unit based on its shortest signaling time, i.e., code elements per second.

bay   A self-contained editing room with requisite gear for videotape editing. This editing area can be part of a larger room or can be broken up into numbered bays, as separate rooms. Also, a bay is an area in a studio or within a soundstage where set properties, grip equipment or operational gear is stored, such as dollies, tripods, etc.

bayonet mount   A snap-in or drop-in mount for lenses that doesn't require machine threading. The lens is inserted into place and held there with a snap-lock which expedites rapid changing of lenses.

bazooka   A balanced converter used for matching an unbalanced coaxial television transmission line to a balanced two-wire system. Also called balun, from BALanced-to-UNbalanced.

BCU   See BIG CLOSE-UP.

BD (block-down) conversion   Lowers high-frequency signals from satellites to more adaptable frequencies used by a receiving unit, professional or home receiver.

beaded screen   A front-projection screen surfaced with high-reflectance beads of plastic or glass.

beam projector   A lighting device that projects a single pattern of light, such as an infrared beam, a laser beam or a focused light beam with variable color frames; for example, a FOLLOW SPOTLIGHT. To be differentiated from MOTION PICTURE PROJECTOR.

beam splitter   A prism or customized arced semi-mirror which reflects part of a light beam while allowing the rest of the beam to pass through. This separates colors or creates two or more images, each in a different place. The effects produced by these split-beams are often used for special effects, particularly in SCIENCE FICTION films. It can also be used to separate colors for special chromatic effects.

Beaulieu   A lightweight professional motion picture camera that is used extensively for news and documentary coverage, handling a 200-foot film roll internally in the 16mm version of the camera, with MAGAZINE attachments for larger film rolls.

bed   The background music for a commercial.

beep   A short spurt of sound. This brief soundtrack tone is aligned with a visual referent, a "slate" light, for example, in order to synchronize sound and picture elements in postproduction. For film, it can be a magnetic-tape sound dot attached to a preset spot in the Academy Leader.

beeper   An instrument used to feed beep tones into an audio system or onto an audio tack.

behind-the-lens filter   A gelatin filter in a holding frame inserted in a slot behind the camera lens and directly in front of the film. It fills the same function as a comparable glass filter inserted into a matted box in front of the camera, or other front-of-camera attachments, i.e., to filter out certain colors, or all colors but one.

behind-the-scenes film   Half promo, half documentary. These films or videotapes chronicle highlights of "the making of" a film or major TV special. An example is Monty Python gang's behind-the-scenes look at the making of *The Life of Brian*.

believability   A style of delivery that is natural, without seeming affected or postured, although "naturalness" can often become stylized and mechanical. Believability in a radio announcer is strictly based on the vocal presentation of the material, or in TV, the total presentation on-camera. For a newscaster, however, believability is intermeshed with credibility, that is, how trustworthy and authoritative the newscaster seems.

Bell and Howell An early motion picture equipment manufacturer of cameras, projectors, and accessories. A pioneer, leader and competitor with Eastman Kodak in the development of the 8mm and 16mm markets.

bellows attachment A lightproof cloth, square-shaped with "accordion-pleat" folds, attached between camera and lens to extend the focal length of the particular lens. It is helpful in shooting extreme close-up material.

belly board A camera-mount accessory board that is used for low angle shots. It is often used in conjunction with a HIGH HAT or placed flat and parallel to the camera plate.

below-the-line Crew, staff and logistic costs of a production, as opposed to above-the-line, i.e., the "creative" aspects. However, a budget is a parameter-making framework that affects all areas of creativity.

bending Videotape distortion caused by physical flaws in the tape or in the playback equipment.

best boy The best boy is second-in-command on the GRIP or electrical team.

best-of-sequence A preferred take or section of a take of a given set of shots with the same slate number. In practice it is chosen by the director while shooting or in the director's final post production selections.

best take The take arbitrarily chosen by the editor to be used in the edit. It may be "best" on its own or be "best" in interpositioning within the other scenes.

best time available (BTA) The best time for a station to schedule a commercial or series of commercials.

BG See BACKGROUND.

bias A high frequency alternating current which, when directed through magnetic recording heads, puts the audio signal in the proper section of the magnetic curve, thereby reducing noise and other forms of electrical distortion.

bicycling Transporting tapes for broadcast, storage or review purposes from station-to-station, or between production facilities and stations. An example of such a bicycled piece would be a videotape copy of a news event (or a feature-film promo clip) covered exclusively by one station and used, with acknowledged courtesy of that station, on a broadcast by another. Sometimes, as soon as one station finishes airing a film print of a motion picture, it must immediately be bicycled back to the studio or distributor. The term "bicycling" is derived from the major studio days where there was considerable acreage for each studio and between soundstages. Department heads would have their own bicycles to shunt from stage to stage. This method of transport still exists today, in a limited way, at some of the main lots: Burbank Studios (Warner's/Columbia), Paramount, Disney, for example.

bi-directional A microphone that is sound-sensitive in front and back, but DEAD on the sides.

big close up A camera shot replaced almost entirely by large close up or EXTREME CLOSE UP.

big eye Massive luminaire with the lighting power of 10kw, i.e., 100,000 watts.

bilateral amplifier An amplifier that both sends and receives signals. See TRANSCEIVER.

bilateral antenna One that is halved in its design and operates in opposite directions 180° apart.

billing The sequence, position, duration and size of performers' or crew member's CREDITS on the screen and in advertisements. For example, the credits could be on a SINGLE CARD or a shared card, the front-end credit can be at the head of the picture or as a closing credit, it can be on a credit roll or stationary and it may be included on posters, ads or releases.

bin A cloth-lined or plastic-lined container that is usually on wheels and has a PIN RACK attached from which to hang film strips. It is standard equipment for the film editor.

binary A base-two system of numbering. The radical dual-numbered system is sometimes referred to as an "on/off," "stop/go" or "hold/activate" system. It is the "yes/no" system for computer programming. The binary system is used as the basic control system in sound recording, videotaping and remixing.

binary channel A channel that is dedicated to the binary system in its transmissions.

binary conflict A theory of dramatic conflict that grew up in schools of communication that derives in part from the philosophical writings on cultural stratification of Levi-Strauss and the book on dramatic writing of Lajos Egri. It emphasizes the conflict between culture and nature, i.e., *Deliverance;* the human culture that defies the inescapable and omnipresent power of the river. Also referred to as binary operations and binary opposition. In Lajos Egri's definitive book, *The Art of Dramatic Writing,* "man against nature" is one of his categories of major dramatic conflicts. Other categories are "man against himself," "man against the world," "man against man" etc.

binaural Literally, to be "heard by both ears." A sound that is separated into individual tracks and reproduced in like manner. In a theatre it can come from different speakers. Binaural has now become multiaural, with many tracks splitting up the sound into corresponding speakers, to create a "surround" system.

binder Gelatin adhesive that fixes light or sound-sensitive emulsions to the tape base.

biographical film A feature film that is centered on the life of a single protagonist or sometimes the lives of a family. Also called biopic and recently, DOCUDRAMA. Warner Brothers, early on, made some notable biographies based, sometimes loosely, on the lives of Juarez, Louis Pasteur, Ehrlich and his "magic bullet." Others followed with *Young Tom Edison, Edison the Man, Madame Curie.* Notable docudramas, a term generated by TV, include *I, Claudius, Ten Who Dared,* and many British-made biographical works. American docudramas have included *Mommy, Dearest* and the excellent biographical documentary, *The Indomitable Teddy Roosevelt.*

biopic See BIOGRAPHICAL FILM.

bio sheet See CREDIT SHEET.

bipack To superimpose TITLES or other images over another piece of film.

bipack printing Film-printing process wherein two pieces of film are run through together in contact, for MATTING or DOUBLE EXPOSURE.

bipost lamp/socket A lamp with two male prongs that fit into female sockets. These prongs can be round or grooved, and match the corresponding receptor device.

bird The name for a communications satellite.

bit A small part in a filmed or taped show. A preset visual or verbal gag within a comedy routine, is also called "a bit." See BIT PLAYER.

In computers, bit is the abbreviation for binary digit, the basic unit of data in the binary system.

bit density The measured number of bits of information within a specific area, e.g., the amount of bits along a particular length of magnetic tape.

bit player A person playing a BIT part.

bit time A serial binary computer term that describes the time at which each bit appears. An electromechanical example of a practical application in media would be the readout numbers in on-line editing in hours, minutes, seconds and frames, calibrated to a bit-time matrix.

black The absence of visible light or any apparent color.

black-and-white reproduction A photographic film process where color is translated into a scale of monochromatic densities ranging from near opacity (black) to near transparency (white). Reproduction in black-and-white can be done by using black-and-white film, or color film, and printing for black-and-white. When the photographic image is viewed on a white screen, it appears in the scale of near-black and near-white. The range of tonalities determines the CONTRAST of the image. In videotape the color can be dropped out, converting the camera to gray-scale reproduction, for black-and-white images.

black comedy When a serious subject matter is treated with a humorous approach, i.e., Woody Allen's *Love and Death* and *Manhattan*. The substantive topics range from murder, treason and blackmail to nymphomania, satyromania and assorted sexual perversions. Political and military corruption are nicely depicted in Stanley Kubrick's *Dr. Strangelove*. Sexual corruption was depicted well

in the French film *Boudu Saved from Drowning (Boudu Sauve des Eaux)*, and later in its American version, *Down and Out in Beverly Hills*. *The Front Page*, adapted from the Broadway stage play by Ben Hecht and Charles MacArthur, with hard-edged, cynical humor, decimated the "honorable" profession of newspaper journalism. *The Front Page* was made as a film in 1931 by Lewis Milestone, starring Pat O'Brien and remade by Howard Hawks in 1940, with Rosalind Russell and Cary Grant as *His Girl Friday*. A re-remake was made in 1974 starring Walter Matthau and Jack Lemmon.

black leader An opaque leader used to block printing light was used originally for A AND B ROLL PRINTING.

black level Specific amplitude in a TV signal that reproduces the black areas of the picture.

black-level control A TV receiver's control knobs or levers for regulating the BLACK LEVEL of TV images.

black net Black-colored netting used to reduce illumination with minimal diffusion, particularly used with exterior light streaming into interiors.

blackout The sudden switching off of scenic lights instead of dimming them. It is used as fast "light curtain," particularly at the end of comedy sketches in a revue or variety format. Also, it is the comedy sketch itself, written with a curtain-line strong enough to justify a light blackout.

A blackout also defines a solar flare interruption of radiocommunications.

In television broadcasting, a blackout is a local area or regional ban of live broadcasts, such as a world-championship heavyweight fight, or other major audience attraction, another sporting event, a rock concert, etc. This limits audiences to those who can attend the live event or who have access to it through pay cable. It generates income for the producer/promoter. Blackouts are also those programs that are banned because of subject matter, e.g., some TV programs in the United States that were on acid rain, plus antiadministration pieces on Vietnam; in England, Margaret Thatcher banned an IRA documentary on British television. In general, a blackout is a ban on carrying a given show on any or all local channels, for either commercial or political reasons.

blackout switch   The master switch controlling all production lights on a theatre or sound stage. Also called master switch.

blacksploitation film   Films that have a black person as hero or superhero and a melodramatic and sensational plot, sometimes played straight, sometimes a send-up. They often have crime-in-the-streets themes and their sex and violence are heavily marketed. Examples would be the *Shaft* films, *Superfly* and *Blacula*. These films flourished in the mid-'70s to early '80s. Sometimes spelled blaxploitation.

blanketing   The dispersion of signals over a wide band of frequencies. This attenuates the signal, often causing it to disappear for all effective transmission and/or reception purposes. This sometimes occurs when a receiving unit is too close to a transmitter in the immediate area.

blank   As in "blank tape," it is tape unused for any purpose. It is analogous to virgin stock in film.

   A blank is also a cartridge for a rifle or handgun that has a reduced mixture of gunpowder and no bullets or pellets. It is used for gunplay scenes in film or videotape.

blanking   A beam cutoff in a cathode-ray tube in intervals when the image is not being formed to allow for the next beam-scanning interval. The beam is blanked as the spot-image comes in from the right to form a new line at the left. Or the spot-image can come from top to bottom, as well as bottom to top. This helps eliminate apparent image dropout.

blanking pulse   The pulsation that BLANKS the video beams of a camera and TV receiver. Blanking must be synchronized with left-to-right, bottom-to-top, top-to-bottom sweep circuits, so that all beams are cut off at the exact time.

blasting   The gross distortion of loud sounds that is caused by overloading an amplifier or loudspeaker.

bleachers   Bleachers are movable studio seats that are used to seat the audience in game shows, audience-participation shows, multicamera sitcoms taped in front of a live audience, etc. Bleachers can be combined to use as many modules as necessary to accommodate a particular audience.

bleed   For the master-shot composition to run off the frame line, as the shot zooms or dollies in, or as seen in a following tighter shot. The term comes from printing; when an illustration bleeds, the colors run off the page.

bleep   To override the existing sound track with an intense sonic tone, with the duration of the tone being as long as the word or phrase that is blocked out. It is used to cover up names or dates no longer relevant in programs or commercials, but is more commonly utilized to erase what has been deemed "offensive language" in broadcasting.

blend-line   The line separating a matte image or image-blocking section of film from the basic action image. It is also used in TV to describe any such line in whatever image separation process is used.

blimp   The soundproof housing that surrounds a camera to prevent the camera noise from being picked up by the microphone on sound takes. SELF-BLIMPED cameras are those in which the camera's normal housing silences the noise of the drive mechanism without the addition of an external blimp.

blimping   Fabrication materials for creating a blimp-housing; structural and soundproofing elements.

blind bidding "Open" bidding on the film rights of a motion picture by theater owners and the follow-up negotiations on a film that has not been seen by them, and probably will not be, until the print of the picture arrives at their theater. Many states now have laws forbidding this practice, as they feel it is discriminatory and an unfair labor practice that puts the theater owners at risk and limits the range of motion picture selections. It is sometimes viewed as unfair competition.

blind booking The booking of a film before its completion or before it has been screened by exhibitors.

blip Synch pop. A circular or square piece of magnetic tape about ¼" in diameter attached to film leader as a signal to the projectionist to let the image be projected, as well as the sound made fully audible. Also used at the end of reels as a changeover signal, or as a standby on a loop in an ADR session.

blistering The tiny bubbling on the surface of a film print or negative caused by extreme exposure to radiant energy. This damage usually makes a print totally unusable.

block To set the movement of actors, crew and gear within a scene. In live theater a director will block actors and alter the placement of scenic props, if necessary. In some productions he or she will work with the set designer directly in devising the stage settings. This happens in some films, rarely in episodic TV.

block booking In distribution, the placement of a group of prints of a film or group of films, in a package-deal, in various theaters in a specific, concentrated area. This practice resulted in film exhibitors having to book films of inferior quality in order to get the better films. This practice has been curtailed, by interpretation of civil law regarding business practices and by industry pressure. However, it still crops up from time to time.

blockbuster A major motion picture with heavy advance advertising and publicity, shown at a limited number of specially chosen theatres on a first-run basis. This gives the film a prestigious opening, good word-of-mouth advertising, and a high first-run ticket price.

block conversion See BD CONVERSION.

block programming Program scheduling by TV networks to hold audiences from program to program, without changing channels. It is a practice designed to obtain and secure high ratings.

blood bag (blood capsule) Plastic containers of artificial blood that can split open by direct physical contact or be set off by mini-explosive caps concealed in the actor's clothing. It helps create realistic action in fighting scenes for stabbings, lacerations and general open-wound injuries.

bloop The punchout, the PATCH, FOGGING mark, painted area or stencil by which the "bloop" (noise made by the SPLICE in joining two pieces of SOUND TRACK) is made audible as it passes over the sound-head of a projector.

blooper An on-camera or on-the-air mistake made by an actor, spokesperson, newscaster, interviewee or announcer.

Also a nickname for any blooping device.

blooping Any method of silencing unwanted noise by the passage of a SPLICE through a sound reproducer. See BLOOP.

blooping patch A small opaque piece of material fixed over a sound SPLICE to BLOOP it.

blow To misread a line, forget the dialogue or make another error. Generally used as a verb, e.g., "I hope I don't blow any lines." In the past tense, "One actor blew half a dozen lines." The crew will sometimes make an error and sometimes admit it with similar language, "I think we blew it."

blow-up Optical printing process by which a picture image on a smaller gauge of film is produced on a larger gauge. A common application is 16mm blow-up to 35mm. Blow-up also refers to the enlargement of the film image in an optical camera. Also, it is a section of a frame enlarged into total frame size. Any print-to-print enlargement by whatever intermediate process, whether on motion picture or still film stock.

blue Adjective synonymous with pornographic.

blue cometing Unwanted light and bluish spots in color film, coming from the developed emulsion. A result of metallic impurities in the film processing baths.

blue gun Electron gun in a 3-gun color-picture tube that strikes the phosphor dots that produce the blue-primary. See GREEN GUN and RED GUN.

blue movie Pornographic film. Also called a DIRTY MOVIE.

Blue Network One of NBC's two networks until 1943, the other being the Red Network. As a result of a 1941 FCC ruling stating that a single organization could not control, and would not control in the future, more than one broadcasting network, NBC sold the Blue Network Company to a private owner in October, 1943. This owner, Edward J. Noble, named it what it is still called today, the American Broadcasting Company.

blue pencil To edit text, blue pencil usually infers CENSORSHIP. Named from the blue-colored marking pen used by text editors, blue pencil usually means to delete, sometimes to transpose, but rarely to add material.

blue screen process A system to use action photography shot in front of a screen or backing of a special blue, to interlock with a MATTE, in order to create a MATTE SHOT.

blur pan See SWISH PAN.

BMI See BROADCAST MUSIC, INC.

BO See BOX OFFICE.

board The working CONSOLE at a recording or mixing session; it also refers to the master control for a lighting matrix. The console is situated in the control room or sometimes on the open sound stage. It is handled by the appropriate technicians of sound, image or lighting.

board fade A FADE IN or FADE OUT of sound or picture done directly at the BOARD.

board wipe A screen WIPE on video that is handled by the technician in charge of video images or special effects.

body In a script, it is the text after the introduction and before the closing wrap-up.

body brace, body frame, body pod A specially designed camera mount for HAND-HELD shots using various frame-mount designs and configurations. It is supported against the body for greater camera stability. See STEADICAM.

boffle A speaker housing with sound-absorbing screens to reduce noise and emit a clearer, cleaner signal.

bomb A motion picture that does poorly at the box office or a TV show that fails to get a respectable audience share. TV audience share is determined by ARBITRON, the NIELSEN TELEVISION INDEX, and other demographic-survey organizations.

boob tube A phrase from the world of print describing the fascination with the glowing TV set and its supposed numbing effect on one's intellect. The term is also used to refer to the audience level of most of its fare.

book Used mainly as verb, meaning to hire or engage a performer, as in, "Go ahead and book the singer for the next show." Setting a motion picture playdate for a specific film or films at a single theater or a contractual group.

booking   Contacting and setting performance runs for live talent, films or any theatrical or entertainment event.

booking agent   The person who arranges the appearance, payment and advertising/publicity for the work or person(s) booked.

booking contract   Full contract or DEAL MEMO between actor and employer (or exhibitor and leasee/renter) stating the details of the obligations and responsibilities of both parties.

boom, camera   A mobile camera mount, usually of a large size, on which the camera may be made to extend out over the set, or be raised above it. Provisions are made for counterbalancing while raising and lowering, rotating, and bodily moving the camera, by electrical motors, hydraulic controls or by hand.
A microphone boom is a simple version of the camera boom, designed to extend the reach of the microphone out over the set, and to turn and twist it in any direction required by the mixer.

boomerang   A semicircular device placed in front of a lamp and fastened on, to hold the color gels that modify the basic lighting.

boom man   Any person who handles the microphone boom.

boom shot   A shot made from a camera on a boom, allowing for fluid movements, or whatever movement is necessary to move in closer or farther away from the scene. Examples: seamless FOLLOW SHOTS, high shots and wide establishing scenes.

boomy   Sound lacking high-level clarity that is caused by over-resonance in the low frequencies. Also called tubby or muddy sound.

booster   A device used to strengthen and retransmit original signals.

booster light   Artificial light used to augment daylight in an exterior scene or, in general, any light used to intensify light level in an area.

boot   A loose, flexible tube of durable plastic, fabric or leather that is a protective cover for a tripod. It is placed on the tripod head when traveling with it, or when it is in storage. There are also boots for the tripod legs, to keep those tripods with pointed metal ends from perforating people and things.

booth   A mini-stage within a recording stage or a motion picture soundstage for isolating a performer who is to be recorded in a soundproof enclosure. It is used for making separate sound tracks that can be mixed later. The performer enters the booth and closes the door to make it sound-secure, and, upon the signal to record, sings, speaks or makes the requisite noises. Also called an isolation booth.

boarder light   A multi-bulbed lighting unit, also called strip light.

bottom pegs   Pegs closest to the animation cameraman when seated in operational position in front of the filming setup. Pegs allow cels to be fastened down for accurate camera-framing and stability of the physical image to be filmed or videotaped.

bounce light   A diffused light created by aiming lamps at ceilings, walls or off-camera reflectors instead of directly at the on-camera subject. This avoids making the person being photographed appear overlit, with HOT SPOTS causing reflective glare on the face or wardrobe. It also gives a more "natural" look to the photographed scene.

box office (BO)   In its broadest sense, money from ticket sales. Box office describes the little room from which tickets are sold.

box office draw   The power of the name of a star or sometimes director to attract ticket sales at the box office, as in, "He used to be a great box office draw, but not any more." The financial pull is often placed in the form of a question in early stages of pre-production, as speculation begins about the projected return. "Will he/she attract enough audience to the box office, to match the salary we're giving him/her?"

B picture   Term from the days of double features in motion picture houses. It is a low-budget, short-schedule film made to accompany the "major motion picture" in a particular theater or chain. The term is still in common use today.

braceweight   Counterbalance or support for the camera brace.

bracketing   Exposing film during shooting at the meter-indicated or extrapolated F NUMBER and then shooting other takes (or still shots) slightly above and below that f number reading. Bracketing is often done in camera tests to find the best exposure.

branching   Computer selection based on evaluated duty to execute the next operation while the program is in operation. This is done to save operational time and to allow for smoothness of output.

break   A mandatory or discretionary stop-and-rest period for crew and performers during production. The Musician's Union requires a five-minute break per hour. Union actors have only a lunch break (½ hr. minimum; 1 hr. maximum). In TV there tends to be more breaks than in film production because of studio scheduling. At a TV station a break is time set aside for commercials or station identification.

breakaway props   Working props designed to shatter, crumble and generally fall apart on impact, such as breakaway chairs made of balsa wood or mal-low-pitch derivatives, and breakaway glass windows and bottles made of safe-shattering plastic. They are used to create shattering and breakage without the attendant dangers.

break down   In film editing, the act of reducing a ROLL of film into its component shots. The term is usually applied to RUSHES when a single roll of film contains numerous, separate scenes and takes.

Break down also defines the activities of the production manager and/or line producer in detailing a scene for its necessary setting, gear, crew, performers and auxiliary services (catering, transportation, etc.); these details are then worked out logistically for budget and schedule, and formalized on the PRODUCTION BOARD. See BREAK-DOWN SHEET in Appendix.

breakup   The distortion or dropout of an image on film or tape, or from a TV set itself.

breathing   A pulsating of a projected film image that causes an uneven focus of the picture. There are any number of causes of breathing: film BUCKLING in the camera or projector, an unstable APERTURE gate in either, or an unsteady rate of the film in moving through either mechanism.

breezeway   (NTSC system) The outgoing edge of a synch pulse and the beginning of the incoming color burst.

bridge   A music cue used to carry us from one scene or mood to another. This can also be done with sound effects.

bridge plate   A movable plate on a camera mount that pivots or slides to move the camera head into a balanced position.

brightness   The physical and psychological effects of the visual perception of a source of illumination. See LUMINANCE.

brightness control   A device in a TV receiver that adjusts the screen image for level of BRIGHTNESS.

brightness range Readings of the light reflected from a set, props or wardrobe, measured by a light meter to determine the correct exposure for a shot.

bring down, bring up Directions relating to light or sound levels, "down" indicates less, "up" more.

broad Squarish floodlight used for general and diffused lighting.

broadcast A radio or TV transmission that is designed for reception by the general public.

broadcast homes Households capable of TV reception that have one or more TV sets per home.

broadcasting station A single station tied into a network, group or syndicated web.

Broadcast Music, Inc. (BMI) A publishing and royalty-policing organization for composers, lyricists and performers who write their own music.

broadcast quality See AIR QUALITY.

B roll See A AND B ROLL PRINTING and A AND B ROLL EDITING.

brute The name of a large and heavy 10,000-watt light that can spot or widen its beam. It is used extensively for nighttime exteriors, to create a bright, sunny day on a gray and overcast one.

BTA See BEST TIME AVAILABLE.

buckle The term that describes how film curls because of heat exposure or shrinks because of pull and strain on the film. This shrinkage results in an unsteady image in the camera or projector. See BREATHING.

buckle switch A trip-device on certain cameras and projectors that immediately shuts off the equipment when the film loop jumps the tracking feed or pull-up mechanism.

buckling The warping of film on the edges, caused by extreme temperatures and exposure to the elements. It can be caused by winding the film too tightly as well.

budget Amounts allocated to specific production categories, singly and in the total aggregate. (See BUDGET FORM in Appendix.) The *adjusted budget* is the revised budget based on new items and cost increases in existing ones. It also includes the finalization of any open-item costs. The *estimated budget* is a rough budget that approximates the cost of production. It is based on industry fees and percentages, and projections of pre-production, production and post-production schedules. The *prelim budget* is more detailed than the estimated budget, normally with more of the above-the-line items established and indicated, and below-the-line costs quoted and tallied. The *production budget* is a fully detailed one, running about two dozen pages, itemized as closely as possible. It is used as a guide to help control production expenses. Used by PRODUCERS, production and unit managers, as well as department heads and the DIRECTOR.

buff An aficionado or fan, in general. In media, it is often used in the phrase "movie buff."

buildup Writing/directing/editing conceptualization of numerous shots arranged in a crescendoing action sequence in order to intensify the rising action of a film or videotape. In film it has been developed most effectively when approached as an extended montage, i.e., montage building to a dramatic climax.

build-up The hype and public relations preceding the launching of a new performer or a comeback of a formerly prominent one. It can be accomplished with on-the-air interviews on radio and TV talk shows, trade ads, and planted stories in media columns in the tabloids, newspapers and "the trades." The personal appearances are often arranged to coincide with the release of a film or launching of a TV series, in which the particular performer appears.

built-in actuator An electrically activated mechanism that aims a satellite dish using a simple control knob. This does away with having to manually position the dish.

built-in light meter An integrated part of the camera in those camera heads utilizing this meter. It greatly simplifies taking a light reading. In specific cameras the LIGHT METER automatically controls the iris diaphragm, opening it wider or closing it, as light levels change. This is especially helpful in filming non-recurring events and in underwater cinematography.

bulb A glass or quartz envelope holding the luminescent elements that radiate light when activated.

bulk eraser An eletromagnetic tool that aligns all iron oxide molecules on a magnetic tape or the magnetic stripe coated onto motion picture film. This process, known as DEGAUSSing, eliminates any pre-recorded sound on them or any sound leaks or static buildup.

bulletin A news notice considered important enough to interrupt the regularly scheduled broadcast.

bullet squib A small charge of pre-planted explosive that is denotated by a direct-wire electrical charge or by radio control to simulate a bullet striking a surface.

bumper A line of dialogue or piece of action in a television drama that is used to arouse suspense or curiosity, planted just before the commercial break, to get the viewers to stay tuned in for the resolution or continuation of the show.

In studio logistics, the bumper is the time allotted in a studio for one production to clear the stage of props and equipment and sometimes scenery before the incoming production group arrives.

bump up To enlarge from one film or tape size to another. It is generally used in reference to VIDEOTAPE.

burned-in image In TV cameras, a burned-in image is one that lingers after the main image has been shifted to another scene; the unwanted carry-over image stays on in its final position. Not to be confused with BURN-IN.

burn-in A superimposition of white TITLES, lettering or graphic images onto a darker background. If color is to be added, the burn-in must be black-matte and filmed separately. A common burn-in is in DOCUMENTARIES, when the name of the on-camera person who is speaking appears, usually in the lower center portion of the screen. Similarly, the subtitled text in foreign films is an example of the use of burn-ins.

burn-out The wearing out of bulbs in a working lamp. Forced burn-out can be caused by excessive use or extremely high temperatures within the lamp unit.

bus Communications path between two switching contacts within a computer. It is used in computer-hookups with both audio and video taping and editing.

business Additional directed action, over and above the blocking, that augments and strengthens the existing moment or the basic theme or idea of a dramatic work.

busing The connecting of two or more CIRCUITS.

bust shot Torso SHOT.

busy Too much BUSINESS. The distracting and random movement within a scene or a scene that is over-full with people and things. Much of the movement is done without motivation.

butterfly A stretched SCRIM on a large oval frame, used in interior lighting set-ups to diffuse luminence directed toward an actor, and in daylight exteriors to soften the glare of the sunlight on the subject to be filmed.

button up To summarize a news or discussion program and close it off.

butt splice An editor's film SPLICE wherein film ends are joined together without overlapping.

buy To accept a scene at its completion, as in "That's a buy!" This phrase can also mean that an entire production concept is agreed upon and the production contract can be drawn up. "That's a buy!" or "It's a buy!" can also mean, "That's it; it's a wrap," i.e., the production is completed.

B wind See A WIND.

byte A byte is a unitary group of BITS processed together. The only limits on the number of bytes depend upon the basic system and how many data bytes are available within that system. Used in timecoding on videotape, and for accuracy and synchronization in post-production.

C

C The symbol for CANDLE.

cable The heavy electrical cords used to power lamps, portable heaters and air blowers, special effects electrically powered gear, camera systems, utility lights etc. A cable is also a wire that may be insulated which transmits electrical currents or impulses. A multi-stranded cable concentrically sheathed in protective insulation can be used for separate or various transmissions. Single-conductor cables are totally insulated from one another.

It is also a general term for a TV system wherein picture and sound are transmitted directly over phone lines and then switched from a local junction near the individual to separate cables leading into each household. Cable systems entail additional costs to install and usually charge a monthly fee for the use of their specific multichannel services. Cable systems are also used within large corporate structure or governmental buildings for in-house telecasting, as well as in hotels and motels for closed-circuit programming.

cable-access channels Franchised channels specifically designated for use in public-access programming with 3,500 or more subscribers. All requests processed by the channel must be handled in a nondiscriminatory manner, with no prejudice shown because of race, sex, national origin, political or religious preference. The requests are to be processed in order received. The programming is for the community audience of the particular geographical viewing area. Also known as public access channels.

cable coupler A joining device for connecting similar or different kinds of CABLES.

cable household A marketing and audience-survey term that denotes a home with some form of cable TV.

Cable News Network (CNN) An all-news cable TV network.

cable penetration A ratio count of homes with TV in proportion to those with cable TV. It is the number of homes in any given area tied in to a cable-TV system.

cable-ready A TV or VCR that is able to receive VHF, UHF, plus midband and high-band channels.

cable release The start/stop device on a motion picture camera or the shutter-trip mechanism on a still camera. The cable release is a metallic-thread cloth or plastic-covered tripwire that moves within that sheath to start or stop the on/off camera mechanism on a motion picture camera. It can also be used for filming stop-frame (one frame at a time).

cable sheath The covering for separate cable conducting-wire that is made of lead, resin, rubber, neoprene or similar plastics.

cable television (CATV) A centrally located master-antenna that transmits signals to subscriber homes over a specially attached cable. CATV gets its operating revenue from a monthly charge to the subscriber of the cable services and from advertising. More powerful cable networks are emerging as they attract a wide range of audiences. They offer the viewer alternatives to programming and less dependence on the major networks. It was developed to serve areas where regular TV transmissions were difficult to receive but soon expanded. CATV augments its network-emanated signals by receiving and retransmitting satellite signals from international sources.

cadmium cell An electric battery or phone cell whose measurement is used as a standard voltage reference: 1.0186 volts at 20°C. Used as portable energy sources in battery belts, walkie-talkies, recording machines, etc., because of their greater durability and reliability.

cadmium sulfide meter A LIGHT METER that uses cadmium sulphide as its active light-sensitive element.

calculator A small cardboard or plastic calibrated and graph-charted device that gives instant read-outs of the relationship between various compensatory filming factors: F NUMBER, COLOR TEMPERATURES, FILTER FACTORS, etc. It is used by camera crews at the studio and on location to determine light settings, how much film has been exposed and how much must be on hand for upcoming

scenes, which filters should be used or replaced by others, and many other general and specific functions.

calibration The marking on the LENS barrels and rings, used to set the effective APERTURE of the lens diaphragm and to control the FOCUS. In general, it is a guide-mark indicating a particular measured point.

call A working schedule for a performance, filming or rehearsal. It is also known as shooting call. The call sheets on the working set or on location are prepared by the production managers and/or assistant directors and given to cast and crew before the next filming. See CALL SHEET in Appendix.

call letters Identification letters for radio and TV stations. "K" and "W" are the commercial call letters used in the United States. Using the Mississippi River as the approximate dividing line, "K" tends to be a western U.S. ID, while "W" is used for those stations in the eastern half of the United States.

CAM See CAM INTERMITTENT.

camera A lightproof mechanism for holding and exposing film; a device used to take photographs.

camera angle The field of view of a camera when it is set up to shoot. The qualifying terms high, low and wide are based on an imaginary norm that roughly corresponds to a 35mm camera with a 2-inch lens pointed at a scene, from shoulder height. The outstanding Russian pioneer filmmaker and film esthetician, Sergei Eisenstein (1898–1948), in his books *Film Form, The Film Sense,* and *Notes of a Film Director* has emphasized dramaturgical and emotional importance in the selection of camera angles, indicating some aspects of their inherent symbolism and metaphorical content.

camera car Any car, truck or customized vehicle designed to handle special camera mounts or specialized BOOMS. It is used for TRAVELING SHOTS and FOLLOW SHOTS or to be able to move rapidly from place to place while on LOCATION. Most professional camera cars are actually flatbed trucks with a preset camera boom bolted or welded onto the platform. Also called an INSERT CAR. See PICTURE CAR.

camera crew See CAMERAMAN.

cameraman The general term for members of the camera crew. The FIRST CAMERAMAN, also called CHIEF CAMERA-MAN, DIRECTOR OF PHOTOGRAPHY or CI-NEMATOGRAPHER, is responsible for the placement and movement of the camera, and for supervising the lighting of the scene to be shot. The SECOND CAMERA-MAN, also called ASSISTANT CAMERAMAN or CAMERA OPERATOR, acts under instructions from the first cameraman, carries out the preliminary adjustments to the camera, and monitors the scene during shooting. The SECOND ASSISTANT CAMERAMAN is the direct assistant to the camera operator. The still cameraman is responsible for taking publicity and production still photographs of the CAST, CREW and SET.

camera, motion picture types A COMBAT CAMERA is one designed primarily for HAND-HELD shooting under combat conditions. See ARRI. A field camera is a nonsilenced camera primarily adapted to shooting exterior scenes, where portability is of first importance. A studio camera is one designed for studio and sound-stage use, fully silenced and carrying every refinement needed for SYNCH-SOUND filming.

camera mount Any camera-holding device that allows panning (see PAN) or TILTING. The mounts are attached to TRI-PODS, flatboards, DOLLIES, BOOMS or customized mount-holders. A BODY BRACE or a STEADICAM are camera mounts. Some mounts are rigid mounts, placed on helicopters, motorcycles, camera helmets, etc., that rely on a person or vehicle to provide movement for the shot.

camera movement Movement of the whole camera as a unit (nonpivotal movement on either its vertical or horizontal axes) while shooting a scene. Also, any integrated movement using a rigid mount. See INTERMITTENT.

camera operator See CAMERAMAN.

camera original The film that was exposed within the camera.

camera left/camera right (screen left/screen right) East-west orientation used by writers, directors, cameramen and editors to help them establish patterns of consistent movement on screen. Analagous to, but not the same as, stage left and stage right in live theatre. When on stage, looking out at the audience, in a proscenium theater, stage left is to the left of the performer, stage right to his or her right. Camera left/camera right are just the reverse; that is, left and right are from the point-of-view of the audience. Anything right of center screen is camera or screen right, anything to the left, camera or screen left. These directions have cultural and symbolic meanings that are not found on the live stage. For example, a train moving from right to left is always assumed to be moving west.

camera report See PRODUCTION RE-PORT.

camera riser Any platform or shoring-up support that takes the camera higher than eye-level.

camera speed The number of FRAMES PER SECOND (fps) or feet per minute that film runs through a motion picture camera or projector. In the take-up chamber of a camera magazine or in the feed-out part of that magazine the speed of transit can vary slightly. It must be at a constant speed as it goes past the filming aperture between LENS and FILMSTOCK. Film sound speed in 16mm and 35mm is 24 fps in the United States and 25 fps in Europe. However, many cameras are now shooting film at 30 fps to match the TV-camera frame count.

camera test   A short length of film used to test the camera's lens system, steadiness of its feed and regularity of the fps rate. It can also serve simultaneously as a film test.

camera tracks   Tracks of wood or metal laid down to carry a DOLLY or camera BOOM in order to ensure smoothness of camera movement.

camera tube   A TV electron-beam tube housed inside the camera. When in operation an ELECTRON IMAGE is produced from an optical image and scanned in a set sequence to create an electric signal.

CAM intermittent   The Cam-And-Claw pulldown mechanism in a camera or projector. This wheel-and-spoke device is often referred to as CAM.

campaign   A series of concentrated and coordinated promotions for a particular product within a given number of days or weeks.

can   Any metal or plastic container used for storage or transport of film, exposed or original prints. Metal cans are preferred for most uses: in-the-field filming, storing prints, original negatives and reversal materials. The cans keep dust, moisture, excessive dryness or heat and light radiation away from the film.

Canadian Broadcasting Corporation (CBC)   Nationally regulated radio and TV network, managed and operated by the Canadian government.

Canadian Television (CTV)   The privately owned and managed English-language TV network that operates coast-to-coast in Canada. Its basic revenue is from advertising.

candela (cd)   The unit of measurement used internationally to designate

amount of LUMINANCE; 1 candela per square meter = 0.2917 FOOTLAMBERTS.

candle   The standard measurable unit of luminous intensity. That specific intensity is defined as light given off by one-sixtieth of a square centimeter of latinum at a temperature of 2042° K.

candlepower   The given intensity of the total amount of luminosity, expressed in CANDLES. This measurement unit is of critical importance to the CAMERAMAN or light GAFFER when lighting a set. What is measured is the strength of white light in the specific area to be filmed. Originally "candlepower" came from the light-strength unit of a spermacetti candle burning at the rate of 120 grams per hour. See LIGHTING.

canned   Material that has been recorded and filed for later use, such as pre-recorded sound effects, programs or music. Laugh tracks for sitcom shows are often referred to as canned laughter.

canned music   See LIBRARY.

canons of journalism   A code of ethics drafted and disseminated during the mid-1920s by the American Society of Newspaper Editors. It was adapted to television in the early 1950s by the NATIONAL ASSOCIATION OF BROADCASTERS. This TV code can be modified and amended to meet social, cultural and political changes.

cap   A LENS cover of metal or plastic or a loose cover of cloth that protects the lens.

capacity   The amount of electrical charge(s) that a system of insulated conductors can receive.

capping shutter   A shutter that is independent of the exposure shutter and functions to prevent light leakage. It is used on animation cameras or special cameras where light leak exclusion is critical.

capstan A drive-shaft, usually operating in conjunction with a pinch-roller, to take up and feed magnetic tape through a recording machine.

caption(s) Superimposed dialogue usually placed at the bottom of the screen. Captions are usually used to translate the dialogue of foreign language films and for the benefit of the hearing-impaired. They are also superimposed over action to indicate the location of a scene, the date and time, and any other explanatory information. Further utilization of captions is to clarify a speaker's words when they are not understandable, either because of overpowering surrounding noise, heavy accent or poor recording. Captions may also be used to convey what the actor is thinking but not saying.

capture effect This occurs when two FM stations are on the same frequency and the stronger station blocks out the reception of the weaker station.

carbon arcs (carbons) Direct current lamps (usually powered by generator unit), which provide lighting from the high intensity burning of carbon arc elements.

cardioid microphone A microphone with a heart-shaped pickup pattern: 180° in front, with minimum rear pickup.

card rate The commercial fees for buying time, predicated on the number of airings, time of airings, and the running time of the commercial. These rate schedules also include broadcasting time slots that are available.

cargo pod A large container in standard use in major motion pictures for air-shipping camera equipment long distances.

carnet An official form obtained from U.S. Customs that is needed to register and transport production equipment for filming or taping to locations outside of the United States.

carousel Multiple 35mm slide holder in a circular form that holds and projects slides in any desired sequence. It is a basic tool of MIXED MEDIA shows and is used in conjunction with such elements as live performers, film projectors, light-beam projectors, audio units, etc.

carrier The constant amplitude wave that sends out TV signals. A frequency wave of pre-set allocations that "carries" television signals from transmitting source to relays to individual homes, or sometimes direct from the source to TV households.

CARS (Community Antenna Relay Station) FCC-designated microwave frequency band of 12.75–12.95 megahertz, used in sending signals to relay antennas in a cable network system.

cart See CARTRIDGE.

cartoon An animated film made from frame-by-frame animation of drawings, paintings or graphics, by claymation or other forms of stop-frame induced movement. See COMPUTER-GENERATED ANIMATION.

cartridge A pre-packaged, self-contained unit for film or tape, designed for simple, non-adjustable insertion, avoiding threading or line-up adjustment. A *phonograph cartridge* is a replaceable sound unit, including the needle, at the end of the pickup or playing arm. A *sound effects cartridge* is one (often on a continuous loop) that replaces sound effect tapes, records, or magnetic-stripe film. A *music cartridge* has the basic form and function as the effects cartridge. Also called cart.

cartridge camera A videotape or film camera that uses CARTRIDGES instead of reel-to-reel film or tape. If inserted into the mechanism of the camera they can be ejected ready for development (if film) or play (if tape). Cartridge-loads are used to avoid threading the film on spools or cores. The film cartridges originally in super-8mm, are being replaced by videocassettes, mostly for non-professional filming. The audio tape cartridges are being used widely in location-taping, particularly for news coverage.

cartridge machine   A cartridge player; particularly one used at a broadcasting station.

cassette   A tape cartridge containing a roll of one-eighth-inch tape with a feed reel and a rewind reel. This is the cassette used in the Walkman players and in home entertainment units in tape-decks. It is also used professionally for music and effects elements in sound mixes.

cassette recorder   A recording machine using one-eighth inch blank cassettes as its audio stock.

cassette tape   The audio stock inside a packaged ⅛″ cassette. It is used extensively by news and general story field interviewers. In order to edit it, the cassette tape is transferred up to ¼″ reel-to-reel and then script-edited and spliced to conform for broadcast use.

cast   The total number of performers needed to fill all roles in a film, videotape, radio program, or whatever dramatic medium is selected. In film this usually breaks down into these categories: STARS, FEATURE PLAYERS, BIT or DAY PLAYERS. The BACKGROUND cast—comparable to supernumeraries (supers) on the stage—would be the EXTRAS, also referred to as ATMOSPHERE. Special cast categories would be actors in cameo roles and STUNTPEOPLE. In musicals there would be further subcategories for dancers and singers. See STAND-IN.

As a verb cast means to select actors for various roles in a film, program or commercial. Often handled by the CASTING DIRECTOR.

casting department   A regular division of major film or TV studios, as well as large, independent production companies, that specializes in casting the dramatic or musical projects of these companies.

casting director   The person in charge of sending out requests for actors to read for roles in SCRIPTS that are to be produced or are already in production. The casting director works closely with the DIRECTOR and sometimes the PRODUCER in setting up the readings. The final selection of performers is done by the director or producer. In casting for COMMERCIALS or INDUSTRIAL FILMS, the client often makes the ultimate choice.

cast insurance   Insurance to cover production budgetary losses caused by incapacity of a performer, particularly a star, who is unable to appear for filming because of a general, unavoidable delay, accident, bodily injury, sickness or death.

cathode   The negatively charged TERMINAL, as opposed to ANODE.

cathode ray   An electron stream sent out from an electric filed of an evacuated tube that is activated by the cathode electrode.

cathode ray tube (CRT)   The basic TV tube that evolved from the simpler diode, but in more complex form. It includes an electron gun that emits a stream of electrons which strike a coated-fluorescent tube widened at the other end, i.e., the TV "screen." When activated, the electron gun emits its grid-controlled electron stream, which forms or reassembles the picture.

cattle call   A mass casting call, sometimes an open audition, for various supporting and minor roles, including dancers and singers.

CATV   See COMMUNITY ANTENNA TELEVISION and CABLE TELEVISION.

catwalk   A narrow walkway suspended above a shooting stage. It is used for the high-rigging of lamps to light the set. It allows ELECTRICIANS and GRIPS to mount and operate lights or drop in overhanging microphones.

CBC See CANADIAN BROADCASTING CORPORATION.

CBS See COLUMBIA BROADCASTING SYSTEM.

CCR See CENTRAL CONTROL ROOM.

cd See CANDELA.

cel A sheet of transparent plastic in width-and-height accommodating screen ratios in size. These sheets, of CELLULOSE ACETATE, cellulose triacetate, or comparable plastic, are used to paint, ink or draw on directly and are used mainly for ANIMATION and titling. The cels have premeasured, pre-punched holes, customized to the particular film ratio and animation-camera system. Cels are put into proper registration by slipping the camera-ready cels over matching pegs on the device that holds these cels while they are being filmed.

cel animation Film made with drawings, full art work, graphics or abstract designs photographed or videorecorded on standardized CELLULOSE ACETATE or triacetate sheets.

celluloid The working name for cellulose nitrate, which was the original flammable film base, that is now replaced by CELLULOSE ACETATE.
  Celluloid is also a slangy name for things dealing with or related to film. In the 1920s and 1930s one of Hollywood's nicknames was *Celluloid City*. A recently operating projection room in Hollywood was *Celluloid Services*.

cellulose acetate Safety-base transparent film for photographic emulsions.

cement A liquid used to chemically dissolve FILM BASE in order to make two pieces of film bond together in a SPLICE.

censorship Arbitrary applied guidelines determining what can or cannot be said or shown. All countries have some form of media censorship. It may be for any combination of commercial, political, religious or social reasons.
  The performing arts in media are particularly sensitive to long lists of "do nots." For example, hard liquor commercials have been banned in the U.S., but ads for wine or beer are acceptable. However, wine or beer cannot be sipped, tasted or gulped but it can be shown in beautiful and glamorous settings, poured in slow motion in rich, glorious color, even lifted right up to the lips. Politically, in the United States in the 1980s, the Department of Energy attempted to suppress films on acid rain for fear of giving a bad image of the oil companies and heavy industry. Their attempt to ban two Canadian films on acid rain raised a great outcry, and one of the two films went on to win the Oscar in the Best Documentary Short category.
  Censorship styles and standards vary from state to state, even city to city, and, of course, country to country. When filming it is vital to know the rules and tacit mores of a given region. For example, in Mexico you cannot film people walking around in bare feet, prisons or military installations. Film confiscation, equipment confiscation and personal detainment are not uncommon punishments if these rules are violated. In Russia, military bases and airports cannot be filmed without high-level permission. In nearly all areas filming permits are needed.

centering control The TV control knob or handle used to move the full TV screen image left and right or up and down. It works in conjunction with the FRAMING CONTROL. Horizontal control moves the cathode-ray tube image left or right; vertical control, up or down.

center of perspective The camera-eye position in which the photographed image will match up dimensionally with the actual subject.

Central Casting The original CASTING service to provide the studios with specific types of EXTRAS: American Indians, wrestlers, swimmers, executives at a conference table, DRESS EXTRAS, for example. These services were paid for by the production company of the studio's production unit. The fee paid is based on a percentage of the extra's gross pay. Since Central Casting there have been many other casting companies and services established.

central control room A main area for audio and video MIXING and/or the generation of broadcast image and sound. It is usually a soundproof, glass-enclosed booth with consoles to accept all input elements for the final selection and mixing into final form. In live television this process may be done simply by selecting shots on multiple monitors.

century stand (c-stand) Basic, metal all-purpose stand, with a special head on top to which arms for FLAGS, CUCALORISES, tree branches, or whatever is called for can be attached. For example, an INKY-DINK light is often cantilevered from a c-stand arm to move into, above or below the scene. Other small lights can also be attached by slipping over the topmost vertical rod extension of the century stand.

ceramic microphone One that is activated for sound production and transmission by a ceramic CARTRIDGE.

ceramic pickup A record-console's ceramic cartridge in the playing head.

changeover Switching from one projector to another so that reels may move sequentially with minimal or no pause. Ideally, this should be an uninterrupted flow from one projector with one reel to the second projector with the next reel, a seamless continuity of sound and picture.

CFI See CONSOLIDATED FILM INDUSTRIES.

CG See CHARACTER GENERATOR.

changeover cue A circular mark flashed a few seconds before the end of the reel, and a direct cue to roll the next reel at only a few frames before changeover. The first visual cue of the circular mark sometimes activates an auditory cue that alerts the projectionist to check for focus on the upcoming reel and activates the projector-to-projector changeover. A twice-recurring cue, as a rule, to the projectionist.

changing bag A light-proof bag with "sleeves" which the CAMERAMAN can put his arms into to handle the exposed or unexposed film. Often used on location for loading and unloading MAGAZINES.

channel A term used more frequently in TV than radio. It refers to a designated circuit for the receipt or transmission of electronic signals. Commercial radio commonly uses the term FREQUENCY. In ordinary conversation the station, or channel, is referred to by call letters or numerical dial position, e.g., "68.5 FM," "92.8 AM."

channel reversing switch A switch device that shifts the output of two speakers in a stereo system, i.e. the previous right-speaker sound now coming from the left speaker, and vice versa.

channel selector A dial, switch or pushbutton that is used to choose a particular channel.

channel separation The difference of sound characteristics between left and right channels. Too little separation can nullify any sense of "stereo" in the sound, while too much separation distorts the "normal" balance.

character One of the parts in a film. A specific ROLE.

character actor/actress A performer who portrays supporting ROLES. However, there are many films with character LEADS, where an actor who usually plays supporting character roles has a leading role. The character actor differs from the more romantic or traditional leads—IN-GENUE, JUVENILE, LEADING LADY or LEAD-ING MAN—in being older, of a different race or nationality, or in other ways that set them apart. Sometimes, as in the Western movies, the HERO's sidekick—the character actor—serves as comedy relief. Noted character actors of the past would certainly include such performers as Marie Dressler, Wallace Beery, Margaret Hamilton, Mischa Auer, Herman Bing and Margaret Dumont. The character actor helps give a richer texture to the dramatic mixture, a greater sense of filmic reality by creating believable characters, dramatic or comedic.

characterization The internal/external delineation of the character the actor is portraying. Characterization derives from three areas: the SCRIPT itself, indicating the human background, environment and personality of each character; the additional interpretive touches added by the DIRECTOR; and the final fusion by the ACTOR, physicalizing all of this in the performance.

character makeup Makeup that in color and texture enhances the actor's physical appearance in relation to the character. For example, it is used to make actors appear to be humanoid, a different race, considerably older, to have distinctive scars or markings.

charger A specialized, small transformer for re-powering batteries usually using an ALTERNATING CURRENT.

chase Standard suspense-creating or intensifying dramaturgical device that creates tension through the suspense of extended or delayed physical confrontation; usually between PROTAGONIST and antagonist. Elements of the chase can include near-misses, immediate danger, deaths of secondary characters, rapid and perilous pursuit, and explosive—literally and metaphorically—dramatic resolution. These high-intensity, fast-action scenes of pursuit in Westerns are on horseback; for

cops-and-robbers the automobile is the standard vehicle, with augmentation of motorcycles, trains and helicopters; for SCIENCE FICTION the proper chase vehicles are interplanetary armed spaceships. In whatever style of drama or using whatever mode of transport, certain elements remain the same in all chase sequences: the situation is life-threatening and the pace is urgent and driving.

chaser The playoff music for a comedy or variety act.

chassis A cabinet or frame for housing electronic elements and their circuitry, which is made of sheet metal or a heavy-duty plastic.

chatter The opening-and-closing of an electrical current, particularly at contact points, that causes irregular video and sound and general transmission problems.

cheat To force a perspective or create an illusion by using real elements to establish an image that is physically not real, but seems so on screen. An example is Harold Lloyd's famous sequence in *Safety Last* in which he is hanging onto a giant clock, high on a building, with nothing below him but the city streets and a sea of traffic. In actuality, Harold Lloyd was hanging only a few feet above a roof that extended from the building at a lower level which was cropped out of the camera composition. In martial arts films, when the hero is seen jumping over a car coming toward him, and it is not a MATTE SHOT or optically-processed SPE-CIAL EFFECT, it's an instance of "cheating the shot." In this case, the hero jumps in a high arc as the car hits a given line-up mark at a given number of feet in the BACKGROUND. Properly choreographed and placed, the effect appears "real."

checkerboard cutting An editing technique that eliminates the unwanted image of the frame-cut line. This is done by covering the immediate FRAMES on either side of the frame line with black, opaque LEADER. By doing this, the transfer of the "splice-image"—emulsion, tape or frame-line—is eliminated. It is called checkerboard because of the alternating frames of picture and black leader on two strips of film (A AND B ROLLS); when one has frames of black opaque leader, the other has picture and vice versa.

check point   In computers, it is an information-storage point that allows computations to restart from that point. In media it is important in backing up and restarting in on-line editing.

check print   Film print, sometimes optical only, that is run off from the negative to see if there are any chemical or mechanical errors in the printing of the film.

chicken coop   A rectangular lighting instrument with multiple globes, covered with protective wire mesh that is usually the same sort of mesh used in actual chicken coops.

chief cameraman   See CAMERAMAN.

chief engineer   The person in charge of the technical aspects of live or taped TV production. The chief engineer works from control room or tech-center.

children's films   Films made primarily for children. These films now have more material in them that are interesting to parents, and the term children's films has been almost totally replaced by "family films." Such films have either a "G" or "PG-13" rating.

chip chart   A chart with various black-and-white patterns on one large test-camera. It is used to check out or correct camera and lens alignment.

chippie   British term for a carpenter on a film or video crew.

chopping   Electronic pre-determination and control of wave trough-crest maximums, by "chopping off" extremes.

This controls extreme audio or video distortion.

chord organ   An electronic musical instrument that reproduces a wide range of chords activated by levers, keys or buttons.

choreographer   A creator of dance numbers, ballet, or dramatically integrated choreographic movements. Choreographers sometimes serve as dance directors. In music video productions the entire physical movement is often the sole responsibility of the choreographer.

chroma   A color-saturation term that indicates the amount of saturation of any particular color. It is handled in live TV or videotaping by the chroma control.

chroma control   A color-TV variable resistor that controls the level of CHROMINANCE. It modulates the intensity-of-hue in the color-picture, starting at zero level, which is black-and-white.

chroma key (chromakey)   A TV-production MATTING technique that is done electronically.

chromatic aberration   A lens ABERRATION characterized by the failure of a lens to bring light of different wavelengths to the same FOCUS. It results in impure color, unfocused color or out-of-focus image.

chromaticity   The combining of the saturation and the hue of a color. It does not, however, designate the brilliance of the color.

chrominance   Measurable variance between one color and another of equal luminance. The reference color has a set, pre-measured CHROMATICITY. Used in TV to balance the three basic colors: red, green, blue.

chrominance subcarrier   See COLOR CARRIER.

cinch marks Scratches on the surface of a piece of film that are caused by pressing down on the edges of a lightly wound roll of film or by drawing it tight.

ciné Prefix from the Greek *kinema,* indicating action and movement. The prefix itself is a back formation from cinematograph, and is used in such words as CINEMATOGRAPHER, CINERAMA, CINEMASCOPE, CINEMA and others.

cinema As a collective noun, cinema refers to the entire physical structure of cinema—real estate, theatres, distribution, commercial transactions—as well as to film as an art and a craft. As a more specific noun it refers to the motion picture theatre itself. It is used as an adjective in such phrases as cinema memorabilia, cinema fan, cinema aesthete, cinema critic, cinema historian etc.

cinema noir See FILM NOIR.

CinemaScope The original wide-screen, stereo-sound process developed by 20th Century Fox that achieved commercial success. Shot on 35mm, with a specially designed set of anamorphic lenses, the images were "squeezed" optically 50%. This compression when projected with a compensating lens added the original 50% to the now "normal" screen image, giving it that percentage of horizontal extension. The system can use magnetic or optical tracks, and this creates a slight variation in the ratio of the screen image. For optical sound, 2.35 to 1; for 4-track magnetic sound, 2.55 to 1.

CinemaScope 55 More sophisticated CINEMASCOPE process, in which a 55.6mm-wide negative stock was used in a camera engineered for the system, the lens of which squeezed the image into a ratio 2 to 1 (2:1). The CinemaScope 55 image was physically four times larger within the filmed frame. This, when reduced to a 35mm image, gave extremely high resolution to that image.

cinematographer See CAMERAMAN.

cinéma vérité A realistic approach, theoretically without directorial intervention, of an improvised scene or actual event. The event could be part of a documentary in which the confrontation of man-and-wife is highlighted to a mass political rally of thousands of people. The on-camera interviews of man-and-wife or members of the vast crowd would probably be done in a straightforward news or documentary style. Many documentaries are in part cinéma vérité, at least conceptually, but the term generally refers to films that are totally in this attitudinal style, or to fictional films that simulate undirected "reality."

cinepanoramic A descriptive term for any wide-screen system, particularly of the viewing screen and sound installation.

cineplex A group of theaters under one roof offering varied film-fare, usually first-run.

cinerama Pioneer multi-camera, multi-projector system used commercially; forerunner of today's single-projector Cinerama system. The original system employed three cameras interlocked to each shoot one third of the total image; theoretically, with no image gapping. But because of problems of matching exact intensity in the projector bulbs, and in physically lining up all projectors, and in seeing that color tonalities were precisely the same in all prints, the result was that slight error tended to compound, and that the seams were always noticeable. The problem of these errant joining lines was resolved by simply doing away with them. A single strip of 70mm film is used with a pre-set curvature distortion. When projected, that image is corrected by the exactly calibrated physical curvature of the screen itself. This maintains the sense of audience-involvement in the Cinerama sensation, while at the same time eliminating the problem of the vertical lines between three distinct areas.

cinesemiotics An academic study that analyses a film or films into its signs and symbols, and its interlinkings and interpretations. It also includes studies for tripartite orientations: connotative, denotative and contextual.

cinex strip A film-lab mechanism that prints frames of the same shot at various exposures. This allows the filmmaker to determine the best light at which to print the entire shot. Also used coversationally as simple cinex, e.g., "Maybe we ought to run off a cinex." (Pronounced sy-nex.)

circled takes Takes that are circled on PRODUCTION REPORTS. These circled takes are to be developed and lab-printed for use as WORKPRINT in postproduction. Cumulatively, they form the main body of footage for the first assembly.

circle shot See THREE-SIXTY.

circlevision The first commercially successful 360° system for filming and projecting in-the-round that was pioneered by Disney Studio's camera and art departments. It is now in use in Disneyland and Disney World, as well as Disney's EPCOT and Tokyo Disneyland for various sound-and-image-surround shows.

circuit A multichanneled electronic wavepath carrying numerous discrete signals that maximizes transmission load and aids access of data or programming; used in offline and online video editing.

circuit capacity The maximum number of communication channels that can be effectively handled simultaneously on a particular single circuit.

circuit dropout A lapse in transmission caused by circuit failure.

circuiting The shipping of feature releases straight from one theatre to another without returning them to the distributor for redistribution, inspection or repair.

circuitry A set of circuits joining the inner complex of a system or its crossconnections with other circuits to form a larger network of systems.

clamps See ALLIGATOR CLAMPS.

clapper boards A pair of hinged boards that are clapped together to get a picture or sound synch-mark. In DIALOGUE filming this is done before each TAKE, or sometimes after the take, using a TAIL-SLATE. Nothing is sound-slated until sound and camera are running at synchronous speed, "up to speed." The first visual film-frame of the full closure of the slate is afterward synchronized in the CUTTING ROOM with the first modulations resulting from the sound of the hinged boards being struck together, thus establishing synchronism between sound and picture tracks. The member of the crew who slates with the clapper board, also can call out an audio slate, e.g., " 'Backstage at the opera,' Scene one, take two." Then, the clapper is clacked. Clapper boards have been replaced, in some systems, with a subsonic electronic beep, or by an electronic slate that lights up with the proper scene number and/or the aforementioned beep. See SLATE BOARD.

classification A rating system set up to indicate which films are suitable for which audiences. In the United States the ratings are: "G"—suitable for the entire family; "PG-13"—suitable for minors over 13 years of age when accompanied by an adult; "R"—restricted from viewers under 17 years old, unless accompanied by an adult: "NC-17"—adults (over 17) only.

clatter Noise from too much tension on the take-up reel or on the projector's gate or not enough film lubrication.

claw A device used in cameras and some projectors to provide internal forward movement of the film. The claw engages one or more SPROCKET holes, and pulls the film down to the height of the frame; it then withdraws to go back to the initial position.

claymation A stop-frame animation technique wherein clay is colored, molded, then filmed one frame at a time to make the clay-sculpted forms change or move.

clean entrance/exit When an actor or object comes into frame from an area completely outside the frame's field of vision, or when exiting, to leave the field of vision, as opposed to being panned, trucked or tilted away from, and suddenly being in or out of frame, or being brought in or cropped out by zooming; a clean entrance/exit implies physical movement on the part of the actor.

clean shot No extraneous thing or people, only the story-point and scenic minima in the shot. This allows the target performer or object to dominate the primary composition of the frame.

clear To set up agreements of consent from network-affiliated stations to carry a network-transmitted program.

Also, clear means to return to the head of the audio or video tape and to zero-count, often in conjunction with DE-GAUSSING or recording directly over existing material, or over-recording to achieve a mixed soundtrack.

clearance Attaining permission to utilize registered, published or copyrighted material in film, radio or TV, like film clips, music or long quotations.

clear filter A colorless glass filter positioned between the lens and the outside of the camera used to protect the lens.

"clear the frame!" A command by the ASSISTANT DIRECTOR or DIRECTOR OF PHOTOGRAPHY directly, to move out of the camera's action field. It is usually given while setting up the shot, for cast and crew to get out of the action area in front of the camera, or a command by a director to an actor, e.g., "Be sure when you leave, you clear the frame."

click track An audio LOOP of a specific length, set to metronome equivalents and marked by an audible set of clicks. It is used to musically score a motion picture or videotape. If there is to be irregular or broken rhythm within a sequence, e.g., a dance number, the editor will scratch the synchronous WORKPRINT used for SCORING on the track itself. When scoring the picture, the conductor listens to the clicks through headphones so that the clicking sounds will not be recorded with the music.

client A person or organization who wants to buy the services of a network, studio or production company; an advertiser who buys TV time, directly or through an agency.

cliff-hanger A film or scene within a film that builds to a CLIMAX of high suspense, through a crescendo of action. It is so-named from the old serials, comedies and dramas where, just before the end of the chapter or scene, the actor or actress was left in the predicament of dire distress, often hanging from a cliff. If the person in the life-threatening situations was a LEADING MAN or LEADING LADY, he/she would always be rescued. Villains, however, might either be saved or done in; in the latter case, they were often terminated by their own villainy. Since the outcome was not certain, this added to the suspense of the cliff-hanger.

climax That part of a dramatic work in which the action reaches its most intense and decisive moment. It is the point of dramatic resolution of the conflict.

Clio An award for the best TV commercials in various categories, presented annually at the American Television and Radio Commercials Festival. The name comes from the Greek muse of history, Kleio; Latinized to Clio. It refers to history in the sense of the glorification and celebration of events rather than critical accuracy.

clip A short piece of film or tape cued in to live TV programming, particularly predominant in news and events coverage. A piece of film or tape (sometimes STOCK FOOTAGE) incorporated into a film or TV show.

clipper   That part of a TV circuit that bifurcates video and synch signals.

clipping   The sound-loss at the beginning or ends of words, sung notes or sound effects that is caused by the faulty operation of sound-activated devices.

clock   To time a scene, segment or entire show. Used as verb, "Let's clock this scene!"

close   The windup of a variety act or show. In general, the end of a program; less commonly, the end of a film. Used as a verb, "Let's close with an upbeat ending!"

closed-captioned   A special system for the hearing-impaired whereby a special TV-set adapter prints captions of the show on the screen. This can only be used on programs that are electronically augmented to provide closed-captioning.

closed circuit   A private TV line or lines for professional viewing or for placement in theatres for events not to be seen on regular TV. These commercial aspects of direct-line monitoring are rapidly being replaced by home-use CABLE or satellite reception.

closed loop   A circuit that continuously feeds back output to the input source for instant electronic evaluation.
   In computers, a closed loop refers to a set of instructions that are continually repeated until they are given a cut-off.

closed set   A set that is open only to the cast and crew of the production being filmed. No crew from other productions, tours, or even VIPs are admitted without clearance by the production company using the set. Sets become closed sets for various reasons: a nude scene, a TV soap sequence which involves a disap-

pearance or mystery, a top-secret SPECIAL EFFECTS sequence, an intense dramatic scene which requires intense concentration on the part of crew and actors, and for other technical, aesthetic and production reasons.

close shot   A SHOT where the action is filmed very tightly, but not as close to the person or object as a CLOSE-UP. Lies in between a close-up and a MEDIUM SHOT.

close-up   (CU)   Head-and-shoulder shot of a performer. A tight close-up is the head only. An EXTREME CLOSE-UP could be one eye only or the lips only. An example of the latter is the shot in *Citizen Kane*, where Charles Foster Kane's lips fill the screen as he says the famous word, "Rosebud!"

cluster bar   See CLUSTER MOUNT.

cluster mount   A LUMINAIRE mount to hold a group of lights. Also called a cluster pipe, cluster bar.

cluster pipe   See CLUSTER MOUNT.

clutch   A spindle device on a film projector that alters the tension, to smooth out the movement of the film in its take-up mode.

C-mount   A standard lens mount for 16mm and home video cameras. Lens must be one-inch wide with 32 threads, with a focal distance of 690/1000ths. It is regular field equipment for the news/documentary filmmaker.

CNN   See CABLE NEWS NETWORK.

coated lens   A camera LENS in which the exterior side is chemically coated to reduce reflection. This magnesium fluoride application allows more light to pass through the lens and onto the emulsion surface of the film.

coaxial cable   A transmission line which (when seen in a cross-section) is concentrically formed, i.e., one line completely encompasses the other. The line uses external fields and has none of its own. This transmission line can effectively carry over 40 channels.

coaxial magazine A magazine for film where feed-out and take-up chambers are directly opposite and parallel to one another.

cobweb-maker/spinner A SPECIAL EFFECTS device that blows strands of rubber cement onto a specified area of a set to give the appearance of cobwebs. It is a container that holds the rubber cement and a fan and nozzle to spray the "webs."

co-channel interference Distortion or discontinuity in signals, which happens when two signals operating on the same channel interfere with one another.

code The codified guide to ideal practices in a particular field, e.g., Motion Picture Production Code, Canons of Journalism Code, Self-regulation Code of MPAA, NAB Code, and others.

code generator Electronic gear that puts visual identification numbers onto videotape. It is comparable to CODE NUMBERS in film.

code numbers Identical numbers printed during the editorial assembly in post-production along the edges of synchronized positive picture and SOUND TRACKS, thus providing synch marks at intervals of one foot from the start of the reel. To be carefully distinguished from NEGATIVE numbers.

coding A way of designating characters internally, within the computer, to be electronically converted to print-out or read-out numbers for videotape editing.

coding machine Device that prints matching numbers onto the optical film picture and optical SOUND TRACK to facilitate synching. See SYNCHRONISM.

coherent video A combination signal consisting of a radar echo and the steadily emitted signals of a continuous-wave oscillator. A functional moving-target system is thus formed and used for specific-signal transmission.

cold A descriptive term referring to reading or performing with either minimal or no preparation: "He gave a cold reading," or "She did the interview cold," for example. Also, a description of a performance lacking warmth, as in "Technically it was excellent, but his performance was cold."

cold lights Fluorescents.

collimated lights Lights with parallel rays (not converging or diverging) that are used to properly align lenses and adjust them for accurate focus.

collimation The theory and technique for making light rays parallel. Critical in camera or lens systems to achieve true image and sharp focus.

color (colour) The nuances and shadings of an actor in line readings, gestures and movements; the added emphasis given to a role by the performer. In writing it refers to the variegated range of the text in its interrelationship to its depth-of-concept, the basis of which is the responsibility of directors and performers to delineate.

color balance In film, accurate color reproduction can be achieved only at the source of filming, all later color-balancing techniques performed at the lab result in varying degrees of effectiveness. Filming color can only be done properly when the film being used has been color-balanced for the specific light source, e.g., tungsten-balanced, daylight-balanced, etc. The appropriateness and quality of the light is measured in degrees KELVIN. Higher color temperatures come from blue light sources, the bluer the light the higher the color temperature. This is the obverse of the red-light source, i.e., the lower the light, the redder the light source. Daylight-balanced film will be set for about 6000° K. Tungsten-balanced, 3200° K. Using a film in light different from that for which it is pre-balanced will result in inferior color reproduction. Sometimes, however, a film stock will be used to work against its specified balance in order to achieve additional grain or deliberate color distortion.

In TV, the state of color intermixing as near to "real" color as possible is achieved by adjusting the light-emitting capabilities of the three basic phosphors in the picture tube on the "screen" surface. The balancing-out is necessary because of the differences in the light-emission potential of the three phosphors.

color bars   VIDEO varicolored stripes are used to check and correct color accuracy before broadcasting or presenting a tape for viewing on any viewing system. Color bars precede the actual program section of a tape and run from ten seconds to a minute.

colorblind film   A type of film with black and white emulsion that responds to only one region of the spectrum, usually the blue, and is therefore unable to distinguish colors. This film allows yellow safelights to be utilized in film processing rooms, since the film isn't sensitive to this yellow light and won't become exposed in it.

color burst   Approximately nine cycles of the chrominance subcarrier are part of the composite color signal. Also called reference burst, it is used in the color receiver as a phase reference for the 3.579545-MHz oscillator.

color carrier   A radio frequency signal used for video transmission that carries color information as a carrier for I ("intensity"—luminous intensity) and Q ("quantity"—of electric charge) signals. Frequency: 3.579545 MHz. Also called CHROMINANCE SUBCARRIER.

color-carrier reference   A continuous signal that has the same frequency as the color subcarrier. It has a fixed-phase interlinking with the COLOR BURST. The color-carrier reference modulates at the transmitter and demodulates at the receiver.

colorcast   A TV transmission that is broadcast in color.

color coder   Circuit or part of a color-TV transmitter that combines camera signals with the COLOR CARRIER. This produces the transmitted color picture signal. Also called color encoder.

color-compensating filter   Lens-mounted filter for color-balancing a shot, particularly for correcting color imbalances in film stock, or for pushing for a particular color to permeate the scene. Used in cameras and PRINTERS.

color-conversion filter   A more radical filter for deliberately giving a specific color cast to a scene; it changes the color temperature of the light illuminating a given scene.

color correction   Adaptation of the lighting of a scene to match cinematographic requirements. For example, a scene may want to lose the blue of the real daylight sky, because the set-up being shot is a DAY-FOR-NIGHT scene, and in color shooting, the daylight blue gives away the true lighting.

color decoder   A section, unit or circuit of a TV receiver that translates the incoming signals produced by the color coder into the TV set's useable color signals and COLOR BURSTS.

color edging   Unwanted extraneous color at the borders of an image.

color duplicate negative (color dupe)   Protection duplicate made from the original negative used for striking off multiple prints and to save the original.

color encoder   See COLOR CODER.

color fidelity Degree of accuracy of color reproduction in a television system or the color values of the actual image.

color film FILM STOCK that is color-receptive and that can be processed for and printed in color. Approximative "color" prints, hand-tinted by the frame, or tinted in one overriding color for different scenes (D.W. Griffith in *Birth of a Nation,* 1915, for example) had been around since the late 1890s. In 1918 TECHNICOLOR launched a red-and-green process, among others. In England, in 1921, the film *The Great Adventure* was in color—Prizmacolor. One sequence in de Mille's first *The Ten Commandments* (1923) was in color. 1932 was a color milestone in film history; it was the year that the first three-color Technicolor film was made. It was a Disney cartoon, *Flowers and Trees.* The first feature film shot completely in Technicolor's three-strip system was RKO's *Becky Sharp* (1935). The three-strip process was replaced by Technicolor's own monopack that used one instead of three negatives. But the three-strip prints in prime condition have never been equalled in color values (in the opinion of many color-film experts). However, with today's fast film stock, flexible and portable cameras and lighting equipment, new color dynamics are being explored, often successfully, by cinematographers. Also, there are improved lab techniques for color-saturating and desaturating film, forcing-for-grain to texturize film, plus shooting in color stock and printing in black-and-white.

color film analyzer Scanning optical-electrical unit in a film lab system that evaluates the color negative and gives a reading for proper EXPOSURE on the print to be made from the negative.

color flicker Fluttering color caused by unwanted fluctuations in CHROMATIC-ITY and LUMINANCE.

colorimeter Optical device that makes color evaluations between a color test sample and a standard synthesized sample. It is used to analyze the technical electronic efficiency of color-reproduction equipment.

colorimetry Technical method to measure and evaluate color in all its phases, from film targeting to reproduction for viewing.

colorization An electronic process which adds color to a motion picture; specifically, to turn a black-and-white film into a motion picture in color.

colorizer A unit that blends COLOR BURSTS with incoming light from the target object to create intensification through distorting, abstracting or caricaturing images.

colorizing Gerundial noun, as in, "Colorizing has opened up new markets in re-releasing old black-and-white films." It is also used as a verb, as in, "Some of the films in our library are going to be colorized."

color lily Color chart photographed for reference at the head of a scene; it is either slated separately or physically attached to the working slate.

color match Shot-to-shot constancy of general color appearance of a film or tape, from beginning to end.

color mixture In TV, the color that is a blend of LUMINAIRES of different colors. Also an electronic mixture of alternating colors at an extremely high rate so that optically they appear as one. Color mixture also refers to colors that can be produced simultaneously if they are immediately contiguous, small and close enough, so that no pattern effect is discernible.

color negative Film that has color images complementary to the colors of the filmed subject. Light areas of the subject appear dark on the negative, and dark areas appear light. See PRINT.

color oscillator A TV set oscillator whose frequency and phase are synchronized at the transmission point by the master oscillator. The TV set's color oscillator functions at a burst frequency of 3.579545 MHz.

color-picture signal   A signal that electrically carries a scene's three color attributes: BRIGHTNESS, HUE, SATURATION. See BLANKING.

color picture tube   Large electron tube that produces a color image by scanning and activating the screen phosphors with changing intensities from image-to-image. The images produced are derived from the preset levels of the selected primary colors.

color print film   FILM STOCK for making color prints from color originals or intermediates.

color processing   The chemical and mechanical development of film to produce color images. See DEVELOP.

color purity   Color at its basic level, i.e., with white light or additional colored light removed.

color registration   Mixture of superimposed colors in a TV monitor: red, green and blue.

color rendering index   A number corresponding to a light source that indicates the approximate effect of that light source as it illuminates colored surfaces.

color reversal film   Film stock which, when camera-exposed and lab-developed, has a positive image (the opposite of the COLOR NEGATIVE). Reversal film has been phased out of filmmaking and has been replaced by negative stock.

color reversal intermediate (CRI) COLOR DUPLICATE NEGATIVE made directly from the color original in the reversal process.

color saturation   Amount of color in a frame using white as a guide. The farther away from white, the stronger the saturation.

color sensitivity   A photosensitive emulsion's response to exposure to various wave lengths of white light.

color-sync signal   Sequential cluster of COLOR BURSTS. These subcarrier reference signals help make up the composite video signal.

color television   Complete color range of TV images from red, blue and green signals, remodulated for reception.

color television receiver   In developing the color TV set from the black and white sets, a regular monochrome (black/white) augmented the receiver with special circuitry, and a "screen" that is sensitive to three primary TV colors (red, green and blue; R-G-B). The colors are produced by PHOSPHORS customized to R-G-B.

color temperature   A value scale for measuring a light source on a set in degrees KELVIN.

color temperature meter   A METER that reads a light source in a graded KELVIN scale, giving the color temperature of light's ambience.

Color-tran   Commercial name for a lighting product that contains built-in transformers on its individual units. These autotransformers boost the voltage delivered to standard lamps, increasing their color temperature and allowing more light to be put into the filmed scene.

color triad   Red-green-blue phosphor dots that carry the color-producing elements.

color wheel   A rotating wheel with circular frames in which to place color GELS. The wheel can be made to rotate at a steady rate for continued color changes, or be used to switch from one color to another. It is used for special on-camera or on-stage lighting effects.

Columbia Broadcasting System (CBS)   One of the major television and radio broadcasting networks.

Columbia Pictures   A major motion picture studio located for many years in Hollywood's "Gower Gulch," that is, fronting on Hollywood's Gower Street. It is now located at the Warner/Columbia lot in Burbank, California.

coma   Aberration in spherical lenses caused by the asymmetrical formation of the rays that form the image; the result is an unclear image.

combat camera   See CAMERA, MOTION PICTURE TYPES and ARRI.

combination microphone   A microphone that uses two or more microphones combined into one.

combiner circuit   TV camera circuit combining LUMINANCE and chroma channels with the sync signals.

comeback   To return to a successful career in the performing arts, after having been absent for a considerable time.

comedy   An attitudinal orientation and structuring of material, utilizing many elements: slapstick, satire, parody, farce, plot situations, bawdiness, grotesquery, burlesque or wit.

comedy of manners   Humorous delineation of dramatic characters, which makes light of or scathingly attacks their social-climbing activities and their petty pretensions.

coming attractions   Short excerpts of a film or tape, edited for maximum impact, with added graphics or special scenes. It is essentially a commercial for an upcoming or currently showing motion picture or TV program. Also called TRAILERS.

command   In computer language, set(s) of signals generated by an instruc-tion. A triggering signal acting within a receiving device.

commentary   Spoken text VOICE-OVER or on-camera for a film or videotape, usually in a news or DOCUMENTARY format. Also called NARRATION.

commentary (news)   Editorialized and interpretive remarks by a newscaster that present a personal viewpoint.

commercial   Word indicating the sales power of a TV program or describing a motion picture with strong box-office appeal; as in, "It's got great commercial potential."
It is also a radio or TV advertisement, broadcast during COMMERCIAL BREAKS.

commercial break   A time slot during or between programs, allocated for a COMMERCIAL or PUBLIC SERVICE ANNOUNCEMENT.

Community Antenna Relay Station   See CARS.

Community Antenna Television   An independent or network cable station fed through a system that transmits programs into homes by way of a COAXIAL CABLE tied into a master antenna.

complementary colors   Contrasting colors; on a color wheel they are the colors opposite one another. An unmixed color has no complementary elements in it. FILTERS absorb their complementaries: for example, red filters absorb blue and green, green filters absorb red and blue, blue filters absorb red and green and yellow filters absorb blue.

completion services   LOOPING, sound transfers, lab printing, CONFORMING of original picture, graphics, mixing, etc., to be done after the shooting of a film. Also known as POST-PRODUCTION SERVICES.

compilation film   A film made up mostly or completely of preshot footage, such as news coverage, OUTS, pickup shots, technical shots or archival material.

The editing of these elements often includes introductory or wrap-around segments filmed or taped especially for the project.

complimentary tickets   See COMPS.

composer   Author of music. In performing media he is often composer-arranger-conductor, or a combination of any two of those elements. With the new electronic musical systems (emulators, synthesizers and the newly emerging computerized master-memory units), the composer is often his own basic orchestra, augmenting the score with acoustical instruments. Sometimes the entire score is electronically produced.

components   See ELEMENTS.

composite   Synchronously   aligned sound and picture on one piece of film.
    Also, a glossy still picture.

composite color signal   TV picture, blanking and synchronizing signals, taken together.

composite sync signal   TV sync signal comprised of horizontal, vertical, blanking and equalizing pulses.

compound move   Having both actors and camera in movement during a shot. It also refers to a camera move where two or more movements are combined, e.g., panning while zooming, zooming back while physically moving back on a dolly, tilting down while dollying in, etc.

comps   Short for complimentary tickets or passes. Originated in live theatre. See ANNIE OAKLEY.

computer   Electronic device for extremely rapid solutions to problems, for instant switching commands, memory retrieval or extensive data storage. Now used in all phases of communications, and every branch of the performing arts. In media arts, computers serve many functions, including: to "store" entire screenplays, production reports, budgets and logistics; to "supervise" a sound mix by specific-assignment programming; to evaluate film processing while in progress, and even compensate for color unevenness; to store talent biographies on performers, ready for instant retrieval; to handle interlocking of electronic hardware with electro-mechanical machines and units, and bring them into synchronous operation; for looping, mixing, multichannel audio recording, sound-sampling and regenerating; to "file" the records—production, budgetary, travel talent and scripts—of a production company or studio; to generate special effects and new colorization within those effects; to colorize black-and-white film. Minimal comprehension of computers is required in any facet of the communications industry.

computer colors   The range of colors that can be generated by a particular computer. Used by production managers to differentiate, in detail, logistical and budgetary items into color-coded categories and subcategories.

computer-generated   animation   Images created by computers and their scanning lines, as well as utilization of pattern-forming devices. Final images can then be fed into a holding videotape or master, or transferred to motion picture film. These electronically generated effects are used for in-house sales videotapes, informational films or tapes, theatrical features, holography and simulated holography, as well as trade shows, mixed-media shows, and graphic enhancement of cassettes. Also referred to as COMPUTER GRAPHICS.

computer graphics   Used as a synonym for COMPUTER-GENERATED ANIMATION, this term also refers to specific SPECIAL EFFECTS wherein computer-generated animation is mixed with live action. Used extensively in science fiction films. Some examples are the *Star Trek* series of films, as well as *Tron, Star Wars, Robocop* and *The Abyss*. Computer graphics were also used in the recent *Superman* series, and most of the Steven Spielberg films like *Indiana Jones and the Last Crusade, Gremlins II, Always* and the *Back to the Future* series.

computer interpolation A computer-graphics system wherein electronically generated computer images change from one image to another. Used in many commercials, as well as FANTASY and SCI-FI films.

concave lens A single lens having one or two recessed circular planes. These spherical section surfaces combined with other surfaces, concave and convex, are put together to create compound lenses.

ondensations/rarefactions Pulsatcing vibration of a string, surface, diaphragm or any sound source. These periodic pulsations rise and fall to create a sound wave. When this wave strikes the receiver, it makes it vibrate sonically.

condense In writing or editing, to exclude all extraneous or secondary materials and to concentrate on the primary theme of the film. This is often done to shorten the film's length to meet exigencies of program timings.

condenser microphone See ELECTROSTATIC MICROPHONE.

condensing optics Single lens or lens system that compresses and narrows light rays from whatever source they are emitted.

conditional breakpoint instruction An instruction switch that makes a computer fully stop or pause, and then to either proceed as coded or to jump to a new instruction in the computer's storage location.

conductor A material that functions as a carrier of electrical current. Whatever medium transmits the electrical current is regarded as its conductor.

It is also a music term denoting the leader of an orchestra or musical ensemble.

cone A vibrating element in a loudspeaker, generally conical in shape, for emitting and physically amplifying sound.

cone light A floodlight that diffuses light.

confetti Splotches, streaks and spots of color caused by "noise" in the color system in the TV set. Because of its chromaticity, confetti is far more pronounced in a color system than in a black-and-white one, the color being extremely noticeable and distracting.

configuration Components in a circuit that are arranged in a particular pattern in relation to one another that are used to create or alter electronic sound or images.

confirmation The contractual agreement and fixing of schedule dates to broadcast the television commercials of a given sponsor or public service organization. Acknowledged by a signed contract, deal memo, or faxed or telexed verification.

conflict The confrontation between protagonist and antagonist or antagonistic forces: man-against-man, man-against-the-world, man-against-forces of evil, man-against-nature, etc. The elements of opposition and struggle within the framework of the plot.

conforming Matching original footage to WORK PRINT. Also called MATCHING.

connector A unit of two matching parts for joining or bifurcating electrical circuits.

console A control panel with numerous controls that can be used in many configurations. It is used for sound recording and rerecording; to enable the input of one or more sound elements coming in from a live microphone, electronic synthesizer, audio tape, optical sound, DAT, or others; and to vary these elements in amplitude and frequency. It makes provision for the MIXER to monitor the signal at the console output.

Consolidated Film Industries (CFI) One of the major film labs in the United States, located in Hollywood.

consonance   Resonance in an electrical or acoustical mode between units not connected to one another.

constant current   An emitted current with an output that is steady, within preset limits; limits conditioned by the voltage range of the power supply.

constant-current transformer   A transformer that keeps a constant level of current in its secondary circuit despite changing load conditions.

contact   A juncture point in a current-carrying system: connectors, switches or relays.

contact microphone   One designed to receive mechanical vibrations from any particular sound source(s) and to change them into electrical voltage or currents.

contact print   Positive film printed directly from the negative, making an emulsion-to-emulsion contact.

contamination   The incursion of dust particles, improper chemicals, or various foreign and corrosive substances, which soil the photographic chemicals.
  In electronics, a bad separation in the color signal paths.

continuity   The dramatic sequence of events in a film or videotape production. The smooth flow from moment-to-moment, scene-to-scene, created by the director and his actors, critically augmented by camera and sound. A common directorial command, especially in dramatic works, is to "maintain the continuity."

continuity cutting   A style of editing marked by its emphasis on sustaining the continuous and seemingly uninterrupted progression of the action of the story. It relates this action as if it were being observed directly by the audience as spectators. To be contrasted with DYNAMIC CUTTING. See FILM CONTINUITY.

continuity editing   Editing a film that is shot in CONTINUITY or editing in script sequence and leadering the areas where scenes are still to be added. See CONTINUITY SHOOTING.

continuity shooting   Shooting the SCRIPT in the scene sequence in which it is written. Entire feature films are seldom shot this way, as it is not ordinarily budget-effective. However, the long, going-downriver sequences in the film classic *Deliverance* was filmed in this manner. SOAP OPERAS are taped in continuity with full scenes or sequences done as uninterrupted performances.

continuity sketches   Drawings by an artist to highlight action and composition, laid out sequentially. They can be simple pencil sketches or multicolored, finished works. They are used by the director and cinematographer, as well as the design crew, as a guide and reminder of scene progression, and the overall "look" of the production. See STORYBOARD.

continuity writer   In radio, the person who writes or edits the materials to be spoken on the various broadcasts.

continuous action   Straight-through action of a scene that usually covers a large area of ground. Sometimes two scenes of intense action are blended and filmed as one scene, covered by multiple and overlapping camera set-ups. Also, the cameras are set at the requisite divergent angles necessary for editing, in order to avoid JUMP CUTS. Often these action-intense scenes involve nonrepeatable action (fires, explosions and car crashes) calling for a one-take situation, thus requiring multicamera shooting. If the action is laid out and filmed properly, it will move seamlessly from one camera position to another.

continuous loop In MIXING, a background effects loop that is joined together to move in continuous circularity over a sound head. The jointure of the two spliced ends often uses a diagonal cut, so that part of the sound of each end overlaps, and obscures the otherwise harsh jump in the sound. In video and audio cassettes, a loop that does not come to an "end," but travels in a continuous path, obviates the need to rewind at the conclusion of the tape, as it is once again in "ready" position from the top. Some units have an electronic signal that shuts the cassette off at the end of the tape.

contract Written agreement between production entity and actors, crew and staff. Unless the actor is under contract to the studio or production company, the contract will be for one film, videotape or specific group of productions. For crew and cast, and sometimes staff, the contract lists working hours allowed, conditions of work, responsibilities of employee and employer. The contract also declares salary base and, when applicable, residuals. Contracts can also be between production entity and the workers' unions.

contractor (musical) Musician supervising the hiring of a musical group. Sometimes the contractor is also the conductor or musical director.

contract player A player under contract to a studio or production company, who works on programs or films as assigned.

contrapuntal sound Sound or music that increases comedic or dramatic intensity by playing "against the scene." It often conflicts directly and deliberately with the implicit mood of the action. For example, a light, happy tune that a young boy whistled in earlier scenes might be played over a sequence showing his funeral; the lilting melody playing in counterpoint to the tragic surroundings is far more potent and poignant than "tragic" music.

contrast Juxtaposition of opposites for dramatic effect. The contest between little David and the giant Goliath, the setting of the luxury apartments directly next to the slums in the play and film *Dead End,* the dainty wardrobe of the petite Eastern schoolmarm in the rough-hewn setting of a Western frontier town with its mud streets and sweaty-masculine look.

In photography, the difference between the brightness of the most illuminated and the least illuminated areas. In a negative or print, the difference between the densities of the most exposed and least exposed areas. Difference between highlights and shadows; maximum/minimum ratio in brightness values. See EXPOSURE.

contrast control A TV receiver's adjustment knob or dial that alters the level of brightness, as seen in the image's highlights and shadows.

contrasty In photography, an image strong in polarity of tones, with well-defined light and dark areas, and minimized tonal gradations.

control room The soundproofed enclosure within a radio or TV studio, wherein the director, producer and technicians supervise the logistics of taping or live broadcasting.

convergence The three-color matching of the R-G-B beams at a set "focal" point, generally at the APERTURE MASK.

convergence pattern TV test signal used to evaluate the monitor picture for distortion.

conversion filter An in-camera or front-of-the-lens filter attachment that allows indoor film to be used outdoors and outdoor film for interiors.

converter An electronic unit that lets a TV set receive additional channels.

convex lens A camera lens with two outwardly protruding spherical surfaces on either side. The obverse of the concave surface.

copter mount Special camera mount designed to facilitate filming from helicopters by decreasing vibrations and lurching. The gyroscopically balanced unit can be mounted inside the helicopter, using an open side door and is controlled directly by the cameraman. The belly or nose mounts are bolted into position and remote-controlled from inside the helicopter. Also called HELICOPTER MOUNT.

cool Referring to a TV image with a green or blue tinge.

copy Text for ads and commercials.

copyright A document that registers a creative work with the United States Register of Copyrights, to protect it from being stolen. Among items copyrighted are: novels, stories, articles, screenplays, photographs, motion pictures, new works of graphic art, musical compositions, lyrics and libretti.

cordless synch, crystal synch, cableless synch Terms for sound-recording units that can maintain synchronous camera-to-recorder sound without being physically connected by a synch-pulse cable. See SYNCHRONISM.

core RAW STOCK is wound around plastic hubs called cores. The developed NEGATIVE is usually stored on cores rather than REELS. Cores are categorized by film width (16mm, 35mm, 70mm), and are either "male" or "female" depending upon the center-core stamping. These plastic hubs have diameters of 2″ or 3″. There is a center hole and a spindle-slot, also called a "keyway," which is 1″ in diameter. Used in the manufacture, development and further processing of film, cores are also used in placing film on a split reel for editing or projection.

core storage High-speed computer storage utilizing magnetic CORES.

corporate image campaign An advertising and public relations push to self-aggrandize a company or a corporation instead of its products. In TV, this "packaging" of corporate images has also been used to package political candidates.

Corporation for Public Broadcasting (CPB) The Washington, D.C.–based corporation in charge of the distribution of federal funds to public TV and radio stations. CPB also funds some programming for radio and TV, in accordance with the Public Broadcasting Act of 1967 to create and disseminate noncommercial programming.

corrective commercial An ad that corrects inaccurate information or misrepresented claims of another COMMERCIAL. For example, in a corrective political ad, retraction of a claim of political malfeasance or a correction of any previous misstatement in a PUBLIC SERVICE ANNOUNCEMENT or commercial. Seldom done voluntarily, these commercials are nearly always made at the command of the Federal Trade Commission.

correlative Similarity in the electronic measurements of two signals. Used to maintain videotape synch, audio and/or picture.

cosmetic makeup Standard makeup to make the performer appear his best in front of the camera, designed by the make-up artist to work in a particular type of lighting setup.

costume That which is worn by actors in a play, film or TV production. The head-to-toe clothing. A costume reflects the personality of the character being portrayed.

costume designer The creator of costumes for any era or place which relate well to the general look of the picture, established by the ART DIRECTOR.

costume house Supply warehouse of basic costume rentals, with staff of tailors, fitters, seamstresses, cleaners and general workers. As studios develop and accommodate their own wardrobes, the large costume houses are being phased out by smaller, more specialized costume establishments, or by the studios doing the majority of costuming in-house. Since much costuming today is contemporary dress, this makes the task somewhat easier.

costume picture   A period piece, as a rule, wherein the costumes as well as the actors seem to "star."

costumer   The hands-on member of the crew who gathers all the clothing to be worn in front of the camera. The costumer works with the designer to see that customized costumes are precisely made and well-fitted to the actors who must wear them. In contemporary films the actors often provide their own wardrobe, or part of it. It is the responsibility of the costumer to provide everything else, by either supervising their manufacture, purchasing ready-mades or securing rentals. In rare cases costumes will be found in the studio's own wardrobe department that will work for the film.

countdown   Stand-by-start cue-signal. It can be given vocally or by hand signals to an on-camera TV performer. It is part of the head-end leader in film or videotape forms, each number representing one second.

counter   A numerical meter that "counts" film length in feet, tape in numbers of FRAMES, etc., and registers these numbers on a dial or readout unit.

counter-key   Light source opposite to the KEY LIGHT that is used to balance light for a more natural look.

counter programming   A network's competitive fight for the highest audience rating in a given time slot, exemplified by that network's putting on its "strongest draw." The purpose of this is to take viewers away from the TV fare of the competitive network and to attract that audience to its own programming.

coupling   The "joining" of two or more circuits so that power can be sent from one to another.

cove   An area at the base of a cyclorama or scenic background piece with a strip of working lights covered from view by an integrated baseboard. As an adjective it is often used descriptively in the term "coved cyc." See CYCLORAMA.

cover   A camera hood or wrapping to keep out dust, moisture and inclemencies of weather. Sometimes serving as an improvised BARNEY.

Cover also means to visually tape an event. To place the camera in such a way that it can pick up the necessary action. Also, to make additional shots to protect the film continuity, in case previous shots don't fit together editorially.

coverage   In dramatic film or tape, additional shots that augment the MASTER SHOT, such as SINGLE, CUTAWAY SHOTS and tight TWO SHOTS. It is from the master shot and COVERAGE that the editor assembles the scenes.

In documentaries and news, the term "coverage" means total tape or film used to record a particular event.

cowcatcher   Sponsor identification prior to but part of the actual program that it precedes.

CPB   See CORPORATION FOR PUBLIC BROADCASTING.

crab dolly   Wheeled camera-mount that can be steered. Usually it has a vertical metal adjustable column for raising or lowering the camera.

cradle   Camera attachment to support heavy lenses. It gives the lens greater stability, protects it from damage and keeps the lens mount from being bent or ruptured from the weight of the lens.

cradle head   Sturdy camera head geared for smooth TILTS and PANS.

crane   A large, vehicle BOOM that lets the camera move in wide, circular movements, or move up to a HIGH SHOT position in a vertical, diagonal or irregular path. It allows for great flexibility in camera movements.

craning   The typical movement of a CRANE, i.e., rising up or down. Movement is on the crane itself or simulated by shooting from inside clear-glass elevators, cherry-pickers, rooftops of buildings or production trucks, etc.

crane shot   Shot made on the crane itself.

crater   Concave depression at the end of a positive carbon. It holds the ball of incandescent ionizing gases that emit the light, resulting in more efficient use of the gases and a longer life of the incandescent element.

crawl titles   TITLES or CREDITS that appear to "roll in" from the bottom of the frame and exit at the top. Also called roll-up titles or creeper titles.

creasing   The lengthwide deformation of the film strip itself. The usual cause is misthreading in the developer or the projector.

credits   The listed names of CAST, CREW and STAFF involved in a given film or TV production that are seen at the beginning or end. Radio credits are spoken by the announcer.

credit sheet   Typed, photocopied or printed sheet(s) giving the background of a performer, DIRECTOR, PRODUCER, or CREW/staff member. It lists past productions on which the person has worked, what his or her function was, and also names the most recent CREDITS. Also called bio sheet or résumé.

creep   The uneven feed of a videotape as it moves around a CAPSTAN, particularly when it slips, which momentarily throws off synchronization and distorts the picture or sound.

creeper titles   See CRAWL TITLES.

crest   See PEAK.

crew   The crew is composed of those who are "behind the cameras" in the physical production of a film or videotape project. This would include soundmen, CAMERAMEN, GRIPS, BEST BOY(s), ASSISTANT DIRECTOR(s), MAKE-UP PERSON(s), PRODUCTION ASSISTANTS, WARDROBE DEPARTMENT, GAFFER(s), GRIPS, carpenters, painters, drivers, etc. Differentiated from CAST and STAFF. See PRODUCTION STAFF.

crew call   A notice either hand-delivered by the ASSISTANT DIRECTOR or PRODUCTION MANAGER, or posted on the CREW's production bulletin board. It gives the names of those on call, and where and when the filming will be held.

CRI   See COLOR RENDERING INDEX or COLOR REVERSAL INTERMEDIATE.

crimping   To add a terminal, contact or splice to a conductor by pressure to make an instant connection.

crisis   Dramaturgically, it is the moment when dramatic tension reaches a high point.

critical angle   The extremity of angle, wherein a radio wave can be sent out from an antenna, and sent back by ionospheric refraction.

critical focus   Regarded as both an activity and an ideal pre-set measurement. The goal: precision focus. Devices that help accomplish this state of focus are an electromechanical focusing unit, photo-sensitive-activated unit, or mini-computerized versions of both. Precision-sharp clarity of image, or an indication that such clarity is mandatory in a specified shot.

critics Film and TV critics are reviewers of produced and released films, plays or videotapes who often possess backgrounds in journalism. Their reviews appear in print (trade journals, newspapers, magazines) and on television.

crop To cut off visual information by FRAMING. Still photographers often crop their NEGATIVES in order to intensify the image. Also a direction to the DIRECTOR OF PHOTOGRAPHY from the DIRECTOR: "Crop off more of the house in the framing so that I can see all the steps."

cross Performer's move from part of the set to another. In a director's or actor's notations, such blocking is indicated by an "X." Examples: "X to desk," "X to doorway and exit," etc.

cross abrasions Little scratches across the horizontal width of the film frame. This happens when the film roll is shifted from side to side during shipping or handling.

cross color Interfacing cross talk from monochrome signals in a color-TV receiver. This cross talk affects the chrominance channel(s).

cross coupling When two separate communication channels or their elements are mistakenly or inadvertently coupled together, this results in cross-coupling.

crosscutting A to-and-fro pattern from one scene in one locale directly to another, and back again, e.g., a chase scene, or where two courses of plot-action are starting to converge toward a CRISIS-POINT. D. W. Griffith, in *Intolerance,* took the form to its most complex level by cutting directly in his summary montage within a matrix of the four slot periods of *Intolerance:* ancient Babylon, Christ's crucifixion, 16th-century France and contemporary America of 1916. By this forced parallelism he was attempting to create stronger metaphors and highly impactive

visual messages. He succeeded, and was a seminal influence on the work of Sergei Eisenstein, and Slavko Vorkapich, who created what we regard today as the fast-cut percussive MONTAGE.

cross-fade The lowering of sound in an outgoing scene—usually to the level of inaudibility—while increasing the volume of the incoming scene. Basically an AUDIO term in FILM and RADIO, but sometimes used as a video term in taped or live TV.

crossing the line An improper camera positioning relative to the target objects (animate or inanimate). It is an apparent shift in the on-camera subjects that is caused by a radical 180-degree change of the camera position. For example: two lovers talking face-to-face, shot in profile, with the girl on screen left, the boy screen right; the 180° change, i.e., shooting it from the other side, would result in the boy being on screen left, and the girl screen right. Such a jump is disturbing to an audience as it breaks tension and disturbs the general flow of the scene. Sometimes *crossing the line* is used for exactly this disorienting effect. When used in proper context and by an experienced director it can be highly effective. Used by an inexperienced director it can range from irritating to totally confusing.

cross modulation An intermodulation caused by an unwanted signal acting upon the specific carrier of the proper signal.

crossover frequency The frequency in electrical dividing network that sends equal power to adjoining frequency channels. It must be kept consistent in all electronic media work to help maintain quality control of image and sound.

crossover network Amplifier filter that divides the output signal into discrete frequency bands. This separation into specific bands allows for the creation of a multispeaker system.

cross-own To simultaneously own a broadcasting station (radio or TV) and a newspaper in the same locale.

crosstalk Interference of an unwanted signal into an audio or video matrix of the primary, selected signal.

crowd burble The sound of a crowd, generally with a background presence. These crowd effects are recorded during a scene and used as is, or are augmented by using the existing burble as a guide track and recording new, more specific burble in background dialogue or general sounds. These crowd noises are defined and listed by general size or activity of the crowd, e.g., "small, excited crowd," "classroom burble," "crowd cheering at football stadium," "crowd at airport," etc. Many of these burble tracks are available in a SOUND EFFECTS LIBRARY.

CRT See CATHODE RAY TUBE.

crutch tips One-inch rubber caps, manufactured to cover the ends of crutches. Used by GRIPS to place on CENTURY STAND legs, especially in on-location shooting, to keep the metal legs or points from scratching hardwood, plastic or marble, or from snagging carpeting.

crystal control Control of an oscillator's frequency using a specially engineered cut crystal. Used in camera and audio noncable synch set-ups.

crystal microphone One that is put into operation when an electric charge is created by causing variations in the basic form of a crystalline or crystalline-functioning object. An object that generates voltage under mechanical stress to create audio signals.

crystal motor Electric unit with speed regulated by a vibrating crystal. Used to maintain CORDLESS or CRYSTAL SYNCH.

CS See CLOSE SHOT.

c-stand See CENTURY STAND.

CTV See CANADIAN TELEVISION.

CU See CLOSE-UP.

cucaloris/cukaloris Pronounced ku-kah-lor-iss. A device for shading direct illumination on scene to be filmed with a cut-out vermicular pattern used to create a mottled lighting effect when placed in front of the proper source light. Often simulates blurred, leafy shadows. Also referred to as kuke and kookie.

cue A signal by word or action for the actor's next speech, reaction or movement. Cues can also be given to the crew, e.g., to the CAMERA OPERATOR to start zooming; to the LIGHTING GAFFER to bring in or take out light with a simple rheostat fader; for a SPECIAL EFFECT technician to activate the working, physical effect, and others. "CUT!" is a stop-cue, as "ACTION!" is a start-cue. There are also cues that activate crew or performers on a visual count, or an audio one if sound is not being recorded while filming.

cue card Cardboard sheets, ordinarily about three feet by three feet square, on which phrases or sentences are printed to prompt performers, or which are often read verbatim for full, on-camera text. These cue cards are held off-camera by members of the production staff. Also called idiot cards or flip cards.

cue light Small indicator light to cue performers to start and stop in VOICE OVER or on-camera narration.

cue mark A scratch, editor's crayon mark or a punched hole on a piece of film or magnetic sound track, serving as a start mark for LOOPING, editing or in an INTERLOCK SYSTEM. In film projection, it is a small circular mark at the end of a reel to cue the projectionist for changeover to the next reel.

cue sheet Logged or listed cues for audio mixing or SWEETENING.

cukaloris See CUCALORIS.

cult film Cult films characteristically have a loyal, enthusiastic following despite usually having a limited audience appeal and poor distribution. The term can refer to a particular film or a genre of films. Examples of cult films are *The Rocky Horror Picture Show, Mommy Dearest, Pink Flamingos,* and *One-Eyed Jacks.*

curl Distortion along the frame width, due to a gap between emulsion layer and the support base of the film stock. It is caused by changes in moisture and the general atmosphere, including storage temperature and humidity levels.

current Movement of electrons through a conducting medium. The magnitude or volume flowing through the conductor is generally measured in amperes. It is evaluated to determine whether it needs to be increased, decreased or remain constant.

curvature of field Characteristic of a lens-formed image where the focal points are on a curved, instead of a flat, plane.

curve (H and D) The calibrated curve perfected by Hunter and Driffield that graphically indicates how accurately the photographic emulsion had recreated the tonal scale of the original scene.

cut An instantaneous transition from one shot to the succeeding shot. In editing, a cut is made by splicing two shots together, with no indication for a fade or dissolve.

"Cut!" is the order given by the DIRECTOR of the film when the action of a shot is completed, to indicate that sound and camera are to stop. A general direction in filming or sound-recording to shut off all filming or recording gear.

Cut also is used as a verb meaning to omit or remove DIALOGUE from a SCRIPT; a piece of action on the SET; or a segment of film when editing. As in, "I think we'll cut this entire segment."

A cut is also an edited version of the material. Used both in film and TV, as in, "The editor screened his first cut." See FINE CUT, ROUGH CUT.

cutaway shots Insert shots, extreme CLOSE-UP SHOTS, LISTENING SHOTS, AMBIENCE SHOTS, as well as shots from another scene used for cross-cutting. Shots allowing the DIRECTOR and EDITOR to "cut away" from the main scene or MASTER SHOT and add additional information, intensification or CHARACTERIZATION to build dramatic tension, suspense, etc.

cut-in See INSERT SHOT.

cutoff Edges of a frame of film or video beyond which no image appears.

In electronics, the high-and-low limits outside of which a particular circuit does not respond.

cutter See EDITOR. Also, in lighting, it is a device that cuts down illumination by blocking part of the lamp with a FLAG, a CUCALORIS, a SCRIM, a BARN DOOR, etc.

cutting action Cutting on movement from one camera position to another. These positions can be from a multicamera shoot or from a sequence of overlapping shots, filmed with the concept of postmatching to the best point of action, with the most acceptable match. This also refers to cutting to a following action or an implied sequential action. For example, a man may exit through a doorway, and the next cut shows him entering an underground parking garage; or after exiting the door, the next cut can be the man already in the car, starting the engine.

cutting copy (British term) The assembled edited version of work print from which will be fashioned the ROUGH CUT and the FINE CUT.

cutting in the camera Filming in sequential order and in the required alternation of framed shots so that there is minimal cutting required on the part of the editor. News is often shot this way.

cutting room   A room equipped with the proper editing gear for the EDITOR of the film or tape.

cutting to the beat   Editing shots that start at a preselected downbeat or upbeat of a given measure of music. Music videos are the prime examples of cutting to—or on—the beat.

cyan   Lab name for minus-red subtractive elements in three-color (red-green-blue) processes.

cyc   See CYCLORAMA.

cycle   Off/on utilization of electrical power calibrated to the crests and troughs of a cycle-wave within a second.

cycle animation   The repeated use of a set of animation cels, used for repetitive actions, like walking, traffic flow, water passing by in a river or an ocean.

cycle counter   A timer or recorder that numbers the rate at which a particular cycle is repeated.

cycle timer   A control device that opens or closes electrical contacts. It is premeasured to a set cycle.

cyclorama (cyc)   White or blue background painted on a smooth wall or on one covered with smooth plastic, used to simulate "limbo" (see LIMBO SET) or sky. The cyc is placed either at one end of a soundstage or insert stage, or curving at one corner of the stage. Larger cycloramas can stretch from one side of the stage to the other, and can be covered and curved at the edges as well.

D

DA   See DIRECTIONAL ANTENNA

d-a decoder   Electronic unit that transfers a digital word into an analog equiv-

alent. One of its uses in media is to control conceptual data into graphics.

dailies   The print delivered or picked up from the laboratory of film materials shot on the previous day. Now applied also to taped materials to be utilized alone or in conjunction with film.

daily production report (DPR)   All departments—sound, camera, music, editing—have their own special DPRs, but on location the term usually refers to the production manager's overall report and record for the studio or production entity. The reports are used substantially in post-production to evaluate materials on hand to complete the film or videotape and to determine completion schedules and costs. See PRODUCTION REPORT.

dampen   To reduce audio echoes and deaden vibrations by surrounding a microphone or speaker area with sound-absorbing materials, including acoustical walls.

damping   To reduce waves or oscillations in amplitude; to stop excessive swings of vibration by friction or resistance.

dance drama   A dramatic form of dance-storytelling utilizing additional elements, i.e., singing, DIALOGUE, MIME. Used often in MUSICAL COMEDY and in TV production numbers.

dance-pantomime   A narrative dance form; a blend of mime and dance.

dancer   Performer, either chorus or principal, whose activities in a given production are primarily dance or dance-oriented.

dark end   Part of a film processing machine where film feeding into the machine for developing and processing requires an area of total darkness.

dark spot   An unwanted electron cluster that splotches the TV image. It is caused by an electronic malfunction in the transmitter.

day SCRIPT indication giving the time of a scene. For example: "EXT. An open field. Day." Or "INT. Jim's car. Night." Sometimes the time of day is given more shading by such terms as "sunrise," "high noon," "dusk," etc.

day-for-night Filming in daylight but with special FILTERS and EXPOSURE to give a "nighttime" look, often augmented by special developing in the lab.

daylight Sunlight and ambient sky-light together, set at approximately 6500° K.

daylight color film Film balanced for exterior shooting, or light filtered to about 5500° K.

daylight conversion filter It is used to alter color temperature of the light coming through the LENS and striking the unexposed film that is set for artificial lighting. Also used for filming outdoors in daylight.

daylight loading Full-flanged metal spool for the FILM STOCK, to protect it from being exposed to light while the camera is being loaded or unloaded.

daylight projection Rear-screen projection onto the back of a translucent screen. Also, shadow box projection.

daypart An arbitrary time segment of a broadcasting day, based on audience demographics, to measure the effective viewing times for target audiences.

dayplayer An ACTOR with DIALOGUE, hired by the day, with no weekly or run-of-the-picture contract. Sometimes referred to as a BIT PLAYER. However, a day player may have a key scene in the film and have been precontracted as a FEATURE PLAYER, with appropriate screen credit.

dB See DECIBEL.

dB meter An instrument calibrated to check sound levels in decibel (dB) readings.

DBS See DIRECT BROADCASTING SATELLITE.

DC See DIRECT CURRENT.

DC noise Extraneous noise that is present when reproducing a tape non-uniformly magnetized. This unwanted noise can have long-wavelength components 20 dBs higher than would have been obtained had erased or DEGAUSSed tape been used.

dead Acoustical terminology referring to a "dry" sound, one with minimal reverberation, as in a recording studio.

dead air A time when there is no sound and picture during a broadcast transmission.

dead end Section of a recording studio with the greatest sound absorbency.

deadline A deadline is the cutoff time for handing in material that is broadcast-ready. It is a term adopted from journalism.

dead mike A microphone not working, either because of a malfunction or simply because it is turned off.

dead side Side of the microphone less sensitive in picking up sound. Opposite to the "live" side.

dead spot Geographic area in which TV reception is poor, wherein other forms of reception must be employed: cable, for example.

dead synch Frame-to-frame synchronization of SOUND and PICTURE. This stage of post-production, with synchronous projectors and editing systems, is the stage just prior to the final mix and running off COMPOSITE PRINT. When a marked soundtrack leader and a picture leader are directly opposite in the upright Moviola, flatbed or gang-splicer, a one-to-one synch is created. Also known as EDITOR'S SYNCH or printer's synch.

dealer spot A local version of a national commercial, using the body of the existing commercial, with an addition of a tag giving name and location of local or regional dealer. Sometimes the tag is directly from local dealer's facility, with the dealer personally acting as local announcer. See LIVE TAG.

dealer tie-in Listing of local or regional outlets that carry the station-advertised product. These names are either burned-in or added on an open-end tag. See BURN-IN.

deal memo It is a formalization of an agreement to do business that sets forth an understanding between the production company and actor or crew member being hired. It sets forth working dates and times and agreed-upon payment. It precedes the full contract, and is often used to set terms within body of the contract itself. See DEAL MEMO in Appendix.

debug To remove technical impediments and correct any working elements that have a mechanical or electronic problem. To correct the nonworking or below-par functioning state of any instrument or unit. The test procedure that accomplishes this is referred to as debugging.

decay Gradual diminution of an image or signal.

decibel (dB) International standard measurement unit to indicate power loss or gain, particularly in the auditory range. A unit of sound measurement that increases exponentially by ten (deci-) and is named after inventor Alexander Graham Bell (-bel).

decisecond One-tenth of a second. Units often used for music editing, particularly when editing to a musical beat.

decor Set furnishing used to dress a scene. Furnishings and decorations for the set are selected and placed by the ART DIRECTOR and staff.

deep field cinematography A manner of filming in which both FOREGROUND and BACKGROUND settings and actions are in FOCUS. This is accomplished by using small f-numbers or lenses with short FOCAL LENGTHS.

definition Sharpness and clarity of a photographic image. Authenticity of production of picture or sound. In sound, this would mean a high signal-level with minimal NOISE.

defocus For a focused image to go deliberately out of focus; used as a transition device. Lenses that are longer than normal are used for this effect. Also called RACK FOCUS.

degauss To electromagnetically erase the existing signal on a tape and to realign the magnetic poles. See BULK ERASER.

degradation A gradual reduction in picture fidelity caused by DUPLICATION, and taking the image one more GENERATION from the ORIGINAL, whether tape or film.

delay Time allotment needed for a signal to move to and past a unit or conductor.
   Also, a production delay caused by the performers or crew.

delayed broadcast When a network affiliated station tapes programs, then puts them on hold for broadcasting at a later date.

delayed contacts Preset delays on electronic contacts that are regulated to be actuated after the beginning of a timing cycle. Used in media, for example, to bring in multiple audio and/or video tracks in editing or mixing at different pre-set times.

delivery The personal manner of performing or presenting written material, whether by the host, newscaster, actor, spokesperson or on-the-air celebrity. The creative and technical abilities of people to put materials across.

Delta PCM (delta pulse code modulation)   A modulating system which takes audio signals and changes them into trains of digital pulses. This minimizes interference while transmitting over wire connections or radio channels.

De Luxe   Informal for De Luxe Laboratories, a film lab; seen in film credits and ads as, "Color by De Luxe."

demagnetize   To overcome undesirable magnetic fields by degaussing, cleaning or coating tape recording units, especially recording heads.

demodulate   To take out a broadcast signal from a CARRIER wave.

demographic profile   A statistical survey of TV audiences, categorized by age, sex, occupation, geographical location, education, income, etc. Used to determine what kind of listener is watching which ads or programs, when and why. Most ad campaigns are designed with a demographic profile in mind.

denouement   Final cleaning up of details; the tidying-up of the plot, right after the CLIMAX. An example: Sherlock Holmes traps and unmasks the criminal in a stirring climax. After the constable has taken the criminal into custody, Holmes explains the part of the mystery that remains unclear. This unraveling is the denouement.

densitometer   An electronic mechanism for calibrating density of photographic images.

density   Measure of opacity in photographic film.

departments   In a TV or major motion picture studio or large independent studio, the various diversions of the CREW into distinct segments and physical areas. Often the diversions are indicated by separate UNIONS: cameramen, editors, directors, etc. Generally, there is a department head and an assistant who supervise these divisions and often handle the hiring directly. Some basic departments are MAKEUP, music, sound, special effects, etc.

depolarizer   In optics, a device for eliminating the polarization in a ray of light. This restores the vibrations of the ray in all directions and at right angles. It is commonly used to photograph through glass that is reflecting sunlight or other light, so that the objects behind the glass can be seen. It is also used for eliminating glare from highly polished surfaces.

deposit for copyrights   It is no longer necessary to deposit film copies of motion picture films with the Library of Congress; full videotapes, in most cases, are acceptable. Check with an attorney or with the copyright office, in Washington, D.C. See COPYRIGHT.

depth of field   Range of distance within which objects can be shot in FOCUS.

depth of field scale   A calibrated camera lens scale that gives a reading to indicate the depth of field at a given distance, and requisite aperture settings needed to make a focused picture.

depth of field table   A measurement graph that lists the DEPTH OF FIELD for various lenses; a matrix also showing focal lengths with their appropriate APERTURE and FOCAL POINTS.

depth of focus   The range through which the image plane (emulsion surface of film) can be moved backward and forward with respect to the camera LENS, as defined under DEPTH OF FIELD. The term depth of focus is often used instead of depth of field. Nontechnically defined, depth of focus is merely the distance between film and lens, wherein sharpness of focus can be maintained.

desaturation   The elimination of color in general, or of one specific tonality, in order to create a monochromatic effect within a filmed scene, sequence or entire production.

Desilu   A group of studios and enterprises set up by Desi Arnaz and Lucille

Ball (whose first names helped form the compound word) primarily to handle the production and syndication of the "I Love Lucy" show and the "Lucy Show," and later on other specials and co-productions.

detail shots   Close-up and extreme close-up shots of people or objects, and details of even smaller sections of close shots, to intensify the presence of the image and its significance. An example would be a full shot of a man drawing a gun, then cutting to an extreme close up (XCU) of his eyes as he aims the gun, then an XCU of the gun barrel itself. Both of these XCU shots are detail shots. When they are shot in general coverage they are usually referred to as CUTAWAY SHOTS or, depending upon how they are used, INSERTs. Other examples of detail shots: part of a person's apparel, clock hands indicating a given hour, a TV dial set on a specific channel, a name on an envelope, an entry on a menu. See also SHOTS.

deuce   A 2000 watt floodlight.

deus ex machina   Plot-resolving device used in early Greek and Roman drama, where resolution to a seemingly impossible situation was solved by bringing one of the gods down from heaven to unscramble everything on the spot. As used in modern theater and mass media, it refers to a gimmicky plot device dragged in from left field and used to unravel bad plotting, structuring and character development. Used often in early motion picture serials to explain the hero's or heroine's miraculous escape from the cliff-hanger jeopardy of the previous episode. A literary device to be avoided, unless used in parody.

Deutsche Industrie Norm   See DIN.

develop   To bring out the latent photographic image on a film original by processing it in the lab.

developer   Liquid chemical mix for developing the exposed film, as it goes through various processing stages to produce the developed negative.

development   The process of developing film to get image.
It also refers to the structuring of plot and character involvement to flesh-out a plot outline.

development deal   Step-by-step contractual agreement to proceed with a motion picture in all pre-production phases. Usually the production phase is covered in separate contracts and agreements.

DGA   See DIRECTOR'S GUILD OF AMERICA.

diadachokinesis   Inherent or developed talent for racing through a long piece of difficult, polysyllabic copy with total accuracy. Common device in certain stand-up comedy routines. Used comedically in some commercials, and desperately in other commercials, e.g., when 30 seconds worth of copy has to be crowded into a 20-second commercial.

diagonal   An expression of distances formed on diagonals within the image area of a film frame.

diagonal cut/splice   When an overlapping oblique cut is used to join or tape film instead of a vertical one. On magnetic film or tape this tends to overlap incoming with outgoing sound, both reducing and covering up the noise of the splice.

diagonal scratches   Scratches aslant on the film; generally caused by film running off the edge of a projector's roller flange, or when the original is misaligned inside the camera when the film is being shot. The latter is rare.

dialogue   The exchange of conversation between two or more characters in a dramatic work.

dialogue coach   A member of the production staff whose responsibility is to run through the lines with the actors—

usually without giving any interpretative comment—to make certain that the DIALOGUE is correct before the scene is filmed or taped.

dialogue replacement Replacing sound of poor quality, often from location shooting, with recording-studio quality. The actors have to be able to LIP SYNCH their own voices or replace other actors' lines, often from playback through earphones while watching original footage, in order to match lip movements. See LOOPING.

diaphragm, lens An adjustable opening formed by thin, overlapping plates, usually placed between the elements of the camera LENS to control the amount of light reaching the film. Also called an IRIS because its action resembles the iris of the eye.

diaphragm pre-setting Choice of F-NUMBER to match the necessary DEPTH OF FIELD, allowing the scene to be lit for the desired exposure.

dichroic filters Color-balanced diffusers of blue glass or gelatin, mounted in front of the light source to reflect excessive red and allow the blue end of the spectrum to pass. Used for balancing an indoor/outdoor mix in conjunction with the proper filter.

dichroic mirror Glass surface covered with a coating of metallic salts, and applied in such a mixture and manner as to reflect back one color, and to transmit all others.

differential microphone A carbon microphone with two packets of carbon granules, one on each side of the diaphragm. This creates a strong back-and-forth action on the diaphragm, increasing signal output while decreasing distortion. Also called a double-bottom carbon microphone.

diffused light Light that is spread out, either by atmospheric conditions or artificially by diffusion materials. It has a

certain softness to its shadows and an unconcentrated luminescence that creates a gentler ambience than bright surfaces of light.

diffuser Piece of cellular diffusing composition placed in front of studio LAMPS to soften the light. A diffuser is any translucent material that spreads the light and keeps it from causing HOT SPOTS, and gives an even more natural look. Also called a GEL.
    Also a panel in a sound studio that can reflect or absorb sound.

diffusion curtain Plastic DIFFUSER to spread light. Its predecessor was a plain shower curtain.

diffusion materials Various plastics, silks and spun glass used in front of the LAMPS to soften light without adding color.

digital video effects Special graphics and SPECIAL EFFECTS produced by a programmed computer control unit based on a numerical system.

dimmer Electrical or electromechanical device to lower or raise the amount of light in a scene. Not generally used in dramatic color photography because the voltage change also alters the color temperature of the LAMPS.

dimmer banks Banks or rheostats used to adjust the voltage and thus the intensity of lamps connected to them.

DIN A European film-exposure referent. DIN is the acronym for Deutsche Industrie Norm.

diode tube A tube for evacuated air with cathode and anode elements, used in radio and TV receivers. Most of these have been replaced by solidstate semiconductors. One of the basic inventions making possible the effective reception of radio and TV signals.

diopter An extension or attachment for the LENS which permits filming of extreme CLOSE-UP materials with sharp definition.

direct   To stage the action for on-camera, on-mike or live performance.

direct broadcasting satellite   A satellite that transmits feed directly to a receiver antenna.

direct cinema   Term popularized by filmmaker Albert Maysles to describe "close-observation" shooting with indigenous sound, filmed and recorded with lightweight portable equipment used to interfere as little as possible with the actual event.

direct current (DC)   Basically constant current, flowing in one direction. See also ALTERNATING CURRENT.

direct cut   An immediate shot to the next one in continuity, without intervening fades or dissolves. See also JUMP CUT.

As a direction in a screenplay, it means that there is an instant cut in the moment, the dialogue, action ends or the scene ends, straight to the next scene. There is no holding on the shot or dwelling on the image.

direction   (by the director) The input of character interpretation, sense of the dialogue, BLOCKing, general scenic intent, etc., given by the director to the actor or actress. The direction may be as minimal as his or her MARKS, or as extensive as going into a full probe of character development, motivation and subtext.

(from the writer) The SCRIPT indications describing the actors' general movements and attitudes, designated in two basic categories: GENERAL DIRECTION and PERSONAL DIRECTION. General directions are nonpersonal ones relating to one or more actors: "The young couple pauses for a moment at the doorway, then leaves." "John takes the book from the desk, glances at it curiously and puts it into his traveling bag." "The horse breaks loose; Marie runs after it, trying to stop it." "General Stuart enters. The men

stand at attention." PERSONAL DIRECTIONS sometimes indicate directions to a single actor or actress, but more often refer to directions included within the person's speeches, to indicate his or her mood, awareness and, sometimes, movements. Example: John (staring at her): What do you mean by that? "Staring at her," in parentheses, is personal direction. See SCRIPT FORM (THEATRICAL), in Appendix.

directional   When applied to certain optical and acoustical devices like loudspeakers, EXPOSURE METERS and microphones, this term denotes a limitation of the angle of dissemination, reflection, radiation or acceptance.

directional antenna   One that receives or radiates signals in one direction better than another. An antenna positioned or electronically adjusted to receive only specific stations.

director   The person who controls the action and DIALOGUE in front of the camera and who is therefore responsible for realizing the intentions of the scripted concept. See DIRECTORIAL REMINDER SHEET in Appendix.

director of photography   See CAMERAMAN.

director's finder   Calibrated optical device with a range of views measured to a given lens. In other words, it lets you see approximately what the shot will look like with a specific lens. For example, if the finder is for a 35mm camera with a lens range of 25mm to 250mm, and you want to see what the shot will look like on a 50mm lens, you focus the lens at the 50mm mark and move to camera position to view the upcoming shot.

Director's Guild of America (DGA)   A national union for professional directors in film and television.

direct pickup   Transmission of TV signals/images without the intervening step of magnetic or photographic recording. Also called live direct.

direct response Advertising term which gives the audience only a limited time to respond to an offer by dialing a number or sending in a response by mail.

direct-to-disc Recording straight to a master record rather than to a tape that can be reedited later. Today the masters are nearly all tape, but the theory is the same: The direct recording cuts out intermediate generations necessary in editing, and it also gives greater intensity by having uninterrupted sound-takes. There are fervid and authoritative advocates supporting and opposing this process.

direct viewfinder See VIEWFINDER.

dirty dupe A film print made directly from another print, used for editing and mixing purposes, where color quality is not vital.

dirty movie See BLUE MOVIE.

disc Blank used for phonograph recording or reproduction-pressing. Common name for a phonograph record.

In computers the "library" elements that can be stored separately from the computer. Hard discs can be used for permanent storage, floppy discs for temporary or permanent storage. Floppies are often transferred to hard discs.

disc jockey Radio announcer who hosts a regular program of popular music.

discontinuity Consecutive shots of scenes that do not match in action. Unless you are attempting discontinuity deliberately, it is a grave dramatic error of directorial misjudgement. Discontinuity can also be caused by a mismatch of DECOR, PROPS or LIGHTING, or any combination of these. See also JUMP CUT.

discovery shot See REVEAL SHOT.

disc recorder An audio recording machine that electromechanically puts sound onto a disc. To be differentiated from TAPE RECORDER.

discrete component One manufactured before being integrated into a unit or system: transistors, diodes, resistors, etc.

dish Nickname for the large parabolic antenna that receives and retransmits images to TV sets. This microwave antenna reflects radio/TV energy entering or leaving the specific receiving/transmitting system.

dishing A roll of film that has been improperly wound, too loose, usually; or too tight, so that it goes "soft" in the center and makes a depression in the roll, convex or concave, depending on how you look at it. The result can be a disastrous spilling out of the center of the film and a consequent inordinate amount of post-production time to disentangle and rewind it.

Disney Studios The name used in daily discussions of what is officially known as the Walt Disney Company. It is a media empire that includes the main studio in Burbank, the theme park division (Walt Disney Imagineering), the feature film divisions, Touchstone, Walt Disney Productions and Hollywood Pictures, the Disney Channel (cable TV), Disney HTV, Walt Disney Educational Media Company, Walt Disney Music, Buena Vista Distribution and numerous marketing adjuncts. The theme parks—Disneyland, Disney World, EPCOT, Tokyo Disneyland and Euro Disneyland—are all run independently under the aegis and supervision of the Walt Disney Company.

dispersion An optical material's capacity to cause some wavelengths of light to be sent through the material at different velocities; velocity in this case is a function of wavelength.

display primaries A TV receiver's R-G-B (red, green, blue) matrix from which all the other TV colors are derived.

dissolve An optical impression between superimposed shots, in which the second shot gradually begins to appear as the first gradually disappears. Called mixes in England. See LAP DISSOLVE.

dissolve animation Motion indicated by fast dissolves or SOFT CUTS from image to image or sequential artwork. Induced animation, created by a series of fast DISSOLVES to move artwork or objects in space or time.

dissolve control Special MULTIMEDIA unit that interlinks CAROUSEL projectors, in order to DISSOLVE from one picture or slide to another.

dissolve lapse Shots of brief duration filmed at spaced time-intervals, and linked together with fast DISSOLVES. Similar to TIME LAPSE in its effect.

distance shot A TV term that is the same as LONG SHOT in film. A shot that looks at the action from afar. "Long" is determined by its relation to the medium shot.

distortion Picture distortion is a warped and incorrect image caused by an optical-system malfunction in the camera. Sound distortion is signal malfunction between input and output of an electrical amplification or transmission system.

distortion filter A specially crafted effect filter that deliberately distorts an image in a given way.

distribution The dissemination of a media product, through various channels: motion picture theatres, TV networks, TV syndication, cable, home video cassettes, educational/informational market, etc. Agreements can be for sales, releases, rights or rentals.

distributor Person or organization that handles DISTRIBUTION. In home video marketing, the distributor is the wholesaler, the middleman. The distributor in this field purchases, or sometimes takes on contingency, products from the supplier, i.e., the manufacturer or producer,

and places them in video store outlets. The video stores buy them from the distributor. Sometimes the distributor is bypassed and the video store owner or operator buys the videocassettes directly from the prime supplier, the manufacturer or producer.

distributor-exhibitor contract A regular play-date contract or a FOUR WALLING contract, the latter now being quite rare. Contract points covered include names and affiliations of contracting parties, name of the film (The team "title" has another meaning in legal terminology.), picture's play-date, and options to extend the run. The contract must set fees, percentages and the method by which they are to be calculated and dispersed.

ditty bag Canvas carrying bag for holding camera tools, camera tape, spare mechanical parts, etc., for use by camera crew. Often suspended under the in-place tripod.

divergence loss Transmission loss of sound resulting from the dispersion of sound energy.

divergent turret Camera turret holding lenses away from one another on metallic convex plane on which the lenses are mounted. The lenses are placed so that long-focal-length lenses will not be in the wider field of vision of the short-focal-length lenses. It also allows two large long-lensed barrels to be mounted on the same turret.

dividing network A network of frequencies that can split the audio-frequency spectrum into two or more parts and send them to separate units: speakers, relays, amplifiers, etc.

docudrama A film or videotape dramatization based on documentary materials drawn from current headlines or immediate events. Some docudramas are controversial and historical in nature. See BIOGRAPHICAL FILM.

documentary A type of film marked by its interpretative handling of realistic subjects and backgrounds. Sometimes the term is applied widely to include films that appear more realistic than conventional commercial pictures; at other times, so narrowly that only films with a NAR-RATION track and a background of real life are so categorized. According to John Grierson, one of the founders of contemporary documentary film, documentary filmmaking is "the creative treatment of reality." Documentary has developed various styles of presentation, as well as overlapping into other film and tape areas—news, special events, travel, biography, among other areas. Then too, fiction films, as well as commercials, have incorporated documentary techniques, as documentary has incorporated techniques drawn from many film and tape forms.

Dolby sound Pioneer sound system that generates sound with a minimal NOISE level, either on optical track or tape. This noise reduction allows for cleaner recording and greater fidelity.

dolly A light and compact wheeled mount for a camera, used for DOLLYING shots and for greater mobility in moving the camera from setup to setup. "Okay, now dolly in!" "We're going to dolly alongside him as he walks to the house."

dollying Movement of the whole camera when making a shot. Sometimes referred to as trucking or tracking.

dolly man A camera-crew person who pushes and guides the dolly when a scene requiring a dolly move is being filmed. He or she usually moves it between shots, although sometimes it is a camera crew member who moves it for the shot and a grip who moves it into place for the next setup where it will be needed. Sometimes, an assigned grip handles all of the moves, depending upon union rules and jurisdictions, production needs and crew size. Also called dolly pusher.

dolly pusher See DOLLY MAN.

dolly shot Moving shot made from a dolly. Regular lock shots can be made from the dolly, as well, the dolly being used in this case for fast and efficient moves from one location to another. Used loosely, a dolly shot is any moving shot, from a wheelchair, a flatbed car or any wheeled device on which the camera is mounted. Dolly shots can be made from either a free-wheeling dolly or one that is on track. Also called FOLLOW SHOTS.

dominant wavelength The wavelength of light that dominates in any given color.

donut The cloth or spongelike eyepiece of the viewfinder. It softens the hard edges of the viewfinder, making it more comfortable and easier for the cinematographer to work efficiently. Called a donut because of its circular shape and center hole for viewing.

dope sheet ANIMATION cue list, used for sequence-by-sequence exposure information. Also called EXPOSURE SHEET. More casually, any sheet of production information.
An analysis of film materials prepared for production or library storage and retrieval.

dot A small, round GOBO; opaque and usually painted black. Used to cut out hot, direct light falling on a specific area within the set.

double Substitute for the star, who resembles the performer and does the physically difficult and dangerous shots for the actor. The double can be used in long shots, especially those shot by the SECOND UNIT. See also STAND-IN.

double bottom carbon microphone See DIFFERENTIAL MICROPHONE.

double exposure Successive exposure of a light-sensitive emulsion to two scenes, so that two superimposed images within the frame are visible after development.

double feature Two films on one theater program for a single admission price.

double image A TV picture with overlapping images, caused by the receiver picking up the same signal coming in over two paths, and not arriving with exact simultaneity.

doubling When one actor does two or more separate voices of characters in radio or voice-over work for movies and TV.

Also, it means working as a DOUBLE for the star.

double perf stock Film stock with perforations on both sides of the film. Used for steadiness of image in cameras with double-sprocket drive, either for MOS or DOUBLE SYSTEM SOUND RECORDING shots.

double system sound recording A method of sound recording in which the sound is originally recorded on a separate piece of film or audio tape, physically apart from but in synch with the camera. See SINGLE SYSTEM.

double take A comedic bit with its roots in ancient Greek comedy. A reaction of delayed awareness. Looking at something twice in rapid succession; usually a look of surprise and agitation.

down link Transmission from SATELLITE to receiving station.

down shot Scene or shot filmed or taped from a high angle, looking down.

downstage From live theater, this term refers to the area of the set close to the camera.

down time Production delay caused by equipment failing or malfunctioning. If caused by performers or crew, it's referred to as a "delay." A good PRODUC-TION MANAGER figures some down time into any production schedule, making projected allowances.

dowser The electromechanical part of a projector that cuts off or blocks off the light beam when reel-changeover takes place from one projector to another.

DPR See DAILY PRODUCTION REPORT.

drain Power loss in a battery.

drama Inclusive term indicating the full body of all work in a dramatic form.

dramatic film A film that is structured in a dramaturgical form, with created characters and a shooting script to work from. The old dictum of a form with a beginning-middle-and-end was answered by the New Wave filmmakers of France with, "Yes, but not necessarily in that order." Often comedy will be referred to as "dramatic," particularly if there is a strong emphasis on character. In general usage, "dramatic film" refers to one that has a strong emphasis on conflict, wherein there is something vital at stake, in various stages and degrees of jeopardy.

dramatic irony Information made known to the audience of which the characters in the script are unaware. For example, a bomb is planted in a suitcase. We as the audience see and know that. We also know that it is set to go off at a a specific time. While people are chatting in a train compartment, the suitcase is riding in the luggage rack above them. Cutaways to wristwatches showing the time, to the conductor's stem-wound railroad watch and to the clock in the train station, all help to build the suspense. Meanwhile, the small talk goes on, playing an irritating, trivial counterpoint to the impending explosion. Another example of dramatic irony can be contrapuntal. For instance, in the Italian neorealistic classic made right after the end of World War II, *Shoeshine,* a little tune heard when the poor children of the bombed-out city "find" a horse—a happy, lyrical and bright tune played on a little flute—is heard again when they find the animal dead, and at other moments of tragic tension. See CONTRAPUNTAL SOUND.

dramatic unity A theory of dramaturgy first propounded by Aristotle in his *Poetics*. Basically, it says that the entire action of a play should take place within a proscribed time and in essentially the same place. While this dictum is sometimes applicable in live theatre, it is totally unnecessary in film, which can compress great lengths of time into a taut encapsulation. This doesn't mean that it cannot be used effectively in film. Two Alfred Hitchcock classics use a somewhat compressed period of time and an almost claustrophobic sense of place: *Lifeboat* and *Rope*. Another example would be Buñuel's *The Exterminating Angel*; from France, *Last Year at Marienbad*. *No Exit*, by Jean Paul Sartre, is in open-time but with extreme compression of "place" and great tension in the relationship between characters. This interweaving of close contact and hyper-awareness of one another is another hallmark of characterization in plays with dramatic unity.

drape A theatrical plain backdrop. Also a nickname for any theatrical curtain.

draw cards Cutaway cards in a holding rack on which are graphics, titles, charts, credits, that are camera ready and in position for filming or videotaping.

dream mode Scenes depicting the dreams or imaginings of one or more characters in a film.

dress To arrange the set pieces, scenic props, regular props or whatever is necessary to make the set ready for filming/taping.

dresser A wardrobe person assigned to prepare an actor in proper wardrobe for upcoming scenes.

dress extra An EXTRA who provides his or her own formal wear or special costuming, and gets an additional fee for supplying them.

dress rehearsal A full rehearsal of a film or videotape which is basically the same as a live theatre dress rehearsal, wherein the show is run in full costume and with the technical cues indicated, prior to the actual filming.

drift An undesirable change in electronic output that can throw off sound and image synchronicity.

drive The mechanism device through which motion is conveyed from the motor to the roll of film in a motion picture camera.

drive-by shot One where the camera car makes a shot by driving by a stationary person or object; or in car-to-car shots, going by another vehicle. In nature films there are drive-by shots of various wild animals on the open plains. For example, going past a herd of wildebeests on the African savanna, either overtaking them or moving by them in the opposite direction.

drive-in A motion picture house designed as an exterior theater where the audience views films from their automobiles. Special long cords allow speakers inside the individual automobiles.

driving signal Television signals from a synch-generator made with pulses at the line frequency plus pulses at the field frequency. They time the scanning of the image.

drive-on pass A studio pass allowing a vehicle to enter the motion picture lot. See GATE PASS.

drop See BACKDROP.

drop-out A sudden total lack of recorded-sound presence, caused either by electronic malfunction, by intentionally dialing down the sound or by inserting a blank leader. It is important that all dropouts be corrected and filled in with AM-BIENCE, SOUND EFFECTS tracks, music or DIALOGUE, or a mixture of any of these.

drop shadow A simulated cast shadow, usually on a lower angle than the object or lettering casting the shadow. Used graphically in lettering so that TITLES and CREDITS stand out more distinctly.

dry-mounting Placement of artwork on artboard by heat-pressing dry-mounting tissue to the board.

dry-mounting press A machine customized to perform the dry-mounting process. Its two heated plates melt the special tissue placed between artwork and artboard, causing adherence of the graphics to the mounting board.

dry run Rehearsal with or without actors to check camera moves and re-check marks for blocking.

dry-type-transformer One not cooled by immersion in oil, but by circulation of air in and around the unit. See TRANS-FORMER.

dual modulation Two types of modulation, each carrying its own particular intelligence, in order to modulate a common carrier or subcarrier wave. See MODULATION.

dual role When one actor plays two roles in the same film, often in the same scene. Some examples: Lily Tomlin and Bette Midler *both* played dual roles in the 1988 Touchstone film *Big Business;* Ronald Colman in *The Prisoner of Zenda* (1937); Richard Dreyfuss in *Moon Over Parador* (1988); Douglas Fairbanks, Jr. in *The Corsican Brothers* (1940), as well as Dustin Farnum in the 1919 silent version of the film, and Richard Greene in *The Return of the Corsican Brothers* (1953); Olivia de Havilland in *Dark Mirror* (1946), etc. See also MULTIPLE ROLES.

dual-track recorder A recording head that covers half the tape width. This al-lows the unit to record on that side of the tape. Then, if necessary or pre-arranged, the reel can be turned over and new materials recorded on the other half. Used only for amateur or semiprofessional work, or in reportage or event situations when tape is running out, i.e., an emergency situation.

dub (dubbing) Synchronization to on-camera lip movement that replaces the existing voice, whether his/her own, or that of another actor. Also, when the language is indigenous, foreign dubbing is usually accomplished by means of loops, consisting of short sections of the DIA-LOGUE that is to be replaced. Dubbing is used to record or rerecord songs, prepare foreign versions of film and videotapes, and replace unsatisfactory dialogue. Um-brella term for RE-RECORDING, ELEC-TRONIC LINE REPLACEMENT, and LOOPING.

dubbing sheets The "scoring" sheets for the DUB or MIX, in parallel vertical and horizontal columns, indicating in graph form what sounds—music, sound effects, voices—are on each track and at what footage count they come in and go out. Used by the MIXER to cue in the necessary tracks from the mixing board.

dulling spray An antireflective spray, applied to a high-gloss surface to reduce their reflection and cut down the high-lights.

dump tanks Large troughs or water-tanks atop spillway, whether a scenic cy-clorama or off-camera functional chutes, that when opened on cue let the water come rushing into the scene. Used to augment heavy surf, simulate a tidal wave, a storm at sea, etc. Often used in con-junction with the studio's "lake," or ma-rine tank. Also called spill tanks.

dupe negative A NEGATIVE film pro-duced by printing from a positive.

duplication Making prints from a film master or videotape copies from a vid-eotape master or a SUBMASTER.

dutch angle An image tilted toward screen left or right, effected by moving the camera from its vertical and horizontal axis and tilting it to angle desired. Used to create dramatic tension or symbolize surrealistic images.

dutching Taping or painting over spots needing repair or repainting on the set or in a PRACTICAL room.

duvetyne A napped fabric that is used for covering scenery, or, in black, as background cloth for shooting props or people "in limbo." See also LIMBO SET.

DVE See DIGITAL VIDEO EFFECTS.

dynalens Gyro-controlled stabilizer that can be attached to a camera to cut down vibration and smooth out jerky or bumpy camera moves. Particularly useful in car-to-car, air-to-air and telephoto scenes.

dynamic cutting In film aesthetics, a type of cutting which, by the juxtaposition of contrasting shots or SEQUENCES, generates concepts or reactions in the mind of the spectator that were not inherent in any single element of the film. It is thematic editing with recurring shots comprising the structure of the overall film segment. The accent is not on visual continuous action, but great use is made of visual and auditory metaphors, dramatic contrast and pictorial analogies.

dynamic frame A film concept and process in which the screen is a full, widescreen size (2.55–3.1 ×1), with certain scenes framed by masking them on a section of the screen to a desired ratio. Full-screen would be used for wide-open spaces, a framed-in standard ratio (1.3 × 1) for more intimate scenes, while narrow vertical matting might be used for hallways. Devised by Glenn Alvey in 1955, only one motion picture was made using the process, the H. G. Wells story *The Hole in the Wall*.

dynamic range The sound spread in amplitude from the softest to the loudest.

Used in relation to sound recording from whatever source.

E

E Symbol for VOLTAGE.

E and O See ERRORS AND OMISSIONS.

earphone Electroacoustic receiver, placed in or over the ear. The smaller receivers that can be effectively concealed are often used by on-camera newscasters. The crew will more likely wear a single combination headset comprised of a minimicrophone and earphone (single or double). Also called an earpiece. See HEADPHONE.

earpiece See EARPHONE.

earth station A receptor unit electromechanism and support building for receiving SATELLITE transmissions.

ease in/ease out Moving up to the speed of motion smoothly and gradually is "easing in"; moving down from that speed, "easing out."

easel Graphics stand to hold title cards, charts, drawings, LOGOs etc., for filming or taping.

east/west Using the top of the screen as North, the bottom as South, this makes left screen WEST and right screen EAST.

EBR See ELECTRONIC BEAM RECORDING.

EBS See EMERGENCY BROADCAST SYSTEM

echo A rebounding wave returning with enough magnitude and delay to differentiate it from the original, received signal.

echo chamber   A term used in the recording industry that originated in radio. It signified a special room that had an intense reverberation-presence, giving words spoken or sung added power and impact. Used for flashback or other worldly voices, or to enrich the narrator's voice. In singing it was used to give fullness to a solo voice, by separating it from its background. This same principle was also used for singing ensembles and choral groups, or in separating solo instruments from the orchestral background. The echo chamber is a separate channel fed into the MIXING BOARD. The echo mike often worked in an isolation booth, and sometimes in a separate studio. The echo effect today is usually built into the mixing board, and can be added as needed. This effect is standard input in many contemporary instrumental and vocal recordings.

Eclair   Initially, the prime camera for shooting synch sound documentaries in the new light-weight portable style. It was almost silent-running with a padded cloth cover or a cameraman's jacket. Its magazines could be changed by a good camera operator in about ten seconds as opposed to the four or five minutes it would take the same operator to change the Arriflex magazine. Today, however, the Arriflex and Aaton or the Frezzolini magazines can be changed rapidly, as well. Its design was such that it made handheld shots easier and smoother. The ACL model was the successful pioneer self-blimped camera. Used for features as well, particularly in Europe.

ECU   See EXTREME CLOSE-UP.

edge fogging   FOGGING along one or both sides of a piece of film, often caused by light leakage in a MAGAZINE or by inadequate taping of the lid of a can of original film, exposed or unexposed.

edge number   One of a series of numbers, combined with key lettering, printed at regular intervals along the edge of many tapes of RAW STOCK. These numbers, incorporated into the film itself, print through to positive stock (much lighter). They mark film lengths so that scenes can be found when editing by winding forward or back to the specific number. Also referred to as footage number, key number and negative number.

edge numbering machine   Electromechanical printer for imprinting EDGE NUMBERS on film optical and audio tracks.

edge track   Magnetic audio strip on the nonperforated side of film stock.

edgewave   An unwanted condition which occurs when one or both edges of the film are too long in proportion to the main frames, i.e., an unstable feed in/out.

edgewax   Trichlorethane solution treated with a small amount of paraffin wax (50 grams per litre of solution) that is used to treat edges only of the emulsion side of the film; lubricant used to protect film in post-production editing or during projection.

edging   Unwanted discoloration at the edges of TV picture.

edit   To arrange and assemble film or tape, prepare it for TV playback or projection by the INTERLOCK SYSTEM, and set it up for final sound mix.

edit code   Data used to store and retrieve information regarding frame count, time count (hours, minutes, seconds), cross-referenced retrieval sources etc., all put onto a control track.

edit control   Synchronous editing setup that is activated when editing videotape. Customized jacks are used to join together two or more VCRs.

edited music track   Sound track cut to match the picture.

editing block   A flat, solid, rectangular device with film-width grooves. Used to cut FILM STOCK with a precision slice, in order to recement or retape it to a similarly cut piece of film. Also referred to as a SPLICER.

editor   Person who physically assembles the running structure of the film or tape, who puts together sound, picture, music and effects into a working whole, ready for release. "Assembling" means re-arranging and re-assembling SOUND and PICTURE, in making editorial choices.

editorializing   An analysis of the news; an interpretation. Both of these words are more dignified ways of saying "opinion." All editorializing is subjective. But then, so is the so-called "objective" reporting. "Objective reporting" is a paradigm and never a full reality, but in non-editorial reportage it is usually attempted. Overt editorializing is more potentially dangerous, and certainly threatening to the truth, than in documentaries where the footage shows "reality," usually—but not always—unstaged, while the narration is assumed to be making a direct, "objective" comment on what we are seeing. This is done subtly in some films and with a heavy hand in others, but whatever the shading, the aim is to disseminate a specific attitude or subjective viewpoint. A commercial is an example of almost total editorialized self-aggrandizement, with a strongly attitudinal preset message. Editorializing is usually genteel propaganda, hoping to bring an audience to sympathy with or belief in the speaker's point of view. Editorializing is, however, only one form of propagandizing.

editorial process   The full range of everything needed and services required to assemble a ROUGH CUT, fine cut and to prepare picture and sound tracks for the mix (crew members, supplies, editing equipment, editorial offices and cutting rooms).

editor's synch   Alignment marking on sound and picture elements, not compensating for projection-mode. Also called PRINTER'S SYNCH, and sometimes DEAD SYNCH.

edit out   To electronically delete or physically take out sections of SOUND TRACK or picture, in film or videotape.

EDP   See ELECTRONIC DATA PROCESSING.

educational film   A film produced and released to the educational market (grade schools, colleges, universities, private and trades schools) in tape or film formats for lease or purchase. Some of these films that have a broad appeal go on to PBS showings and cable network playdates. The films can be informational, educational or motivational, including OPEN-ENDED FILMS, which are designed to stimulate discussions, and "how-to" films.

educational television (ETV)   The original name for PUBLIC BROADCASTING SERVICE (PBS). The change was prompted by a general consensus that the word "educational" alienated a substantial portion of the viewing audience. See PUBLIC BROADCASTING SYSTEM.

effective aperture   Functional ratio of a lens between the focal length and the diameter of aperture. This diameter of the lens-opening is controlled mechanically by the parameters of the iris, from totally closed to completely open.

effects   Sounds or images used to enhance a scene—to add humor, suspense, pathos or whatever mood is required. These effects can be visual, through lighting, texture, setting, composition, rhythm of editing, or combinations of these and other elements: aural, with synchronous, fabricated or surrealistic sound effects; combination of picture and sound, augmentative or contrapuntal; or SPECIAL EFFECTS.

effects bank   Control panel that activates direct electronic or computer-generated effects. It works from a control booth or in a portable unit from the studio floor.

effects filter   An optical filter that distorts the rendering of natural objects to such an extent that a special effect such as light at night or a fog effect is produced.

effects projector   A special projector for front-screen or rear-screen projection of film, video or stills, or front-projection onto any customized surface required for the particular effect.

effects track   A separate track for SOUND EFFECTS. There may be more than one track for sound effects—up to two dozen on large productions utilizing numerous sounds. The SOUND TRACKS are differentiated in editing and MIXING from music, narration and dialogue tracks.

EFP   See ELECTRONIC FIELD PRODUCTION.

EHF   See EXTREMELY HIGH FREQUENCY.

EHS   See EXTREME HIGH SHOT.

eight ball mike   Developed originally as a radio mike, with a lower black spherical section holding the microphone's electrical voice-receptor unit with a circular protective sound-screen over the top. Called "8-ball" because of the appearance of the lower part of the microphone, it's used for single-voice or sound effects.

eight-millimeter (8mm) film   Film used for home movies, although some footage, reportage or event not available in any other format, can be and has been blown up to 35mm for professional film release as inserts in documentation segments of a film. The stock for home use is now being phased out by new lightweight video-cameras that record picture and sound. See CAMCORDERS.

electrical degree   Time-measurement division into discrete units, for measuring alternating current.

electrical drive motor   Synchronous or variable-speed device, used to drive a camera, audio recorder or projector.

electrical generator   Mechanical engine that converts mechanical into electrical power. Used in studio situations to augment existing power supplies, and on location when power is not available.

electrical interlocks   Open/close switches activated by the rods or levers that run the electrical-contact operations.

electrical motor   Motor driven by electricity that uses the electrical energy in order to transform it into rotating mechanical energy. Used internally in film/video cameras as drive mechanisms.

electrical noise   Electrical energy extraneous to the primary signals. It is necessary to reduce or eliminate it to ensure sound or image clarity.

electrical reset   Putting a relay back into potentially operational mode, after it has completed a function. This allows instant spotting and replay for ADR or rapid access to a frame in offline and online editing.

electrical transcription   A recording on disc of a radio program, or a segment of that program, now replaced by tape recording and digital recording. In the golden days of radio, a common phrase from the announcer introducing a previously recorded program, went something like this: "The following program is an electrical transcription." If it was a west coast re-broadcast of a program broadcast earlier to the east coast, the announcement would add, ". . . recorded from an earlier broadcast."

electrical truck   Specially rigged hauling and utility trucks for lights, cables and other electrical equipment. Some trucks are equipped with self-housed generators or attachments to haul and connect to generators.

electrical wave filter   A filter separating electric waves of varying frequencies.

electric discharge lamp   Sealed glass envelope with an electrically charged metallic vapor or inert gas to create the luminescence. It operates at lower temperatures than arc lamps, uses less space and maintains consistency of daylight-balanced light at the proper color temperature.

electrician Person responsible for placement and adjustment of lights, and for the supply of electricity to them. See GAFFER.

electroacoustic Adjective describing a unit which utilizes both sound-frequency pressures and electrical current.

electroacoustic transducer A device that either receives impulses from an electrical system and transmits them as output to an acoustic system (e.g., a loudspeaker), or the other way around, transmitting them for reception (e.g., a microphone).

electrodynamic braking A gradual deceleration and stopping of the reels on a tape-deck, by activating a pre-set voltage to the motor(s).

electrodynamic speaker A direct-current driven, magnetically-activated speaker used in recording live events. The sound recordist will often tap directly into the feed mike, rather than record from the loudspeaker, to control and ensure sound quality.

electrographic recording Image created by an electrical current and originally transferred in direct analog by an electromechanically powered pen or stylus. Now the term refers primarily to transmitted facsimile reproduction. A fax is an example of electrographic recording.

electromagnetic communications Frequencies for so-called wireless communications, i.e., radio, short wave and microwave transmission (also visible light), and microwave transmission requiring lower frequencies. Once this is achieved, the systems may be said to be in a state of electromagnetic compatibility.

electromagnetic   compatibility (EMC) For electronic communications systems to operate acceptably in their intended environments they must be free from unwanted electromagnetic radiation.

electromagnetic horn Large horn-shaped device or structural unit that emits directional radiation of radio waves. It operates in high frequency (100-megahertz) range.

electromagnetic lens Electron-focused lens that aligns electron beams to achieve sharpness of image.

electromagnetic spectrum The full range of electromagnetic radiation.

electromagnetic-type microphone Mike whose voltages are altered by an electromagnet. Examples would be the RIBBON MIKES, MOVING-COIL MICROPHONES, dynamic microphones and moving vane/reluctance microphones.

electromechanical timer Motor-driven timer. The clutch that drives the numbers may or may not be electrically operated. If not, then it is operated and calibrated mechanically. Used for numerical readouts in filming/videotaping and in production, and in editing in postproduction.

electronic Theoretical and applied science term that describes the movement of free-electron currents and the modes of their emissions in a gas, vacuum, photosensitive tubes, conductivity materials and semiconductors. To be differentiated from electric, i.e., strong currents carried by metallic conductors. Also refers, adjectively, to units handling these currents: control devices, transmitting and relay equipment, instrumentation gear for all units, augmentative circuitry, etc.

electronic beam recording (EBR) The transfer process for making a film print from videotape. Based on a digital gray scale, it is done by stop printing from three gray-scaled black-and-white negatives.

electronic data processing Data operations carried on primarily by electronic equipment, with minimal manual handling.

electronic director Live TV or video multi-camera director who calls the shots to feed into the live outgoing broadcast or the master videotape. Works from the control room in direct contact with the switchers, and phone line contact with the TECHNICAL DIRECTOR (TD). Sometimes the electronic director is the same as the staging director.

electronic editing Audio/visual editing of materials without mechanical splices, lifts or reprints all selected and assembled electronically.

electronic field production (EFP) Location production that utilizes lightweight, portable video gear. It is used extensively in news-gathering and documentary work.

electronic flash tube See FLASH TUBE.

electronic line replacement (ELR) A video looping process in which lines are re-recorded to match the existing synch movement of the actor's lips to the picture, or to specific action. Dialogue has been re-recorded by the original actor or a replacement. Sometimes only a near match is needed if the original soundtrack is in one language and the replacement track is in another. ELR is the name for the entire lip-synching process (usually computerized) as well as for the session itself. ADDITIONAL DIALOGUE REPLACEMENT is the name for this function in looping for film. See LOOPING, DIALOGUE REPLACEMENT.

electronic news-gathering (Eng) On-the-spot news coverage, employing highly portable videotaping systems in place of motion picture cameras. Now the standard practice for TV stations.

electronic slate Name for an internal electronic device that is part of the camera that simultaneously flashes some film frames and emits a synchronous audio signal of the same frame duration. This allows picture and sound elements to be in synch not only during production but also in post-production.

Also a lighted, digital, battery-powered hand-held slating device, external to the camera, giving numerical readouts.

electron images Images produced by electrons sent out by a scanning gun that are—as nearly as possible—in a one-to-one relation to on-camera objects.

electron lens A squeezing down of electrons into a narrow beam. This is done inside a cathode-ray tube electromagnetic or electrostatic deflection device. This function is similar to an "optical lens," hence the term.

electroprinting A system where sound is transferred from the master magnetic track directly to the release print, thereby avoiding the need for the additional element of an optical sound track printing master.

electrostatic microphone A microphone activated by variations in its electrostatic capacitance; also known as a condenser microphone.

electrostatic process Video image information brought about by changes in light rather than electrical input.

elements Units of original film (reversal or negative), plus SOUND TRACKS that are used to make the COMPOSITE PRINT.

Editorial elements include all the various units of picture, sound, graphics, titling, music and effects that are to be used to put together the final version of the film or videotape. The assembly of these elements takes place in an editing bay for videotape or an editing room for film.

Lens elements are the individual lenses (either separate or sealed together) that in combination form a photographic objective lens, corrected for ABERRATIONS. Lens elements are also called components.

elevation drawing Term for architecture (and later theatrical design) that gives the vertical measurements of buildings; and for stage, the sets. In film, an elevation drawing lays out the vertical schematics and measurements.

elevator shot One in which the camera moves straight up and down, as if shot from an open elevator or fork lift, which it sometimes is. It is not a crane or tilt shot.

ELF See EXTREMELY LOW FREQUENCY.

ellipsoidal spot Hard-beam spotlight utilizing spherical optics to achieve its effect.

elliptical cutting An editing style in which action is compressed by avoiding literal sequential editing and eliminating intermediate shots, even deliberately using JUMP CUTS.

ELR See ELECTRONIC LINE REPLACEMENT.

ELS See EXTREME LONG SHOT.

EMC See ELECTROMAGNETIC COMPATIBILITY.

Emergency Broadcast System (EBS) The United States warning network that, in case of a national emergency, can place all broadcast stations under federal authority to broadcast emergency instructions.

emergency network Radio or TV frequencies earmarked for emergency usage, or a name for the assembly of commercial stations that will sound an emergency tone, instructions and information in case of a national disaster.

emission Waves in space that are sent out from a transmitter, their emission allows signals to be beamed to attuned receptors.

Emmy TV's equivalent to film's "Oscar." The Emmy awards are chosen by the Academy of Television Arts and Sciences.

The name Emmy comes from "Immy," a nickname for the image-orthicon tube, the basic TV tube. "Immy" was changed to "Emmy" and the award statue became a woman.

emote To portray the required emotion required by the script or improvisational situation. Originally it meant to act, but over the years it has gained a connotative meaning that ranges from humorous acceptance to openly derogatory rejection of the word that is synonymous with "overact." Some examples of use are "Wow! She was really emoting!" and "Never mind the emoting, let's see a real performance."

empathy In general, sharing another's concept or emotion. Dramaturgically, it is the involvement of the audience so that it emotionally participates in the actions and moods of the characters on screen.

emphasis Dramatic stress achieved, for example, by an actor's highlighting of particular words in a sentence, a sudden increase in volume or tempo in the music, a physical gesture, special sound and visual effects or punctuated editorial rhythm.

emphasizer A piece of electronic equipment or a circuit that gives a deliberate increase in signal strength at specified audio frequencies.

emulsion Light-sensitive layer on film base that is exposed to the scene to be filmed. It is this emulsion that holds and stores the LATENT IMAGE of the filmed scene that can be made visible by DEVELOPING.

emulsion batch See BATCH.

emulsion number A three-digit number on a RAW STOCK film container and can, immediately following the numerical film code number, that indicates film-base stock. See BATCH.

emulsion position   Whether film going through the projector is emulsion facing in to the projector or out. If it is facing in toward the projection lamp it is in A WIND projection position, if facing toward the motion picture screen it is in B WIND projection position.

emulsion speed   An emulsion's photosensitivity; it is measured using an index number which gives working suggestions and instructions for exposure conditions as well as specifications for the developing lab.

emulsion side   The side of the film that is emulsion-coated.

end credits   See END TITLES.

end-of-tape marker   Warning marker at the end of a magnetic tape, such as a section of transparent or photoreflective material, indicating the end of the recording surface of the tape.

end synch marks   Synchronizing points, marked at the ends of sound and picture, that allow printing to be carried out in both directions. End synch marks can also be usefully applied in recording SOUND TRACKS.

end test   Footage exposed toward the tail end of a film roll that is developed and viewed before the rest of the roll is developed. This helps to choose more accurately the exposure rate for developing the film.

end titles   Closing CREDITS or cards that are run at the conclusion of a film or tape. Also called END CREDITS.

energize   To activate a switch, coil, or relay by feeding the predetermined voltage into it.

energized   Activated into a "live" or "hot" condition by electrical connection.

ENG   See   ELECTRONIC NEWS-GATHERING.

engineer   A person who handles the technical operation of a studio: recording, television, radio, electronic editing, as well as CATV or satellite transmission and reception.

enhancer   A processor of signals that can sharpen focus, change coloration, alter contrast, etc. Used for tape-to-tape, film-to-tape or tape-to-film corrections or augmentations.

enlargement printing   Optical printing that increases a small frame area e.g., 16mm to 35mm. See BLOW-UP.

entertainment film   One produced for commercial release and distribution to the largest market possible; it is designed for showing in theatres, on television, and in secondary outlets, like videocassette markets, in-flight screenings, etc.

entrance   The emergence of an actor or actors upon the scene. The entrance may be highlighted and set up with crescendoing anticipation, or it may be unexpected, even surreptitious. But once onstage or in front of the camera, the actor has "made an entrance." Entrance also refers to the physical location from which the actor enters.

entrance cable   One that taps into an outside power line and brings it into a studio or general-use building.

environmental sound   Actual background sounds recorded within the filming or videotaping range of a particular scene. Traffic sounds, background conversations and crowds cheering are all examples of environmental sound. These sounds can be "WILD" RECORDINGS and the editor can LAY IN the tracks to match picture, or they can be recorded synchronously, whichever expedient is dictated by the necessities of production.

epic   A big film about a hero who is usually larger than life and sometimes semilegendary or folkloric.

episodic A style in which events occur sequentially, but without nuance of character or shadings of plot, and sometimes without dramatic logic. Although used mostly as a negative term, it can also describe a film in which episodes that are seemingly unrelated can build on top of each other to come into perspective as the film progresses, and into resolution as it ends. *Citizen Kane* is an episodic film in the best sense of the word. An episodic novel would be the picaresque masterpiece *Don Quixote*.

episodic TV Dramas with continuing stories in various episodes, as in a miniseries, or with continuing episodes, as in SOAP OPERAS.

equalize To adjust and balance the qualitative and quantitative electronic characteristics relating to the frequency and signal-power of the sound or picture.

equalizer A recording device for balancing music, NARRATION, DIALOGUE and SOUND EFFECTS tracks in a sound-mix session. This is done by altering the frequency characteristic of the electrical circuits.

equalizing Working from the coordinating master panel that coordinates and adjusts all the various SOUND TRACKS in conjunction with the equalizing devices.

equal time Part of the 1934 Federal Communications Act which assures equal time availability and privileges for air time (radio first, later for TV) to major political candidates running for the same elective office. Extended to include those with opposing viewpoints to any station's in-house editorial(s).

equipment chain Interlocked units of equipment that work as a unified system; the failure of any component results in down time until it is repaired. See DOWN TIME.

equivalent loudness Sonic intensity measured on a chosen referential scale, e.g., a 1000-hertz pure tone. Any standard for "normal audibility," above and below that range being evaluated as above or below "normal." Sound level using an arbitrary, numerical reference of intensity, e.g., a 1000-hertz pure tone, which auditors deem to be equivalent in loudness.

erase To remove recorded signals from an audio or videotape, to clear it for reuse.

erasing head A degaussing and over-recording device for removal of original signal.

erasure Signal-removal process on audio/video tape. This gives the tape the potential for recording uses.

erect image An image that is seen topside-up instead of reversed or upside down as in some portrait still cameras or early motion picture viewfinders.

errors and omissions (E and O) One of the various forms of essential production insurance. E and O insurance protects the producing company or corporation from those who would state that the idea of a produced program was taken from them—stolen directly, or by having had access to it in the past. For example, a plagiarism case was brought by syndicated columnist Art Buchwald against Eddie Murphy, Arsenio Hall and Paramount Studios regarding *Coming to America,* which Buchwald asserts was taken from the story he submitted to Paramount: The court agreed, and Buchwald won the case. The loss to Paramount would be covered under E and O insurance. It also is a shield against people who charge that the producer has invaded their privacy, defamed, slandered or libeled them, or held them up to ridicule. This is extremely important insurance to have in documentary and news reportage, and particularly investigative reportage.

establish In radio or TV, to let the music or effects stay on long enough to make a dynamic point, then fade out or cut abruptly.

establishing shot Traditionally, a wide shot introducing locale, weather conditions (if relevant), and the introductory or complete action of a scene. The establishing shot can sometimes serve as the MASTER SHOT if it runs for the length of the complete scene. However, an establishing shot may be a CLOSE SHOT or a MEDIUM SHOT, depending upon dramatic necessity. The establishing shot, over and above giving information, should also set the mood and style of a scene or, if it is the opening establishing shot, the entire film or videotape production.

estar A film base developed by Eastman Kodak Company to give great strength and durability to film prints. Now Fuji film has a comparable stock, as do other international film manufacturers.

estimate Budgetary educated/guess; a projection of total production costs, based on above-the-line and below-the-line demands of a given production. A rough budget usually typed up on a one-page budget summary sheet. It is the tentative budget preceding the long, multipaged, fully detailed working budget.

ethnic film   A film that is designed to highlight one or more races or sociocultural groups through the use of set, cast or plot. *The Milagro Bean Field War* is a recent example. Films on the Mafia and its extended family are instances of ethnic films, as are *A Man Called Horse* and *Dances With Wolves,* films on the American Indians from POINT OF VIEW. The pioneers in this genre were the black filmmakers Oscar Micheaux and Spencer Williams. Two of Williams' films were *Blood of Jesus* (1941) and *Go Down Death* (1944). Oscar Micheaux was a producer/director with over 200 films to his credit, including *Exile* (1931), *Ten Minutes to Live* (1932) and *The Notorious Elinor Lee* (1940).

ethnographic film A professional documentary, graduate-student or de-

partmental film that tapes any image as is, then adds evaluation and commentary in postproduction, while editing. The subject matter is sociotribal, racial or religious, studied as entities, or a single person or family can serve as typical of the entire group.

ETV See EDUCATIONAL TELEVISION.

excess noise Noise caused by a current passing through a semiconductor material. Also referred to as low frequency noise.

exchange In projection, a place to store theatrical reverse prints for transfer to various theaters. At these exchanges the prints are checked in, inspected and sent out to subdistribution points, i.e., the theaters and secondary venues.

exciter lamp A light that "excites" a current in a phototube. Often the lamp output is modulated by placing a light modulator, such as a SOUND TRACK, between the lamp and the tube.

exclusive run Exhibition of a film at only one theater in the greater metropolitan area of a city, usually at a FIRST-RUN theater.

exclusive videocassette marketing Franchise to a store or chain of stores that handles the display, sales and rentals of home video cassettes; an agreement to give them exclusivity on a title for a particular geographical area for a specific length of time.

executive producer Producer in charge of procuring and disseminating production funds. On production lots at the major studios, this title is also given to a staff producer working for the studio who keeps track of schedules, BUDGETs and all general production areas.

exhaustion Depletion of developing capacity in photoprocessing chemicals; a wearing-out of their efficiency due to time or use. Reduction or loss of their reaction-causing abilities.

exhibition Commercial showings of motion picture films, particularly in commercial exhibition houses.

exhibitor Owner or manager of a motion picture theater who supervises showings: bookings, advertising, accountancy, etc.

existentialist films A simplistic misnomer derived from a total or limited misunderstanding of existential philosophy, based on popularization by Jean Paul Sartre of the concepts of Kierkegard, Nietzsche, Husserl and Heidegger. In film critic's terminology, it is synonymous with FILM NOIR.

exit To leave the scene, either in front of camera or onstage. Also, the physical point at which the actor or actors leave.

expanded cinema See EXPANDED FILM.

expanded film A name given to films that incorporate breakthrough technology, such as computer-generated visuals, holograms and videographics. Also called expanded cinema, it came to prominence in the early 70's. The term is occasionally used today to indicate digital sound, colorization, and other terms reflecting state-of-the-art techniques, such as PAINT BOX and HDTV.

experimental film A subjective work of the FILMMAKER, using new technological or conceptual approaches or old ones in a new manner. Many films from students in the media schools apply the newest film and video techniques with state-of-the-art hardware, when possible. The product is often a totally subjective view of a person, thing or event, or an abstract work of form and movement, the latter using many superimposed and overlayed images. A film made independently as a personal vision or statement.

expiration date Final day for filming with a roll of film, after which there is a risk of decreased reproductive efficiency. The date is stamped on the film box or can.

exploitation film A feature motion picture with obligatory sex, violence, horror, catastrophic events or a mixture of any or all of these elements. The film exploits and builds its advertising campaign around these elements to attract audiences.

exposed Film that has been fed through a working camera subjected to light and images; it cannot be used again.

exposition Dialogue that explains story points that cannot be brought out by visual storytelling alone.

exposure Exposing a photographic film to any given intensity of light in such a manner that it may produce a latent image on the emulsion. According to the reciprocity law, exposure is determined by the product of time and intensity illumination. Overexposure is an exposure greater than optimum for a particular photographic emulsion, developing condition and range of brightness; it usually results in an image that is too light.

exposure calculator A wheel graph that shows suggested exposures for given light conditions.

exposure guide Portable data sheet or card that gives the best exposure for a range of light conditions.

exposure index A number based on emulsion speed and latitude, EXPOSURE METER characteristics and techniques, and the conditions of development, which enables the user of a film emulsion to determine the correct exposure using different light conditions, estimated by an exposure meter or from tables.

exposure latitude The range and limits of a film's overexposure and underexposure.

exposure meter A device for determining the light flux incident upon or reflected from a scene to be photographed, the corresponding instruments being known as INCIDENT LIGHT METERS and REFLECTED LIGHT METERS. The most common type in motion picture photography uses a scale calibrated to measure extremely small currents in microamperes. The meter is activated by a photovoltaic cell. Also called LIGHT METER.

exposure sheet Exposure level and duration of exposures on a sequential cue sheet to film a sequence of ANIMATION.

expression Interpretation in the delivery of dialogue, including facial appearance; the visual and spoken indication of a range of feelings. Also called a dope sheet.

expressionism A distorted world picture seen "subjectively." In film this is achieved by forced perspectives, irregular planes, tilted buildings, fractured composition, distorted lighting and costumes—all elements representing a forced visual metaphor of a personal reality. Used to express inner disturbances and solipsistic reality.

EXT See EXTERIOR.

extended play (EP) EP records were developed from the LPs, i.e., LONG-PLAYING records. The EPs were geared primarily to garnering the popular market, rather than widening the classical one. An EP plays at 45 rpms, and has eight minutes of running time per side, as opposed to the four or five minutes on the old 78 rpm records. All discs—33⅓ (LPs) and 45 rpm (EPs)—are now being phased out rapidly by audio cassettes and CDs, just as the EPs and LPs phased out the 78 rpm discs.

extension tube A tube extended the distance between camera and lens in order to extend the focal length of the lens and increase its properties of magnification. Used in TABLE-TOP PHOTOGRAPHY, detailed exploratory camera work and overall close-up photography.

exterior (EXT) Outdoor scene.

exterior lighting Outdoor lighting using available exterior light as is and adjusting to it, or augmenting the available light with dichroic-filtered light and reflectors in daylight. Night lighting on an exterior street is usually bounced light or brighter-than-standard lamps placed in street lamps and other "source" lights.

external device Input or output unit such as a tape recorder, secondary readout screen, line-printer, etc.; all under computer-control.

extra A film supernumerary; ATMOSPHERE, BACKGROUND. There are union and nonunion extras. Screen Actors Guild has expanded its membership by allowing SCREEN EXTRAS GUILD (SEG) members to become SAG members. Extras pay is less than Screen Actors Guild pay and unless specifically contracted, extras receive no RESIDUALS.

extraneous response Unwanted response in a recorder, receiving unit, or any device sensitive to given input signals. This response is caused by distorted or undesired signals that cause poor reception and reaction.

extraterrestrial noise Radio interference from outside the Earth's atmosphere; cosmic or solar noise.

extreme close-up (XCU or ECU) A shot concentrating on parts of an actor's face, i.e., eyes, mouth, nose; or other parts of the body—hands, the feet, an arm moving, the shoulders shrugging, etc. Also, detailed shots of various objects: a phone-button on a telephone, hands of a clock, date on a calendar, etc.

extreme high-angle shot See EXTREME HIGH SHOT.

extreme high shot (XHS or EHS) One that looks down on the scene of action from far above. Examples are: a shot made from a giant crane, the roof of an adjacent building, a high geographical prominence contiguous to the scene, an airplane, an aerial balloon, a helicopter, etc. Also called extreme high-angle shot.

extreme long shot (ELS) One made at an appreciable distance from the scene. For example, the cavalry appearing on the horizon.

extreme low shot Made from a point below the action, below eye level. For example, a POV shot of a gladiator knocked to the ground, as he looks up at his antagonist towering above him.

extremely high frequency (EHF) Frequency band of 30 to 3000 GHz.

extremely low frequency (ELF) A frequency below 300 hertz.

eyelight Low-intensity light that is as close to performer's face as possible without coming into frame; it highlights the eyes of the on-camera performer.

eye piece lens VIEWFINDER lens on which cameraman places his eye to look at a shot.

F

f The letter that stands for the evaluative distance between the camera lens opening and the focal length. This measurement is vital for focusing, lighting and for film development notes for the lab.

face The section of a meter with the scale markings.

faceplate Front part—the viewing surface—of a TV picture tube.

facial expressions Important indication of on-camera personage, whether performer, or real-life interviewee in a news, game-show or audience-partici-

pation situation. Facial expressions in acting for TV are usually lower-key than in film, since more close-ups are made in TV fare than in theatrical films. Then, too, the TV medium itself is more intimate than the motion picture screen; this simplifies all nuances of expression.

facial makeup A large percentage of all makeup (excluding sci-fi prosthetics) is facial. Hand make-up is optional while body makeup is rare. Thus, facial makeup is the core makeup discipline that makeup persons must master first. As facial makeup progressed from heavy, stage makeup to today's lightweight panchromatics, the makeup was adjusting to better lighting, new awareness of the critical nature of the closeup, clearer images, color, etc.

facts Raw data forming the core of news coverage, documentary reportage, investigative reports and informational films in general. As to when an estimate, extrapolation or interpretation becomes a "fact" is still hotly contested in general philosophy, semiotics and applied media. A rule-of-thumb definition: "Facts" in media are objective, raw data, prior to interpretation by commentators, newscasters or their writers. Facts can be of places, persons, things, time or number. Of course, the "persons" may be individually spotted, as in a story of a murder suspect or celebrity, or handled in the aggregate, "the Red Army," "American high-school dropouts." One fact by itself usually has little relevance. It is only its relationship to other facts or circumstances that gives it depth and/or perspective. For example, the numerical standing of American education is of little importance, unless we compare it to the educational levels of other nations. Facts that are minimally descriptive and that deal mostly with numbers are sometimes referred to as "facts and figures." Facts relying on figures are only as accurate as the reputability of the data gatherers and the methods of their extrapolation. The old saw in the facts-and-figures trade is, "Figures can't lie, but liars can figure." Data is best synthesized from multiple reliable sources. One source, even one that is highly reliable and fully reputable, is not enough. Also, the more specific and detailed a fact is, the clearer it becomes in its social and semantic contexts.

factual film   An educational, documentary or informational film.

factual programming   News documentaries and on-the-spot reportage as scheduled by TV networks, cable systems and independent stations. Often, open forums or panel discussions are included under this heading; however, these programs are more often programs of opinion than fact.

fade   An OPTICAL EFFECT occupying a single shot, in which the shot gradually disappears into blackness or another color (FADE-OUT) or appears out of darkness (FADE-IN). The most prevailing convention for the fade is to use it to denote the passing of time, as opposed to the DISSOLVE, which ordinarily indicates related or continuing action or longer periods of time than symbolized by a CUT. In music, fading out is a lowering of sound to inaudibility; fading in is coming from inaudibility to the required audible level. Regarding color, it is degeneration and attenuation of chromatic intensity of any color from its original state.

fade-in   To start from black or a color wash and let the picture fade into a full, delineated image.

fade margin   Maximum number of weakened decibels that can be included in a frequency propagation path. After reaching a certain critical point, the signal-to-noise ratio becomes functionally audible in the signal area.

fade-out   When the vanishing image goes into black or into a color wash.

fader   Part of a console or similar device that increases or decreases sound levels, or lightens or darkens picture image. Multi-unit switch-over control, taking out one live microphone or camera and bringing in another. In film projection, a sound rheostat for volume control that is used for fades in or out.

fade scale   Marking or read-outs interlinked mechanically or electronically to a fader unit. The speed and smoothness of a fade can be evaluated by the fade scale indicator.

fading   Reduction of field strength of a transmission in an electronic fade-out; an increase of same in a fade-in.
Also the verb form of FADE.

failsafe   A projection-room device mounted on, or separate from, the projector; it senses film that has split or is damaged and automatically stops the projector.

fair comment   In critical evaluation of aesthetics of the arts and adjuncts to the arts (museum curators, gallery owners, film exhibitors, TV programming executives, etc.) it's a no-holds-barred situation, as long as it is clear that the comments—written or spoken—are the opinions of the critic(s). Also, the facts must not be grossly distorted or abrogated. Analogous commentary in the sociopolitical fields is referred to as "editorial," since it is interpretative. See EDITORIAL.

Fair Marketing Amendment   Name used in the home video field to refer to the 1983 Consumer Video Sales/Rental Amendment. This amendment has explicit language against the practice of misrepresenting or mislabeling merchandise, and an implied message not to sell pirated tapes.

fairness doctrine   Federal Communications Commission ruling that requires stations to make readily accessible, and provide availability for TV time to air, opposing viewpoints on matters of public importance. This includes responding to a station's on-camera editorial comments, which state the station's viewpoint on such issues.

fall-in Descriptive of the moment that a synchronous motor reaches synch speed.

fall-off The diminution in the amount of light on an object caused by increasing its distance from the direct light source. In film projection, the lessening of luminance from the center of the screen to the edges.

false move An error in blocking or gesture by a performer.

false reverse A reverse from an angle not congruent with the left-right orientation of the characters or objects, so that it appears to be an improper orientation. See CROSSING THE LINE.

fan An avid follower of media performers. There are groups of fans for composers of motion picture music, film directors, even writers. Also called a buff.

fanfare A musical flourish—usually on brass instruments, sometimes accompanied by percussion—to open a drama or an important/regal scene within the work. Example of a fanfare used on TV would be Masterpiece Theatre's "Fanfare for Trumpet" by Jean Joseph Mouret. A fanfare, in a looser sense, is any PLAY-ON/PLAY-OFF, and can be orchestral, a solo instrument or a musical electronically-generated cue.

fantasy film A work of free-roving imagination in creation of bizarre and sometimes grotesque characters and in their pictorialization. Films can be animated or live, or a mixture of both, as in *Who Framed Roger Rabbit?* It is a broad category covering films as diverse as Disney classics like *Dumbo* and *Fantasia* to *E.T.* and *Star Trek.* The category includes fairy tales, abstract film such as Bach's Toccata and Fugue in *Fantasia,* science fiction, motion picture versions of comic strips, "Batman," "Superman," "Popeye," etc. In general, the fantasy film brings us into a totally imaginary world with outlandish characters. In the

better films of this genre, however, even the most incredible characters have empathetic universal character traits: compassion, fear, cowardice, courage.

farce Comedy based on situation and plot; written and played broadly. Farce in films, because of the close-ups and close shots, could be played a little less noisily and with the mugging done less obviously. TV, moving in even closer, could pick up further nuance of reactions, and interplay of back-and-forth looks between characters, through fast cutting or switching. However, TV farce is still played broadly, with stock gestures and reactions from stock characters. It has become almost as stereotypical as the old-fashioned melodrama was for its time.

far shot Synonym for LONG SHOT, now seldom used. See LONG SHOT.

fast A high ASA or ISO film speed that allows film to work at low levels of light because of its high degree of light sensitivity.

Also refers to camera lenses which have a speed value of about one. This allows filming in minimal light.

It can also refer to the manner of processing, when pushing a film. See PUSH.

fast cutting Rapid succession of shots, sometimes only a few frames. A MONTAGE is an example of fast cutting; or a chase scene, as it cuts swiftly back and forth from pursuer to pursued. See KINESTASIS.

fast forward Accelerated drive-motor setting to make tape roll ahead rapidly in the direction of PLAY. This speeds up the search-and-select process for starting a sequence or finding a specific segment. The opposite is either indicated rewind or fast rewind; reverse or fast reverse.

fast forward control The knob, hand or button on a tape recorder to put the tape in or take it out of a fast forward mode.

feature A full-length dramatic film made for theatrical release. Feature-length made-for-television films or videotapes are often referred to as TV films, movie-of-the-week, TV specials, etc. When used as a verb, it means to give billing to a performer just below that of the leading STARS. To give him or her prominence dramatically, or to concentrate on a particular performer in a scene; to favor, by lighting or placement.

A story that opens a TV news program, and is scheduled later in the program in its proper news subheading, SPORTS, weather, local events, etc.

FCC See FEDERAL COMMUNICATIONS COMMISSION.

feature length A film that runs at least 70 minutes; few features today run less than ninety minutes. Under the rules of the ACADEMY OF MOTION PICTURE ARTS AND SCIENCES, a "feature documentary" is 30 minutes or more in length.

feature player Principal performers in a film or TV show; supporting players to the stars. Today's feature-player CREDITS, particularly on television, may be included in a list headed by the words, "Also starring . . ."

Federal Communications Commission (FCC) U.S. governmental organization initially set up in 1934 for the purpose of overseeing the nation's radio broadcasting. Later it took over the same function for television. Among other things, it supervises the interpretation and policing of the FAIRNESS DOCTRINE.

Federal Trade Commission (FTC) The federal agency that among its other functions, oversees the regulation of TV advertising. The FTC monitors commercials for accuracy and for honest representations of products or messages.

feed To broadcast programming to sub-receptors or directly to households.

Also, it describes the process of taking in, sending through and guiding film into a camera, processor, recording machine, printer or projector. Used more often as a film term. The head end of a film that is put into the take-up mechanism first is called the feed end.

feedback Electronic circuit that returns a signal separate from the output, indicating the proper functioning or malfunctioning of that circuit. This special returning signal is part of a closed-circuit link that makes it into a "closed-loop" system.

feed end See FEED.

feeder line Household TV lines branching out from a main coaxial cable and into the individual receiver sets.

feed lines Lines delivered from OFF-CAMERA for the benefit of the on-camera actor. The lines are delivered to cue in the on-camera actor or to give that actor DIALOGUE to which he or she can react.

feed reel A metal or plastic reel from which film or tape is fed into a take-up device and sent on through a camera, projector, recorder, etc.

feed spool Spool on which original film can be loaded to be run through the camera and exposed.

feed sprocket A sprocket that unspools film from a supply reel or magazine.

feedthrough Unwanted electronic leakage and drifting of a signal from one track of a multitrack tape to another track where it does not belong. This can interfere with the desired signal of the host track or completely overpower that signal.

feet Measurement unit of film length used to describe 200', 400', 800', 1200', 2000' film reels. Also used as totals: "We shot 40,000 feet in 16mm for the project!" In Continental Europe, the "footage" count more often used is in the metric scale.

female plug Receiving electrical plug for a joining MALE plug. Female plugs have receptor sockets for male prongs.

ferric oxide The reddish coating of iron oxide that is standard for most magnetic recording tapes.

ferrite core Doughnut-shaped oxide core, i.e., iron oxide and others. Because it can be swiftly magnetized or demagnetized, it is used in magnetic memories to store information for later application or retrieval. The ferrite core is also used in many varieties of electronic circuits.

ferromagnetic When certain materials are caused to be polarized, a field change is created that results in an electromotive force. This force can result in an electrical current that is used to activate audio or videotape.

FET See FIELD EFFECTS TRANSISTOR.

FG See FOREGROUND.

fiberglass A basic plastic in fabricating lightweight scenic props, such as massive rocks, park benches, storefront facades; in brief, "heavy" items in a lightweight, easily portable form.

fiber optics Fabrication and application of bundles of parallel optical fibers extended to whatever length is required. Used to transmit pictures from one point to another with minimal loss of light and delineation. This is accomplished by total image–reflection.

fiction film A film that is adapted from a novel, short story or other literary work, or authored directly for the screen.

fictitious characters Even in cases where characters are created by an author for a specifically designated film, TV or live theater project, the rights regarding use of those characters in film sequels, a TV series or a work of fiction remain the author's. This is true regardless of the nature of the contractual agreement with the producers of the film or TV project that introduces such characters.

fidelity The degree of accuracy of reproduction in the output of a sound or picture system, or specific part of that system, as seen or heard in the final product.

field Physical portion of the scene that is framed for filming or videotaping. The framing of the picture. Also called action field.

field camera General location camera used by SECOND UNITS. Also the name for easily portable, lightweight cameras used in DOCUMENTARIES and for news coverage. For news today, these are nearly all TV cameras which have rapidly phased out 16mm motion picture cameras. See CAMERA, MOTION PICTURE TYPES.

field chart A transparent, acetate guide with concentric rectangles indicating areas covered by gradation of camera positions. It is mounted onto an animation table or plate by pegs that are premeasured to match peg holes on the acetate sheet. Also called field guide.

field effects transistor A semiconductor in an amplifying system.

field guide See FIELD CHART.

field magnet Powerful, permanent magnet that creates a forceful magnetic field microphone, speaker, phonograph pickup, etc.

field pickup See REMOTE.

field producer Producer in charge of crew or crews sent out to gather news in the locations of occurrence. Sometimes an active part of a newsgathering team, going with the crew to the scene of the event; or the field producer can work from the studio to designate and dispatch crews.

field reporting On-the-spot reportage by a news reporter for radio or TV. In radio, the reporter often audio-records the happenings and augmenting interviews to be transferred from his audio cassette to ¼" reel-to-reel tape and edited for broadcast. "Phone-in," on-the spot reports can come from any worldwide location where a phone is available. This system is used in TV when there is no time to set up an electronic satellite feed; for example, action footage, as well as a pictorial ID of the newscaster might be shown as the phone-in commentary is heard. This is raw, unedited reporting that can be edited later for rebroadcast purposes. TV on-camera reporting can be detailed more definitively by voice-over, later recorded by the reporter and played over matching visuals.

fifteen (15) IPS Recording audiotape speed for professional studio production, musical recording or postproduction pre-dubs and mixes. Much location sound is recorded at 7½ IPS and later transferred up to the 15 IPS rate.

figures of speech Active metaphors or similes, used widely in news and documentary reportage. In writing such texts, it is important to avoid such tired tropes as "trees standing like sentinels," "The city is a mixture of the old and new," "Our corporate staff is like a team," "foregone conclusion," "at this point in time," "tip of the iceberg," "ax to grind," "compare apples and oranges," "clear as crystal," etc.

fill Additional materials recorded to be run over the picture of an on-camera stand-up reporting introduction, segue or close, where the sound might be lost; summary backup material.

fill leader LEADER laid into an editing film roll to indicate where a shot or scene is to be placed. Or a temporary indication by a leader of the exact length of the scene to be replaced, repaired or reprinted. The leader can have this exactitude, or merely indicate that a scene of

a given length and/or time will be inserted. The same term applies to sound as well as picture.

fill light A light near the camera that is used to kill or minimize shadows resulting from the strong key light. Fill light can be either direct or bounced in from a reflector. Also it's a term that indicates the resultant illumination.

film A thin flexible ribbon of transparent material base that has perforations along one or both edges and bears a light-sensitive layer or other coating capable of producing photographic images.

Film can refer to the cinema, in general or in particular to a specific film.

As a verb it means to shoot a motion picture, in part or whole.

film aesthetics An academic, philosophical approach to film. In one sense, film aesthetics refers to the application of technical and creative ability to turn out a completed motion picture. Also, the unconscious or deliberate sociopolitical subtext of the film's structure. In another sense, film aesthetics refers to the use of cinematic elements to generate a particular audience response, or even to motivate audiences.

film archive A reference library of film, to be used for research, STOCK FOOTAGE in DOCUMENTARY or documentary-type films, or for establishing shots, in some cases, of foreign locales for feature films. Archival material use is billed on the basis of the linear film footage and running time of the shot or scene.

film base Flexible, transparent foundation material upon which emulsion and magnetic coating is placed.

film capacity Maximum amount of film that a camera, projector or other piece of film equipment can handle.

film chain Electromechanical hookup projecting film into a television system for broadcast or for the transfer of a closed screening.

film chamber A light-secure holder for exposed or unexposed film. A film magazine itself might be regarded as being made up of two film chambers, the feed-out and take-up chambers.

film checker Person who inspects film for any faults or damage.

film commissions A group of business and cultural leaders who solicit organizations to advertise the advantages of filming in their state or city in order to attract production dollars to their immediate area. All states in the United States have such commissions, or an analogous group that handles the liaison functions between filmmaker and local officialdom. Also, the larger cities (like New York City, Los Angeles, Chicago) have their own film commissions. These groups expedite filming permits, help assemble local crews, and, in some cases, even procure on-camera talent.

film clips A small portion of film from a long motion picture or an out-take. A film clip may be used to set foreign locale, show a massed battle or other historical re-creations. Archival clips are often used in films or videotapes on motion picture history. Also used for assembling the proper shots to be used to create previews of coming attractions and commercials for the film.

film continuity The straight-through or fractured-time flow of action that is "filmically" correct: matching direction of movements of camera itself or on-camera subjects; matching of picture and sound from one shot to another; appropriate rhythm of FADES, DISSOLVES and CUTS; matching screenplay text; and the clear visual and auditory delineation of the film's intended theme.

film exchanges The regional centers from which films are distributed to individual movie theaters.

film festival A special commercial, social and cultural event featuring the showing of numerous and varied types of films (depending on the occasion). It usually takes place in one city over a period of several days and is climaxed by the presentation of commendations, awards and prizes.

film-footage table A conversion table equating 35mm and 16mm footage to time, and vice versa. See TIME-FOOT-AGE COMPUTER in Appendix.

film gate A camera or projector device consisting of combined PRESSURE PLATES and APERTURE PLATES that help guide film through, and maintain the proper focus distance between, the film and LENS.

film gauge Standard width of basic film stock: 16mm, 35mm, 65/70mm.

film grammar Term devised and demonstrated graphically in worldwide lectures by the man who brought the montage to international cinema, Slavko Vorkapich. A logical/psychological approach to the graphic "statement" of film, with guidelines for avoiding the most egregious errors. For example, the "subject noun" was whatever was being featured in front of the camera; the "verb" was the action, from a subtle internationally recognized facial expression of the on-camera actor to two armies charging one another. Any physical movement had a real denotative direction and an implied connotative direction; that is, a man could be moving to the left, in order to go out the door. If the actor has been established and oriented in the room and we have seen, denotatively, a number of times, that the door is toward frame-left, then even if the door is not in the shot, we know that, when an actor in that room moves in that direction, the connotation is "the actor is moving toward the door." If two armies are established first by different personages, uniforms, equipage and banners, these differences may not be immediately discernible or identifiable in extreme long shots, or even with closer camera placements. But direction-of-movement, especially mass movement, is perceived instantly. If one army is established as moving screen/frame left-to-right and the other screen/frame right-to-left in the close shots in the beginning when they all first ride out to meet the adversary and as they pick up speed in the attack, then, when the long and extreme-long shots are used, the screen direction tells us which army is which—that is, until they clash and mingle, at which time closer shots are used. At the end of battle sequences, extreme-high shots are often used to show scenes of either desolation or of the continuing melee, as in Bondarchuck's magnificent extreme high-shot in his film of Tolstoy's *War and Peace*. What is shown is the largest scene of extras ever filmed, over a hundred thousand of them milling about in a swirl of opposing uniforms and battle gear, all identifying screen direction being totally obscured in a vortex of warfare.

filmic space The aesthetic/technical power of the film medium that enables it to combine shoots of widely disparate origins into a single scenic framework of space.

filmic time/space Most film sequences deal with compressed time, with the exception of SLOW MOTION segments or something as detailed and expanded as the celebrated Odessa steps sequence in Eisenstein's *Potemkin*. Transposition of time through compression, extension, FLASHBACKS and FLASH-FORWARDS are all examples of filmic time. Movement in space can be accomplished with a direct CUT—from Moscow to Paris—almost instantaneously. Then too, outer space can be simulated and "travel" through it speeded up or slowed down as required. The connection between otherwise disparate shots can sometimes be delineated by either a linking musical leitmotif or a SOUND EFFECT.

film island An area in a TV studio housing motion picture and slide projec-

tors that are ready for broadcast use. This term is now being used less frequently as technologies continue to interlink and overlap.

film leader See LEADER.

film library The organization of the film material in possession of a film studio, production company or specialized film research group, correlated by means of a cross-index system.

film literacy Comprehension of basic structural and narrative techniques of filmmaking. Film literacy deals with time and space in condensation or expansion and the related information necessary in a context of ongoing continuity. See FILM GRAMMAR.

film loader On a strictly union crew, the person in charge of loading, unloading and marking rolls to be developed. Sometimes he is also responsible for fixing camera jams caused by uneven flow of the film through the camera, although this is usually handled by the assistant cameraman. In a small nonunion crew this is handled by the assistant cameraman or the OPERATOR.

film loop Lengths of FILM or SOUND TRACK spliced end-to-end to form a continuous loop for PLAYBACK, used in LOOPING and DIALOGUE REPLACEMENT sessions.

A piece of master or original film run through a printer for multiple copies.

A continuous loop of completed film or videotape in finished composite form (music, EFFECTS, DIALOGUE, NARRATION) on a special cartridge or system for projection.

Slack film—in projectors or cameras—between SPROCKETS, rollers and the DRIVE and track-up mechanisms.

film magazine Detachable, light-proof container for holding film as it is fed through the camera and exposed. The exposed footage is taken up in a separate compartment. One compartment is for virgin stock, the other for exposed film.

filmmaker A person who individually supervises all of the production steps necessary to create and produce a complete film.

film noir Films whose story lines are built on "dark" characters—thieves, con men, prostitutes, paid killers, night people—who are portrayed, often violently, in situations of high action and confrontation. Also called cinema noir. See EXISTENTIALIST FILMS.

film pickup System for telecasting shots or scenes from motion picture film, that primarily consists of a film projector linked to a TV camera.

film reader Computer-scanning device that "reads" photographic film—transparent, translucent or opaque—and sends the readout information on to the receiver system of the computer.

film recorder An electronic machine or system that performs the reverse function of the FILM READER. The film recorder takes information from the computer and records it on photographic film.

film review A critical report by a reporter or columnist of a newspaper, magazine, periodical, radio or TV. Shorter film review forms are often printed in TV and film magazines or media sections of periodicals, as well as encapsulated on TV and radio programs about film and TV, such as "Entertainment Tonight." These compressed minireviews name the leading players of the cast, give an indication of story and, sometimes, add a truncated critical evaluation.

film running speed The speed of the film as it runs through a camera or projector, measured by frames-per-second (fps) or feet-per-minute, or in the metric system for footage in meters. See TIME-FOOTAGE COMPUTER in Appendix.

film scanning The process of "reading" film and transferring it into interfacing electrical signals which can then be sent out for reception by a telecasting system.

film speed Working term meaning the EXPOSURE INDEX of a film stock.

film splicer See SPLICER.

film stock The basic raw material that goes through the film camera to give the final pictoral image. The RAW STOCK, unexposed and unprocessed, will hold the latent image from the film production period of the filmmaking process.

film storage Optimal holding of the original exposed film footage, and sometimes work print, that is stored in specially designed dust-free and temperature-controlled vaults (45°–50°F), either separate from, or part of, a film-developing lab. Unfortunately, most film is not stored under ideal conditions, instead, it is relegated to closets, shelf space or indifferent areas in homes or offices, and at whatever temperature is prevalent. Improper storage causes color and texture degeneration of both the prints and the original.

filmstrip A frame-by-frame piece of film, usually 35mm, which projects single frames of a film or still pictures onto a screen; special projectors can project these images directly or in a rear-screen system.

film structure The architectonics of the conceptual skeleton that holds a film together; PLOT, CHARACTERIZATION, recurring motif, time progression, etc.

filter Optical unit for the camera's LENS system, that absorbs specific elements of the incoming light spectra. See FILTERS.
  A sound filter is designed to thin out preselected narrow-frequency bands.

filter factor A numerical factor by which the length of a photographic exposure must be increased to compensate for the absorption of an optical filter through which the exposure is to be made.

filter holder Any slot, frame or attachment that holds the required filters in front of the camera LENS during filming or videotaping.

filter mic   A microphone with low-re-verberancy frequencies minimized, giving a flat, slight nasal sound to voices and a "thinner" sound to music or effects. It is used to simulate old recordings of speaking or singing voices or to simulate voices heard over a phone receiver, intercom or public loudspeaker.

filters (optical)   1. *Black and White.* The basic uses of filters when shooting in black and white are for making the sky appear darker or for cutting through overcast or hazy weather. Since almost no black and white is shot today, this principle can still be translated to color in concepts of contrast. Most footage seen today that has been newly released in black-and-white has been actually shot in color and printed in black-and-white. 2. *Color.* Good color can be brought to its optimum potential by correct filtering—using the proper lighting to its full effectiveness. 3. *Daylight.* The #85 filter is the "daylight" workhorse. It can be used in conjunction with high-speed film by using an ND .30 (NEUTRAL DENSITY) filter. 4. *Diffusion.* Diffusion filters are for taking the hard-edged lines off camera subjects: people, places or products. These softening filters should be used judiciously so that they can innercut effectively with the nondiffused footage. 5. *Fog.* A special type of diffusion filter available in a widely varying scale, with a slightly different effect for each grade of filter. Tests are recommended for these filters before production commences. 6. *Neutral Density.* A gray filter that reduces the amount of light striking the lens. It has an omnicolor function, i.e., it maintains a natural color balance and affects all colors equally. Therefore, ND filters do not change the color balance, but cut off light, to increase the lens aperture, and lower the CONTRAST. 7. *Polarizing.* Filter used with sunlight, reflections on glass or water, or glare from white sands or snow. It controls or eliminates unwanted reflections. The desired effects of the polarization filtering must be determined by viewing through the finder while rotating the filter. 8. *Pro-*

tection. Prime quality clear glass, mounted in a filter holder, to keep dust, snow, rain and other unwanted "invaders" away from the lens.

final cut   The last fine-tuning of all elements immediately following acceptance of the FINE CUT. In this ultimate cut, sound is fully mixed and the picture conformed and made ready for the lab to run off the FIRST-ANSWER PRINT.

finalize   The term originated in advertising circles then spread to the media, and means to put something into definitive, final form or to make a decision, as in "Let's finalize that deal," or "Get them to sign off on the script concept, so we can finalize it!" It is now fading into obscurity, where it will soon be finalized.

financial reporting   What was once a restricted media area of short segments of a few new shows has now become a regular feature or occasional feature on many TV programs. Today there are financial news stations and a loosely affiliated financial news network that only report on financial news. Presenting financial news on TV requires extensive research, background checks and constant updating as in radio or print, but it can be augmented in the area of retention by strong visual, on-the-spot reports, plus news footage, charts and graphics.

finder   See VIEWFINDER.

fine cut   The version of the WORKPRINT that follows the ROUGH-CUT stage in the film's progress. At each successive stage, the cutting is refined and the unnecessary footage eliminated.

fine-grain   Term used to designate film emulsions in which the GRAIN size is smaller or finer than the older type of emulsion commonly employed prior to the mid-1930s. Fine-grain film is usually slower (requiring a longer exposure to light) than other films.

fine-grain dupe   DUPE NEGATIVE from a MASTER POSITIVE, taken from the original black-and-white negative, or a dupe negative made directly from the contact reversal-printing process, derived from the original black-and-white negative.

fine-grain master positive Next processing step (in black-and-white film) that comes after the original NEGATIVE is made. This both protects the ORIGINAL and allows for printing of OPTICAL EFFECTS.

fine slow Digitalized slow-motion, smoother and more realistic than prior videotape or film forms. Also called natural slow.

fine-tuning control A device that controls received signals or directs input by varying the local oscillating frequencies. This corrects drift and allows for more precise adjustment in a station's carrier frequency.

finger A long, thin GOBO for blocking out a small area of incoming light. It keeps glaring shapes of light away from the person or object being filmed or video-taped.

fire doors Metal doors, either solid or metal-surrounded, that close off areas of high-risk flammability (like a projection booth) from other "safe" areas. It is also the name for the metal closure-plates in front of the viewing ports, which can be closed mechanically by hand, as well electro-mechanically in some cases, but always operable manually. They can be closed to keep fire or hazardous fumes in one area from moving into another. The term also refers to the safety shutters over the small projection room windows (the "ports").

fire shutter Internal projector mechanism directly behind the film aperture of the projector-gate unit. It is set to open only at the point that the projector gets up to operating speed. Conversely, it closes down once the projector speed falls below a safe operating speed. Originally called a fire shutter because it was

designed to close when the projector's interior overheated or the film caught fire.

first Describing the head of a particular crew, as in first grip, first prop man, first assistant director.

first answer print First conformed and sound-mixed COMPOSITE film print from the lab. It is this print that is checked by the lab timer and producer for color-timings, sound-printing and synchronization to see if they are correct and totally satisfactory. Also present at screenings of the answer print are the DIRECTOR, ART DIRECTOR, DIRECTOR OF PHOTOGRAPHY, sound recordist, and possibly some of the leading actors. Any combination of the above is usually at the discretion of the PRODUCER.

first cameraman See CAMERAMAN.

first-generation dupe A reversal print made from a reversal stock original film (now mostly archival use) or master tape, often for the purpose of producing further prints or tapes, which are known as second-generation dupes.

first paragraph A key attention-grabber, even more important in TV reportage than in print, it is the opening of shows and segments that gets the audience's attention initially and attempts to recapture it after the commercial breaks.

first run The premiere cycle of the exhibition of a film.

first sale doctrine The existing law that there is no accounting for residuals or royalties on a home video cassette once a sale is made at the counter.

fishbowl Originally the sponsor's booth (or VIP booth) in a radio station, with a large soundproof glass panel behind which the special guests sat, watched and listened to the radio broadcast. The name has been adopted by TV.

fisheye lens Extreme WIDE-ANGLE LENS. The curvature of the exterior convex lens element gives this lens its name. It provides a forced perspective of extreme closeness in the center part of the image, with barreling curvature at the outer edges. It is used to attain deliberate distortion and to create comedic caricature or parody, as well as images that are grotesque, menacing or surrealistic.

fishpole A lightweight rod or pole on which a microphone is mounted. It is hand-held by one of the sound crew during shooting.

five (5) Eastman Kodak motion picture film designatory initial number for its 35mm stock, such as #5247 (daylight-balanced, with 85 filter), #5296 (fast, low-weight, tungsten-balanced), and #5381 (print stock for lab use).

fix To set and stabilize the developed film image by processing it in its chemical bath—the fixative or fixer. Sodium thiosulfate.

fixed focus A lens designated and crafted to hold the maximum depth of field when set in a position calibrated to the exact film plane. It holds people and objects in focus, despite their distance from the camera.

fixed-focus viewfinder One in which an image can always be brought into sharp focus regardless of the distance between the filmed action and camera.

fixed position The prescheduled and firm time slot allocation for a TV commercial. The rates for fixed position commercials are of the highest on the play-rate card.

fixed-transmitter Transmitter operated from an established locale.

flack A press agent as well as the materials placed by a press agent: notices, stories, special articles, photos with captions, etc. Flack also includes all news releases in all media referring to clients of the press agent.

flag A miniature rectangular GOBO (a light-shielding device), made of plywood, plastic or cloth mounted on or in a metal holder, and usually attached to a stand. See SCRIM.

flagship The major station of a commercial TV or radio network, syndicated group or cable TV network.

flaking Chipped-off emulsion particles that lodge and build up in the projector's image area as film is moving through the gate. Usually caused by improper edgewax lubrication. Flaking can injure or destroy film.

flange A metal or plastic disc against which film mounted on a rewinder is wound onto a CORE. One side of a film reel.

flare Area of highlight intensity in the NEGATIVE film image, caused by internal reflections in the camera lens or by starry reflections from bright objects or a section of a TV tube with a hot, washed out, glaring light that obscures the image being televised, caused by the oversaturation of light. See also HOT SPOT.

flash A generally unwanted and unwelcome bright spot generated through the overexposure of the film, or by something that throws a distracting and disturbing reflection into the frame area during filming.

flash-ahead See FLASH-FORWARD.

flashback A scene or full sequence looking backward in time from the "present action" on screen. Some films, such as John Huston's classic *The Man Who Would Be King*, have only a few opening and closing scenes, and the entire balance of the film is told in flashback. Current examples would be the *Back to the Future* series of films.

Flashback action refers to those things that happened before the film's "present" time reference.

flash cutting Rapid cutting of shots of short duration.

flash-forward Anticipatory shot or scene indicating future action. Also called flash-ahead. The flash-forward can be a foreshadowing image, an action scene, or partial segment of a full scene to be shown later in the film.

flash frame A shot of one or few frames inserted within another shot or scene to give a rapid, percussive image, or an insert blank frame that creates a momentary, subliminal flash. Used often as dynamic film punctuation from scene to scene, especially effective in creating a highly energized, kinetic sequence. See SUBLIMINAL CUT.

flashing Deliberately exposing film to a weak light prior to, or immediately after, making a shot or shooting a roll of film to reduce contrast.

flash tube Tube that emits high-intensity flashes of light in short bursts. In professional and even amateur photography, it has almost completely replaced flashbulbs and cubes. Also called electronic flash tube.

flat Tonal neutrality, with minimal contrast.
In a lens, "flat" refers to the lens or its image as not anamorphic; not squeezed.

flatbed An editing machine with a horizontal bed instead of an upright working area. It consists of matching pairs of circular plates, one for feed-out, one for take-up. There are at least two sets of these plates, one pair for picture, one for sound. Other plates are for additional SOUND TRACKs, and in some models, for additional picture.

flat glass Fine, distortion-free glass used in front of the camera for keeping water, dust or any foreign particles from striking the lens.

flat light Lighting the on-camera action or objects so that an overall even quality of light is obtained and CONTRAST is avoided.

flat, scenic Plastic, wooden or light metal framework covered with stretched cloth, painted as a background (realistic, stylized or neutral) for performers in live theater, film or TV.

flicker Fluttering produced in the picture on TV. This is caused when the field frequency falls short of being able to synchronize images. It is similar to FLUTTER in motion pictures. In film projection, a rate of fewer FRAMES PER SECOND than PERSISTENCE OF VISION can fuse into a continuous mental image. It also refers to the intensity of light thrown upon the screen as it fluctuates, caused by the passage of the SHUTTER across the light beam.

flip Optical effect in which the frame of the film seems to turn on either a horizontal or vertical axis and "flip" to another image on the "other side."

flip card See CUE CARD.

flip lens Optical printer device for making flip-overs.

flipover wipe A WIPE in which the image appears to turn over, revealing another image on the "back," the axis of rotation being either vertical or horizontal.

flip stand Rack or easel for holding FLIP CARDs for videotaping.

float The time period allowed to home video store owners by the manufacturer or distributor of a film, before calling for the payment of the product.

floating lens Originally it referred specifically to a lens suspended in a liquid balance, but now it refers to any lens that could give a floating effect. Shots made with Steadicam systems are sometimes described as floating shots.

floating release Film available to all theater venues; not precontracted or booked into exclusive circuit release.

flock paper Nonreflecting paper; opaque sheets for use in special effects' mattes.

floodlight Any lighting instrument that emits wide beams of light.

floor Set or studio performance area.

floor crew Crew members who operate from the floor as opposed to the control room. The floor crew includes camera operators, boom operator, technical director, audio engineer, light board operator, production assistants.

floor manager Directs FLOOR CREW from the floor, while in constant touch with the control room by using headphones to maintain communications.

floor plan Drawing of a set to scale, with the point-of-view of looking down from directly above.

flub For an actor or actress, a flub occurs when he or she blows a line or makes an error of movement. For the crew, it is any technical error during filming or videotaping.

fluency A smooth, unfaltering and unstammering direct delivery of speech.

fluff A blunder or mispronunciation in speaking. See also BLOW.

fluid head A camera mount filled with a viscous fluid device that allows for smooth camera movements.

fluorescent light Light from a fluorescent coating contained inside gas-filled tube. Radiation is generated when the gas is heated.

flutter Unwanted erratic movement in a camera, causing pictorial jumps or unevenly exposed FRAMES. In a projection system, it is a loss of screen image sharpness because of improper positioning of the film image itself in the projection aperture. Focusing or refocusing will not solve the problem. In sound recording systems, flutter means slurring, speedups or DROP-OUTS. This can happen through improper feed or take-up in a unit, and can take place during playback, recording or duplicating/reproducing.

flux The amount of light within a given area, measured in lumens.

fly To suspend scenery above a set by ropes or cables, so that it can be lowered or raised as needed.

flying erase head Instead of being mounted off the VCR head drum, the flying erase head is on the drum with the record and play heads. This positioning gives clean audio breaks, noise free, between separately recorded scenes.

FM See FREQUENCY MODULATION.

f number/f-stop A number with decimal gradations denoting the geometrical progression of LENS speeds. It is a numerical scale based on the division of the FOCAL LENGTH of a lens by the diameter of the lens opening. Critical accuracy is important in f-stop readings in order to obtain proper f-stop lighting. The "full stop" range is: 1.0, 1.4, 2.0, 4.0, 5.6, 8, 11, 16, 22, 32, 45, 64. A full-stop change from one f-stop number to the next immediate higher full-stop number will cut the exposure by half; going to the number immediately lower will double the exposure. In lighting with fine gradations, many exposures requested by the DIRECTOR OF PHOTOGRAPHY are between f-stops.

focal length Distance between the film plane and the "center" of the lens, determined optically, and focused on infinity.

focal point Spot behind a lens where a point in the action field comes into focus. This occurs when the lens is focused at infinity. See BACK FOCUS.

focus   The point at which parallel rays meet after passing through a convergent lens. In more general usage, that position at which an object must be situated so the image produced by the lens may be sharp and well defined; hence, an object is spoken of as "in focus" or "out of focus."

The focus is the point of concentration of reportage, news, commentary or documentary.

focus band   Part of a lens that is rotated to the proper imprinted markings or added tape markings, in order to focus the lens. The distance-scale gradations are marked in feet and/or meters.

focus control   A TV-receiver device that fine-focuses the electron beam that forms the picture.

focusing   The art of moving a camera lens toward or away from an emulsion plane to bring the image of this plane into FOCUS.

focusing microscope   An optical device in some cameras of superior design for magnifying the image formed on a GROUND GLASS by the camera lens.

focusing viewfinder   A VIEWFINDER with a shallow depth of field. As the distance from the camera to the object or action varies, the viewfinder must be refocused.

focus plane   Spot closer than infinity where the lens forms an image.

focus pull   Refocusing while shooting to let one area drop out of focus and another come into focus. When the image to be brought into prominence becomes sharply focused, the original subject drops into a soft or out-of-focus image. See RACK FOCUS.

focus puller   Assistant cameraman whose duties include following the proper focus points during shooting. A term used in U.S. early on but which fell into disuse,

however, still used in credits in British films. Also referred to simply as focus.

It is also the handle attachment on the lens barrel for following focus.

fog   Exposed areas of film that were unintentionally lightstruck due to improper loading into the camera or from structural light leaks within the camera itself. Also, in the developing process, the light hitting the unexposed film and "developing" it.

fog density   Basic density of a film stock when it has been developed without being exposed to light.

fog filter   A special camera filter that approximates the look of fog. Since it has a diffuse, softening effect it is often used in shooting close-up shots of actors and commercial products.

fogging   To fog the film. Also, the deliberate exposure in the lab to achieve this effect or the accidental occurrence of the same from improper handling.

fogmaker   A machine that puts out controlled amounts of "cooled" smoke so that it will settle low to the ground, creating the illusion of fog, mist or smoke.

foil cues   Cue marks on the projected film to make a smooth and accurate changeover much easier. In certain systems of projection—automated and semiautomated—the cue can consist of a piece of metal foil attached to the film print, at the edge, or a metal circle in center-frame of one cue frame.

foley   To add postproduction SOUND EFFECTS to a picture by first watching, timing and annotating the inherent scene cues, then SIMULATING effects to match the ACTION. For example, a scene may be shot without the sound of a man walking in the snow. The foleying sound effects man will watch the scene—usually on a LOOP—and rehearse it, then go for a TAKE. The takes that match the action the closest are the ones selected, noted and turned over to the film editor. Foleying can be used to add sound when the scene is filmed without sound, when the sound needs to be augmented, or where existing sound has to be replaced.

foleying session Time and place reserved for recording the foleyed effects. See FOLEYING STAGE.

foleying stage Soundstage set up to handle "the FOLEY." These stages are especially equipped with free-standing doors that open, close and lock, a starch box for walking on snow, a gravel box for walking on gravel, coconut halves or plumbers plungers for horses' hooves, a tank for water sounds, buzzers, bells, etc.

follow focus A continuous change in camera focusing, necessitated by relative movement between the camera and its subject, greater than can be accommodated within the DEPTH OF FIELD of the basic shot. Follow focus often requires correction of viewfinder parallax and framing. Following focus is usually the function of the first assistant cameraman.

following blacks/whites Edge effects. In following blacks the edge following a white object makes the image appear as if it has a trailing black border. Following whites creates an opposite appearance, when the edge that follows a dark gray or black object has a trailing white border.

follow shots A shot in which a moving camera follows the action of a scene. Another name for DOLLY shots.

follow spotlight Spotlights used where there are great light-throw distances. They work from an electric arc that radiates light between two carbon elements. Used in sporting events, MUSICAL COMEDIES, rock concerts, ballet and other programs requiring long-throw spotting illumination.

follow up To investigate subsequent actions of an earlier story; or to follow a story lead to its source and then report on it.

foot End of a film roll. Also called TAIL.

footage Film length based on a scale of feet, although "footage" is also used in metric measurements and in frame-count indications. The amount of film run through the camera in filming the production.

footage counter Electromechanical readout unit that shows the number of feet run through a camera on a specific camera load, it sometimes indicates balance of film left to shoot. In postproduction the footage counter is either on the editing machine or sound reader. In screening dailies and subsequent cuts, including the final cut for mixing, the readouts are on a large readout box, illuminated, and placed at the lower center edge of the screen.

footage number See EDGE NUMBER.

footage-time calculator A linear or wheel-shaped chart giving correlations and direct ratios between running time and FOOTAGE. The calculator is calibrated for various film gauges at various speeds. See Appendix.

footcandle A basic lighting measurement of the illumination striking a spherical surface from a distance of one foot from the light source.

footcandle meter A light meter calibrated to take its readings in FOOTCANDLES.

foot irons Specially designed metallic hardware used to secure scenery to the floor. Designed originally for live theater.

footlambert An illumination measurement of one LUMEN per square foot of a light-source.

force To slow down the film developing process, giving more development time to correct for underexposure. See PUSH.

foreground The action area nearest to the camera. The antonym is BACK-GROUND. The term middle ground is the intermediate area between the two and is used most often in describing shots that cover a great area, especially in depth of scene.

foreground treatment Compositional approach to a pictorial arrangement of people or things, or, if outside in nature, a selected placement of the camera that will emphasize the FORE-GROUND element. The goal of all this is to create an arrangement that is eye-catching and will further the dramaturgy of the work, through information, mood-setting, plot-jointure or counterpoint. Such pictorial treatments draw heavily from the graphic arts, particularly representational drawing and painting.

foreign release Domestically made film distributed or exhibited out-of-country.

foreign version Film made in one country with a redubbed soundtrack or subtitles added for a particular FOREIGN RELEASE.

foreign works Foreign films, tapes, books or other creative works; they are protected by copyright laws drafted and empowered by the Universal Copyright Convention.

forelengthening The induced appearance of depth in filming with wide-angle lenses. The effect is lessened the nearer that image is to center screen or is viewed from that vantage point.

foreshortening Compression of depth obtained by using telephoto lenses. Again, the effect is minimized when viewed from the center of the perspective circle.

format FILM-STOCK dimensions giving the measurement of the FRAME area, perforation size and total area.

Format also defines the working space or framed action area of a show to be filmed.

It can also be the standard structure of a daily or weekly TV show; program outline.

In programming, format describes a station's orientation and accustomed policy (open or tacit) as to selection and time placement of programs.

Finally, in projection, format is the size and ratio of screen images in theatrical projection. This means the width of the projected film, the projection grid required, the sound system (optical, magnetic, stereo, surroundsound), and whether the image is a standard flat one or anamorphic.

Fortnightly decision It establishes by legal adjudication that closed-circuit TV can be broadcast in that circuit without being restricted by copyright, usually without payment. Named for Fortnightly Corporation in suit brought against it by United Artists.

forty-five (45) record Seven-inch disc with a 1½-inch hole in the center, sometimes filled in, with only a standard-spindle opening. Recorded and played at 45rpm. The popular format for SINGLES.

four-track recording Setup that allows four separate tracks to be recorded on ¼" tape. The four tracks can be recorded monophonically, i.e., each track handled separately, or stereophonically, with two sets of two tracks.

four-walled set Surrounding set, with no opening on one side while filming. The set totally encloses the action area.

four-walling The exhibition of a film where the distributor pays the theatre owner a preset, negotiated price to cover operational out-of-pocket expenses that the theater must incur, as well as covering for prorated cost of loss of theater income for the four-walling period. These fees are paid for the use of the theater, wall-to-wall. Whoever pays this fee for "the use of the hall" also promotes and advertises. Of course, all monies that exceed the wall-to-wall costs go directly to the distributor. Concession sales are negotiable.

fps   See FRAMES PER SECOND.

frame   The individual picture on film, tape or videodisc. Used as a verb, it means to select and compose a shot.

frame counter   A readout unit on a film counter that, in conjuction with feet or meters, indicates the FRAMES. In 16mm, which has forty frames per foot, a footage number might be 246 feet, 14 frames; after 40 frames the counter moves to the next consecutive foot.

frame line   Separating line between FRAMES.

frames per second (fps)   FRAMES moving through a camera or projector measured by total number of frames moving past the aperture gate in one second. It is also a measure used in film printers.

framing   Setting up and positioning of a camera prior to the shot, for rough-framing, and the refinement of that shot immediately before filming it.

To projectionists, framing means to align the film in the projector gate to obtain the proper centering of the image on the screen.

framing control   Knobs, levers or dials for centering and correctly adjusting the height and width of the TV picture.

franchise   Ownership of a company name and a supply of its videotapes, information sheets and additional merchandise. "Franchisee" is the store-owner; "franchisor" is the supplier. Franchisees will often share the costs of general advertising to promote the chain, thereby reducing advertising on a cost-per-store basis.

fraud   In media, the most prevalent form of fraud is the misrepresentation of a film's potential by a producer to a backer. It is a dangerous policy for a producer to claim (for example) that a given film will earn "at least a certain number of dollars once it's completed." Problems occur because the film may not get distribution or the proper distribution, the ad campaign may be deficient, or audiences may not want to see the picture. Since backers can be liable for any indebtedness, like crew salaries or lab bills, fraud is a very serious and costly crime. Each party (and their attorneys) should carefully read the contract before signing it to understand what responsibilities they are accountable for so that they will not be fooled by misrepresentations.

Freedom of Information Act   A federal act mandating that the government must make available to a person or group documents, records and proceedings that are deemed to be in the public interest. The Freedom of Information Act went into effect in 1967, and was amended in 1974 to give the public greater access to public information.

free-lance announcer   An announcer who is not on the staff of a station or network but gets his assignments on a job-to-job basis.

free-lance assignment   An assignment given to an independent producer, writer, or director, who will often provide these assignment services or handle them on a subcontractual basis, billing the funding source through the company or corporation.

free-lance producer   A producer who does not work for a studio or as a staff producer for a large production company. Also referred to as an INDEPENDENT PRODUCER.

free-lancer   One who works on a job-to-job, contract-to-contract basis. The contracts are usually in effect only during the active production phases of a project. Sometimes, however, the free-lancer will be contracted to remain in an advisory capacity until the finished product is placed into the proper distribution channels.

free-reel   Reel on a recorder that feeds out magnetic tape.

freeze   For an actor to forget lines; to draw a blank. See also BLOW.

freeze frame   A single FRAME that is reprinted for as many frames as the running time of the freeze-frame shot requires. It visually stops and holds the action for accent and emphasis for whatever length of time is desired. Also called stop frame.

frequency   Number of repetitions of a periodic phenomenon within a given amount of time. Electrical frequency time units are given as "hertz," with an accompanying number. Radio frequencies are measured in kilohertz up to 30,000, after which they are regarded as megahertz. Frequency is indicated by the lower case letter "f."

frequency allocation   The assignment of available broadcasting frequencies to a station under the auspices of the Federal Communications Commission.

frequency authorization   The paperwork and documentation from the FCC that legalizes a frequency allocation.

frequency discount   Bulk discount on commercials given to advertisers who contract for a full cycle of 13 weeks, or at a specified minimum number of plays per week.

frequency measuring equipment   Devices for testing an electrical signal's frequency or pulse-repetition rate.

frequency modulation (FM)   Modulation of frequency of the carrier wave in phase with music, sound, speech, or whatever signal is required. The method of broadcasting that utilizes these signals. The opposite is amplified modulation.

frequency modulation broadcast band   The allocated band for frequency-modulation (FM) broadcasting. The range of the FM band is from 88 to 108 megahertz. This band is divided into 100 channels, each channel being 200 kilohertz wide. These channels are for use in FM broadcasting only.

frequency range   Frequencies of a transmission system which allow that system to transmit power without seriously weakening it. A particular portion of a frequency band.

frequency response   Equipment's effectiveness in transmitting or reproducing a part or all of the frequencies of a sound signal.

frequency spectrum   The full range of electromagnetic radiation frequencies.

Fresnel lens   The concentric rings on a circular glass lens that narrow and concentrate the rays of emitted light and spread the light evenly. The word is derived from the inventor, the French physicist Augustin Jean Fresnel, 1788–1827. It was originally developed to be used with lighthouse beacons.

Frezzolini camera   Popular in Europe and North America, this lightweight camera can be loaded and unloaded rapidly. It is usually used for documentary style news-gathering but also to make feature films.

friction head   A PAN-AND-TILT HEAD set on a TRIPOD or other camera support. It employs a smoothly sliding friction device to secure smoothness of the camera movement.

fringe area   Area immediately outside of the workable service area reached by a television transmitter. In this area, signals are attenuated and unpredictable. In order to assure acceptable reception, a high-gain directional antenna, coupled with a sensitive receiver, must be used.

fringe time   TV broadcasting time segment from 5:00–7:00 P.M. and 11:00 P.M.–1:00 A.M. In between these fringe times is PRIME TIME (7:00–11:00 P.M.).

fringing   Degeneration of image at the edge of an insert MATTE.

from the top   A directorial term, meaning to start again from the beginning of the scene or sequence during rehearsal or filming.

front end   Preproduction costs, as well as accumulated costs prior to active, salaried preproduction: optioning the property, paying for re-writes, working out a fully detailed budget, etc.
   In electronics, the front end is the part of a receiver/tuner that selects a particular radio (AM/FM) or TV band.

front lighting   Lighting coming from the immediate area of the camera position and aimed at the action area.

front porch   Portion of a composite television signal that precedes the horizontal-synch pulse at the tail end. Operational at the blanking or black level.

front projection   One method of projecting background images onto a special screen behind the actors. Compensating lighting is added to eliminate the projected image that falls on the actors.

f-stop   See F NUMBER.

FTC   See FEDERAL TRADE COMMISSION.

full aperture   Widest opening of the iris of a LENS.

full coat   Film that is magnetically coated on one side of the stock with iron oxide.

full immersion contact printer   Film lab printer that has original and print stocks totally immersed in liquid chemicals and a cleaning "bath." This stops scratches from being printed.

full net   TV hookup and feed to all network affiliates.

full network station   One that carries in PRIME TIME the network-available programming. These network-affiliated stations carry more than two-thirds of network prime time programming.

full shot   One that includes the full height of the actors, head-to-toe. It can also mean a shot that includes everything in the scene at its widest angle.

full-text database   News and documentary filmmakers use this as an invaluable resource for in-depth evaluation. The full-text database carries complete contents of designated newspapers, periodicals, reference publications, documents and reports.

full track   All the audio-sensitive surface of a tape utilized for recording. Used both as an adjective and a noun.

function switch   Switch that selects whether an audio system plays or records in a monophonic or stereophonic mode. It has a range of switching options: paralleling the speakers, switching one off while leaving the other(s) on, reversing channels, etc.

fundamental tone   Lowest-pitched component of a complex tone.

fungus spots   Nature's blotches on film, from fungoid growth, which remind us that film emulsions contain chemicals with a vegetative base.

funnel   See HIGH HAT.

furniture pad   Insulated cloth pad used by moving van companies. Originally obtained from moving companies, the pads are now specially manufactured for filming needs: a ground pad on which camera and cameraman can be situated for a low angle shot; an improvised sound baffle; a buffer for carrying delicate equipment; etc.

fusible link Safety device of two sections joined together by an alloy with a low melting point. Used in projection booths. When intense heat melts the alloy, it will activate a sprinkler, sound an alarm or drop a safety shutter.

fusion When live action, special effects or animation are blended together, as in *Who Framed Roger Rabbit?*

fuzz The deliberate, distorted tone on an electric guitar. Also known as fuzz tone.

fuzz tone See FUZZ.

fuzzy An adjective describing an image with an unclear FOCUS or one that is not sharply delineated. Said of soft-focus or out-of-focus images.

G

gaffer The chief electrician who is responsible for the LIGHTING of SCENES. Lighting is supervised by the DIRECTOR OF PHOTOGRAPHY.

gaffer's tape All-purpose cloth or plastic adhesive tape, utilized for improvised and standard functions during production. It is often used to attach GOBOing devices to CENTURY STAND arms or even to the body of the camera itself, or to stabilize PROPS, give actors their marks or hold IDIOT BOARDs in place.

gag A verbal or visual "joke," or a comedic situation.

gain A power increase in a signal as it is being sent from transmitter to receiver.

gain control A control device (knob, dial, switch, lever) that can increase or decrease the total gain of an amplifier; in other words, the volume control.

gain, screen The measurement of reflected light striking a screen. No screen reflects back all of its incident light, but if it did, its ideal rating number would be 1.0, representing 100%. A professional viewing screen has a gain of about 0.85.

game show TV show in which 'the game' is played by preselected contestants or contestants chosen from the audience. Rewards for playing the game are prizes or money.

gang control Interlocked control of various parts of electromechanical or purely electronic gear with one knob or control device. This simultaneous adjustment allows greater quality unification of an operation.

gang synchronizer This term is usually preceded by a number that tells how many sprocket wheels the unit has. A three-gang synchronizer can handle three strips of film; a four-gang, four; and so on. On most gang synchronizers there are SOUND HEADS, so that sound and picture synchronism can be determined. Used for matching SOUND TRACKs to a WORKPRINT, and for matching a print to the ORIGINAL. See also SPLICER.

gap A section in a magnetic circuit without ferromagnetic coating; space between the poles of a recording head; or a time or space interval on tape that designates the end of a word, phrase or record.

garbage in/garbage out Phrase for computer-operations that have defective input, resulting in defective output. In media it refers to a signal that is not clean going in; coming out it will either be the same or degenerated. Also known by its acronym, GIGO.

garbage matte   Basic, original-image matte that is discarded as optical work progresses and cumulative steps are completed.

gate   The APERTURE unit of cameras and projectors.

Gate also refers to the gross amount of money taken in at the BOX OFFICE, or in any other pay-for-view medium for a given attraction or viewing period. Originally a circus term, later applied to "legitimate theater," and then to mass media. Derived from ticket gate.

A gate is also the device that holds the film to the aperture in projection position.

gate tension   Restraint of film movement by adjustable, floating guide tracks (or "rails") to maintain an even and constant projector feed.

gate pass   A signed pass left at the studio gate for a particular person that permits access to the studio. See also DRIVE-ON PASS.

gating   Blanking pulse in a TV cathode tube or grid that applies voltage during sweep-time, to sensitize it for the production of an image.

gator clamp lamp   A small lamp with a permanent GATOR-GRIP attached, allowing for immediate placement for lighting its particular area.

gator grip   A strong, multipurpose metal clamp, often insulated on the clamp handles with plastic as protection against electrical shock. Jump-start battery cables use gator grips. These grips are used in film production and videotaping to attach foliage branches to a scenic support, lightweight lamps to set furnishings or CENTURY STANDS, to give some common examples of production utilization. They are also used to clamp sound-baffling sheets or white reflector cards into place.

gauge   Millimeter measurement of professional film widths: 16mm, 35mm, 65/70mm.

gauze   A translucent fiberglass or similar material that looks like gauze, that is used to soften a light source and diffuse the light striking the photographed person or object. It is often used in making beauty shots of women.

gear head   A type of PAN-AND-TILT HEAD set on a tripod or crane, which incorporates two gear drives with various single or compound movements, operated by crank handles.

gel   Short for gelatin. A transparent or translucent plastic color piece that fits into color mounts and color frames. See DIFFUSERS.

gelatin   See GEL.

gelatin filter   Serves same rudimentary purpose as a glass filter, but can be cut from small gelatin sheets to fit the gel frame either within a camera or on the gel mount external to it. As their glass counterparts, these gelatin filters modify light received by the camera through light filtration.

general direction   Direction in a script, usually starting on the far left margin of the page, that describes general actions and reactions: ENTRANCES, EXITS, movements, group reactions, and so forth. To be differentiated from personal direction, which pinpoints feelings within the body of the player's dramatic speeches.

general movement   Mechanical unit inside a projector that provides intermittent film movement; at normal projection speed, this is a rotation rate of 24 times per second. The movement is a combination of rotation cam-and-pin that engages a four-slotted star wheel, this formation resembling a Maltese or "Geneva" cross. The star-wheel shaft with its intermittent sprocket rotates 90°, or one frame, at the 24-times-per-second rate.

general release   The full distribution (nationally and world-wide) of a motion picture.

genre   A particular classification of film by its style or subject matter: cops-and-robbers, western, sci-fi, zany comedy, horror or any other standard category.

geosynchronous satellite   A communications SATELLITE that moves in an orbit analogous to the Earth's rotation.

gesture   On-camera movement of the upper body that is intensified by closeups: a hand gesture, a head nod, a shoulder shrug. Body language may be international, but some gestures that have a good or neutral connotation in one culture may have a rude or obscene meaning in another. Repetitive broad gestures, if used in today's films, become distracting and are even more so in television, which is a much more intimate medium. Gestures should be used sparingly and to make points or set something apart for greater emphasis, but they should be, or seem to be, natural. On TV, where shots tend to be tighter than on film, it is not easy for the camera to follow swift, sudden gestures.

ghosting   Image disturbances or distortions, double-imaging and other extraneous errors. Sometimes, double-imaging and strobing are used deliberately to create the effect of ghosts, spirits or "ghostliness." Unplanned ghosting can be caused electronically by improper TV camera alignment or bad transmission or reception. In film it can result from improper image transfer or technical or operational problems in projection.

GIGO   See GARBAGE IN/GARBAGE OUT.

gimbal mount   Dual ring mount that allows free-tilting in any direction. A camera head is attached, and the movement is smoothed by the addition of a pendulum weight attached below the mount itself. There are updated hydraulic flotation variations of this mount. See DYNALENS.

glass filter   Any filter, neutral or colored, layered in between two distortion-free pieces of glass. The filtration layer is gelatin or customized plastic. All elements of the glass filter are calibrated to the size required for attachment to cameras. A glass filter can also be a fully tinted piece of solid glass.

glass shot   A shot or scene filmed with and through a plate of glass on which is painted or printed titles or art work, against which action is filmed in superimposition.

glint   Artificial glimmer of incoming light created by a star filter or special diffusion filter.

gliss   See GLISSANDO.

glissando   This musical dipping and rising effect was used in dramatic radio in a similar manner to a STING. The direction gliss sting was not uncommon. It is used in comedy shows as well and is usually followed by a crash, splash, slide whistle or explosion. The term was never widely used in film or TV. Derived from musical terminology, it is analogous to a musical "dipthong" or sliding. Electronically, it is a tone that moves unobtrusively and easily from one pitch to another. Often referred to as gliss.

glitch   An electronic disturbance on tape or a film misfunction: a SPROCKET jump, a color mismatch, a sound dropout, etc.

global village   A "village" that is our entire earth, joined electronically by the "cool fires" of television. A concept of Buckminster Fuller, "cool fires" was introduced by Marshall McLuhan.

glossmeter   Photoelectric measuring instrument for evaluating the gloss (the area reflectivity) of a surface.

glossy   A high-reflective finish on a still photo. Used for most professional photos in actors' portfolios. The opposite of a MATTE FINISH.

gloves   White, lintless cotton gloves are worn by film editors and lab technicians when handling film raw stock and fresh prints in the lab. They keep body oils off the film stock.

gobo Specifically, a black wooden screen placed so that it screens one or more studio LAMPS, thus preventing light from entering the camera lens. Usually mounted on adjustable stands, it can be in many shapes and sizes. Generally, a gobo is any shielding device that keeps light from directly striking the camera lens.

gofer From "go for this, go for that." Any assistant who runs production or staff errands.

Goldwynism Tropes and malapropisms attributed to Samuel Goldwyn, many of them apocryphal like, "I'll say it in two words: 'im,' 'possible' " and, "A verbal contract isn't worth the paper it's printed on."

golden time The time period following overtime (after 14 to 18 hours, depending on union and contract). Golden time pays appreciably more than overtime at anywhere from double to quadruple the rate of regular time. The term is also applied to working calls on holidays and Sundays.

gothic film Derived from the literary term gothic novel, a novel that has elements of grotesque fantasy and a pervading mood of decadence and danger. Examples of such novels are the early gothic work *The Castle of Otranto,* by Walpole, *Frankenstein* by Mary Shelley, or *Wuthering Heights* by Emily Brontë. The last two were made into gothic films. Other such movies with sinister and foreboding locales, would be the *Fu Manchu* films, the *Dracula* variations, and werewolf and assorted monster movies. Gothic films typically occur during an indefinite historical period, and use fogbound moors or castles for locales.

gradient microphone A mike where output increases and decreases directly with the sound pressure.

graduated filter A filter for motion picture or still cameras with monochromatic color in one segment that gradually tapers off into a "normal, clear" area. An example of use would be a filter that is dark at the top and normal at the bottom to darken the sky in an exterior shot, while leaving the rest of the shot in "normal" light. See FILTERS.

grain The grouping together of fine particles of film coating too small to be seen under normal viewing conditions. This clustering can cause particles to become visually distinguishable, thereby resulting in what is described as GRAININESS.

graininess The grain cluster on film that is seen as separate particles when projected, to cause degeneration of the image. Sometimes a filmed scene or an entire film will deliberately use graininess to create a feeling of another time or of unreality, or conversely, of gritty, documentary-like "truth."

grammar Active use of applied grammar in writing for media has generated some good habits (terseness, directness and energized verbs) and some bad. A local TV station carried an ad of a furniture store that specialized in kitchen and bar furniture, or as they put it with participles dangling, "We're number one in eating and drinking furniture." However, good grammar isn't always the first priority for ad agencies that try to sell products in a limited space or time. They don't necessarily need good grammar to convey their message, and sometimes they use bad grammar deliberately, so that audiences will remember the commercial.

G-rated Motion Picture Association of America's rating for a film that has been judged by the MPAA to be "suitable for general viewing," regardless of age.

graticule Transparent or translucent screen with calibrated lines of measurement put in front of a cathode-ray tube and used for technical evaluations. It helps determine accuracy in all areas of the received TV image.

gravel box   A wooden box filled with pebbles and crushed rock used for SOUND EFFECTS in FOLEYING, or in radio, used to create the sound of a person or persons walking on gravel. A standard piece of apparatus on a foleying stage.

gray scale   Gradation of "steps" in gray fields, from white to black, represented on a check chart—a gray card—used by labs and cameramen.
It is also a scale of TV brightness values and used in black-to-color digital conversions as a reference guide and calibration tool.

greenery   Foliage used to dress a set consisting of augmented existing growth or totally artificial plant life.

green-gain control   Adjustment device used to balance the color in a TV set in conjunction with analogous blue and red elements of a three-gun color TV receiver. The green-gain control increases or decreases the green intensity of a signal.

green gun   Electron gun emitting a beam that strikes the green phosphor dots in the electron tube of a TV set, activating them. See BLUE GUN, RED GUN.

green-man   Person in charge of dressing the SET or location site with greenery. The actual plants can be live and growing or trimmed and remounted branches, flowers or tree trunks.

green print   A film print just out of the lab, so freshly processed that the emulsion may not have properly hardened. In this condition care should be taken when projecting it. The projectionist should apply edgewax lubrication to avoid damaging the edges through tension-ripping or perforation.

grid   A piece of studio RIGGING, consisting of interlocking metal pipes—aluminum or steel—that are suspended hor-izontally from the ceiling area immediately above the soundstage filming area.

grip   The person on the studio SET who is in charge of minor adjustments and repairs the PROPS, CAMERA TRACKS and the like.

groove   Phonograph record track, cut into the record by the stylus and copied in duplicating the record. Groove also refers to the track in which the needle travels when a record is played back.

ground   A connection between an electric current and the earth.

ground glass   A piece of glass with a finely ground surface on which an image can be formed. It is used in the VIEWFIND-ERS of cameras.

ground modulation   When various channels, separate within a specific frequency range, are modulated to transfer them over to another frequency range.

ground wave   A radio wave that moves along the surface of the earth rather than through the upper atmosphere.

ground wire   An electrical conductor connected to the earth or a substitute ground.

guarantee   An advance payment on projected potential earnings from the acquiring distributor, paid to the producer or owner, to attain rights to a property or production. The advance is proportional to the estimated sales or rentals of the property in all markets, domestic and international, in theatrical, cable network, commercial network or home videocassette venue.

guard band   A band left clear as a buffer between two channels to avoid interband interference.

guard circle   On disc records, the inner concentric groove that keeps the pickup from jumping to the center of the record and rebounding, to protect the grooves and the pickup head.

guided propagation   Radiation radio wave that is bent sharply by refraction in the lower atmospheric layers. This generates something similar to a wave-guide in the atmosphere, a duct to direct some of that radiation energy over greater distances than normal.

guide-line   An editor's marking that moves onto, across and off the screen, to serve as a standby and direct cue to the actor who is LOOPING the lines. Often the direct cue occurs immediately after the line clears the FRAME.

guide rails   Vertical rails above and below the projection aperture that, steadies and reduces lateral movement of the film while it travels through the projector gate.

guide roller   A flanged roller that directs and restricts movement as the film passes through a camera, printer or projector.

guilds   Another name for "union." Some of the entertainment industry unions are Screen Actor's Guild (SAG), Screen Extra's Guild (SEG), American Guild of Variety Artists (AGVA), American Federation of Television and Radio Artists (AFTRA), Director's Guild of America (DGA), Writer's Guild of America (WGA), and others. See UNION.

guillotine splicer   Editing apparatus that properly aligns the two film strips to be butt-spliced. It not only trims but often perforates the splicer tapes.

gyro head   A camera-mount device that is stabilized by an internal mechanism that drives a rapidly spinning flywheel. This smooths out the erratic movements of the camera, especially in shots made on or from a moving vehicle, or in HAND-HELD shots.

H

hair stylist   Person whose job it is to dress the hair of the on-camera performer and maintain its appearance during the filming.

halation   A diffused halo-like glow on a performer or object that is caused by overspill of reflected light.

half-apple   See APPLE BOX.

half-inch   Standard-width tape for home VCRs; VHS is the most common format in the United States.

half-track recorder   One whose recording head covers just half the recording tape's width, so that the reel may then be turned over to record on the other, unused half.

halogen lamp   A light that reuses part of its own burned-off tungsten to give it longer life and a more even color temperature.

ham   Amateur radio station operator. Licensed hams are not allowed to be paid for any of their services or to broadcast advertisements. Their stations are run as a hobby. It also refers to their portable two-way radio communications gear.

hand camera   Lightweight motion picture or television camera, ideal for HAND-HELD shots, which gives it its other working name, hand-held camera.

H and D curve   See CURVE (H AND D).

handgrip   A special handle-mount for cameras, used for making HAND-HELD shots. Also called handhold.

hand-held   A shot made without benefit of TRIPOD, DOLLY or CRANE, where the camera is held directly by the cameraman/operator, and the movement of the operator's body determines the camera's movement. See STEADICAM and CAMERA.

handhold See HANDGRIP.

handlebar   mount Dual-handled camera mount, allowing the camera operator to use both hands for tilting or panning.

hand model A person who is hired for photographing his or her hands only. There are also lips, legs, feet and eyes models.

hand props Easily portable and lightweight PROPS, carried by the performer or handled within the scene. Some examples are a box of candy, handgun, telephone, bouquet of flowers, knapsack, or alarm clock.

hand receiver A hand-held earphone, pressed to the ear to receive auditory transmissions.

hand signals Floor director's cue to on-camera TV performers, newscasters, host, etc. "On the air," "You're on," is analogous to the called cue of "Action!" in films. It is simply a direct hand cue ending by pointing directly at the on-camera person who is to speak or sing. "Switching cameras" is a broad wave of the forearm while pointing to the camera which is now hot and ready to receive input from the on-camera talent. "Speed up": a finger twirled rapidly in a circle. "Slow down": a slow motion drawing apart of both hands as if lazily pulling taffy. "Cut": a brisk, basic throat-slitting gesture with one extended finger moving across the throat. Minutes left in a program's on-the-air time or before a commercial break are usually counted down from two or three minutes; three fingers held up meaning, "Three minutes left," two for two minutes, one for one minute. For 30 seconds, the forearms can be crossed or the index fingers of both hands may be used. Counting down prior to

"You're-on-the-air" direct-pointing cue, is given usually, from five seconds; the five fingers of the cue hand are counted off by reducing the number of visible fingers to two and then standing by to throw the "On-the-air" cue at zero.

hardener The HYPO, or other chemical mixes, that harden and hold the film emulsion during development.

hard light A concentrated, narrow beam of light, making hard edges and sharply defined shadows.

hard news Coverage of an important or newsworthy event as it is in progress, rather than as seen in a later news report or integrated into a documentary presentation.

hard sell Commercial announcement with an aggressive, pushy delivery, that drives home the name of the product and its attributes.

hard ticket Ticket printed on regular ticket stock, and paid for by the holder. A paid admission, not a COMP, two-for-one or press pass.

hash Unwanted interference signals from various sources, including the immediate environment itself.

hazard pay Additional fees over and above the daily rate for any work involving risk. A cameraman receives such pay any time filming is from a plane or helicopter. Fees for STUNTPERSONS are hazard-fee rates, predicated upon the degree of risk involved in any particular stunt. The director is now held responsible for determination of risk.

haze filter A lens filter that removes ultraviolet light thus minimizing or eliminating haziness. Also called haze-cutting filter.

HBO See HOME BOX OFFICE.

HDTV See HIGH DEFINITION TELE-VISION.

head The sensitized optical or magnetic tape reader for playing or recording sound. It is also the front end of a roll of film or tape (audio or video).

head, camera The revolving/tilting mount on which a camera is fixed, and which in turn is fixed to a tripod, HIGH HAT, DOLLY, VELOCITATOR or BOOM. The head also refers to the combination of the mount and camera.

head demagnetizer Electromagnetic unit for clearing magnetism build up in a recording head.

head end Start of a reel where film is threaded for projection.

head gaffer First electrician in a film production. Works directly with the camera crew.

head leader Leaders that are at the very beginning of a film. In work-print assembly, junk leader; later stages, opaque leader or Academy leader.

headline writing News writing that uses catchy, compressed phrases to convey the essential, basic information of the story. Audience-arresting, simple, direct wordings are best while technical terms, wordiness, overblown imagery and cliches are usually avoided.

head-on shot Action moving directly toward the camera, often implying a collision course.

head-out A reel of film so wound that the first FRAME is on the outside, ready to project. Also called head-up. The opposite term is tail-out.

headphones Minireceivers fitted to the ear, singly or in a pair, and mounted on a flexible headpiece. Used by the recording engineers or persons recording onstage for playback to evaluate the level and quality of the sound.

headroom The margin between the top of an actor's head in the frame and the top line of the frame itself. The frame's upper edge is larger for film cutoff than it is for TV-CUTOFF.

heads Sound recording or PLAYBACK units, custom-sensitized for such requirements. Used on sound recorders, MOVIOLAS, playback equipment, etc.

headset Sound-receiving unit for one or both areas, similar to headphones but with attached minimicrophone.

head sheet A still picture, usually an $8'' \times 10''$ GLOSSY, with various head shots of an actor on one print. Also called composite.

head shot A tight CLOSE-UP in which the on-camera performer's head fills the FRAME.

head stack Two or more heads arranged in a single, mounted unit; for multitrack recording or playback.

head-up See HEAD-OUT.

heat filter Optical filter used in a projector to absorb or reflect arc-lamp heat and prevent this unseen energy radiation from reaching the projector's film plane. Unreflected heat can injure or destroy film.

heavy The antagonist, who is usually the villain. The opposing force to the PROTAGONIST.

held cel An animation cel to be photographed for many frames without a change in position; it is tied into other cels which are in movement. This makes it unnecessary to redraw many elements in particular scenes. For example, a cel of a forest background against which foreground characters are running would be the "held cel."

helicopter mount See COPTER MOUNT.

helios noise Wave transmission interference caused by a SATELLITE passing between the earth-based tracking station and the sun.

hero, heroine The leading character, the PROTAGONIST, who opposes the ANTAGONIST, the HEAVY.

hero product The sponsor's item used in a commercial and treated as the STAR. Sometimes there's an antagonist—brand "X," or "others."

hero shot The video or film take that is the best; the winning take; the chosen one.

hiatus A break in production, particularly on a TV series, during which decisions are made about the next shooting. In general, any production or programming break.

hickeymajigger Spring-loading locking device that holds a takeup reel onto the spindle on the reel arm.

hi-con See HIGH CONTRAST.

hi-fi See HIGH FIDELITY.

high band Frequency range of 174-216 MHz, TV channels 7-13.

high contrast Stark differentiation from blacks to whites in a motion picture, TV image or in still photography. High contrast film obtains this effect by minimizing the emulsion grain in the print when matting. Known in its abbreviated form as hi-con.

high concept A program or film that can state its premise succinctly and strongly. The sort of one-line definition that can serve as an instant story line for the program description in *TV Guide*. It should be a sentence that not only says what a show is about, but raises a question that can only be answered by watching the show itself.

high definition television (HDTV) Television system developed and now in use in Japan, with 1100 lines of density.

In comparison, the American NTSC system color telecasts have 525 to 550 lines. It is highly superior to the NTSC system, and is easily convertible to film without excessive loss of clarity or overall color quality.

high fidelity Sound reproduction made as close as possible to the original by using a frequency response that is stable and uniform.

high frequency Frequency band ranging from 3–30 MHz (megahertz), i.e., 100–10 meters.

high hat A very small solid TRIPOD of fixed height that can be attached to the floor or to a moveable, flat board for LOW-ANGLE shots.
 Also, a metallic snoot, usually painted black, that fits over a light and cuts down the spill, thereby more sharply delineating the light-pool area. Also called a funnel.

high intensity arc Lighting instrument utilizing a transformer and carbon arc to create a powerful, bright light.

high key Infusing the action area with illumination to stress and accent the lighter tones.

high-key lighting Lighting preset to produce strongly accented and fully lit images.

high-level "Loud" sector of given sound range.

highlight To pinpoint an object or person with maximum illumination so that it stands out in a scene.
 The highlight is also the measure of the greatest amount of light the photographed person or object can take without having its image obscured or distorted by glare and bounce-back.

highlights Within a lighted scene of action, the brightest areas of illumination that have a high level of reflectivity.

high-pass filter   Electronic filter used on an audio system to attenuate any frequencies below a preset frequency, but allowing all other frequencies to pass in an unattenuated form. Used in re-recording to clean up background of spillover noise or unwanted sound.

high-pass speed-duplication   High-speed duplicating equipment that repro-duces programs much faster than at real time. This cuts costs and allows for greater productivity.

high shot   A shot above eye level of the action, as opposed to LOW-ANGLE shot.

high-speed camera   A camera that moves the film rapidly through the GATE at speeds greatly exceeding the normal fps rate. This can be a few hundred frames to thousands of frames per sec-ond. The effect of this high-speed cine-matography is one of extreme SLOW MO-TION when shown at normal projection speed. Used for product analysis, re-search and SPECIAL EFFECTS.

high-speed film   FILM STOCK with added perforations, to use in high-speed cinematography. It is film with a high ISO (formerly ASA) rating, very sensitive to light. Used in situations where a minimal amount of light is available.

hiss   Prolonged sibilant noise in audio frequency range. Such noise on playback of audio tapes is generally from distortion of high-frequency signals.

hit   A successful film, TV or radio pro-gram with good box office or listener-rating numbers. Also, a command given to the cast or crew. For example, from the head GAFFER to the lighting crew: "Hit the lights!" Or from the director to an actor or camera crew to land on the proper, preset positional floor markings on the right word, cue or countdown: "Be sure to hit your marks."

hit radio   Format based on top forty singles in rock, country and western or any pop-music category. One classical station used to have a top forty format. The shows are usually loud, high-energy programs, where announcers use fast, frenetic deliveries.

HMI lamp   One that gives a warm light simulating daylight. Used to add "sunlight" when shooting on dark days or at night.

hold   To rephotograph one frame of action or one cel in animation. See HELD CEL.
    Videotape set aside for later use is said to be "put on hold"; also used in de-scribing a performer who is waiting for his call to the set, i.e., "He/she is on hold."

holdback   Number of days, weeks or months a title is held back from other media outlets once it has been put into the home videocassette market.

holdback sprocket   Sprocket which prevents forward-jumping action of the takeup reel from being sent along the film. This keeps the film flow at a regular speed, especially as it passes the sound-scanner.

holding control   A device or set of devices in a TV receiver that change the horizontal and vertical sweep circuits.

holdout matte   That element in a mo-tion picture matte that follows the con-tour of an image. The "image" is black, playing against a clear background. The real backgrond can be added on a sec-ond pass.

hold takes   See KEEP TAKES.

hold under   Fading music and keep-ing it at a low level behind the spoken words or, in some cases, sound effects.

Hollywood   Geographically, a part of Los Angeles between Beverly Hills and the Los Feliz district; commonly, wher-ever a studio is situated in the greater L.A. area. MGM was located in Culver

City; Warner and Columbia's main shooting stages and corporate offices are in Burbank; Twentieth Century Fox is in West Los Angeles; Disney's collection of buildings have sites in Burbank, Glendale and in northwestern regions of San Fernando Valley. It is a name that signifies the image of a place more than a specific locale.

Hollywood Blacklist A roster created in 1947 by the House Committee on Un-American Activities with the names of writers, actors and directors who had been identified with communist or pro-communist causes. Performers who had been named to the blacklist, while not necessarily being communist sympathizers, found themselves suddenly out of work and unable to get a job. The result of this series of investigations was to stifle the creative community, resulting in the general blandness and banality of the films of the late '40s and early '50s.

Hollywood Ten The key target of Hollywood's most well-publicized "witchhunt." These were writers and directors who were working regularly in the industry until they were sent to prison for one year for declining to testify to the House Committee on Un-American Activities (against their peers), on the charge of "contempt of Congress." After serving their prison terms they were blacklisted. These were the ten: Alvah Bessie, Herbert Biberman, Lester Cole, Edward Dmytryk, Ring Lardner, Jr., John Howard Lawson, Albert Maltz, Samuel Ornitz, Adrian Scott and Dalton Trumbo.

hologram A three-dimensional image made with laser photography.

holography Photograph designed to produce HOLOGRAMS.

Home Box Office (HBO) A TV cable syndicate; one of the early cable networks. It now shows top feature film attractions. HBO is a major competitor of network television.

home terminal Plug-in device to hook up a home TV receiver to a cable system.

It also means the electronic attachment with knobs or dials that allows two-way voice or video use. There is now an accelerated development in various modes of informational and educational interactive TV.

home video recorder One that receives and records TV programs as they are broadcast. Theoretically it is only for personal use in playback situations. However, recorders are often used to reproduce programs for personal use and for sale. The owners and distributors of the programming consider such replication an infringement of copyright laws. Though replication/duplication are regarded as illegal, cases are still pending on appeal on many levels of these rights.

homophonous words Words that sound the same but may or may not be spelled differently. "Bear" (the animal) and "bear" (to put up with) being examples of the former, "here" and "hear" being examples of the latter. Since these words are not often spelled out over radio or in front of the camera, it is important that the context in which the homophone is situated is as clear and unambiguous as possible. Words such "as a strike of minors" will certainly be accepted, normally, as "a strike of miners." But if minors really are on strike, it's best to make it obvious who is striking.

honeywagon Vehicles that are portable makeup rooms, toilets, wardrobe or dressing rooms, or any combination of these.

hook A bit of action or dialogue that immediately captures the attention of the audience at the beginning of a film or TV program. It originated in radio, was then used in film and finally in television.

hooked tooth A sprocket tooth so worn it resembles a hook. Such a deteriorated condition demands immediate replacement of the sprocket to avoid damaging the film perforations or ruining of the film itself.

horizontal lock Circuit that controls and keeps constant the horizontal synchronization in a TV receiver.

horizontal track camera A motion control that travels back and forth along a horizontal track. Analogous to a regular camera moving on dolly tracks. It is used for filming scale models or forced-perspective models, graphics, products for commercials, art work, matte paintings, etc.

horror films A film creating intense fear or dread and sometimes great repugnance. Designed to instill terror and dismay in the viewing audience. Stephen King's *Cujo* is an example, or *The Shining,* directed by Stanley Kubrick.

horse opera A western feature film or TV segment. Also called an oater.

horseshoe staging Staging in which the audience sits in front and on both sides of the performers, often utilizing a thrust stage. Used especially for audience-participation shows, musical groups and variety material. Developed from legitimate theater staging.

hosted interview One in a standard set in a TV studio, or on location. The former is more common on talk shows, the latter in documentary and reportage. The commercial network talk show hosts, like Johnny Carson, Phil Donahue and Oprah Winfrey, usually have a permanent set in a given numbered studio in a particular station, although they may vary the locales of emanation from time to time. Documentary hosting can be on- or off-camera—on-camera for intros, segues and closings; off-camera for voice-over. Often in documentary the interviewer is not seen, and the ''hosting'' responsibility is only to supply voice-over narration.

hot A scene that is too brightly lit. See HOT SPOT.

hot box A lighting junction box for cables.

hot frame One that is deliberately overexposed so that it can function as a visual cue for editing purposes.

hot-press A titling method using multicolored transfer papers, pressing heated type against them or against an animation CEL.

hot property Originally referred to a book, play or other literary or dramatic work that was a best seller or highly publicized, or a Broadway hit. It was regarded for purchase by the motion picture industry with that evaluation, which could serve both as caveat and inducement. It now also refers to a star at the height of his or her career, to a director with a fresh box office hit, or a writer with the same level of success. Used particularly by the agents who represent them.

hot splicer Editor's SPLICER that electrically heats the SPLICE, to accelerate the holding effect of the film cement.

hot spot Unwanted HIGHLIGHT caused by LIGHTING that is too strong for the given area.

household Demographic term meaning any home in the USA with one or more working TV sets. Used in this context originally by the Nielsen organization, and now a standard demographic word.

house reel Professional projection reel used in theaters. Made of heavy metal, it can handle 2000 feet, although there are now super-reels that can project footage in the 10,000-plus range. These are used in automated theaters and sometimes in regular theatrical houses. These reels are part of the permanent projection equipment.

howl An unwanted and irritating electromechanical yowling, in a speaker due to electrical or acoustical feedback.

howler An electronic device that produces audio frequency tones.

how-to film A motion picture that explains and demonstrates a skill, concept or mechanical process.

hue Gradation of color.

hum A constant sonic vibration in the low-frequency range caused by an error in the alignment of the circuits.

human interest Story that has personalized detail instead of generalities. A lead story might be the number of homeless in the United States, but a human interest story would follow a homeless person in documentary style, conduct a detailed on-camera news interview, or both. In a fictionalized or actual story, it is this human, emotional appeal of individual identification that creates the basis for human interest. How effective the human interest story is depends upon the story-teller as well as the story. In newscasts, the human interest story is often a specific feature, usually at the end of the program, featuring a story of an animal saving the life of a child, woman and child reunited after a long search for one another, the winner of the national chili cook-off, etc. It is often lighter than the mainstream, high-profile news; it is a story that must evoke audience empathy and have wide appeal to be memorable.

humor Humor is used in media in many ways. On news programs it can be inherent in the story itself: in an unintentional malapropism on the part of the interviewer or the interviewee, or humorous anecdote used to illustrate a point. Humor in dramatic works is derived from character and situation, especially certain characters in totally inappropriate situations. Conflict of aims can also produce a humorous impasse, or a tragic one. Humor must grow naturally in good dramatic works, as opposed to mere gag-insertion in run-of-the-mill TV SITCOMS. Real humor takes great skill and application to write and perform. Also, in performing, it seems to take a natural, inborn talent. Not every one—sometimes not even excellent actors—can do comedy. Humor at its best is based on character,

and the character of the person creates the situation. Wit is cerebral, and what it gains in sharpness it often loses in warmth. It is humor that can create both the warmth and the laughter. It is important to realize that humor varies from country to country, and what is hilariously funny in one country might be only mildly amusing, or even unintelligible, in another.

hype Publicity and advertising, including personal and TV talk show appearances, newspaper and magazine articles, talk-radio interviews, etc., to promote and publicize a film or TV program or series.

hyperfocal distance When a camera lens is set at infinity, the hyperfocal distance is the distance between the lens and the nearest object that can be held in sharp focus.

hyperspace A special effect wherein pinholes of light simulate a field of stars that seem to stretch to infinity before collapsing. Used extensively in outer-space sci-fi films.

hyphenate One who works in more than one PRODUCTION capacity, often with UNION cards for each function: writer-director; actor-producer; producer-director, and other combinations.

hypo (hyposulfite) A solution that chemically stops the development process of film by lifting out undeveloped particles and hardening the gelatinous coating.

I

IATSE See INTERNATIONAL ALLIANCE OF THEATRICAL STAGE EMPLOYEES.

IBEW See INTERNATIONAL BROTHERHOOD OF ELECTRICAL WORKERS.

icon A term used in academic discussion of communications in media, and communications generally. The American philosopher C. S. Peirce, brought the term into prominence in its contemporary sense. It refers to the resemblance between objects and copies. A copy, for example, is a still photograph of an object or a drawing of it. An ongoing debate in some circles is whether work in abstract fine art, or such movies and TV that use abstraction, are icons.

iconoscope   Tube for electronic TV cameras. This cathode-ray unit converts color and tone values into electrical impulses that correspond to the visually recorded images. The image-scanning is done as an electron beam sweeps back and forth, at a rapid rate, across a light-sensitive screen.

iconoscope camera   TV camera, the heart of which is the iconoscope pickup tube.

ideas (copyright of)   Ideas, unless particularized, cannot be copyrighted. For instance, a generalized story plot of "Aliens from outer space invade, and our hero repels them," would obviously not even be considered as "copyright" material. In literary, musical, dramatic or whatever artistic/creative form, the need is for specifics of plot, character and setting. Also, differentiating details that will set off the elaborated ideas from others of a similar nature. In brief, you cannot register for copyright an idea for a motion picture, TV program, play, story, or any other form or artistic work. To secure copyright the completed work is needed as close as possible to its production or publishable form. This includes such properties as: dramatic compositions for all media; scripts of lectures, panel discussions, variety programs, commercials and speeches written for radio or television.

identification   In commercials, the norm for product identification is repetition—oral and visual. Product identification used to be inserted constantly into motion pictures and in dramatic works on TV, until the payola scandals forced a pay-for-play situation, or an acknowledgement of services provided in exchange for product mention—or both. The scandals revealed high prices were paid for on-the-air plugs inserted by on-the-air performers and announcers. The payments were usually made under the table. Product identification on PBS programs used to be restricted to corporate names, shown and spoken. Then, due to cutbacks in federal funding, the logos of the companies were permitted. Now, programs are introduced and closed with company and corporate identification, and often with minicommercials. So far, they do not interrupt programming with such identifications.

idiot board   Cue cards with CUEs and DIALOGUE for reference of the actor/actress. In some cases this is replaced by systems in which an electronic roll's images—usually the words and cue marks—are transmitted to a reflective glass plate in front of the camera, beveled at an angle so as to be read by the performer and yet not visible to the camera lens. Also called flip cards. See also Q-TV and TELEPROMPTER.

idler   Rubber-tired wheel that can be locked in or left neutral. It transfers power from a phonograph motor to the turntable rim.

idler roller   A free-rolling, neutral, undriven roller in a projector or lab developer. It supports a film thread-up pattern, and is free to move in opposite directions when the film movement is in forward or reverse. Rollers carry the film web. Used extensively in loop cabinets in conjunction with multiprojector shows or exhibitions, as well as regular professional and home-use projectors.

illiteracy   Because of widespread illiteracy in the United States and the changing demographics of a population, where many people speak foreign languages, the speech in media should be as clear and direct as possible. Unnecessary polysyllabic words should be avoided when a shorter word will suffice. However, this does not mean reducing materials, particularly the raw materials or reportage, into simplistic inanity. In dealing with technical terms, the full terminology can be used as long as it is explained in an immediately understandable context. Sometimes charts and graphics will help clarify obscure points of information. Remember, "visual literacy" is high in the United States, even if the ability to read words is not.

illuminaire In a broad parlance, any light source—LAMP, candle, a REFLECTOR bouncing light into a scene, flashlight, SUNGUN, etc. Any unit that provides illumination. Illuminaire is an international filmmaking term, and it appears in many academic glossaries and guides. It is seldom used professionally.

illuminance Density of luminous flux, i.e., the flow of particles at a specified distance from the core of a source.

illuminant Whatever light is used in the projector to throw image onto the screen: high-intensity incandescent bulb, carbon arc, etc.

illustrate To give examples of what a story is about, particularly in reportage coverage like statistics, anecdotes, briefly delineated historical precendents, and graphics.

image The reproduced likeness of the object, person, or setting that is scanned or photographed. A latent image in photography is a virtually instantaneous one in TV or videotape. The framed picture first seen through viewfinder or camera, and then on the screen.

image distortion A great difference between the object scanned and the reproduction of that image on the TV screen. Distortion can be at the transmitting end, from a faulty camera or transmitting system, in the relay-and-feed from an intermediate transmitter or from the TV receiver itself.

imaginary line A line that passes through two or more performers which should not be crossed. The crossing of this line results in a filmic mismatch that will not edit correctly. This error is known as crossing the line, crossing the one-eighty (180), or false reverse.

Imax Superlarge-screen process developed in Canada, using a special camera with a horizontal film-through-camera movement to achieve maximum image surface on the film stock itself. The Imax can easily be ten times the size of a conventional motion picture screen. Wider than Cinerama, the screen is also taller, creating an effect far more compelling than basic wide-screen. A standard Imax screen measures 75 by 100.5 feet, as compared to regular wide-screens of 19 by 45 feet, or Cinerama's 31-by-64-foot screen.

imbibition print A print made using a dye-transfer process. In this case, the transfer is of magenta, cyan and yellow-dyed matrix films, in strict register, to a special clear film base; or prepared paper, for stills.

improvement threshold In FM radio receivers, a level of minimum signal power needed to overpower inherent thermal noise. The more the noise is overcome, the greater the signal-to-noise ratio, in favor of "signal."

improvise For the performer to invent on-the-spot DIALOGUE or action. It's also a term used behind the camera, meaning to work out production problems, using backup planning or instantly devised methods suited to the given situation.

impulse A pulse with such a minimal duration that it may be expressed mathematically as infinitesimal, even through the change caused by the pulse may be finite and measurable.

impulse buyer The idealized buyer for those wishing to sell by motivating other's reflexes. When triggered by words such as "sale," "now," "operators waiting to take your call," "never before a buy like this," plus repetitions of the number to call, the impulse buyer must and will buy, buy, buy. There are inveterate impulse buyers just as there are alcoholics and other addicts, but even the purchase-wary consumer is impulse-motivated from time to time.

in and out of focus   Uneven breathing of the film in the projector gate, resulting from extreme heat energy. This creates images that are clear then fuzzy. This alternating level of sharpness is an internal mechanical error that can't be improved by refocusing.

in-camera   Shots made within the camera itself by rewinding and double-exposing, by shooting mattes and then fill-ins, by filming stop-frame in kinestasis form or time-lapse, etc.

in-camera matte shot   One where a portion of the action field is masked off by a black cutout device, formed to coincide with scenic specifications. This is placed either directly in front of the focal plane or mounted in a MATTE BOX in front of the camera.

in camera range   Anything observable within the camera frames, inside the framing edges and not too distant to be indiscernible.

incandescent lamp   Sealed, gas-filled bulb, generating emitted light from a tungsten wire filament. The common household light bulb is an incandescent lamp. Also, a professional lighting unit—LUMINAIRE—employing incandescent bulbs.

in character   Correct attitudinal identification by the ACTOR or ACTRESS with the role he or she is playing. DIALOGUE that seems natural to the part.

inching   Running film through viewing or synchronizing equipment, a frame or two at a time.

inching knob   A turning handle that interlocks with the drive mechanism of a GANG SYNCHRONIZER or other piece of editing or projector equipment that can take the film forward or put it in reverse in accelerated or decelerated moves. These moves can be made by hand or be motor-driven.

incident light   Light from all surrounding sources (intentional and otherwise) that illuminates the on-camera subject.

incident light meter   One that measures the cumulative amount of light from whatever sources that falls onto the on-camera subject.

independent   Filmmaker not working on staff for a major studio or production company but who seeks out and completes projects, either as an individual or as a company.

independent production   TV or film production not affiliated with a major studio or production company. Independent productions range from full UNION to subcontracted crews, as well as non-union casts and crews, and mixtures of all of these.

independent station   A radio or TV station not network-affiliated, or a network carrier-station that programs less than a dozen hours of network fare per week. An international or cable network, or any group of owned-and-operated stations.

index counter   Counter that measures and indicates, with an odometer-like mechanism, the amount of tape fed out or reversed. This allows an operator to spot a particular section of a tape for cueing, or inserting a scene or a segment of a scene.

Index of Copyright Registrations   This extensive file has a record of all copyrights filed. The copyright office will, for reasonable fees, search its files and report back on information found. It is a good way to determine, among other media information, what films are in the public domain.

indicate In acting, to point out something nonverbal—a shrug of the shoulders, a change of expression, a gesture of the hands, nodding toward something. Examples in GENERAL DIRECTION in a screenplay: ext.: The farmyard. Tom and Jody walk toward the car. Tom stops. Indicates to Jody to look into the front seat. Examples in PERSONAL DIRECTION: Tom: (indicating front seat of car) Look at that!

indicating meter A meter with a visual indicating device, readout electromechanism or simple printer, that registers the short-time immediate average of the measured quantity.

indigenous sound The real sound (matching or synch) of the location that is being filmed. Its PRESENCE or ambient sound.

indirect light Light from a source that is not in itself luminous, but is reflected or bounced into the scene, altering the overall light level.

indirect quote A summary phrase or sentence that gives the gist of a particular statement without quoting it directly. This compressed summary can gain power by being succinct, but this same terseness can also oversimplify, and even distort. An indirect quote can be "misquoted" as easily as a direct one.

indirect view TV A projected and enlarged TV image on a big viewing screen.

industrial film An informational, motivational or propaganda film, the subject of which is a factory, industrial group, utility or conglomerate. Sometimes such films are included in the term corporate image film.

inflection Vocal range of stress, rhythm, pitch and mood used to intensify and clarify meaning. Inflections can also be used to gloss over, obscure and even reverse meaning. Improper inflection plus the wrong stress on key words can make a hopeless muddle of the most clearly-written report. Inflection sets the scene for a story, including a factual one, and determines the dynamics of it, as well as its energy level.

informational film/tape A structured presentation setting forth facts, procedures and conceptual themes.

informational programming Program of an educational or documentary nature, informational in character and considered "nonentertainment." Often scheduled by TV stations to fulfill their PUBLIC SERVICE requirements set by the FCC.

information-gathering Other than on-the-spot news with eyewitnesses, the amassing of information is a slow, deliberate process accelerated considerably by computer databanks. Other sources for reference and research are library materials, government public documents and files, experts in a special field, interviews with people directly involved in a past or ongoing event, informal and structural surveys, etc. See FREEDOM OF INFORMATION in Appendix.

information theory Philosophical and scientific approach to accuracy and inaccuracy in message transmission, in whatever medium or form the message is in. Pure information is sent out from its source to its receptor; along the way it meets the impurities of transmission failure, noise and distortion.

infomercial A "long" commercial of 90 seconds plus in running time. It gives information about the advertised product, but has more of an institutional attitude, and less of the hard-sell edge. It talks about "quality" and "service" more than discussing costs and venues of sales.

infrared, projection Radiation in the long wavelength range that is not visible but manifests itself in radiation from a carbon or xenon arc. This greatly intensifies the heat-up of film and projection gear. Infrared motion picture film is used for haze penetration and for producing special non-panchromatic effects.

infrasonic   A sound wave with a frequency below the audible range.

ingenue   A leading woman who is in her late teens to mid-twenties.

in-house   A film or TV presentation designed to be used internally by a corporation, government agency or special group. The film is used for various purposes: process explanation, orientation, information, motivation.

in-house agency   An advertising agency wholly owned by a company or corporation, which handles all advertising for the company. Generally, it handles the corporate owner's account exclusively but occasionally; it will take on additional accounts outside the parent company or corporation.

ink-and-paint   Filling-in on the various animation cels and other graphic elements for final filming.

inker   Animation artist who draws details and outlines with acetate ink that is applied to the top surface of cels.

inky-dink   A popular term for a miniature incandescent lamp, usually 250 watts. Its main use is for highlighting part of a person or a prop. It functions as a minispotlight, not a FILL LIGHT. It is the smallest focusable lamp.

in phase   Two waves of the same frequency with coinciding crests and troughs of their undulations. When they move through these maximum/minimum polarities at the same time, they are described as in phase.

in-point   Frame-count number at the beginning of a shot, scene or sequence, in film or videotape. "Frame-count" is

the final indicator. In film, there are ordinarily 24 or 25 frames per second; in videotape, 30 frames per second.

input recorder   Any electrical equipment that records input signals.

insert car   See CAMERA CAR.

insert shot   A DETAIL SHOT from the main scene, relevant to the action or mood. Used as CUTAWAY SHOT to intensify and heighten the specific scene or to give necessary dramatic information: a key sentence in a letter, a date on a calendar, a newspaper headline, a face in a group photo, etc. In TV, it is a local station's insertions into network broadcast materials.

insert stage   A small shooting stage for shooting commercial product shots, TABLETOP PHOTOGRAPHY, MACRO LENS photography, and close-up and extreme close-up photography of whatever objects need to be filmed or videotaped.

instantaneous recording   One that is made and released as recorded, without any sweetening, overdubbing, or any remixed re-recording.

instant replay   Live telecast playback of any selected part of the program. Most commonly used in sporting events, in real time or SLOW MOTION, or the playback can stop the motion with a FREEZE FRAME.

institutional   A film or video piece that promotes a company, corporation or organization (including the government) that pushes image instead of product.

institutional copy   Writing that creates a favorable image of a particular organization; it may show the people as community leaders, loyal Americans pursuing the great free-enterprise dream or friendly neighbors who have provided years of service. This may or may not be true, but it is the composite image most often desired. At the same time, they want to appear future-oriented and openminded.

instructional film A classroom or orientation film. For example, films used in the armed forces showing servicemen how to handle gear and arms, or films demonstrating to tellers "how to handle the window." Insurance companies have films and videotapes highlighting the key points of a sale. Many companies have audio-video programs teaching their employees how to work with computers. An instructional film is designed to help teach or improve skills, obtain straightforward information or foster certain attitudes.

insurance Producers, studios or production companies should be customized-insured for areas that are appropriate to the need of production. For example, no insurance is needed for injuries received from high-risk stunts if there are no stunts in the particular production being filmed or videotaped. Common headings for media production insurance are: completion-on-schedule against production-interrupting weather conditions; against fire, burglary, property damage; workmen's compensation; and life insurance of principal performers, and sometimes, producer or director.

in synch In technical use, the phrase means that sound and picture match.

integrated circuit (IC) A miniature interconnected circuit made up of many electronic and semiconductor components, all contained in a single, discrete electronic element.

intelligence bandwidth The full range of audio or video frequency BAND-WIDTHs. Bandwidths can carry one or more channels.

intelligence signal One containing information. A signal of picture, voice, facsimiles, printed or handwritten message, code, logo, etc.

intensity Amplitude or relative strength of energy: electronic, vibrational, magnetic.

Regarding light, intensity is the emitted power of a single light source, or a measurement of the aggregate.

It is also the luminant power of a light source, and the complete visible radiation that it produces.

interaction The listening and speaking rhythm of interplay between interviewer and interviewee. It is a key element of on-camera interviews. It is the responsibility of the director and interviewer to set the pace and tone of the interview, and to put the interviewee at ease.

interactive An adjective describing such personal video programming techniques as video games, freezing frames or repeating scenes on a video cassette; hardware or software combinations that let viewers make decisions about the course or even outcome of a program.

interactive television A system where the TV audience uses gear especially designed to signal reactions and answers to questions and situations to respond and have the responses monitored and evaluated by the transmitting entity. Used for Q-and-A instruction, or for in-house seminars in different locations, and for other related uses such as how-to demonstrations, impact presentations or concentrated information, multilingual interchanges, etc.

intercutting The point-counterpoint of filmmaking, now being used more often in videotaping (production and post production). Shots of and from other scenes and contexts are inserted into the structure of an existing scene or SEQUENCE, for CONTRAST, suspense or comic effect.

intercommunication system (intercom) A two-way interlink; a simple, direct communication system with two or more connections, without a switchboard. In media, an example would be a two-way system between a TV control room and the studio stage.

interior A scene that takes place indoors. Abbreviated "INT." in SCREENPLAYS.

interior framing Framing the foreground to give special emphasis to particular foreground objects or people.

interlacing The TV scanning process where the picture is formed by two complete but separate sets of interlacing lines. By this interlacing the flicker is reduced or virtually eliminated.

interlock Connections used to control operations of various devices in synchronicity.

interlock system Independent motors so controlled that they all turn at precisely the same speed. This can be done mechanically, with an electronic system or a mixture of both. The term is usually applied to any system by which picture and sound readouts (on tracks or other discrete units) may be screened synchronously, especially in flatbed editing machines and projector systems.

intermediate To protect the original, an intermediate is film that is used to make duplicates.

intermittent Movement at equal intervals, but not continuous, e.g., the movement of sprocketed film through a projector at 24 fps. Intermittent movement can also be preset or controlled to allow for "randomness." In most projectors and cameras with 24 fps, the movement is functionally "continuous," but mechanically "intermittent."

intermittent sprocket Camera or projector sprocket that gives intermittent drive to a film when moving it forward or in reverse through a camera or projector.

International Alliance of Theatrical Stage Employees (IATSE) The union for most of behind-the-camera film crews. See NABET.

international broadcast station Station operating by international agreement, within frequencies of 6000—26,000

kHz. The programs it broadcasts are for worldwide public viewing. See SATELLITE.

International Brotherhood of Electrical Workers (IBEW) A union that began with stage electricians, expanded to the craft unions for stage and live TV and now includes taped TV and motion pictures.

international copyright A copyright that protects an invention or creative product throughout the world; but such protection is only workable in nations that have signed the international copyright treaties. If a nation is not a signatory, you can be assured it offers little or no copyright protection, even if that protection has been contractually agreed upon between parties.

Copyright convention law has slightly different methods of registration in each country where such law is in effect.

International Telecommunications Union The United Nations has set up this group to deal with telecommunications internationally. The agency works to achieve professional standards in communications usage and procedures; for example, to allocate frequencies to stations.

international track A separate track, independent of music and EFFECTS TRACKS, on which NARRATION AND DIALOGUE can be recorded.

internegative Color NEGATIVE dupe struck from a color POSITIVE. Used for making RELEASE PRINTS in an effort to preserve the original.

interpositive A POSITIVE dupe used for making prints.

interpretative reporting Analysis of a news story in order to delineate not just what happened, but how it came about, and why. A personal examination that has been researched or experienced, and explored for its causes by extrapolation, direct evidence, quotations, statistics, and a historical perspective. The personal aspect creates the dilemma of addressing the personal conviction and insight to a story, while relaying an uprejudiced and fair view of it.

interviewing Effectiveness in interviewing procedures starts with the questions that are appropriate to the topic and for the interviewee. The interviewer should study every aspect of an upcoming interview. The person being interviewed will also expect professional journalistic courtesy. This does not mean that the interviewer should not press hard to get an accurate response. But at what point "pressing hard" becomes "bullying" has never been unequivocally determined.

in the can Exposed film, ready to go to the LAB. Also used when filming is completed. "The picture's in the can!"

intonation Frequency at variance with the accustomed audible frequency of a musical note that makes the note sound sharp or flat.

introduction (intro) In a radio or TV program, the standard opening of a show, the ID. The same regular opening that tells the audience week after week, or day after day, the name of the program and whose show it is, i.e., who the producing and starring entities are. Also, an introduction is a lead-in to presenting a guest artist, a panelist, a game show contestant or a noted person in the news. Obviously, all introductions should be suitable to that which follows, in text, delivery and program placement.

invasion of right of privacy Invasion of privacy covers a host of improprieties, some of which are regarded as constitutional rights infringements. Among such invading acts into a U.S. citizen's private realm are: films, books or videotapes that reveal the "new" identity of a person who, under another name or geographical placement, leads a life of crime or was involved in a high-profile scandal;

publicity spotlighting a person's deviant sexual behavior; publicity pinpointing a person's anatomy, particularly genitalia, including showing unauthorized pictures used for medical reports.

These are regarded as public disclosures. But there are also physical "invasions" which include: using a wiretap to gain information about a person; monitoring deposits and withdrawls of a person's bank account, without authorization; securing information on a person's voting record in closed balloting; and securing information by surveillance of a person at home: calling that person by phone, often or at unreasonable times, photographing comings and goings.

Such invasive disclosures can be dangerous when they unmask a police informer, reveal the location of a person hiding from an international terrorist organization, or reveal identities of undercover government agents. A constant concern or even danger in investigative reporting for both interviewer and interviewee, invasion of privacy is also a problem in regular in-studio news and informal, chatty nonsubstantive shows such as "Entertainment Tonight" or "The Tonight Show." Any flip, offhand remark can be interpreted by amateur attorneys as injurious to character or slanderous.

Also, there is the problem of how far to probe or how strongly to make a negative statement of character. Does the fact that the statement is made with humor or wit mitigate the fact, or make it worse?

investigative reporting In-depth reporting of stories that some people, often those in positions of high authority or socio-political power, do not want to have come to light, because the truth will reveal improprieties or even criminal activities. For example, the squirmings and sidesteppings of President Nixon and his White House intimates to torpedo the investigation of Watergate by reporters of the Washington Post. The probing documentaries of Peter Davis for CBS, "Hunger in America" and "The Selling of the Pentagon," and later, independently, "Hearts and Minds," on the disgrace, hoax and folly of the Vietnam War. Investigative reporting at its best is one of the highest and most involving forms of reportage.

invisible cut   A cut that is imperceptible because it is made on action and follows the flow and rhythm of the action.

iris   A closing out of the screen image as a circular wipe tightens up to the smallest point and then goes to black. The reverse is to iris out, with the circle opening up and disappearing off the screen. The iris movement can also stop halfway, setting off the scene in a circular frame. See DIAPHRAGM, LENS.

iris shutter   To be used in front of a SPOTLIGHT to go from a pinpoint beam to a large area and all gradations in between. Its mechanism is similar to the iris shutter of a camera.

isochronous circuits   Circuits operating with same resonance frequency.

isolation booth   See BOOTH.

issue   The essential element of a news story: What's the issue? What's at stake? If the issue is the Iran-Contra scandal and its adjuncts, it is complex and multilayered by its nature. If it is a natural event such as San Francisco's 1989 earthquake, the issue is simpler but still with various interpretive facets: Could the city have been better prepared? If so, how? What is the human loss in lives, injuries, property and emotional shock? What, if anything, can be done in the future to prepare for another quake? When will science be able to predict them more accurately?

J

jack plug   A direct-connection device between audio components that plug in at one or both ends.

jack tube   Telescopic support for a LUMINAIRE braced between two walls.

jam   A bunching up of the film going through the camera or projector so that it stops the mechanical drive or take-up movements.

jamming   See ACTIVE JAMMING.

jargon   Specialized language of a profession. This dictionary is mostly jargon. The broker, the attorney, the accountant, the clergyman and the thief all have their own jargon. Whatever the jargon may be, it is the business of those in performing media—particularly in reportage, to clarify it when it must be used and to get rid of it whenever possible, using substitute and denotative language instead. In dramatic characterization where jargon is essential to the feeling of authenticity, jargon sometimes has to be used. If used sparingly and selectively, it can be fully effective. If overused, it can be a distraction and an unwanted irritation.

jellies, color   Gelatin FILTERS placed in front of LAMPs. Also called GELs.

jenny   Electrical generator; common terminology for a portable one.

jingle   The repetitive words and music used in a commercial to impart the sponsor's name and product.

jitter   The jiggling of the entire picture on the TV tube, caused by improper synchronization. Generally, signal inaccuracy and instability caused by wavering amplitude or phase.

jog   Used as both verb and noun, referring to the deliberate frame-by-frame movement forward or in reverse, in videotape helical scan editing.

joint circuit   A link in a communications system that carries various elements that complement each another in a cohesive signal. Set up from control areas, operation bays, augmenting relay stations, etc.

journalism Journalism is, in its general sense, the occupation of reporting the news. This includes on-the-spot-observation, writing, televising, photographing and radio or TV broadcasting of the news. Considered for many years a minor craft and never "deep" enough to be an art, journalism is now being treated much more seriously, especially by those who are targets of investigative journalism. Its immense power has given journalism a grudging and wary respect. This is especially true in TV journalism, which accounts for over half of America's major sources for news. The old definition of journalism being synonymous with "pandering to the popular taste and sentiments," "superficial research," and "top-of-the-head" decisions, should be carefully applied, i.e., only when a negative description is accurate. Certainly, the writing of in-depth news stories requires rapid research, but this doesn't mean such writing lacks research requisite for the story. Modern researchers can use the computer data banks with great and precise alacrity, and often their writing style is clear and has a sharp cutting edge. For example, had it not been for the combined journalistic forces of press, TV and radio, the Iran-Contra scandal or Watergate may never have been uncovered. "60 Minutes" alone has looked under many rocks that people in power would just as soon not have had turned over. The TV reportage of the Vietnam War had a powerful impact, which had much to do with bringing that chapter of military intervention right into the homes of the American people. The image-journalism of American servicemen's corpses in body bags actively stimulated the grassroots end-the-war movement.

There are many serious ethical questions to consider regarding newsgathering and news presentation. In gathering news, there is often a breach of hospitality by the interviewer and his crew, and sometimes an overt INVASION OF RIGHT OF PRIVACY. There is also the ploy of obtaining an interview under false pretenses although in investigative journalism this is often the only way to get the interview. In writing the news or documentary reportage, there is always a personal slant or bias to guard against, as objectivity is a goal. The spirit of fairness must be carried through in both gathering and writing the news. News can be easily colored or distorted by deliberate or accidental interpretations, to give it an entirely different skew. A common ethical dilemma is caused when the right to privacy meets head-on with "the public's need to know." This need is interpreted by some as a right—even an extension of constitutional rights of free speech. Another moral quandary is the aspect of treacherous duplicity on the part of the interviewer, who acts in a warm, friendly manner to a prospective interviewee, while setting up an interview situation in which the latter, given the requisite amount of rope, will hang himself/herself. Even if you are exposing fraud and unethical behavior in a scandal that needs to be exposed, this does not whitewash the act of obtaining the story in a fraudulent, unethical manner.

joy-stick Two-way zoom-control, cable attached to a motor that operates a zoom lens.

joystick zoom control Two-way switch (forward or reverse) attached to a cable connected to a ZOOM-LENS drive motor. It can move the LENS for zoom-ins or zoom-outs, with either preset or variable speeds.

juice Electrical power.

juicer An electrician, particularly one who handles the main power source.

jump cut If a section is taken out of the middle of a shot and the film respliced across the gap, a jump cut is said to result, since there is a jump in the shot's continuity. When the shot is motionless, this is a useful device for eliminating dead footage. Shots, however, are usually moving, and if there is movement, a visible jump will usually occur. Sometimes deliberately used by directors to fracture time and movement, and give a sense of freneticism or surrealism.

jumper Power cable extension.

junction Connection between two or more conductors or between two or more transmission lines.

junction box Electrical box into which cables or wires are plugged or connected.

junior A focusable studio LAMP using a 2000-watt bulb and a FRESNEL LENS. The studio-lighting "basic" lamp.

justified camera move Organic camera movement which is motivated and determined by the action of the scene. A movement for a reason as opposed to a random, distracting or unnecessary movement.

justify To properly align data relating to a specific reference.

juvenile A young male in his teens to twenties, in a dramatic work. The male counterpart to the INGENUE.

K

K A call letter for radio and TV stations in the western half of the United States; for the eastern sector (mostly east of the Mississippi) the letter "W" is used. Examples: KSL (Salt Lake City, Utah), KOCE (PBS station, Huntington Beach, California), KMPC (radio only, Los Angeles). WGN (Chicago, Illinois), WNET (PBS station, New York City), WQXR (radio only, New York City), WETA (PBS station, Washington, D.C.). There is some geographical overlapping.

"K" is also an abbreviation for degrees Kelvin measured on the KELVIN SCALE.

In lighting, K measures luminosity in lighting gear; lamps are referred to as "1K," i.e., one kilowatt; "that's a 10K," 10 kilowatts, etc. A 500-watt lamp is sometimes called "half-K."

keep takes Takes not annotated as out-takes (see OUTS), but as potential editing material out of which to make the complete film/videotape. Takes that are to be printed are generally circled by the assistant cameraman and/or the SCRIPT CLERK. Also called hold takes.

Kelvin A scale used to measure and indicate color temperature. A Kelvin scale has the same gradations as Centigrade, but absolute zero is at 0.

Kennedy-Nixon debates The pilot miniseries that started a trend. Now, every four years, there is a new programming of the format. The opponents are either the incumbent president and the contender for the presidency, or, if the presidency is open because the incumbent has served two terms (and under the constitution cannot run for a third term), then the debate takes place between the two major contenders for the presidency, usually a Democrat and a Republican. The reason for the debates is to show where the aspirants stand on various issues and how quickly and accurately they can think on their feet.

key Device for switching part of a simple or multiple circuit. Hand-operated by a push-button or handle. Also called a key switch.

keyed rainbow signal Signal that generates color-bar images from a continuous sine-wave (3.56 MHz).

key grip Head of the GRIP crew.

key light The main light used for the illumination of a subject within a scene. High-key lighting means that the key light forms a large proportion of the total illumination on the set, resulting in an effect of general brillance. Low-key lighting is when the key light forms, in comparison to high-key lighting, a smaller proportion of a smaller total area of illumination on the set. The result is that many objects are allowed to fall into semidarkness or even total blackness, thus throwing other objects into correspond-ingly stronger relief. This more dramatic style of lighting, which has now won general acceptance for certain types of commercial motion pictures, makes greater demands on emulsion characteristics and on PROCESSING techniques than does high-key lighting.

key number See EDGE NUMBER.

key station The prime originating station for a TV or radio broadcast. Also referred to as the master station.

keystoning Image distortion caused by projection at an angle other than perpendicular to the axis of the THROW, or caused by filming at such an angle.

key switch See KEY.

key words The important words in a phrase or sentence. These words demand interpretative stress, not just louder reading. For example, if the Nationalist party is running a new candidate, "The Nationalist party announced today it would be introducing a *new name* into its political roster . . ." If, however, the public is expecting the opposing party to introduce a new name, but the Nationalist party does it instead, the same words would have a different stress: "The *Nationalist* party announced today that it would be introducing a new name into its political roster . . ." So, both denotation and connotation determine the interpretative stress of key words. Connotative readings are determined by the context of the spoken word.

kicker A light news story with strong human interest that is used to lead into a commercial. This, in turn, creates a demand for kickers and helps de-emphasize straight news.

kicker light A LAMP that puts light on the subject from behind and to the side and the illumination resulting from this.

kill To turn off certain lights, as in, "Kill the JUNIORs!" Or to turn off all the lights and stop the sound: "Okay! Kill everything!"

kilohertz Name replacing previous term "kilocycle." 1000 hertz is one kHz.

kilowatt (kw) 1000 watts.

kinescope The primary large tube in a TV receiver; converts cathode ray input signals into the picture that is viewed on the "screen" end on the tube. Also, a copy of a TV program made by directly filming the TV screen and simultaneously recording the sound. Preceding the development of videotape, kinescopes are the only records of TV shows from the 1940s.

kinestasis A neologism from the Greek, denoting movement ("kine") and standing still ("stasis"). The word refers to rephotographing photos, one frame at a time, for as many frames as necessary, usually one to 24 frames. A 48-frame shot (two seconds' duration, at standard 24 fps projection rate) is one of extended length in kinestasic terms. When projected, the rapid cuts give a feeling of frenetic, staccato movement.

Klieg light Lights used originally in live theaters and eventually motion picture production. "Klieg light" in the 1920s and 1930s was synonymous with "movie light." It is a trade name.

knuckle Metal circles with matching, grooved surfaces that fit together or in which piping or light stems can be clamped. They work on extension arms on C-stands and can be used with piping to cantilever a small light or microphone over the action, or to fasten and secure cutter arms.

kookie/kuke See CUCALORIS.

kw See KILOWATT.

L

lab (laboratory) In film usage, a company specializing in developing motion picture stock for image and for optical sound. The lab also makes MASTERS, DUPE NEGATIVES, WORKPRINTS, and copies of COMPOSITE prints for release, i.e., RELEASE PRINTS. Many of the labs also have full postproduction videotape facilities for transferring tape-to-tape, film-to-tape, and in more specialized labs, tape-to-film.

lab effects   Those OPTICAL EFFECTS that can be handled in lab processing and printing, such as pushing light, printing for night effect, sepia-coloring selected shots.

labels   Words on the screen to point out certain items and name them or their function. These words can be superimposed over a scene or in the bottom third of the screen, as in a subtitle. Or they can be brought in with animation, special effects or simply popped or dissolved in sometimes with indicator arrows. Used in training films, particularly step-by-step how-to films, such as "Changing Your Car's Oil," "Computer Operation," "Cleaning your Rifle."

labor relations   Special department in major studios and at the unions to handle negotiations, public news releases and the general dissemination of information, usually partisan. In a studio or production company, this is critically important and extremely complex. For example, a major shoot can involve a dozen unions or more. Or the contract for services may be a subcontract to another company or corporation to provide postproduction mixing, catering, second unit photography or any other requirement. In securing these services, a temporary partnership may be formed.

lace   To thread a projector. See THREADING.

lag   Time difference between two waves of the same frequency, indicated on a scale of electrical degrees. Also, the time interval between signal transmission and signal reception.

lambert   Luminance unit equal to $1/\pi$ candle per centimeter. As a theoretical

ideal entity, it is uniform luminance of a flawless diffusing surface, either emitting or reflecting accurately one lumen per square centimeter.

lamp   General term for an electrical globe used in lighting the SET. Originally the term referred to the entire lighting unit, and still does in some working situations, depending on what is common usage with the crew. When referring to the lights themselves, the globes referred to go from INKY-DINK to 10K.

lamphouse   A self-contained light unit using either a carbon arc or a xenon arc, with interlinking optical and operating devices; for professional projectors.

lamp operator   Crew member in charge of a large LIGHTING unit that requires special, individual attention because of complexity or bulk weight.

lap dissolve   A long, overlapping DISSOLVE that has to be handled as a special optical printing. Sometimes synonymous with dissolve.

lapel microphone   A small mike with a clip-on grip to attach to clothing, as near to the performer's mouth as possible.

lap switch   A fast DISSOLVE from one video signal to another. "Lap" is merely a truncation of the word "overlap."

laser   A laser is a unit for taking diffuse, incoherent light of different frequencies and focusing it into a narrow, concentrated beam of intense coherent light. LASER is an acronym from Light Amplification by Stimulated Emission of Radiation.

laserdisc   See laser videodisc.

laser videodisc   Software for the laser videodisc player. Optical reflectance material, scratch-resistant plastic of great durability, reflects the laser light back into the hardware, which then retransmits it as image and/or sound superior to videotape. CDs are the audio version of the videodisc. Also called laserdisc.

latensification Special lab-handling of a LATENT IMAGE, to increase light in a frame area needing more exposure.

latent image The invisible image registered on a photographic emulsion which becomes visible after development.

latitude The range of exposure of an emulsion. The latitude of exposure is normally greater than the latitude of an emulsion.

laugh-track A SOUND TRACK of audience laughter used to augment actual studio laughter or added to a composite track that has no response on it at all. There are various kinds of laughter, from "tittering" to "thunderous," categorized and filed by their levels of laughter in the sound effects libraries.

lavaliere microphone A mike held to the performer by a cord around the neck.

lavender print British term for FINE-GRAIN print.

lay an egg To fail badly on-stage or on-camera, particularly in front of a live audience. Said often of comics.

layback Fusing all audio and video tracks. Final transfer of synch elements onto a working MASTER of whatever tape width: 1/2", 3/4", 1".

laydown Copying of production elements (tracks) onto a multitrack tape such as a 24-track (2") unit, as well as adding sweetening and the SMPTE time code. All this is then mixed down to a four-stripe track (usually 1"), with newly mixed discrete elements of one track each: music, effects, dialogue, plus time code.

lay in To spot and place sound or picture segments while assembling and structuring the film.

laying tracks Preparing and synching the multiple tracks necessary for the final MIXING sessions.

layout Director's notes and sketches for cast and crew movement within a complicated scene. Common talk from director to assistant director: "Okay, let's walk through this, and lay out the shot." In ANIMATION, the chart, guide or sequential shot list. Sometimes the STORYBOARD is referred to as a layout.

lead The primary acting role in a SCREENPLAY or teleplay. From live theater terminology; usually there are two leads— one male and one female.
In cinematography, to pace the on-camera performer moving cross-screen, so that there is a greater screen and FRAME space in front of than behind the actor.

leader Film consisting of a coated or uncoated stock used for THREADING in film-developing machines, and sometimes for assembling WORKPRINT and re-recording SOUND TRACKs that contain only short segments of audio track. Often, different kinds of leader are designated by their color. (See also ACADEMY LEADER.) Audio tape leader is the blank nonmagnetized portion at the beginning of a tape.

leader tape Plastic, nonmagnetic tape for use in audio or video recording splicing that can be used at the head or tail end of a roll. Also it can be used as tape for separating cues, particularly with 1/4" audio tape or for pausing between sections of recorded material.

lead-in A direct or transitional introduction to a program segment or to a full program or to a variety act or guest star. An introduction or transition by host, announcer or master of ceremonies into a song, musical number or specialty. Also, a TV program immediately ahead of another. In ELECTRONICS it's the conductor carrying radio frequency energy between the antennae and the radio or TV receiver or transmitter creating the frequency-energy path.

leading lady   The female star of a production.

leading man   Male star of a production. This term and the one above are from the stage, and apply, in working parlance, mainly to theatrical forms.

lead, news reporting   The opening sentence of a news story. It must immediately capture the attention of the radio listener or TV viewer. If it doesn't, the channel might be switched or turned off.

lead-out   A TV show that comes immediately after another program.

leading questions   Leading questions are really "loaded questions." That is, there is a subtextual or direct implication that indicates the way you should answer. For example: "Nearly every legal expert feels that this law is unjust and should be repealed. What do you think?" "Only a person who is artistically ignorant and insensitive would want to see this work hung in our museum, don't you agree?" Interviewers who ask leading questions sometimes do it in order to get a strong response from the person being interviewed. It has a dubious ethical place in the etiquette, if not morality, of interviewer/interviewee protocol. Probing, in-depth, to-the-point questions are better, but research and a thorough look at the discussion theme or specific topic take more work to come up with.

lead sheet   In broad terminology, a sketched-out musical accompaniment. In more specialized use, the term refers to a musical synchronization sheet for either animation or live action. This is a horizontal bar graph, indicating exact cues, either visual or auditory. Or sometimes, by count number alone.

lead time   The time a media film or videotape begins production (including active preproduction) and the target delivery date of the complete work.

leaf shutter   Rotating disc or blade in a camera or projector that momentarily blocks out light. The intermittency is determined by the number of "openings"—one to three—in the device. It is calibrated to reduce FLICKER and to eliminate visible frame lines.

leaser/owner   Agreement between equipment owner and production unit renting the equipment or leasing it for an extended period of time. Leasing can be flat-rate or with option to purchase. The agreement applies to all media equipment rented for production: audio gear, motion picture or TV cameras, grip paraphernalia, walkie-talkies and bullhorns, production vehicles and any other primary or augmenting bits and pieces.

left/right signal   Sound emanating from a source that comes primarily from the listener's left side—or right, if it is a right signal. Left or right is determined by regarding the performing area as center.

left/right stereo channel   Left or right signals in stereophonic transmission/reception.

legal forms   Standard forms used often in reproduction or distribution. These include SAG, WGA and DGA basic contracts, property permits and releases for filming agreements between distributors and producers, personal on-camera releases and injury/risk waivers. Many of these forms can be purchased at stationery stores specializing in media clientele. See Appendix.

legal issues   In media, there are many legal issues; perhaps the most recognized conflict occurs between the privilege of the First Amendment versus the corpus of law on responsibility in media (libel cases). Other legal issues in news or documentary reportage are such potential snares to the reporters as: trespassing to obtain or augment a story; freely extrapolating and prejudicially interpreting governmental excisions from materials required under the FREEDOM OF INFORMATION ACT; breaching security requirements in disseminating a story; stepping out from behind the shield of privilege; and exposing confidential legal information from plaintiff or defendant prior to a trial. A reporter, documentary-maker or news-gatherer must understand the basic legal rights of reportage and how they apply to individual reporters.

legs   Another name for tripod.

lekolite   An ellipsoid spotlight with individual push-SHUTTERS for "shaping" the emitted light. A live theater standard, and a "special" for film and TV.

lens   A transparent glass optical device that transmits an image to the photographic emulsion within the camera, produces a screen image through the projector, or is used in similar technical manner in various optical instruments. A photographic lens consists of precision-mounted transparent pieces called ELEMENTS. A long-focus is a relative term, describing lenses of greater FOCAL LENGTH than normal, consequently giving greater-than-normal magnification. Inaccurately called a TELEPHOTO LENS. A normal focus lens, shooting in 16mm, is a one-inch lens; in 35mm, a two-inch lens. A short focus lens is one with shorter focal length than normal, consequently giving lower than normal magnification and a wider field of view. Also called WIDE-ANGLE LENS.

lens adapter   A camera device allowing a lens not ordinarily used on a given camera to be fitted onto that same camera. This lens-holding device allows extended use of differing lenses.

lens aperture   See F NUMBER.

lens cap   Plastic or metal cover, with a snap-on or threaded fitting that attaches to the end of a lens to protect it from scratches, dust and dampness.

lens coating   A protective chemical layer that guards the exterior glass lens element and allows more light to reach the film emulsion by cutting down the reflectance of incoming light.

lens element   See ELEMENTS.

lens extender   Name for any number of devices that move the lens farther from the camera and closer to the object to be photographed, or for giving an "induced" closeness. Used for detail photography work, particularly when requiring extreme close-up shots.

lens flare   A glint of light seen on the developed image that is caused by sunlight or other bright illumination hitting the LENS.

lens hood, lens shade   A device used to shield unwanted light from the lens. It can be mounted on the lens barrel itself or directly in front of the camera.

lens markings   Calibrated numbers and reference marks imprinted on a lens to designate f-number, FOCUS and DEPTH OF FIELD.

lens mount   A simple mechanism to attach a lens to a camera.

lens speed   A measurement of the amount of light a lens will allow to pass through to the receiving medium (film, videotape). The number is determined by the focal length divided by the lens diameter.

lens stop   An iris opening setting for a lens, indicated by these standard f-stop numbers: 1.4, 2, 2.8, 4, 5, 6, 8, 11, 16 and 22. These numbers are derived from the formula:

$$f = \frac{focal\ length}{diameter\ of\ opening}$$

lens support   A metal or plastic brace at the front end of a camera mount, used to support a long lens.

lens tissue   Very soft paper sheets with minimal lint, designed for cleaning the delicate glass lenses without scratching.

lens turret   A lens-mounting plate that can be rotated to accommodate two or more lenses. This allows for quick movement from one lens to another for varying FOCAL LENGTHs. Used often in early newsgathering on film, and for documentary shooting. Now largely replaced by the ZOOM LENS.

letters   Letters or notes are common plot devices, going back to Richardson's *Pamela*, and more recently, in mid-twentieth century America, to John O'Hara's *Pal Joey*. Cryptic notes or seemingly nonsensical or innocuous ones are often the unraveling key in many a mystery story, such as Poe's "The Gold Bug," Sir Arthur Conan Doyle's "The Dancing Men," and many an Agatha Christie classic. The letter has been a pivotal plot point in such films as *The Letter to Three Wives, Letter from an Unknown Woman, Dear Ruth, Address Unknown*, and others.

level   Volume of sound that is usually registered by a needle-pointer on a calibrated readout meter.

libel   A false or malicious statement, written, spoken, graphically depicted or otherwise communicated that holds a person or persons up to public ridicule, with subsequent damaging of the reputation of the person(s). In reporting or news analysis there is much that is open to public comment, i.e., open governmental hearings, political speeches, court preceedings. However, the fact that these activities are "open" does not mean that it is "open season." Public comment must also be fair comment. Fairness is often difficult to determine in court, much less in on-the-spot or under-the-deadline situations, when one is caught up in the fervor of the event. If it can be proven that in the reportage ill-will or prejudice were integral factors, then malice aforethought may be charged.

library   Titles of films contracted for lease or purchase by a videocassette manufacturer. The number of acquisitions constitutes the "library."

The catalogued repository of general music, effects and shots.

library research   For researching in general or for media, the sources of data are many and international in points of origin. Sources include: world-network databanks; regional/national and in-house databanks; Library of Congress in Washington, D.C.; local public, college and university libraries and archives; newspapers; trade journals; periodicals; dictionaries and encyclopedias; books on special subjects; government documents, including files now available through the Freedom of Information statue.

license   An FCC station permit to operate and broadcast.

lift   To incorporate a segment of one TV program or motion picture into another. For example, to show a segment of a TV program from the 50's playing on the home TV set in a film about that period. To incorporate part of the first film of a series or TV program into a subsequent show, as a FLASHBACK.

light   Radiant energy in the general range 3800 to 7000 Angstrom units. This is the spectrum that the human eye is sensitive to. Light is a broad term for "visible radiant energy."

light-balancing filter   Camera filter, lightly tinted, that alters the color temperature reflected from the photographic subject. The light-balancing filter compensates for color-temperature differences in interior or exterior lighting. Exterior lighting variations would be caused by sky conditions and by the time of day. The filter is tinted in different shades to match the correction necessary or the effect desired. These filters are also used for achieving specific light effects, both interior and exterior. See also FILTERS.

light batten   A light batten is a long piece of pipe with electrical outlets in it. Luminaires are plugged into these outlets. It is suspended above the performance area or just at the periphery, and then the luminaires are spotted or focused in. Developed originally for live theatre, now a staple in all visual performing media.

light board A control board for distributing electrical current to a group of luminaires. Used for dimming, adjusting intensity or for direct "on" and "off" cues.

light board operator Person in charge of seeing that the lighting in the studio is properly set, and that the performing area light can be cued in and out at the necessary times. The person who handles the light board.

light box A unit with light bulbs inside covered on one side of the box with a translucent heavy plastic or frosted glass sheet. Used as a background for the direct photography of titles, or for photographing small objects without casting shadows.

light comedians Dramatic comedians who are deft and agile, openly quick-witted and fast-reacting, or wisely aware of what's going on despite a bumbling, fumbling appearance. Cary Grant is an example of the former. Charlie Chaplin of the latter. The light comedian should be able to blend, in various ratios, the comedic and the romantic.

light filter A transparent sheet, colored glass or dyed gelatin. This light-absorbing sheet is used to give a special cast to, or to control the colors of, a projected image as it passes through a particular plane.

lighting One workable method of differentiating types of lighting has proved most effective, that is, to define lighting in its subcategories by indicating the direction from which it comes. For example, *backlighting* is when the illumination source from behind the SET or the performer, lighting that is pointing toward the camera. The actual light source is, of course, shielded so as not to shine into the lens. Backlighting ranges from a bare indication that a shot is backlit to fullcon-

trast silhouette, wherein all front-lighting is eliminated. *Front-lighting* is the fundamental lighting of a set, from behind and from the side of the camera. The greater the proportion of front-lighting to other kinds of light, the "flatter" (less contrast) the lighting. *Cross-lighting* is intermediate in its direction between front-lighting and back-lighting. *Highlighting* is additional illumination applied to a small area. *Top-lighting* is light from sources mounted above the subject and shining down onto it.

lighting director In TV, the lighting director works directly with the TECHNICAL DIRECTOR with light-board patterns, presets them with the LIGHT BOARD OPERATOR, who physically runs the cues. In smaller TV stations, the lighting director may also serve as the light board operator.

light level Light intensity expressed in FOOT CANDLES.

light meter Photosensitive device to measure light levels. The meter is activated by a photocell powered by a minibattery. See EXPOSURE METER.

light plot Schematic drawing indicating placement of lights on a SET or LOCATION. Information on the plot gives LAMP names, wattage and placement.

light positive Light with positive photoconductivity, which means that the conductivity increases when exposed to light.

light sensitive Having a photoelectric reaction to irradiation. As seen in "electric-eyes," e.g., a photovoltaic light meter.

light-struck Film that has been unintentionally exposed to light, causing EDGE FOGGING or full-frame FOGGING. For almost all purposes, this renders the film useless.

light-struck leader Film deliberately exposed to light, to be used as LEADER.

light tight Cameras, magazines, changing bags and other camera equipment that excludes light is said to be "light-tight."

light trap A darkroom entry with double doors, staggered black panels or other arrangements, to let people in but keep light out.

lily See COLOR LILY.

limbo set A SET suggesting open space, reaching to infinity. A CYCLORAMA is often used for a limbo set.

limited animation ANIMATION wherein the main figures remain in place, but segments are in motion; for example, the head remains still but eyes or lips are in motion.

limiter An electronic unit that does not allow, in sound or image, a particular aspect of a multiple signal to exceed a preset limit. Used for eliminating unwanted noise or intrusive background sound, or to alter image to a truer chromatic balance.

limpet mount Suction-cup camera mount which can be fastened to smooth surfaces, such as car hoods, tabletops, linoleum floors and even-surfaced ship decks. Named for the tenacious rock-clinging little gastropod, the limpet.

line The part of TV picture covered in one full horizontal sweep of the electron beam, moving from left to right across the screen. United States standard, at present, is 525 lines per picture.

line filter Device to block noise signals. In preventing unwanted noise signals from entering a receiver, it passes through the desired signals for proper reception.

line noise Noise interference of signals coming from transmission lines.

lines Principal foreground DIALOGUE, as opposed to the BACKGROUND burble of the crowd. Collectively, all the words in a script to be spoken by the performers.

line synchronizing impulse Impulse applied to the video signal at the end of each spanning line. This synchronizes reception of picture and sound.

lining up The process by which a CAMERAMAN sets up his or her camera to cover the desired field of view. Also the adjustment of the MONITOR viewfinder to correct for PARALLAX. Lining up is also called FRAMING.

lip mike A microphone sensitive to actual lip proximity or contact. Used in live performance situations, particularly rock concerts.

lip synch To match sound and picture to the actual movements of the lips as they say the recorded words, as opposed to matching FRAME numbers, edge-coded numbers or other references.

liquid-gate process Machine that immerses a film master or dupes in a chemical solution that fills in the scratches, thereby eliminating the refraction caused by them and ensuring that the scratches will not be projected onto the screen. The immersion liquid has the same index of refraction as the film base.

listening shots A CUTAWAY SHOT of the person listening to the actor delivering the dialogue. Used to intensify reactions, to break up long speeches or to cover a synch mistake by cutting to a listening shot and substituting a better audio take of the same dialogue.

live action On-screen action of live performers, as opposed to ANIMATION.

live announcer Station announcer who does live intros, segues and other required voice-overs for commercials, programs and special events.

live broadcast On TV or radio, an event—sports, news, interview—that is being aired as it is taking place.

live direct See DIRECT PICKUP.

live end Part of a radio studio or sound-recording studio where the sound reflectance is the highest.

live-on-tape Broadcast that is taped live in real performance time, not to be postedited.

live room One with a high degree of reverberance. This is accomplished by having many sound reflective surfaces in a room, with a minimal number of sound-absorbing items: drapes, rugs, etc. Used for basic high-reverberancy recording; or in conjunction with an echo chamber.

live sound Sound recorded on-the-spot during filming, as opposed to sound reproduced from prerecorded effects. Also refers to dialogue.

live tag Live portion of a commercial left open for local or regional announcements made live by a staff announcer. For example, a hit Broadway show might be on tour, and is currently playing in Omaha. The basic commercial, fully produced with composite sound, music, voice and picture, is played, and when the open spot is reached (usually at the end of the commercial, with music under), the local announcer gives the time and place of the Omaha performances. Or an automobile commercial might have a similar open section where the local dealer can insert his specific plug. This is sometimes referred to as a dealer spot.

load To put film into a camera, either internally threading it, or by attaching a film MAGAZINE. Analogous use for VIDEO-TAPE.

loader One who handles the above tasks, particularly in film.

local channel Standard broadcasting channel used to service several stations in an area. Range of approximately 200 watts to 1000 watts maximum per station. A channel taking incoming signals from the main station and rebroadcasting

them, or taping them for a later broadcast.

local control Hands-on supervision at the transmitter, in contradistinction to REMOTE CONTROL.

location Any film or videotape setting, interior or exterior, outside of the studio or production company.

location fee Permit fee paid to use any locale for filming or videotaping purposes.

location lighting Lighting set up on location sites, interior or exterior. Location lighting, when possible, uses lightweight gear and on-the-spot cabling, with or without a generator.

location manager Production staff member in charge of scouting and/or logistics of a LOCATION shoot. Sometimes this is a line producer, UNIT MANAGER or production manager. See LOCATION SCOUT.

location scout A person who goes ahead of the PRODUCTION UNIT, often weeks or months in advance, to shoot still pictures of potential LOCATION sites, check out contacts, accommodations, permits, and gather all charts, production sheets, names and statistics relating to the upcoming location shoot. See LOCATION MANAGER.

log A detailed film report of shoots and sound, as well as schedule and logistics. Each department makes out its own special log or report. See REPORT.

Also, a complete in-house list at a radio or TV station of every program broadcast, and on what date and at what time.

Also, an official governmental roster, or one that is privately published, both covering the same materials: station (radio or TV) frequencies, power, geographical location; listed by call letters.

logo A visual symbol that immediately signifies a product or organization. Sometimes the logo is also the trademark.

lo-mode (STEADICAM term) A camera mounted below the Steadicam arm instead of above, at ankle level instead of eye-level, and monitored with a TV-assist or approximated by eye. Used for fight scenes, particularly when the two fighters are grappling on the ground; as an animal's point of view as it stalks or runs; for shots of men marching while concentrating on the masses of feet moving in cadence; for natural-motion low shots, in general.

longitudinal scratches Marks running through a specified length of film.

long play records Or more commonly, "LPs." The term came in the late 1940s with the appearance of numerous speeds that extended the playing time of recorded discs. Eventually 33⅓ rpms became the standard. To this was added shorter selections on 45 rpm "donut" discs—because of the large hole in the center for an adapter disc that slid over the spindle. The 45s were dubbed EXTENDED PLAY, or "EPs." These two speeds, and lighter weight discs than the 78 rpm standards, are now being replaced by cassettes and CDs.

long shot (LS) Shot including the subject and surroundings, or one of the subject at a great distance. The latter is sometimes referred to as an EXTREME LONG SHOT. Formerly called a FAR SHOT.

loop A slack section of film that provides play when the film is being fed from a continuously moving to an intermittently moving SPROCKET. For DUBBING or SOUND EFFECTS, a loop is a continuous band of film or tape that passes through a projector or other viewing device or through a sound reproducer, particularly when repeated playings are required. Loops are used for instructional purposes, as guide tracks for DUBBING, and as vehicles for continuous SOUND EFFECTS in re-recording.

looping Sound and voice augmentation or replacement of the existing tracks.

Voice looping often requires LIP SYNCH; at other times, it can be to a specific CUE, e.g., an OFF-SCREEN voice, but it still must fall on the exact FRAME. It is done by utilizing a continuous visual LOOP that is locked into a recording unit and making a number of TAKES, one after another, until the desired take(s), and often a protection take, are laid down. The SCENE-numbered takes are voice-slated and marked as to those preferred. (To voice-slate is to call off take number into a recording microphone.)

loose framing A shot with a considerable amount of space between the subject and the frame edges, allowing for movement within the frame.

lose light To reach a point in the day's exterior shooting where it is too dark to get the necessary light meter reading to make a shot. "Hurry up and get your shot, before we lose the light!" is a common admonition to the cameraman from the director or to both of them from the production manager. This late-afternoon warning, or earlier on if it's clouding over, is an alert to push to the maximum to get as much filming done before the sky becomes too dark, for whatever reason. Or if the shooting is taking advantage of the A.M. LIGHT, the shooting must be done quickly in order to capture those few prime minutes.

lose the loop For film loop to slip out of the drive-mechanism threading pattern; for it to "jump the film track." If a loop is lost, either in the camera or projector, the device must be shut off immediately, or sprockets will be bent, spindled and mutilated.

loss Energy diminution in a signal while it is being sent from one point to another. This decrease in power transmission is generally measured in decibels.

lot The entire land area of a motion picture studio, including buildings, scene docks, standing exterior sets, etc. The back-lot is a name for special scenic areas with building facades and streets, e.g., European street, western street, waterfront and spill tank.

Louma State-of-the-art crane with a camera that is remote-controlled. Since the crane has a minimum arm of 26 feet, this extension and flexibility allow for many styles and combinations of sophisticated camera moves. Cameramen control its multiple or simple moves with hands-on controls. The results are checked with video monitors.

low angle A camera position in which the camera is pointing upward. Low angles tend to make the on-camera performers look larger than life. The low angle can also intensify the threat of a HEAVY or make the protagonist more heroic in stature. Also called low shot.

low band TV channels 2–6, which have a frequency range of 54–88 MHz. An FCC band allocation.

low contrast An extended range of tones in either color or black and white that soften the edges of "contrasty" images.

low definition TV A total TV interlocked system using less than 200 scanning lines per frame, as opposed to the commercial or professional 525. See HIGH DEFINITION TV.

low filter One designed to filter out turntable's rumble, system-operations interference of signals, player-head resonance, etc. This audio circuit removes these low-frequency noises from audio material.

low frequency noise See EXCESS NOISE.

low hat A truncated version of the HIGH HAT, used for mounting on a board or metal plate base in order to lock in the camera at an extremely low level; or for a tripod extension that doesn't require

quite the additional height provided by the HIGH HAT.

low-key Lighting that emphasizes the darker end of the lighting scale. See also HIGH-KEY.

low-noise lamps Lamps manufactured to emit minimal or no NOISE. This is so that the unwanted light-hum sound can be overcome and not picked up by the recording microphones.

low shot See LOW ANGLE.

lubricant Generally, a wax compound in a volatile solvent such as carbon tetrachloride. This lubricant is put onto the film itself, particularly at the edges, to reduce friction. This in turn makes the feed-through of the film much easier.

lumen A measuring unit to determine the rate of luminous flux, the level at which light pulses are emitted or received.

luminaire A full lighting unit: housing, lamp, cord and, sometimes, lamp stand.

luminance Calibrated measure of BRIGHTNESS. Light measured on motion picture screens in footlamberts, or CANDELAS per square foot.

luminance channel The color-TV path for carrying the luminance, i.e., the black-and-white matrix of the color-picture signal.

luminescent screen One that exhibits luminosity in areas excited by electron beams. These luminous displays are most often seen on the picture-end of a cathode-ray tube encased in a TV set.

lux Working reference-unit of illumination in the metric system. One lux is equivalent to one meter-candle. It is the illumination of an area of one square meter wherein there is an evenly spread flux of one lumen.

M

macrocinematography   Filming of small objects and details within photos, drawings or objects themselves by using a MACRO LENS, extension rings, diopters, etc.

macro lens   Detail LENS for extreme CLOSE-UP cinematography; tabloid filming. It can focus on details quite close to the camera.

made-for-TV movies   Films or videotapes made primarily for release on television; regular network, syndication, cable network; as well as film movies that hold up as regular theatrical fare for movie houses. The nature of the more rapid financing and production pace of made-for-TV movies allows them to be more "immediate," with subjects that can range from a recent terrorist act to an ongoing political scandal, to disease-of-the-month, or to current causes. But movies that have been miniseries have been effective with a fairly high percentage of the potential audience share. For example, *Roots, Shogun, Marco Polo,* the first two from best-selling novels. More recently, with the advent of upgrading of made-for-cable fare, we have seen miniseries, dramatic, docudrama and documentary coming to the fore.

magazine   Film container forming an integral part of a camera or projector. Camera magazines are light-tight; the film enters and leaves them through light traps.

magazine format   A TV program structure with stories that are current but not as-it's-happening news. The stories are usually shot in varying locations and may be augmented by earlier news coverage. They run two minutes or more— longer than the news "stories" on the regular newscasts. The magazine style can be used within a news program, or by using a series of such stories to comprise a full program. This format serves for such sensational shows as "Current Affairs" to the much-honored, respected and feared "60 Minutes."

magenta   Purplish color obtained by a mixture of red and blue light. A scene is color-balanced by reducing or increasing the magenta, or by letting it stay as it is.

magnetic   In media pertaining to magnetism as a working force, i.e., magnetic as opposed to optical tracks on film, as an adjective describing recording in general.

magnetic cartridge   The electronic element in a phonograph pickup arm that takes recorded sounds and converts them into electrical energy, which is reconstituted as emitted auditory sound signals.

magnetic film   Sound film, sound-striped or full-coated with iron oxide, for recording and reproducing sound: dialogue, music, effects; and for mixing.

magnetic recorder   As opposed to optical recorder. A SOUND CAMERA or separate machine that can play back sound immediately after recording it, without further processing.

magnetic starter   An electromagnetically activated starter in a system or device.

magnetic storer   An information storage unit that uses magnetism to retain data.

magnetic transfer   An electronic copy of a tape from one medium to another, like from videotape to master.

magoptical projector   One that takes both optical and magnetic track films.

magoptical release print   Print with both stripes on it: optical and magnetic.

main title   The graphic title that presents the name of the film. It also refers to the music that accompanies this title.

makeup Face and body cosmetics for on-camera people. Also used as a verb, to apply makeup to the performer.

makeup artist See MAKEUP PERSON.

makeup person One in charge of applying MAKEUP to the performers for their appearance in front of the camera. For bodily areas other than the face and hands that require makeup, or for nude scenes, a special body makeup person is used. Also called a makeup artist.

makeup table An extension of a projection unit or a separate table for assembling film reels as they are received into one long continuous reel for projection on a large feedout platter.

male plug Electrical connection plug, the prongs of which interlock with the receiving female plug.

management of news The constant monitoring and attempted instances of governmental or private organizations to neutralize stories, change the slant, or totally suppress them. During the breaking of the Watergate story the federal government brought pressure on newspapers and television against carrying the story, pleading security breaches, privacy invasions and lawsuits against the offending media would be swift and expensive. Nevertheless, the media persisted, particularly the *Washington Post,* and what had been a "current event" became history. Sponsors on radio and TV will often complain that the news coverage is too "liberal," i.e., it targets sacred cows indiscriminately without giving them what the rich, powerful, conservative or orthodox regard as "proper preferential treatment." Station executives themselves have been known to suppress investigative reporting, particularly of stories that are directly critical of long-time sponsors. For example, an oil-spill scandal can be minimized by surface reporting, without commentary, particularly if the same company or one of its subsidiaries advertises heavily on that particular station.

Political groups—left, right and off-the-wall—are constantly threatening to carry out boycotts, demonstrations and write-in campaigns to sponsors against news programs that either ignore them or, in their eyes, give them unfair treatment. It is, though, impossible for a newscast to please everyone.

M and E tracks Music and effects tracks used in mixing; one track can contain both elements or one track can have composite music, the other composite sound. This allows for dialogue replacement or narration lay-ins in any language necessary for the re-mix, or for a music video where the dialogue is not used.

man-in-the-street A reportage technique starting with on-the-spot radio reporters, who would ask questions regarding the on-site event from passersby who happened to have witnessed it. Also used to take an informal opinion poll. The technique was later used in commercials, on both radio and television, using the actual on-the-spot people or actors who simulate them. Such simulations must now be identified as "dramatizations." This is done to avoid misleading the audience, as sending out erroneous or slanted information is a breach of public trust.

manual dimmer Hand-operated light-dimmer board.

mark Visual guide to indicate where an actor is to be at a point in the scene; anything preselected and agreed upon by actor and director as a stopping point is a mark. On floors inside a studio, GAFFER'S TAPE or chalk is used for marking. In an open field an "X" might be drawn on the ground, or a rock put down as a stopping guide. An example of a preset eye-spotted mark would be an actor driving up to and stopping at a gasoline pump where the mark is the center of the first pump.

market research In media studies market research is the gathering of data relating to audience composition by nationality, age, sex, occupation, etc. This information is used to determine viewing habits and the potential of the viewing audience to use a sponsor's product(s) or service(s). Nearly all information for use in determining demographic viewership and buying tendencies is now computerized from the raw field-data and made available to the media for a databank service fee for access. Also, such information is sent to users in printed newsletters, special update sheets, monthly or quarterly reports and magazines.

mark it Direction to the camera assistant with the slate to put the scene-numbered slate into the shot; if it's a sound take, to voice-slate it as well as clapping the STICKS together. Sometimes, it has been pre-voice-slated by the soundman, and just the slate needs to be clacked.

marquee A signboard that is often cantilevered out in front of a theater. It has movable letters that spell out the names of the attractions and the stars. Most contemporary marquees are built flush to the building area that houses the theater. This is especially true of the new multiple minitheaters.

married Picture and sound put together on one strip of film. Also used to imply "burdened with," as is in, "Are we married to that piece of dialogue, or can we change it?"

Mary Tyler Moore (MTM) A major producing organization for series and movies-of-the-week; it's known by its kitten-in-a-circle logo—a parody of the MGM lion.

mask A frame-device for limiting passage of light, mounted in front of a TV picture tube. This defines the viewing area of the TV screen.

In photoprocessing, a blocking-out device for shielding special pre-set areas of the photosensitive material.

masking A projected image that is restricted in size by black borders, either from the screen or due to specially-cut aperture plates.

mass culture The quantitative, majoritarian arts that are disseminated through mass media, in the performing arts and publication, as well as graphic arts, sculpture and architecture when publicized by such media. The *Mona Lisa,* Taj Mahal, Beethoven's Fifth and Ninth symphonies are now part of mainstream mass culture. Mass culture reflects society and major movements in the arts, and influences those movements directly. For example, motion pictures have influenced writing for live theater and the novel, as well as using novels and plays as bases for screenplays. It is still being vehemently argued whether democratization of the arts has given more people a wider view of all the arts, or cheapened the more substantive arts by forcing them to be competitive in the marketplace. Other ongoing debates include whether TV and movie violence is socially disruptive, even leading to "copycat" acts of brutality, or is cathartic, as is the violence in Greek tragedy; whether TV is "honest" in its news coverage, or is hemmed in by sponsor pressure and governmental caveats; and whether or not mass culture is basically "inferior" in artistic quality, driving out material of better quality, like Gresham's law in economics of bad money diluting and driving out the good.

mast Pole for an antenna. This vertical metal pole can also serve as the antenna itself.

master Cut original negative ready for printing in composite form. Synonym for ORIGINAL. Prints are often struck from a SUBMASTER (one generation away from the master), while the master itself is vaulted for later runs of additional submasters or direct prints.

master brightness control In a three-gun video tube, a variable control used to adjust the bias on all three color-guns.

master control A control board of interconnected elements housing the main operating device. The switching matrix for TV programs, where signals are switched control-board-to-transmitter(s), or to other terminals or relays.

master positive A color-corrected and timed print struck from the original negative.

master scene See MASTER SHOT.

master script The final SHOOTING SCRIPT from which all others are duplicated for use by cast, crew and production staff.

master shot The complete scene covering all dialogue and action in the widest and longest shot. Into the COVERAGE of this scene are added medium shots, CLOSE-UPS, CUTAWAY SHOTS, etc. All of these shots are slated with variations of the basic master shot number. In coverage, the problem of matching physical actions is sometimes handled by simultaneous multicamera filming. In whatever manner it is made, the master shot is the referrent to which all else is edited, and to which all other action must be matched. Also called a master scene.

master station See KEY STATION.

master switch See BLACKOUT SWITCH.

match cut Straight CUT from image to image in which the second image relates visually and directly to the previous image.

match dissolve A DISSOLVE that joins together filmically similar or symbolically analogous images, like from a cross on a steeple to a cemetery cross.

matched load Electronic method for terminating transmission lines or waveguides so that all the energy from the signal force will be fully absorbed.

match-image cut A CUT in which we go directly from one image to an analogous one, from a spinning dancer to a spinning top. From one shot to another

that is kindred in movement, feeling or form.

matching In NEGATIVE CUTTING, a frame-to-frame lineup of original material for execution of the final cut. Also called conforming. In live-action filming, the conformity of movement and camera direction. For example, coverage of a prizefight is always handled so that it can be properly innercut with the MASTER SHOT to the matching FRAME. In SCRIPT CONTINUITY, the visual conformity from one day's shooting to the next, in order to have consistency of wardrobe, hair, props, etc. A mismatch would be to see a man shaving, fully lathered; he hears the doorbell ring, turns and he is already half-shaved. Mismatches happen often when two or three pieces of contiguous action within a scene are filmed on different days or with a lunch break intervening, or when one SCRIPT CLERK is replaced by another in the middle of a shoot, or through error of notation, and many other reasons relating to the fact of production pressures and human fallibility.

matching stock FILM STOCK of the same EMULSION NUMBER or lab batch number, or a stock that will effectively intercut with it. It also means the process of editing staged action, using film or videotape to match the existing STOCK FOOTAGE, or setting up the live action shots to match such footage.

matrix The mould to duplicate disc recordings. Rapidly being phased out in favor of CD and audiocassette manufacturing techniques.
  In a color TV set, matrix refers to the red, green and blue elements that create the corresponding signals.

matte An optical device or process for changing or obstructing light, on its way to form a photographic image. Mattes are not essentially different from masks; but the term "matte" is employed more often to the camera and its functions, "mask" to the color and optical printer. When in synch with film rolls being duplicated, they are called "matte rolls" or "traveling mattes." See also MATTE FINISH.

matte bleed An imperfect matted image, resulting in the appearance on screen of the MATTE lines around the matted-in image.

matte box A mechanism mounted in front of a camera LENS that is designed to hold MATTES used in SPECIAL EFFECTS photography. The matte box is usually combined with a sunshade, and also accommodates FILTERS.

matte finish A softer, duller finish than GLOSSY, giving a more diffuse image.

matting Optical placement, filmically or electronically, of an image within a shot or scene.

matting out Eliminating the matte shot.

matte scan Computerized directions transmitted to, and carried out by, the camera filming of the matted scene. It was designed for greater accuracy-control of movement and the elimination of matte lines.

matte shot One in which one action is matted out and another piece of action (or static image) is laid in.

MC (emcee) A master of ceremonies or program host.

MCU See MEDIUM CLOSE-UP.

MDS See MINIMUM DISCERNIBLE SIGNAL.

mean carrier frequency The carrier frequency of a transmitter averaged to its at-rest mode within that frequency system.

means of communication Classic concept of defining the "messenger" by function or medium: message runner, wigwag signalman, radio announcer, sound waves, video signals, etc.

mechanical bandspread Tuning dial, lever, digital button, vernier device or other mechanism used to extend the rotation of the control knob, lengthening the selection field. This allows more accurate tuning in wave bands that are bunched closely together.

mechanical special effects In contradistinction to OPTICAL EFFECTS. Some on-camera "live" effects include ground fog rolling in, explosions, window shattering, fires, part of a building crumbling and ship models in tanks.

medium The particular communication form used in presenting the written material: radio, TV, CABLE, cassette, film, live performance, HOLOGRAPHY, AUDIO recording, or whatever medium or media are chosen. This could also include print media (newspapers, magazines, periodicals), which are not the subject of this dictionary but are also referred to as media.

medium close-up (MCU) A shot framed to show part of the torso, and the head and shoulders of the on-camera actor. In scenic terms, a shot between an already established medium shot and a CLOSE-UP. See also CLOSE-UP.

medium frequency The band-range of 300 to 3000 kHz (3 MHz).

medium lens One that is or approximates the normal focal length in the film gauge or mechanism being used.

medium long shot (MLS) Between a medium shot and a LONG SHOT. These terms are therefore relative to what have been established as close and long shots. In general parlance, a medium shot is one that frames part of a person or object; in reference to a person, it would be from the waist up and with sufficient headroom. The word *medium* is also used to produce the term MEDIUM CLOSE-

UP and medium-long shot. "Medium close" and "medium long" as script indications are being replaced by the all-encompassing *medium shot*, or by more descriptive and detailed instructions by the writer, which are often changed by the director. Many scripts are now written in MASTER SCENES as basic structural elements, and leave the camera placement to the DIRECTOR.

megahertz (MHz)   One million hertz.

melodrama   A film form in which the structure is built around plot and action, then characters. Melodrama tends toward sensationalism and overwrought emotions. Opera plots are usually rich in melodrama.

memorandum agreement   See DEAL MEMO.

men's costumer   An independent crew member or part of a studio's wardrobe department who supplies and maintains the men's costumes.

metaphor   Literal extension of a simile, i.e., assuming that something is something else, not merely like something else. For example, "The train snaked its way through the deep valley, crawling smoothly on its metallic belly, wiggling and twisting forward." A snake becomes the metaphor for the train. Metaphors are used to force comparisons ("an army of ants"), personalize the impersonal ("The hinges sang shrilly in warning as he opened the door"), create a sympathetic fallacy ("The stars wept when she left me"), legendize a character ("Paul Bunyan's pick-axe dragged along the ground for just a moment or two, long enough to create the Grand Canyon"), and for other language-intensifying purposes. In film, the metaphor is omnipresent, since metaphor is what film is all about—if not intentionally, then by symbolization and personification. For example, symbolization: In films where explorers or troops are dying of thirst in the deserts or on arid plains, water is not "like" life; water

is life and life is water—a coalescent metaphor. Personification: in Fritz Lang's 1926 silent classic *Metropolis,* the machines themselves take on personalities, at times heroic but usually threatening and sinister, until finally it is the city itself that becomes the antagonist, the "villain."

meter   A measuring device. As in light meter, voltometer, sensitometer, etc. Also, a unit of measurement in the metric system. A meter, used in most nations except the United States, England, and a few others, is the standard measure for film "footage." The meter is 39.37 inches or 3.281 feet.

method acting   Introspective and self-examining style of acting based on the work of Konstantin Stanislavsky of the Moscow Art Theatre. It employs techniques such as emotional recall, inner monologue, goal selection, and motivation. The goal of these elements, used singly or in combination, is to concentrate the actor's energies in creating an inner reality. All of these procedures are known collectively as "the method." Some well-known "method" actors are Dustin Hoffman, Jane Fonda, Shelley Winters, Montgomery Clift, Marlon Brando, James Dean, Sir John Gielgud, Maureen Stapleton and Eli Wallach.

Metro-Goldwyn-Mayer   (MGM)   One of the major motion picture studios, located in Culver City, California. The Goldwyn part of the name was from Samuel Goldwyn, who left MGM to set up his own studio and production company in Hollywood, on what was formerly the original United Artists lot. The Goldwyn Studios are now part of the Warner Communications complex, and are called Warner's Hollywood. Meanwhile, Lorimar Pictures took over the MGM studio and lot, while MGM merged with UNITED ARTISTS to form MGM/UA, with their main thrust being film and television distribution.

MGM   See METRO-GOLDWYN-MAYER.

mic   See MICROPHONE.

mickey mouse   To over-accentuate sound effects and music to match image, e.g., for the music to mimic a duck's waddle when we see the duck walking.

microbar   A unit of acoustical pressure. One microbar equals one dyne per square centimeter.

microphone   A transducer in which sound waves are produced electroacoustically; it emits equivalent electric waves. An electronic audio-input device. Also called mic or mike.

microphone amplifier   Audio amplifier that increases microphone output before signals arrive at the main audio-frequency amplifier.

microphone boom   A pole to hold a microphone so that it can be moved into a scene—usually above it—rapidly and silently. It can be part of a whole boom unit with a telescoping arm, impelled with a pulley cable mechanism or a simple metal pole, held by the boom man.

microphone cable   Fully encased and protected cable connecting the microphone to the microphone amplifier.

microphone fade   A fade made not from the board, but by the performer moving into the mike (fade on) or away from it (fade off). This physical movement creates a different "ambience" than that of an electronic fade. Mic fade for short.

microphone filter   Electronic device for screening out high and low frequencies. Informally, and in working situations, "mic filter."

microphone mixer   A basic audio-mixing unit for two or more microphones, balancing input coming in to an audio amplifier. Each microphone input line has its own adjustment knob, button or lever, so that it can be controlled separately.

microphone placement   Situating microphones to achieve the required sound balance in a filming, videotaping, live broadcasting or recording session.

microphone shadow   A shadow cast by the microphone onto some object or person in the field of view of the camera. These shadows must be eliminated before shooting can begin, through the alteration of the microphone, camera, lights or actors.

microphonics   Internal noise generation within the microphone's connective system, not coming from the microphone itself.

microwave   Frequency level of radio waves in the 1000-megahertz-plus range. Used extensively for point-to-point communications, since they can be generated and transmitted as a concentrated beam. Widely used for telephonic communications, and to satellite transmissions of audio and video signals to line-of-sight target receivers up to a range of approximately 50 miles. The microwave system is used often for cable TV and general television linkage, as well as for telephonic and data transmissions; and, of course, microwave ovens. See MICROWAVE RELAYS.

microwave relays   A system of ultra-high-frequency transmitters that can be interlinked in various combinations. For communications: audio, video, data-bank. Predominantly multichannel.

middle ground   See FOREGROUND.

mike   See MICROPHONE.

mimetic   Imitative, as in mime. The basis of all acting. The make-believe mimicry of the craft attempts to elevate it to an "art" without fully understanding that a master craftsman is an artist. The early Greeks drew no line between "craftsman" and "artist." From the Greek word *mimikos,* to initiate, particularly in the style of a mime.

miniature A model used in films to appear its "normal" size. For example, if a building is seen blowing up, a scale model is usually used, for obvious reasons. Another example would be a square-rigged ship burning and sinking. A miniature can be anything from a scale-model PROP to an entire SET or street.

minimum discernible signal (MDS) The smallest input signal going into a receiver that will result in discernible output from that receiver.

minimum wages In union parlance, these minimums are referred to as scale. Each union has its own scale, plus a schedule for overtime and rules of employment for both employer and employee. See SCALE.

mirror An optical device designed to focus or reflect light moving through a camera's viewfinder to the eyepiece. In PROJECTORS, the light moves from the lamphouse unit to the projector's film plane, and onto the receiving screen. Generally any device that gives a high, accurate reflectance of a given image.

mirror reflex shutter A shutter with a silver coating. When closed it reflects light coming into the camera into an integral viewfinder. This allows direct viewing of the filmed image instead of approximating it with parallax viewfinder.

mirror shot A shot that includes a mirror in which the actor's reflection is seen. An ingenious use of the mirror-shot is in the original British horror classic *Dead of Night,* in which we see the man and his reflection in the mirror. But the room we see in the mirror is not the same one in which the man is standing, but a strange and sinister room, with a blazing fireplace and deep shadows. Also, a mirror shot refers to shooting with a semitransparent mirror for superimpositions of either live action, mechanical or projected images.

miscast Wrongly chosen for a part in a film or videotape; being the wrong type for the role or not having the requisite qualifications.

mise-en-scène The total action-image, created by elements such as performers, the setting itself, costumes, LIGHTING and PROPS. The full visual effect.

misplaced emphasis In creating an attention-arresting lead, it is vital to open with the most dramatic details of the story. In TV news, the attention must be caught and held from the first sentence, or the viewer may switch channels.

miss the mark Opposite of "Hit the mark." To not quite reach or to overshoot a preset mark for a camera move or a move by an actor. In broader usage, it means not to come up to performance level, or to go off on a tangent not directly appropriate or even relevant to the TV program or motion picture.

Mitchell One of the major picture camera manufacturers. Most of the leading motion picture studios in the United States, and many international studios, relied on the Mitchell as "the" camera from the days of sound to the advent of the wide screen. It began to be replaced in the 1950s and early 1960s by the new, less-expensive, lightweight and quiet-running cameras, or by the self-blimped models from Europe like the Arriflex or Eclair.

mix The process of combining separate SOUND TRACKS into a single track. Also, "the mix" is a noun, describing the final product of the mixing session.

mixed highs Color TV transmission of extremely fine detail for accurate reproduction. This is accomplished by transmitting high frequency elements within the luminance signal matrix, resulting in achromatic reproduction.

mixed media A blend within one program or presentation of many media elements: LIVE ACTION, tape images, film, slides, graphics, special lighting and music, and customized sound effects, e.g., Disney's audioanimatronic shows often incorporate live performers, film, simulated holographic images and videotape. The intermeshing of STILL slides or film with LIVE ACTION is a common combination. Often used for trade shows, corporate-image extravaganzas and direct dramatized sales pitches.

mixer   The senior member of a sound-recording crew, in charge of balance control of the DIALOGUE, music, or SOUND EFFECTS to be recorded. Today, more often on less complex mixing sessions, the "crew" is often one person.

Also, the sound recording or reproducing system or device, capable of handling two or more inputs, in conjunction with a common output.

mixing board   Another name for the CONSOLE used in a mixing session. It allocates separate channels for the audio tracks that are to be mixed and blends them into a mixed track.

MLS   See MEDIUM LONG SHOT.

mobile transmitter   A radio or TV TRANSMITTER mounted and operated from a plane, train, automobile, truck, boat or ship.

mobile unit   Self-contained production unit for location filming or taping. It started with radio remote trucks, then to TV units for on-the-spot coverage to transmit sound and picture back to the station, to be broadcast over the station's channel. With the advent of the Cinemobile in the early 1960s, the same term now applies to motion pictures.

model   A person on-camera who demonstrates clothing or a product as someone describes it. See HAND MODEL.

A model is also a small replica, usually to scale of objects or people that is used in MECHANICAL SPECIAL EFFECTS.

modeling lights   KEY LIGHTs and FILL LIGHTs, for example, LIGHTING units that create BACKLIGHTING, HIGHLIGHTs, shadows on actors and setting. Distinguished from BACKGROUND or SET lights.

modulated wave   Carrier wave whose amplitude, frequency or phase varies with the composition of its intelligence signal(s).

modulation   An altering of a sound signal by itself or as it is visually manifested on an optical sound track, or as it stands, nonvisually, on a magnetic track.

modulator   Final audio-frequency stage in a transmitter, in which the a-f signal combines with the r-f carrier signal.

module   An interlinking component in an electronic system. A unit within that system with a specially designated, and usually repetitive, function.

moiré   An originally unwanted rippled effect caused by imprecise overlapping of the image lines of a televised image. It is now used for special backgrounds on commercials, industrials and music videos. Unplanned-for moiré effects, however, are still unwelcome.

monaural recorder   Signal channel recording unit, in contradistinction to stereophonics, binaural, multichannel, etc. Technical nomenclature, rarely used, is "monophonic recorder."

money line   The story line that can be compressed and presented succinctly and dramatically, for use in ads, publicity releases, mini-identifications in TV logs, etc. Also, the strong dramatic plot line of a dramatic work.

monitor   The screen on which televised images can be evaluated, either in the studio or in the control room. Actually, one's TV set is a mass-produced monitor. In a TV control room situation, each camera has its own corresponding monitor screen, augmented by a master screen that shows which camera has been chosen for a given segment of coverage.

In the verb form "to monitor," the reference is to overseeing production sounds and images.

monitoring viewfinder See VIEW-FINDER.

monkey chatter Noisy burble of interfering music, dialogue or sound effects from sources outside the desired channel. This happens when channels ajoining the selected program channel impinge on that signal.

monochromatic Photographic images in the white-to-black range, with intervening shades of gray.

monochrome Black-and-white photography.

monochrome transmission TV transmission of gradations of a single color only.

monologue Extended speech for a single person. A monologue can be part of a scene, e.g., an instructor briefing a class. Or it can be isolated, as when Hamlet walks away from the others in the scene to deliver his monologue, or when he is discovered alone and gives the speech. In film or on videotape the monologue can be delivered by the performer's voice-over, while the camera holds on the actor as his reactions are seen to be his own inner monologue. This technique has also been used at times on stage in live theater productions.

monopack Cinematography with a single strip of film, as opposed to the Technicolor three-strip system or multi-camera systems.

monopod A one-legged camera support for rapid shots demanding instant set-ups; a surrogate tripod for reportage situations.

montage In common American usage the term refers to a type of editing assembly using numerous CUTS, DISSOLVEs and superimpositions rapidly following one another, to produce a unified visual effect. Broadly, all putting together of film, cut by cut, is montage assembly.

mood music Synonym for BACK-GROUND MUSIC, particularly music that arouses appropriate emotional responses in the audience, relevant to a specific scene.

MOS An early film abbreviation for "minus optical sound." It is a slate indication noting a SHOT that is without sound.

motif A theme identification, used repeatedly throughout the film, to refer to a particular person, or a recurring mood-of-scene: heroic, mysterious, romantic (the "love theme"), warfare, etc. Used originally in the first Italian operas, it was later rediscovered and codified into a musical philosophy by Richard Wagner, who was much imitated by motion picture composers.

motion picture Also called a "movie" or "film." The film itself as seen projected is a series of images that, because of their speed and contiguousness, give an appearance of motion. This induced motion is the basis of all motion pictures. With television videotape moving at 30 frames per second, however, the motion picture cameras, in some cases, are now being converted from 24 to 30 frames per second. This makes the filmed images more compatible to TV conversion. The use of videographics integrated with film today makes many "films" into living examples of mixed media. This is particularly true in the field of SPECIAL EFFECTS and in filmed MTV presentations. But filming primarily in motion picture stock still makes the total unit a motion picture, especially if the end product is on film print for viewing.

Motion Picture Association of America (MPAA) A group for promoting the international dissemination of American films. Also, one of its functions is the assigning of audience rating: "G" for general audience; "PG" for parental guidance; "PG-13" for parental guidance when viewed by children under the age of 13; "R" for restricted; and "NC-17" for adults only.

motion picture camera   A machine for filming. It is a lightproof device with a film-drive mechanism to move the film through the camera's threading pattern, exposing it. The exposed film moves to a light-exclusion chamber; when the roll is completely exposed, the film is unloaded in a darkroom or with a changing bag, placed in a black lightproof bag, which is then placed in the film can and taped shut to eliminate any chance of light striking the film. This camera-exposed film is then marked "exposed," and properly identified as to production company and film title or number, and taken to the lab for development.

motion picture copyright   Films can be registered with the copyright office in Washington, D.C. "Motion picture" includes not only films, but also video tapes that can be projected or exhibited. See COPYRIGHT.

motion picture film   Long film strips in professional gauges of 16, 35, 65mm; light-sensitive and packaged in rolls of standard lengths: 100, 200, 400, 1000 and 2000 feet. The basic stock used for making motion pictures. Also referred to as FILM STOCK.

motion picture music   Basic ownership of the music, if obtained from a composer not working on staff, resides primarily with the composer. Any fractionated rights are usually for a specific medium, and for a specific time period. This applies to background and title music as well as songs and production numbers.

motion picture projector   A machine that throws film images onto a screen. Projectors in motion picture theaters are all sound equipped and usually 35mm or a widescreen 65/70mm, some-times with anamorphic lenses. For home movies, the most common widths are Super 8, 16mm and at one time Super 16, with projectors to match the filming gauges. Such projectors come in both silent and sound models. Currently, however, the home video cameras are rapidly replacing their motion picture counterparts.

motivated action   In the Stanislavsky "method," an internal reaction that externalizes itself in movement. A movement of a camera or performer for an apparent dramatic reason, rather than just for the sake of frenetic dynamics.

motorboating   Irritating noise from misaligned film passing over the sound drum. The sound "reading" beam reads the perforations, not the soundtrack.

movie   Another name for MOTION PICTURE.

moving coil microphone   One that employs a coil moving through a magnetic field, in reaction to the movement of the microphone diaphragm. The diaphragm vibrates in response to SOUND waves, and the coil's movement creates an electrical signal.

Moviola   The trade name of a portable motor-driven film-viewing machine, upright or table variety, with the latter replacing the former. It is used for viewing but primarily for editing. Although there are now numerous flatbed editing units manufactured by numerous companies, they are still often referred to, no matter the mark, as "moviolas."

MPAA   See MOTION PICTURE ASSOCIATION OF AMERICA.

MTM   See MARY TYLER MOORE.

MTV   See MUSIC TELEVISION.

muddy   See BOOMY.

multi-image   Two or more pictures appearing simultaneously on the film or

TV screen. This is done by fractionating the screen into discrete images, as in the SPLIT SCREEN process, or by overlapping the images as in a DISSOLVE or superimposition. Fast-cut images, because of the persistence-of-vision, as seen, for example in KINESTASIS, are sometimes described as multi-image.

multimedia See MIXED MEDIA.

multiplane Shooting animation through various horizontal or vertical transparent layers to give a greater sense of depth and allow for more detailed backgrounds.

multiple camera A filming approach of simultaneous shooting with two or more cameras, placed in predetermined position so that the action can be properly innercut in the editing process.

multiple exposure Re-exposing the same length of film to a new image while in-camera or in the lab for as many times as necessary to achieve the requisite interlocking, overlapping or superimposed image.

multiple-frame printing Repeat printing, as needed, of one frame at a time, as in a FREEZE-FRAME.

multiple image Various cleanly delineated images within one frame; sometimes shooting the graphic that is already prepared to appear as it is filmed. It can be regarded as a montage of still pictures within one frame.

multiple roles Many characters in one dramatic work, played by *one* actor. For example, Alec Guinness in *Kind Hearts and Coronets,* Tony Randall in *The Seven Faces of Dr. Lao,* Peter Sellers in *The Mouse That Roared,* and Danny Kaye in *The Secret Life of Walter Mitty.* A more recent example of actors playing multiple roles is Eddie Murphy and Arsenio Hall in *Coming to America.* See DUAL ROLES.

multiple screen A filming-and-projection process. The simultaneous or contrapuntal showing of two or more images on two or more screens. Sometimes the same image is repeated on all screens for emphasis and impact, at other times each screen is showing different material, and in multiscreen presentations (at places such as world expos or at the various Disney theme parks), two, three, five, or nine screens are all showing a single motion picture image fractionated into the number of matching screens. See CIRCLEVISION.

multi-track magnetic system Recording with two or more magnetic tracks.

musical comedy A musical-dramatic form often filmed or televised. Developed from the English musical stage and the Spanish zarzuela. The original form included songs with spoken dialogue that was punctuated by musical numbers. Later developments in America and England have resulted in many of the newer works being musicals that derive their structure more from opera. There has been a further tendency for book and lyrics to be less formulaic and more substantive, so that the "comedy" part of a so-called musical comedy is often seriocomic or even tragic. This has resulted in the more frequent and simplified term, "musical."

musical contractor The person responsible for hiring the musical performers or orchestra members, or for subcontracting a complete musical-performing unit.

musical director Person in charge of seeing that music is composed or selected for the film, and is orchestrated and copied. He or she also supervises the scoring sessions and in some cases conducts them. Sometimes the musical director is also the composer.

music and effects tracks See M AND E tracks.

music clearance Establishing the right to use published music or that in the public domain. If published, there will be a royalty fee which can be negotiated or waived. See COPYRIGHT.

music library   An index or catalog of music cues and SOUND TRACKs of which a studio may wish to make repeated use—also, the tracks themselves.

Music Television (MTV)   A cable-TV station that plays music videos and features music-related news, interviews and concerts. MTV primarily plays rock and pop videos. This station has reinstituted the art of montage by intermingling live action, special effects and computer graphics.

music track   The final tracks to be used for the mix, to be blended with DIALOGUE and EFFECTS TRACKs to create the COMPOSITE sound track. Music tracks are often released, along with the motion picture, in specially re-recorded or rebalanced audio albums.

mute print   One without a sound track. Term used more in Great Britain than in the United States.

muting circuit   One that cuts off receiver output. When the circuit or carrier falls below a set limit, the circuit detector activates the shutdown.

mylar   Trade name for du Pont's strong, transparent plastic film. Used as a base in many magnetic tape stocks and in insulating uses in other electronic applications.

myriametric waves   Very low frequency band: 3–30 kHz.

N

NAB   See NATIONAL ASSOCIATION OF BROADCASTERS.

NABET   See NATIONAL ASSOCIATION OF BROADCAST EMPLOYEES AND TECHNICIANS.

Nagra   Standard state-of-the-art portable tape recorder, using ¼" reel-to-reel magnetic tape.

narration   OFF-SCREEN commentary spoken by a "name" NARRATOR who is a well-known personality, or by a professional-but-anonymous "voice-of-God" narrator who gives the words their tone of authority. Most INFORMATIONAL FILMS use an anonymous narrator. In a dramatic work, the narrator may be one of the characters in the story.

narration script   A reading script of narration text that is double- or triple-spaced, allowing for insertions and corrections. When necessary, SCENE indications are given.

narrator   The voice-over commentator who relates the story or explains points of information.

narrow band   Communication channel of a less-than-voice-grade level.

narrow-gauge film   Any strip of film narrower than the standard 35mm.

National Association of Broadcast Employees and Technicians (NABET)   A technical union that originated in the television industry to oversee filming assignments of TV crews.

National Association of Broadcasters (NAB)   Group of station owners, managers and their executive staffs. The NAB code sets standards of broadcasting practices. It sets ethical and business procedures in programming and advertising for members of NAB.

National Broadcasting Company (NBC)   Along with ABC and CBS, one of the three major television networks.

National Cable Television Association   The organization of cable system owners and operators.

National Television System Committee (NTSC) The American system of telecasting using a 3.58 MHz signal. The name is derived from this original group that created the United States' television standards for black and white transmission (between 1940 and 1941). The NTSC set up color television specifications that were accepted and approved by the Federal Commerce Committee. NTSC standards are now supervised, monitored and updated by the Advanced TV Systems Committee in Washington, D.C.

naturalism A style of realism showing characters in social events over which they have minimal or no control. Human values are implied rather than didactically stated.

natural light Exterior or interior visible sunlight, with enough candlepower for filming. Sometimes moonlight can provide enough light for high-speed film and fast lenses. Natural light is not man-made.

naturalness The look of casual, off-handed action or conversation. A style of acting used often in DOCUDRAMAS or regular dramatic works in which the appearance of reality is the goal. In commercials this means a delivery that has rough edges.

natural slow See FINE SLOW.

nature film Film of plants or animals in their natural geographical habitat. These documentaries are a typical staple of PBS and CABLE-TV.

NBC See NATIONAL BROADCASTING COMPANY.

NC-17 The new rating for films formerly released as X. See X-RATED.

NCTA See NATIONAL CABLE TELEVISION ASSOCIATION.

needle Vibrating tracking stylus used to play recorded discs. In equipment, an electronically-driven indicator of power levels.

needle drop MUSIC LIBRARY term referring to a single use of a music cue.

needle scratch See SURFACE NOISE.

negative Negative can refer to any of the following: RAW STOCK, specifically designed for a negative image; the NEGATIVE IMAGE itself; negative raw stock that has been exposed but not PROCESSED; or processed film bearing a negative image.

negative cost Refers to the total film costs, not merely the negative. The total is that of costs in all aspects, prior to RELEASE. It does not include costs of distribution and exhibition.

negative cutting Cutting the original NEGATIVE to match the edited work print, SHOT-by-shot and FRAME-by-frame. The large amount of footage to be catalogued, the necessity for exact correspondence of frame with frame, and the irreplaceability of the negative, impose exacting conditions upon negative CUTTERS. Also called negative matching.

negative filter An optical FILTER that attenuates those parts of the spectrum which are predominant constituents of daylight: the blue from the sky and the greens reflected from trees and grass. Consequently, night filters are *red* and used to produce night effects by day.

negative image A photographic image in which the values of light and shade of the original photographed subject are represented inversely. In a TV picture, the reverse of lights-and-darks; whites are seen as black and vice versa. This happens because the picture signal has a polarity opposite to a normal signal.

negative matching See NEGATIVE CUTTING.

negative numbers Same as EDGE NUMBERS, but a more commonly used term by manufacturers of RAW STOCK. An editor is more likely to refer to them as negative numbers.

negative-positive process Generic term for the normal process of 35mm black-and-white reproduction, whereby positive images are printed as NEGATIVES and vice versa.

negative pull Taking out the original film from the vault, and preparing it for NEGATIVE CUTTING.

neorealism Style that emerged in Italy after World War II, with films such as Rossellini's *Open City* (1945), and De Sica's *The Bicycle Thief*. It derived from the literary movement of NATURALISM and the stark realism of writing in the 1920s and 1930s. Often it had the feeling in style and diction of the street and real people in real situations. Amateurs were used completely or mixed with professional actors.

net DIFFUSER made of spun-glass gauze or metal.

network Group of intercommunicating stations, under one organizational head office. ABC, CBS, and NBC stations are run independently, as a rule, with access to NETWORK FEED.

network feed Programs emanating from the central network flagship station, or major affiliate, and picked up by regional network affiliates. The three major networks mostly program in New York and Los Angeles, with some programming from Chicago. The Turner Broadcasting System's main network and programming center is in Atlanta, Georgia.

neutral density A group of gray FILTERS with graded densities, used to minimize CONTRAST and cut down EXPOSURE.

news director Administrative supervisor over the production of news programs. Sends reporters and crews out on assignments and, if the station is small, he or she will also report a story from the field. The news director may also serve as broadcast anchor.

new versions An extension of the copyright, which allows for a new copyright of a work if it has been substantially altered and revised to constitute a new version. This allows the work to have a full copyright life, from the date of renewal.

New Wave *(Nouvelle vague)* Encompassing term for a group of young French filmmakers of the late 1950s, and their films: Francois Truffaut, Jean-Luc Godard, Louis Malle, Alain Resnais and others. The films used the new professional and lightweight sound and film equipment. Real-life settings avoided use or need of soundstages, and the directors attempted to achieve a more deeply psychological approach to their characters rather than stressing plot. The "realism" allowing such insights was also to be found in the true-life locales. When the New Wave movement emerged, French traditional filmmakers protested the New Wave's semi-improvisational and seemingly formless style. At a film conference in Paris, one of the traditionalists chided the new filmmakers with, "A film should have a beginning, middle and an end." One of the New Wave exponents replied, "Yes! But not necessarily in that order!"

NG takes Unusable shots, made so by error on the part of equipment, crew or cast. NG is an abbreviation for "no good." The term is also used for shot records, sound reports, and production and SCRIPT CLERKS' notes: "NG sound," "NG action," etc.

nickelodeon By compounding nickel and the classic Odeon theater of ancient Athens, the dryly humorous name for the early nickel-a-show storefront motion picture theaters was created.

Nickelodeon Network A cable network with programming for children in the morning and the entire family at night. The evening fare features such classic sitcom series as "Dennis the Menace," "Father Knows Best," "The Donna Reed Show," etc.

Nielsen Television Index (NTI) A rating index that regularly issues reports estimating TV networks' head counts. By using data available from sample households, the NTI can measure the networks' viewing audiences.

night filter One that cuts down EX-POSURE, or changes the overall color tint of a daylight shot, so that a nighttime effect is created.

night-for-night Nighttime equivalent of day-for-day. Filming night scenes at night, instead of shooting day-for-night.

nixie tube Glow tube converting electrical impulses into visual displays.

noctovision A no-light-necessary system for use indoors or outdoors-at-night. Usually utilizing invisible infra-red rays for scanning.

nodal points Two points on a lens that sends back the light ray, with the bounced-back ray being parallel to the original direction by which it entered.

noise Any extraneous sound tending to interfere with the proper and easy perception of desired sounds to be recorded. Unwanted noise can be internal or external to the systems like electrical shorts, power drops and miswirings or air conditioners, outside traffic and airplane fly-bys.

noise-cancelling microphone One that works effectively close to the mouth, thereby cutting out or reducing much ambient sound. Used in rock concerts and newsgathering in the field, especially when there are loud, surrounding environmental noises.

noise filter Choke coils/capacitors inserted between the cord of a radio or TV receiver and the electrical outlet, usually

in the wall. The FILTER blocks noise interference coming from the power line, preventing it from reaching the receiver.

noiseless camera A camera that has no internal NOISE-traps; self-BLIMPed.

noise level The ambient audible extraneous sound; its strength and duration, at a particular location. Or the presence and strength of unwanted noise within a circuit.

noise reduction Elimination or significant diminution of audio system noises by special circuitry.

nonconductor Material used for electrical insulation.

nondirectional microphone One that picks up sound equally from all directions. Also called omnidirectional.

nonhero Leading character in a literary or dramatic work who is not noble, uses wiles to seek certain ends, and often does not attain them or attains them only to find them empty. Alfie, in the film of that name, is an example, as is Archie Rice in *The Entertainer*. In literature the first "modern" nonhero was probably Fielding's Jonathan Wild. Also called AN-TIHERO.

nontheatrical Referring to films or videotapes outside a commercial venue, i.e., movie houses, special nonadmission locales, social clubs, churches, etc.

north Upper area of an animation field chart.

notching Practice of making a "V" cut on a film print to remove damaged perforations. Otherwise, a splice would be made by removing the problem frame(s). Notching should not be used if avoidable as it can and does lead to more extensive damage of the print.

nonsaturated color Impure color, tinged with white, or with its complementary color.

nonsynch See WILD RECORDING.

nonsynchronous Not in phase with another device, neither by frequency nor speed.

NTI See NIELSEN TELEVISION INDEX.

NTSC See NATIONAL TELEVISION SYSTEM COMMITTEE.

nudie A motion picture film exploiting the nude form, male and female, in a lightly scripted "story." Nudies made their prominent appearance in the 1950s as precursors of the X-rated, general-admission porno films.

null Balanced zero-output condition in a device or system.

numbering machines Machines for printing EDGE NUMBERs at regular intervals on RAW STOCK. The term is sometimes used when CODING MACHINE is meant.

nuts-and-bolts film A straightforward film discussing, describing and picturing processes or skills or implanting information. A 'HOW-TO' FILM is an example of a nuts-and-bolts film.

O

oater See HORSE OPERA.

objective camera Looking at a scene from the viewpoint of a spectator (the audience). As opposed to SUBJECTIVE CAMERA.

objectivity To present factual material without suffusing it with subjective bias. This paradigmatic ideal of certain journalists is an impossible goal, considering the matrix of survival instincts, prejudices and misinformation of which we are all composed. Perhaps "approximate truth" would be a better goal, aiming at the highest percentage of truth, as seen through the viewpoint of one individual. It is still a superior form to "truth by committee." Subjectivity at least allows for personal involvement and, sometimes, insight. See also EDITORIALIZING.

obligatory scene Mandatory scene that resolves plot points, crises and problems that have been introduced in telling the story. It sets up climaxes and the DENOUEMENT. In the media markets the term refers to a scene that must be included, in order to insure optimum audience-viewing. This includes the nude scene, the superviolent scene, the graphic sex scene, and other such miscellany. In this sense it is a synonym for the "gratuitous" scene, one called for not by dramaturgical logic, but by eager distributors.

obscenity Material offensive to one's moral concept. What is considered obscene varies from person to person. What is one man's obscenity is another's creative self-expression. X-rated films (now NC-17) can be given an adults-only rating for excessive violence as well as explicit sex, but that seldom happens.

octave Interval with a 2:1 ratio, between two frequencies. The U.S. reference frequency is 440 cycles, which gives us the musical note A.

octave filter Band-pass filter allowing passage of frequencies from a lower to higher limit, to twice the value.

off-camera Outside of the viewing range of the scene that is filmed; outside the perimeter of the action.

off-mike Outside or at the edge of the live-range pattern of a microphone.

off-screen (OS) Not in the FRAME, but immediately at hand.

off-the-record A caveat given by an interviewer to the newsgatherer or documentarian that means, "What I am going to say is totally unofficial and not be used in any way," or, "You can use what I say as long as you don't name the source." Whether or not the journalist names the source is more of an ethical point than a legal one. However, if a source requesting anonymity *is* named, the reporter is considered to have made an unethical breach of trust.

ohm   Unit of resistance. One ohm is the rated-value resistance of one volt maintaining a current of one ampere. The Greek letter omega (Ω) is the symbol for OHM.

oil switch   Electrical switch immersed in oil at the switch juncture, to minimize the activated arc and to reduce any damage to the contact points.

OK takes   As opposed to NG TAKES. These are the good takes that the editor can select from to make final choices in assembling the film or videotape.

omnidirectional microphone   See NONDIRECTIONAL MICROPHONE.

Omnimax system   Special wide-angle lens system to be used with the IMAX camera. The term also refers to the specially designed and custom-equipped theater in which Omnimax films are shown.

on call   A CREW or CAST member officially notified and waiting for the time and place to be given for filming.

on camera   Any person or thing in the shot that is being made.

one-light print   A noncorrected print, using one printing light level preset for the development of all the shots on the film original.

ones   In animation, the one-to-one EXPOSURE of one FRAME per one drawing: "We're shooting it in ones!"

one-shot   A shot of a single person. Also called a SINGLE. Two-shot means two people; three-shot, three, and so on. Over four or five is commonly referred to as a group shot. One-shot in its more general parlance, refers to a live special event, usually nonrepeatable, at which you have only "one shot" to get it, on film or videotape, like a live rock concert, a marathon race or a presidential inauguration.

In electronics, a circuit emitting a signal of fixed duration, despite duration of the input signal.

one thousand hertz tone   1000 Hz is the standard tone for audio measurement and adjustment.

on hold   Having been given a work STANDBY call, to be fully paid for the day, but not necessarily having to report to the SET or LOCATION. When the CAST or CREW member is on hold, he or she must be immediately accessible by phone. This ensures instant availability if called to the production locale on short notice. No additional assignments can be accepted that conflict with the "hold."

on-line   All pre-edited tapes tied into the tape-mastering units for the full mix. (See also MIX). The state of doing the final tape-edit, utilizing audio and video components prepared in the OFF-LINE sessions.

on location   Filming at a venue different from that of the studio, either emanating from the studio (i.e., for direct transport) or at a locale outside studio area; customarily, a circumference of 30–50 miles from the studio center. Union cast and crew receive per diems for distant locations, as well as hotel accommodations and travel expenses.

on mike   Speaking straight into the microphone within LIVE mike area.

on-off control   A switch with two simple stages, "on" or "off," with no stages or gradations in between.

on the nose   At the exact exposure indicated by the light meter.

Also, a radio and sometimes TV cue from the booth or floor director, given by touching the forefinger to the tip of the nose. It means, "You are right on time; no need to stretch or speed up."

opacity   Nontransparency. The quality of obstruction transmission of radiant energy in general, light in particular. Opacity is in contradistinction to TRANSMISSION.

on spec (speculation)   Producing a film with no negative pickup or distribution deal, one designed to make all returns on sales and rentals. In more general usage, any project developed by writers, directors or producers, in which they are not paid any advance money or development fees.

on-stage   Physically present on the performing stage, as opposed to OFF-STAGE. This term is also used by directors to refer to the lighted performing area of a TV or film set.

op amp   Short for "operational amplifier."

opaque leader   Optically opaque filmstrips of the same size as the film being edited. Used to space frame-to-frame in A-ROLL and B-ROLL cutting.

open call   Advertised call, not restricted to actors with agency representation. Also known as a cattle call.

open-end commercial   An ad that has an open section, usually at the end, where the sponsor can add his local message.

open-ended films   Those that state in dramatic and/or narrative style a given problem or situation, deliberately leaving it unresolved, in order to stimulate group discussion.

open-end program   One that has no set completion time, only an approximated one like for the Academy Awards or the Olympics.

open up   To widen the LENS aperture.

operating circle   Full sequence of operations in a properly functioning piece of equipment.

operations   Department in a TV station that handles scheduling of TV programs.

operator   The hands-on member of the camera crew who does the physical shooting with the camera after the DIRECTOR OF PHOTOGRAPHY has set up the shot. In nonunion shoots and most newsgathering and documentary shooting, the DIRECTOR OF PHOTOGRAPHY is also the OPERATOR. Also called CAMERA OPERATOR.

optical effects   Modifications of the photographic image, filmed in a motion picture camera of normal type, produced in an optical printer. Many of the new optical effects are now, initially or in final form, computer-generated.

optical house   A technical and business house that specializes in customized optical printing and SPECIAL EFFECTS.

optical-flop   Reversing an image optically.

optical negative   Original used to make the final prints.

optical print   One runoff in an OPTICAL PRINTER.

optical printer   Machine with an internal camera/projector interlink, designed to make the final OPTICAL NEGATIVE. Can also be used for superimpositions, titling, and special effects.

optical reduction   Going from one gauge of film to another, smaller gauge, by optical printing. 35mm to 16mm is a common reduction.

optical sound   That which is recorded directly onto film and developed as such. As opposed to other means of sound recording: magnetic-strip film, disc, magnetic audio tape.

optical-sound recorder   Equipment incorporating means for producing a modulated light beam, and for moving a light-sensitive medium relative to the beam for recording signals derived from sound signals.

optical track   The original track for final printing, or the track laid down as that print.

optics   Science relating directly to vision. The study of the elements comprising electromagnetic radiation in infrared, visible and ultraviolet areas.

optical viewfinder   See VIEWFINDER.

option   Negotiated instrument of access to allow for the purchase of a film or TV program, usually secured by payment of an option fee. The contract specifies a given date by which time the film or TV production must be under way (in its filming phase). If not in production by the time the option has expired, an extension is negotiable or the property reverts to the author or representative of the author.

order of appearance   A listing in the screen credits of the performers as they are seen onscreen. These chronologically-listed credits make it easier for the performer to be identified and often solves problems of BILLING. Another way of presenting credits is alphabetically.

original   A film term applied either to a film scene or the first recording of that scene. Since film processes are qualitatively indicated by noting how many generations away the print is from the "original," this is of great importance in setting up standards of comparison. The original negative is also called the master.

original screenplay   A SCRIPT that is created by a writer from his or her own concept and not adapted from a book, play or other literary work. See SCREENPLAY.

origination   Locale from which a network program is sent out to its affiliated stations.

orthicon   Upgraded form of the iconoscope TV camera unit. Also called orthiconoscope.

orthiconoscope   See ORTHICON.

orthocromatic   Applied to film emulsions, it refers to a type that is sensitive to blue and green, but not to red. This emulsion of red and reddish colors, orange among them, is used to attain a basic color-balance that is accurate. The term, when applied to photographic reproductions, means REPRODUCTION of colors in black and white.

OS   See OFF-SCREEN.

Oscar   The nickname—which has become the fully accepted name—of the statuette awards for various categories at the annual ACADEMY AWARDS, presented by the ACADEMY OF MOTION PICTURE ARTS AND SCIENCES.
   Three people are credited with giving the name "Oscar" to the statuette: Bette Davis, columnist Sidney Skolsky and Academy librarian, Margaret Herrick.

oscillator   An electronic device that generates frequencies.

oscilloscope   A voltometer with a cathode-ray screen that visually indicates rapidly varying quantities.

OTS   See OVER-THE-SHOULDER.

outboard   reels   Ultralarge-capacity reels mounted vertically on a power drive, free-standing and unattached, though immediately adjacent to the projector.

outcue   Last few words of the spoken narration or dialogue that cues in another segment of narration, dialogue, sound or music.

outline   A structural skeleton that extends a basic story idea or concept of a film or TV production. A rough sketch of the author's intended approach to the subject.

out of character   Conceptually in the writing, dialogue or actions that are inconsistent with a particular character. In acting, for speech, movement and approach to be at odds with the written, directorially-delineated character.

out of frame   Not in camera range; outside the action area.

In projection, an image not vertically centered on the screen, so that a portion of the frame above or below is seen at the top or bottom of the screen.

out of phase   Waveforms of same frequency that do not pass through corresponding values at the same exact moment. In media work, this can cause audio problems. For example, electrical input could be out of phase just enough to throw off the audio track by one field—analogous to one visual frame—which would disrupt the synchronicity of sound and make the audio totally uneditable. Since it cannot be edited while out of phase, it must be put back into phase before going ahead with the audio edit.

out of synch   When the picture doesn't match up with the sound. For example, when a person is seen talking, but for a moment or two no sound is heard, or conversely, if dialogue is heard before the lips begin to move. See SYNCHRONISM.

output   Current, voltage or power emanating from a live circuit.

output meter   An AC voltometer for measuring the signal strength of the output of an amplifier or receiver.

output transformer   A device for coupling the output of an amplifier to a load.

outs   Rejected takes of the same subject matter, not used in the completed version of the film. Also called out-takes.

out-takes   See OUTS.

overcoat   A clear or dyed thin layer laid over the emulsion side of a film strip. This gives the emulsion protection from scratches and abrasions during exposure, processing and projection.

overcrank   Running the camera more rapidly than standard speed. This faster-than-normal operation results in a slowing down of the motion on the screen, slow-motion.

overdevelop   To let the film stay in the developing processor longer than necessary, causing it to fog. Unless planned and done deliberately, this results in unusable footage.

overexposed   A darkened negative and bleached-out print is the result of overexposure. Caused by having too wide a lens opening when making the shot, or by a slower-than-standard shutter speed. Filters can sometimes help correct this but usually this film is unusable.

overhead shot   From directly above, looking down at the action.

overlap   In DIALOGUE cutting, the extension of a dialogue SOUND TRACK over a shot to which it does not belong. In action, to "overlap" means to keep the dialogue moving, one line starting before the lead-in line is completed. This creates a more naturalistic scene, reflecting more realistically the way people talk, as opposed to "stage direction." In postproduction, the overlapping is sometimes done by the editor, the lines having been recorded separately. See "WILD" RECORDING.

overlapping action Picking up the action of the next sequential shot with part of the concluding action of the preceding shot, then "matching" them to the right frame in the process of editing, to create continuous action. Obvious overlapping with repeat segments of shots can be used to give stylistic emphasis of the action of a scene, if so required.

overlapping sound Sound from the preceding shot carried forward into the following shot. Or, sound from the shot coming up that is heard at the end of the preceding shot. This latter use is called foreshadowing sound.

overlap splice Film spliced together with one frame or more overlapping at each film end to be joined.

overload Pulling more current than the immediate electrical system can supply, often causing a fuse or circuit-breaker blowout.
　　Sound distortion caused by recording at too high a level, resulting in NOISE or feedback.

overmodulation Amplitude modulation that exceeds one hundred percent, creating distortions and unwanted radiations.

overnights Ratings derived from TV sets plugged in directly to a computer. Nielsen provides these services in the major market areas: New York, Los Angeles and Chicago. Results are received and stored instantly and are ready for the markets the following morning.

overpower To diminish the presence of fluorescent light by using a sufficient amount of light of the proper color temperature to overpower the fluorescent.

overscanning When the beam of a cathode ray tube is deflected beyond standard picture size.

overshooting Filming beyond schedule or footage that has been allocated or required. Sometimes overshooting is deliberate, as in commercials, for example, to allow for numerous possible choices.

over-the-shoulder (OTS) A shot from behind and to the side of the FOREGROUND actor, including part of the head and shoulder.

ozone Chemically-active oxygen that can build up in projector lamp-housings, and can be injurious to the projection system. This is the reason why the projector's ventilating system must be monitored constantly and carefully.

P

P An indication on camera reports or script supervisor's records that means "print this shot."

PA See PUBLIC ADDRESS SYSTEM and PRODUCTION ASSOCIATE.

pace Rhythm of a completed film or videotape; its structure and internal tempo.

package A comprehensive presentation of the key elements needed to produce a film, TV series or special. The professional package consists of a SCRIPT, BUDGET, SHOOTING SCHEDULE, and often commitments by a STAR or stars, and a director. The package can be further enhanced by indicating agreed-upon deferments (payment delayed until after release of the film, at various stages of repayment) from LAB, performers or director, and having part of the funding already raised or agreed upon when the corrected ANSWER PRINT or final edited videotape is delivered to the distributors.
　　In news, the total and self-contained report by a media journalist. Often a field report—audio or video.

packager Company or individual that puts together packages such as above, in return for a given fee. The packager can be a fund-raiser, production company or agent.

packet switch Message transmission term indicating a complete message that is assembled into one or more packets that can be transmitted through the network, then reassembled at the receiver destination into the original message.

pad To extend the length of a film by adding additional material (outs or re-shoots) to the existing videotape or film footage. At the screenplay level, adding dialogue to a part, to make it bigger. Often done to satisfy demands of the star(s).

padding The material added when one pads a script or particular part.

pad roller Pressure device to hold film with steady-but-flexible touch against a sprocket or other roller.

page A unit of production-time measurement: "How many pages did you shoot today?" A dialogue page averages about 45 to 60 seconds depending upon the density of copy and the page style. This measurement of running-time has been relevant from the silent days, even when shooting from a sketch or outline, and became more pertinent as film production moved into the age of sound, with fully scripted scenarios becoming the norm. Of course, if the fully scripted ⅛ of a page reads: "The two armies engage, and battle to the end," the running time of the page will probably be longer than 60 seconds. But even with these variations, the screenplay pages will average out to a little less than a minute per page. It is working practice in film, and also in videotape, particularly in dramatic forms, to schedule a given number of pages per day. "We're a page and a half behind," is a common complaint of PRODUCERS and PRODUCTION MANAGERS.

Also, a large TV station's usher for program audiences. Also serves as a guide who takes groups on tours of the facility.

paid spot A commercial-announcement segment of time paid for by a sponsor, instead of having the time provided by the station as in a public service announcement. Also refers to the taped or filmed COMMERCIAL itself.

paint box Electronic graphics generator, using a free-form small main-frame computer.

painted matte A matte that has painted images on a section or sections of action areas. These painted images fill out the total composed-frame image.

painter light Meticulously calibrated and regulated source of illumination in a lab printer.

paint pots TV-console dial-rheostats for setting color levels.

PAL See PHASE ALTERNATION LINE.

PAM See PULSE AMPLITUDE MODULATION.

pan Movement of the camera, right to left or left to right, on a horizontal plane. Sometimes used to describe movements of the camera unit or camera head on any plane or angle. Examples of use: "That was a smooth pan." "Pan to the left!"

pan-and-tilt head Camera mount allowing camera rotation around both a vertical and horizontal axis.

Panavision Copyright name for a lens/camera/projector system for professional widescreen presentations.

pancake Makeup that can be mixed with water or a wet sponge for application and removed with soap and water. Standard TV and film makeup.

pan focus A DEPTH OF FIELD setting deep and wide enough to allow everything in the action field to stay in FOCUS.

panorama What you get from shooting a wide outdoor PAN SHOT, i.e., a full vista. Used informally for outdoor shots, as in, "Okay, let's get the whole panorama!"

panoramic display For electronic control and balance, the display of all signals received at different frequencies on a computer screen or instrumentational panel.

panstick Greasepaint-based makeup, not soluble in water so it requires a special makeup remover. Only used when heavy makeup is required and for special effects makeup.

pantomime Silent portrayal of a dramatic incident or mood without using vocal speech. Pantomime is used often in COMMERCIALS, using realistic mime, stylized or classical, white-faced mime. The silent films relied upon mime, mimetic action, dance or acrobatics.

paper edit To write out the descriptions and editing numbers of all the shots for a given sequence or entire film, audio or videotape. This is done to the exact frame if it is a final edit.

paper print Motion picture print made on stock with an emulsion with a paper base. Used for making prints of old or damaged film, which must be handled with great sensitivity.

paper-to-paper Film marked off by paper tape or paper insert tags, indicating "start here/stop here." Used in rolling down rapidly to a section of ORIGINAL film to be printed in a lab, or to a film scene to be projected or transferred to VIDEOTAPE.

parabolic reflector A large concave dish-shaped receptor to pull in the maximum range of signals and pinpoint focus them into an attached microphone. Used for sporting events, political conventions, parades and other occasions where great areas or distant spots must be covered.

parabolic spotlight One that uses a parabolic reflector to make a narrow beam of light.

parallax The difference between the image seen by the eye through the VIEWFINDER and that seen by the camera LENS. In FRAMING a shot, this has to be taken into critical consideration, since some areas may be cut off due to this error. Parallax is eliminated in cameras with reflex viewing systems, since the eye sees through the lens itself.

parallax error Faulty framing of an image caused by not correcting the compositional shift from the parallax finder. Not compensating for the parallactic distortion of the apparent angle.

parallel A tall platform, wheeled or semistationary, that can be set up in the studio or on LOCATION, to raise the camera and crew above the ground for HIGH SHOTS. It can also be used for holding lights.

parallel recording Where record heads in a head stack receive electrical energy simultaneously to record a group of split signals.

Paramount One of the early studios that started as a nickelodeon establishment headed by Adolph Zukor. Studio and lot still remain in Hollywood. One of the few major studios that was ever actually situated in Hollywood. MGM, before it stopped production and went into distribution with UNITED ARTISTS, was and is in Culver City; Columbia Pictures is centered at the Burbank Studios, formerly Warner Brothers, and Twentieth Century Fox is in West Los Angeles. The old RKO studios, after being DESILU for about two decades, joined geographically, if not organizationally, the Paramount complex.

parental guidance Now PG-13, a movie rating meaning suitable for people 13 years and older with accompanying parent.

parody A satirical send-up; a burlesque; a caricatured imitation. Parodies
have historically been of literary, dramatic or operatic works or of current
personalities of the times. Media parodies
tend also to lampoon these same things,
with the addition of such categories as
specific genre types, even specific titles,
in the fields of radio, film, television and
popular music. A good example of a film
parodying a film genre would be *Airplane,* or Mel Brooks' *High Anxiety* (the
Hitchcock films) and *Blazing Saddles*
(westerns).

part An actor's role; his character designation. Parts are classified in distinct
strata beginning with the leading or starring parts. Feature parts refer to supporting roles, including character parts. Bit
parts means small parts, usually comprised of a few lines of dialogue in one
or two scenes.

participation The placing of SPOT
commercials in programming. Products
must not be competitive with those in
other commercials aired during the same
program.

passive communication satellite
One that reflects, but does not amplify,
a signal. A satellite "mirror," it needs a
large, reflective surface on the satellite
itself, augmented by high-tech, high-
powered ground stations.

patch A film overlay, cemented or
otherwise affixed to two abutting pieces
of film, joining them together. The purpose: to repair a damaged NEGATIVE without losing FRAMES.
   In electronics, to join circuits together
with a patch cord.

patching jack Interconnecting jack
plugs for joining together circuit elements.

pathos Emotional texture in a work of
art that evokes a feeling of sympathy in
the audience.

pay assignment See ASSIGNMENT PAY.

payola Special gifts, particularly those
that are not officially approved by broadcasters. These improper payments to station staff members or executives, TV game
hosts or contestants, disc jockeys, etc.,
are made to get additional, favorable
publicity and TV or radio exposure.

pay tv Television or cable connections
that charge a monthly fee after initial
hook-up. Sent out to individual homes
by special transmission, culminating in a
cable that goes directly into the viewer's
home.

PBS See PUBLIC BROADCASTING SYS-
TEM.

PD See PUBLIC DOMAIN.

pea-bulb Mini-lamp inside a film
camera that puts a FLASH FRAME onto the
film stock.

peak Temporary high level, lasting for
a short interval, in amplitude. Also known
as crest.

peaking Tuning or adjusting a sys-
tem-component in order to increase a
circuit's response.

peak load Maximum electronic load
produced or used within a given period
of time.

pedestal A support, usually dolly-
mounted, for a camera. It can also be
used for lights or balancing (or locking
off) a sound boom.

pencil test A procedure using pencil
drawings to check out an ANIMATION move
for speed and smoothness before going
to painting the cels.

Pentagon Papers Key legal case in
determining the rights of reporters and
what constituted invasion of privacy.
Daniel Ellsberg was found "not guilty"
for his receipt and use of government
documents taken without permission from
U.S. government files. It established his

rights of access to materials without being compelled to reveal sources.

perceived noise level   A standard for determining human reactions to noise over a wide range of frequencies. The level is measured in decibels.

perforations   Sprocket holes in film or coated sound stock, with holes on one side (single-perf) for SINGLE-SYSTEM sound, or on both sides (double-perf) when sound is recorded separately, DOUBLE-SYSTEM sound.

persistence of vision   A phenomenon that causes an image on the retina to be mentally retained for a short period, so that if a second similar image takes its place within a period of about $\frac{1}{16}$ of a second, no visible discontinuity will be noticed. This is the visual basis for the motion picture.

personal direction   See SCRIPT FORM in Appendix.

personal manager   A business and talent representative for a performer, director, writer or producer and, more recently, for cameramen. Many work also as licensed agents or in conjunction with a talent agency. In some cases, the personal manager also serves as a business manager.

PG-rated   See PARENTAL GUIDANCE.

perspective   The viewer's sense of depth and space, and the relationship of the objects placed or moving within the composed field.

phase alternation line   The full name for the PAL system. As U.S. uses the NTSC TV system, Europe—with the exception of France, the Soviet Union and former Eastern bloc countries—uses PAL. It is a 625-line system featuring pre-corrected color hues.

phasing   TV-camera alignment process, also used for videotape recorders.

phone line   Refers to the headphone-microphone set going from taping area to control room used for communication.

phonemes   Elemental speech sounds from which all words in a language are composed.

phonetic alphabet   International alphabet of pronunciation symbols.

phonetic spelling   Writing out the pronunciation of words in phonetic syllables, i.e., *Rue de la Paix:* ROO-DUH-LAH-PAY—or *Illinois:* ILL-UH-NOY. See PRONOUNCER.

phosphors   Layers of materials that are photosensitive. These chemically coated elements are found inside picture tubes, and are activated to luminescence when triggered by electron beams.

photoflood   High-wattage, incandescent bulb.

photogenic   A person or thing that photographs well. Used more often to describe people than objects. "He's extremely photogenic; really looks great!"

photometer   A measuring device used to evaluate light intensity. A LIGHT METER.

photometric brightness   Intensity of brightness that can be measured by a photometer.

photoplay   Early name for screenplay, script or scenario.

pickup arm   Long, narrow element on a pivot with a sensitized pickup head for sound reproduction. Used on sound players and recorders (for playback). Contains a stylus which tracks the record's grooves and transmits the sounds that are picked up; the vibrations of the stylus are converted to electric energy.

picture   The completed film. Or the visual image only, as opposed to sound.

picture black   Signal produced by scanning an area having maximum density.

picture brightness   TV-picture measurement to designate level of BRIGHTNESS of the highlights of an image, measured in foot-lamberts.

picture car   Any vehicle that appears in front of the cameras as an "actor." As opposed, for example, to a CAMERA CAR or HONEYWAGON.

picture frequency   TV pictures, full-image scanned per second.

picture head   Projector unit that focuses and projects the film images onto the screen.

picture image   The visual likeness of a person or object, recorded photographically on film, videotape, HOLOGRAM or VIDEODISC.

picture line standard   In TV measurement, the full number of horizontal lines in a full televised image. Standard in United States: 525 lines.

picture monitor   TV receiver on a closed-circuit system for viewing a program image with or without sound.

picture safe   Framed properly to fall within TV CUTOFF; preframed on shooting day to fall within in-camera grid lines.

picture signal   TV signal coming from the scanning process.

picture size   Functional viewing area of a TV receiver's screen, measured in inches.

picture tube   Image-reproducing element that forms the screen in a television receiver.

pilot   Opening program of a TV series, sometimes produced separately and previewed to see if it can attract viewers and sponsors. If long enough in running time, it may be released as a MOVIE-OF-THE-WEEK. The point of all these activities is to procure series funding and achieve longevity.

pilot tone   Tone sent over a narrow audio channel, the frequency of the tone activating a specified operation or testing the channel.

pincushion distortion   A LENS characterized by concave curvature of the lines of a rectangular grid image, caused by magnification that is less at the center than at the edges of the field.

ping-ponging   See YO-YO.

PIO   See PUBLIC INFORMATION OFFICER.

pipe   Plumber's pipe or specially made pipe for rigging overhead or banked lights.

pirate   To copy or retransmit a broadcast without permission or to run off an unauthorized copy of an audiotape or film print. See COPYRIGHT.

pirated copy   Film or tape (audio or video) reproduced illegally from another print or tape copy or from the original.

pistol grip   Handle allowing for a firm grip and good control on hand-held cameras or microphones.

pitch   Distance from the leading edge of one perforation to the next. These measurements are critical for proper camera or projector operation. Film that has shrunk or has incomplete perforations can jam cameras or projectors as well as ruin the in-motion film stock.

In sound it is the wave frequency.

pix   Popular trade-journalese term for "pictures" popularized by *Daily Variety* and *Billboard*.

pixels   Electronic units that make up the SCANNING LINE. Transmission rate: 8½ million pixels per second. The word *pixel* is compounded of *picture* and *elements*.

pixillation Rapid cuts of sequential stills, sometimes with a duration of only a few frames, to produce an erratic induced sense of motion and progression. See KINESTASIS.

PL See PHONE LINE.

platen The flat-glass transparent plate that holds down ANIMATION material to be filmed on an ANIMATION STAND.

play A dramatic form for one or more actors in one or more acts. A stage term designating a piece designed originally for live theater, serving as the basic matrix out of which the screenplay and TELEPLAY were born. Plays are often adapted for film, TV and radio, or the concept purchased as a basis of a new program, film or series.

playback A term denoting the immediate auditing of a sound recording upon any stage of completion.

It is also a method of filming singing, dancing or other actions that must match prerecorded music, words or sounds. These tracks are played back through loudspeakers on the soundstage to enable the performers to do their prerehearsed actions to the tracks. This allows performers to move without picking up unwanted sounds, as only the visual image is being laid down; thus, such filming sessions can be carried out under imperfect acoustical conditions. This action is afterwards synchronized with the original recording made under "perfect" acoustical conditions.

player The ACTOR or performer. The term is often used in contracts as a comprehensive name for any on-camera person.

play-on/play-off Music to introduce and to end the scene or effect an exit for a performer or scene.

plosive A percussive sound from the mouth. "P" is the one phoneme that gives the most trouble to performers who

are in close to the microphone and causes concern at the mixing panel. "B," "F," "T" can also cause plosive problems.

plot The skeletal action-outline of a dramatic work that gives it its inherent structure; to be differentiated from THEME, SUBTEXT, CHARACTERIZATION.

plug To work in a mention of one's product or upcoming TV program or film; a self-advertisement interwoven into interviews or live performances, with varying degrees of subtlety.

plug-in unit A separate subsystem of components easily plugged into or removed from a circuit; handled as a discrete unit.

pointer A measuring indicator needle.

point of view (POV) A subjective-camera viewpoint; looking at the scene of action with the camera serving as the "eye" of one of the characters with the setting and movement seen from that viewpoint.

polarized lens One using a POLARIZING FILTER.

polarized light Light matrix that allows in only light on its same plane, through a system of lenses or plates. Polarizing gives greater saturation of tonality and sharper edges of images by cutting down glare.

polarizing filter Lens filter that lets in or keeps out polarized light, with gradations between these two extremes.

Polaroid Name for a Polaroid still shot. Used on the set as visual record, it establishes performers in the wardrobe they are wearing in a particular scene, as well as hair length or style, scenic exterior setups, onstage sets, performers' positions at the tail of scene when the scene is going to be continued later.

polyester Name given to a strong, durable film base by its developer, E. I. du

Pont de Nemours and Co. Abbreviated name for polyethelene terephthalate, a film-base product with great strength and durability. Du Pont has given it the trade name Cronar; in Kodak products it's called Estar.

pool-hall lighting   Lighting that comes froh, or seems to come from, one light source, as a lamp hanging above a pool table.

poop sheet   Page of relevant information used by a TV host or announcer, from which he can AD LIB.

pop   Current "in" music, or general mass culture.

In recording, the percussive overmodulated sound in speaking or singing that pops the microphone; particularly on initial hard "p," "f" and "t" sounds. See PLOSIVE.

popcorn noise   Electrical noise from live amplifiers that has a similarity to the random soundbursts of popcorn popping.

pop filter   Audio filter used to reduce popping during recording.

pop-on/pop-off   For an image to appear or disappear instantly. Done by shooting a frame at a time and stopping the shooting, then taking the object or person out of the frame or putting him/her/it *into* the frame. After placement or removal, the filming continues for as long as required.

pornography   Technically, pornography is the practice of writing or pictorializing those physical acts of sexual intercourse that are practiced by a prostitute (*porné* in Greek), so as to arouse sexual desire. However, what constitutes pornography can vary from person to person or area to area. Also called a BLUE or DIRTY MOVIE.

portable dressing room   Dressing room on small wheels that can be rolled from one shooting stage to another, to augment permanent dressing room space facilitating work closer to the set. A dressing room that can be trucked or hauled as a trailer, or a mobile home that can be used on LOCATION. See HONEYWAGON.

portamento   Continuous descending or ascending change of tone pitch.

positive film   Film stock for use as master positives or RELEASE PRINTS.

positive image   The processed picture made from the negative and printed onto positive film. This image is the framed one seen by the cameraman's eye as it was being shot.

positive modulation   TV modulation where brightness increases with an increase of transmitted power, or lessens with a decrease of power.

post assembly   The first rough sequential assembly of the materials after completion of filming.

post-production   Putting the film into final release after shooting is completed. Typical post-production work includes editing, scoring, ADL, graphics, special effects, mixing, and negative cutting.

post-production services   See COMPLETION SERVICES.

post-recording   Recording after filming is completed. Includes FOLEY sessions, scoring, dialogue replacement sessions, mixing and remixing.

post-scoring   Recording and laying in the track to the beat or fractionated beat.

post-synchronization   The addition of speech or SOUND EFFECTS to synchronize with picture images already incorporated into the film. See DUBBING and FOLEY.

pot   See POTENTIOMETER.

potentiometer Electromechanical resistance control that can alter electrical resistance. It regulates audio or video levels in the studio or from remotes. Called POT for short.

POV See POINT-OF-VIEW.

power Broadcast transmitter's potential for output emissions, measured in watts.

power amplifier Used to drive more than one transducer or transmitter. This amplifier's output has been forced to greatly extend itself, due to the demands from rock concert producers.

power dump Removing electrical power, by accident or intentionally.

power frequency That level of frequency at which power is generated and sent out. In the United States it is 60 Hz.

power pack A unit that serves as both a minitransformer and a power generator. A BATTERY BELT is a power pack. Power converter taking alternating currents or direct currents and changing them to the voltages necessary to operate an electronic device. A simple example is the plug-in unit that ties into a 220 line and converts it to 110/120 for an electric razor. Used in filming and videotaping to recharge batteries in locations or countries with supplied voltages higher than 110/120.

power zoom One that is made with an electromechanical zoom unit.

practical An operational prop that functions during the filmed/videotaped scene, i.e., a working typewriter on a desk within the set.

practical set A real LOCATION, not a studio SET. An actual drugstore might be used, instead of constructing a "drugstore set," or a real schoolroom instead of a "schoolroom set." As location sound improves and studio construction costs

rise, there is a great financial incentive—and sometimes an aesthetic one—to shoot more and more scenes on practical sets.

preamp See PREAMPLIFIER.

preamplifier Electronic unit to strengthen weak signal voltages and bring them up to workable transmission levels. Called preamp for short.

preempt To exclude existing programming for a given time slot with programming of a higher broadcast priority—a special, a movie-of-the-week, an open-ended major event such as a political convention or a fast-breaking world-involving news story.

prelay To prerecord all ELEMENTS for a final MIX; to ready them for that MIX.

premier An official opening of a theatrical film in a specially chosen theater, or the screening of the first segment of a new TV series.

premix Mixing of a number of tracks onto one, so that it can be handled as a single sound element in the final mix.

preproduction All arrangements made and work done directly prior to, and interfacing with, PRODUCTION.

prerecording Recording of music, voice or sound effects prior to the shooting of the film to accompany it, and in predetermined SYNCHRONISM. Examples would be commercials with playback music, a jingle, or voiceover, in order to give the actors cues, mood and energy level of a scene. This is sometimes done when filming scenes without sound in feature films.

presence The sound AMBIENCE of a specific locale, recorded separately before or after a sound take. Used to fill in sound DROPOUTS. It is either a "wild" sound presence recording in the same spot where the scene was filmed, or a simulation of the "presence" of that locale. See WILD RECORDING.

prescore To record any or all of the film musical score before filming begins.

presentation Written concept or outline of a program (special or series) or picture idea. The more detailed the better, particularly for an unestablished writer. The presentation is part character delineation, part plot and part sales hype, indicating its broad audience and the high entertainment value of the project.

press-to-talk switch Used in the control or recording booth to talk to the sound stage; usually a button or switch that is live as long as it is held down, and cuts off when the spring is released. Also known as a push-to-talk switch.

pressure microphone One that has an electrical output equivalent to the immediate sound pressure of the sound waves.

pressure pad A pad that holds audiotape, as it is being recorded or played, against the proper sound-heads. Generally, a fine felt material or something similar is used, to achieve uniform pressure with minimum friction.

pressure plate In a camera, projector or optical printer, a plate—usually metal—that presses on the back of the film in order to keep the emulsion surface even with the FOCAL PLANE of the LENS.

pressure roller Rubber-coated or sheathed roller that holds film tape against the capstan. This allows the capstan to take the tape from the feed roll and on to the recording heads at a constant speed.

presync See PRESYNCHRONIZATION.

presynchronization Refers to dialogue already prerecorded, to which animation can be set, or to voice-over actors mouthing to animated working figures, such as the animal characters and sci-fi creatures in fantasy films, or to the life-sized puppets on such shows as "D.C. Follies." Called presync for short.

preview Showing preceding a PREMIER, to gauge audiences' responses.

previews of coming attractions A hyped-up sample of scenes from a forthcoming film, presented to motivate audiences to see whatever film is being touted. Also a commercial advertising a film "coming soon."

primary colors In TV they are red, blue and green. Primaries are those colors from which all others can be compounded.

prime time Time with the highest viewership aggregate on TV; 7:00–11:00 P.M.

principal focus Lens point where light coming from photographic "infinity" comes into focus.

principal photography In a feature film, all the footage shot by the first unit. It excludes pick up shots, second unit shots, graphics and special effects shots.

print Positive reproduction of a negative image onto PRINT STOCK. This refers to dailies or to a completed motion picture. In production it is a TAKE that is okay and should be printed. See also P.

printer Machine that copies (prints) from original, exposed film.

printer's synch See EDITOR'S SYNCH.

print stock Film on which prints are made—as opposed to filming or shooting stock.

print-through The signal leaking through from one layer of audio or videotape to another.

prism lens Camera lens attachment or self-contained lens that breaks up single images entering the camera into multiple images.

process To develop and print ORIGINAL film.

process camera One devised for special effects shooting, using various processes: bipacks, multiplane, mattes, etc. Not a live action camera.

processing The group of operations comprising the developing, fixing, hardening, washing and drying of film. Any procedures required to produce either a NEGATIVE or POSITIVE visible image from a strip of film; to bring out that picture from the corresponding latent image.

process photography Photographic images projected onto a background, for PROCESS SHOTS.

process projection A composite-procedure studio technique whereby ACTORS, SETS and PROPS in front of the camera are combined with a BACKGROUND that consists of a translucent screen on which the picture is projected from behind. Also called back projection, rear-screen projection, background projection, transparency process, and, with the advent of a frontal process, FRONT PROJECTION.

process screen A screen used for PROCESS PROJECTION and general special effects.

process shot One made using the process projection system.

producer The person who carries ultimate responsibility for the original shaping and final outcome of a media project. See EXECUTIVE PRODUCER.

producer's contractual agreements Full contracts, letters of agreement, basic employment forms, etc., signed by a producer to state the rights and responsibilities of all parties. These documents are typically between producer and writer, director, performers (in above-the-line categories), and sometimes with the cinematographer. Other typical agreements are made with the various unions and guilds, distributors, producer's working staff.

product bonus An extra print or tape given as a bonus when a school system or corporation buys a large number of prints or tapes from the distributor.

production The general term used to describe the processes involved in making all the original materials that are bases for the finished motion picture or videotape.

production assistant Producer's direct aide.

production associate (PA) One who is assigned to carry out production staff assignments.

production calendar See Appendix.

production designer A term that has come into vogue since the late 60s, though used earlier in rare instances. It describes the person who creates the overall co-ordinated form, color and texture of the film. It is the ART DIRECTOR who executes the scheme, working in conjunction with the director of photography and SET DESIGNER.

production house Production facility for coordinating filming and videotaping; the executive or line-producing locale.

production manager (PM) Person who supervises the daily production of a film, working directly with the PRODUCER, DIRECTOR and ASSISTANT DIRECTOR. The PM relays orders from director and producer to the art director, as well as seeing that contracts are signed, catering is arranged, daily accountancy is up-to-date, locations are scouted and permits are in place for filming in all nonstudio situations. The production manager's role is similar to, but more detailed than, that of the assistant director. Also, the PM generally has a wider range of responsibilities.

production notes Notations and reports made during the filming in all phases and aspects of PRODUCTION: cameras and sound reports, PRODUCTION MANAGER's reports, SCRIPT SUPERVISOR's notes, etc. Used as direct references during production and in postproduction. Also called PRODUCTION REPORTS.

production number A working number for all reports, billings and scripts that are used, filed or computerized on a film or TV production. The number must be the same on all records relating to the specific production. In a musical, the big extravaganza number with dancers, singers, actors and elaborate sets. With musical accompaniment, this singing-dancing catchall often carries the title of the production, as "Hello, Dolly" in the film of that name, or "Babes in Arms."

production operations staff The crew, including cameraman. Production managers are sometimes included with the production operating staff, or are on salary as part of the production company's own staff.

production report Daily report showing full cast, crew and others involved with the production. Lists the hours of the call as well as hours actually worked, the total footage shot, and other informational details. For use by PRODUCER and his immediate staff and co-workers. See PRODUCTION NOTES.

production still A still shot of a scene itself, to be used for advertising or publicity purposes to promote the film or TV show. Also used to show the crew at work, for behind-the-scenes shots that can be filed for the archives as a pictorial record of the shoot, or released with accompanying stories to various trade publications.

production unit A self-contained group of DIRECTOR, camera crew, sound crew, ELECTRICIANS, etc., that works on a soundstage or on LOCATION to shoot an assigned picture, or section of a picture. See SECOND UNIT.

professional A performer or crew member who is paid for his or her ser-

vices. More broadly, an attitude of maturity and responsibility.

program A TV show. News, sitcom, special event, miniseries segment, talk show—any TV presentation.

program channel In a three-position console the middle panel is generally the on-off switch, the left panel the audition channel, the right panel the program or on the air channel. The audition channel is for private-use monitoring or for rehearsal-viewing.

projectionist Person in charge of the projector and projection room.

projection lens One designed for the projection of films. As such, it is balanced optically to reduce aberrations of color, specifically such aberrations as would be seen by the eye rather than the filming camera.

projection room A fireproof room, isolated and soundproofed for the housing of projection and sound equipment.

projection speed The rate at which film is projected. Standard frame-rates are 16 fps for silent film (unless corrected for sound-speed) and 24 fps for sound film.

projection TV Big-screen TV system in which the images are projected either from the front by a special electronic projection unit onto a separate screen, or integrated into a rear-screen TV set that throws the image immediately behind its translucent screen.

projector A machine that allows films to be viewed by throwing images onto a large screen.

promo Short for promotional story or piece. A TV version of the movies' PREVIEWS OF COMING ATTRACTIONS. The promo can be an ad that touts the upcoming event, a news-plant item with film-clip, or a short behind-the-scenes film showing the film as it is being made. Primary use is for television broadcasting, with a secondary use in media conventions and a tertiary and infrequent use as a theatrical short.

prompter   Roller-fed device that can give cues or full dialogue to the on-camera talent. It can work immediately next to either side of the camera or be projected onto a reflective glass plate so that the actor can read it and still have the words remain invisible to the viewing audience. This latter way of using these prompters is now used almost exclusively in newscasts. There are several trade names for these prompter units, such as TELE-PROMPTER and Q-TV.

pronouncer   Written guide to unfamiliar words. See PHONETIC SPELLING.

property   The script or book to be made into a script, with all its attendant rights—which can be assigned in toto or fractionated as the property is multimarketed. A script, story or treatment, sometimes with musical rights attached if music is integral to the production. The literary package that is to be transformed into a produced entity, either on film or videotape.

props (properties)   Same meaning in film and video production as in live theater. Items to be used in a scene, usually portable, ranging from furniture to cigarette lighters. See ACTION PROPERTIES.

protagonist   The person in a play or film who carries the leading role, as well as the role itself.

protection master   Video, film or audio dupe from which copies can be made.

protection shot   A special coverage shot to interlink or cutaway to two other shots, in case there is a mismatch. Shot made by the director to cover possible holes in continuity; it can be a reaction shot or straight cutaway.

proud edges   A projection room term referring to a section of a film roll that

sticks out from the tightly wound film roll and can be easily damaged.

proximity presence   The intensified bass range effectuated by certain microphones, or a deliberate mix to achieve this sound. It gives an intimate, resonant effect.

public access   Availability of cable channels to groups or individuals, allowing members of the viewing audience access to television. Usage fee is nominal.

public address system (PA)   The basic combination of microphone, amplifier and speaker.

public affairs   Community, regional, national and international events: social, business, government. The raw matrix for news and documentary. Today there are public affairs stations throughout the world that show governing bodies in session, legal hearings, media meetings, etc.

Public Broadcasting Act of 1967
A congressional act signed by President Johnson to create the Public Broadcasting System from the originally FCC-allocated stations. This network of about 80 VHF stations and 160 UHF stations was established in 1952 and became known as the National Education Network. The act also created the Corporation for Public Broadcasting. This organization channels government funds to stations and also helps to secure additional funding from the private and public sectors, especially foundation funding. Both stations became fully operative in 1969.

Public Broadcasting System (PBS)
A loose affiliation of stations that started as the Educational Network, and has now expanded to in-depth news and documentaries, travel and nature programs. It still carries educational programs, especially during school hours. PBS funding by the federal government has been radically slashed forcing PBS to hold fund-raising drives. In addition, dwindling tax write-offs have caused a

decrease in private corporation grants to PBS.

public domain A work on which a copyright has never existed, has expired, or was never needed. This usually means that it can be used without payment made to the creator (author, composer, artist) or that person's estate.

public information officer (PIO) A press representative for an organization who gives the press no more or no less than the organization wants the public to know. A PIO may be helpful in steering a reporter to the appropriate interviewee, but based on the corporate parameters of the concept "appropriate."

public relations (PR) firms Organizations dedicated to spreading affirmative images of their clients through all media outlets. Their clients might include an individual celebrity, agencies of the United States Government, multinational corporations, foreign dictators, cultural or scientific organizations.

public service announcement (PSA) An announcement in a time spot reserved for a commercial. The announcement is presented without a time-fee by the radio or TV station as a public service. This is done to fulfill part of the station's community service responsibilities as set forth in the FCC station-licensing requirements. PSAs are for nonprofit and charitable organizations such as United Way or American Red Cross.

published motion picture "Published" means completed and ready for showing, preferably with copyright mark; "motion picture" includes videodiscs and videotapes as well as films.

pull A term used by the electrical crew to indicate how much power will be drawn off and used by particular lamps. "What does it pull?" "It's pulling ten amps!" Editorially, to remove original film footage from the vault in order to prepare it for negative-cutting, or take out a special scene for evaluation or reprint.

pull back To move the camera away from the point of action. Also given as a direction, even when using a ZOOM LENS to achieve an apparent pullback. "Okay, get ready to pull back!"

pulldown The generally downward action of the device in the projector that moves the film, in rapid intermittent movements, through the projector gate.

pull focus See RACK FOCUS.

pull-up torque Minimum time for the torque to get up to rated target-speed.

pulse amplitude modulation (PAM) System which causes a modulating wave to amplitude-modulate a pulse carrier.

pulse mode Finite sequence of pulses with preset pattern, for selection and isolation of a communication channel.

pulse modulation Series of pulses modulated for information use; to send information on a pulse carrier.

pulse transmitter Transmitter for generating pulses and transmitting to a receiving device.

punch Hand-punch for making a hole in the film LEADER to indicate the starting point for editor, MIXER or LAB.
   A mechanical device for making holes on the edge of an animation CEL or title card, to match the pegs on an ANIMATION STAND or easel.

punchline The last line in a sketch or a joke, which in a review can be the "blackout" line; in a gag it is sometimes called the laugh-line, as opposed to the setup lines. The closing line of a comedy routine.

punch-up The monitor carrying the camera shot chosen by the director, i.e., the one being broadcast. "Punch up camera two!"

push To allow the film to stay in the developer for the length of time necessary to add however many STOPS are required. To give such instructions to the lab: "Push it two stops." To add this additional exposure-time is known as "pushing" the film.

push in   Direction to move the camera closer in to the area of action. A ZOOM-IN is an apparent "push-in."

push-to-talk switch   See PRESS-TO-TALK SWITCH.

push-over wipe   A wipe in which the first image moves horizontally across the screen, as if nudged by the second on-coming image, much as in a lantern-slide projector when slides are being changed.

Q

qualified privilege   Government pro-ceedings in all branches and agencies are shielded by absolute privilege. This means that elected officials at the city, state or national levels cannot be sued for libel while speaking in their official assembly venues (city council chambers, courts of law, the Senate) or in making official pronouncements. Qualified privilege covers the media that report these events. The media cannot be sued for presenting these stories in a fair, reasonable manner and as accurately as possible.

quarter-inch tape   Reel-to-reel stan-dard-size magnetic recording tape.

quartz   Glass-like material with the ability to withstand high levels of radiant energy without shattering.

quartz lamp   A unit with a TUNGSTEN-HALOGEN bulb, the iodine gas of which extends filament life and stabilizes its color temperature until burnout. These longer-lasting globes are becoming the basic lights for professional production, aug-mented by other lamps such as arcs and incandescents.

question-answer format   A working structure for game shows, news inter-views, talk shows. Questions must be researched and customized to the partic-ular type of program.

questioning   Form of investigatory probing. An interviewee in a news or documentary interview will be warmed up with general, offhand questions to open the interview. At the right time, the interviewer will move from the introduc-tory questions to the specific and hard-edged queries.

quiescent period   Pause between pulses, in pulse transmission.

quiet tuning   Tuning of a receiver where the audio output is quieted until the receiver is properly tuned to the exact frequency of the desired carrying wave bringing in the signal.

quickie   A film or videotape put to-gether rapidly, filmed and released on a short schedule in order to save time and money or make a release deadline on time. As a rule, synonymous with low-budget. A quickie often carries with it a derogatory connotation as to the quality of the film.

quick study   Performer who learns his lines and blocking on-the-spot and swiftly.

quiet   A command called out directly or amplified over a bullhorn or loud-speaker. It precedes the command "ROLL," the response "SPEED," and the command "ACTION!" It is ordinarily given by the ASSISTANT DIRECTOR, who then signals the DIRECTOR when the appro-priate state of working silence has been achieved.

quip   A witty or sarcastic fast retort. A rehearsed (or sometimes real) AD-LIB, used in COMEDY routines or to provide co-medic flavor in an interview program or game show.

quotation   If integrated properly and seamlessly into a program, the quotation can be an effective intensifying device and can delineate or summarize a major conceptual point. It is important that the quotation is accurate, and that its attribution is correct. It is also important to clearly indicate to the audience when the quotation starts and when it stops.

Q-TV   The trade name for a film or TV cueing system in which the reflected image of the DIALOGUE is seen on a slanted sheet of plate glass directly in front of the camera. Because of the angle of the glass, it is not "seen" by the camera lens.

R

R   See R-RATED.

rack focus   A lens-shift to bring an out-of-focus background image into sharp focus, which simultaneously throws the foreground out of focus, or vice versa. An example of a rack-in would be to go from a blurred and indistinguishable image to a sharp, identifiable image. Rack-out would be to go from the clear image to the blurred one. Also called PULL FOCUS.

rackover   A mechanism used with a VIEWFINDER, allowing the finder to be lined up directly behind the lens, so that the exact framing for a scene can be determined.

radio   Electronic communication using electromagnetic waves for transmission and reception.

Also used as a direction or command in walkie-talkie or two-way radio communication when DIRECTOR and camera are separated. "Radio us from the helicopter when you start filming," for example, is a typical ground-based director's request to a cameraman making an aerial shot.

radio beam   Radio wave with a narrower path, because of its smaller angle of energy emission.

radio broadcast   A program sent out from a radio transmitter to individual radio receivers.

Radio Corporation of America (RCA)   A parent corporation that holds patents on radio and TV components, designs, trademarks, etc. Early on, it put together the NATIONAL BROADCASTING COMPANY and Victor Records as major adjuncts of its corporate structure.

radio engineering   Handling the technical aspects of the generation, transmission and reception of radio; now extended to TV. Also refers to the research and development stages in designing, manufacturing and testing of equipment.

radio frequency (rf)   Any audio-discernible electromagnetic frequency for carrying speech, music, sound or control signals.

Radio Keith-Orpheum (RKO)   Known as RKO Radio Pictures, it was a joint enterprise of Radio Corporation of America and the Keith-Orpheum theater circuit, mostly motion picture houses. *Cimarron, Suspicion, King Kong, The Informer* and others were made under the RKO banner. At one time, Goldwyn, Selznick and Disney released through RKO. Studio control was acquired by Howard Hughes in 1948. In 1957, production was closed down at the studio and it was sold to Desilu TV.

radio mike   Microphone not connected by cable, but operating on a matching radio frequency with the receiving unit. A microphone and minitransmitter are clipped or taped onto the performer. DIALOGUE goes from microphone to receiving unit, which feeds directly into the recorder or to a premix and amplifying unit.

radio receiver   Receptor that converts waves into distinguishable signals: programs, messages, information.

radio signal   One transmitted by radio.

radio spectrum   The frequency range of the radio spectrum, from about 3 kHz to 300 GHz; wavelengths of 100 km–1 mm.

radio station   Loosely, any grouping of equipment for transmission and reception. A building housing technical and administrative areas for radio broadcasting.

radio transmission   Signals sent out by electromagnetic waves that are neither light or heat waves.

radio waves   Waves sent through space without an intervening guidance system. Frequency is below 3000 GHz.

rain-barrel effect   Unwanted echo-like sound on an overcompensated, equalized line.

rainbow generator   Electronic generator that can create a full color spectrum on a television screen.

ramp   Structural or improvised slanted incline, with or without tracks, on which to move a DOLLY alongside actors as they move up or down stairways or over rough terrain.

Rank-Cintel   State-of-the-art film-to-tape transfer system. MOS transfers or with interlocked sound.

raster   Pattern of scanning lines in a TV receiver. The part of a TV screen illuminated by the scanning lines when no program signal is being received.

rate card   Printed rate information, listing fees for the broadcasting of commercials. Fees are based on commercial's length, broadcast times, and airing frequency.

ratings   Statistics measuring viewing (TV) or listening (radio) audiences. Ratings are researched by organizations specializing in this branch of demographics, for clients that include stations, networks, advertising agencies and sponsors.

rating service   Audience survey organization that gives stations or sponsors researched information on viewing habits of general or target audiences.

raw stock   Film that has not been exposed or processed.

raw tape   Blank tape, usually tape on which nothing has been recorded before. Also called VIRGIN TAPE.

reaction shot   One in which an ACTOR reacts to what is happening or being said at a given spot in the script. This is usually a CUTAWAY SHOT. However, a reaction shot is any shot where an actor looks out into the scene—even as a master shot—to which he or she reacts.

reader   Prescreening person who reads screenplays, treatments or books being considered for dramatization, evaluates them and, if it is relevant, passes that information on in a verbal or typed report to the producer. This is the initial step in selecting properties for production.
    In sound, an editing unit with manual or motor-driven mechanism to roll magnetic or optical sound through the machine. The sound is audited on a self-contained loudspeaker in the reader, or by jack-plugging into it with earphones.

reading   Also called run-through. A sitdown, read-through of a script, with minimal input from the director.
    In lighting, a metered evaluation of light available within a lit scene; it can be measured by various light meters.

rear-screen projection   See PROCESS PROJECTION.

recommended practice   SMPTE recommendation of the engineering committee that sets up acceptable levels and practices for specific technical areas in film or television.

record   To lay down sound on audiotape, film (sound-coated or striped), disc, or any other process by which sound is recorded.

recording   Producing a copy of an audible or visible event in the external world.

recording, live   A RECORDING of an original sound, as distinguished from RE-RECORDING. Also called an original recording.

recording studio   Soundproof facility for live recording or re-recording.

recording system   A combination of microphones, mixers, amplifiers and film recorder originally used in recording motion pictures. Now almost totally replaced by the simplified Nagra-system, with its small crew, easy portability and high quality.

recordist   Originally, the operator of the sound camera; now, the hands-on recording person.

rectification   Changing   alternating current into direct current.

rectifier   Electronic   converter   that changes AC to DC, for running xenon arcs, exciter lamps, carbon arcs, etc.

red gun   TV-picture-tube gun with a beam designed to strike only the red primary phosphor dots. Used in conjunction with the green and blue guns to obtain full TV-color range.

reduction printing   Printing down from a larger-gauge film to a smaller, in order to get a COMPOSITE PRINT in the narrower gauge.

reel   A metal or plastic spool carrying a small positioning notch and spoked FLANGES or side pieces on which the film is wound. In prevailing professional practice, POSITIVE film is at all times kept wound on reels after it has left the laboratory.
   The metallic or plastic circular holder for feeding out and taking up film in filming, editing or projection.
   Used as a term of measurement to describe the approximate length of a film:

"It's a thousand-foot reel; 35 mm; runs about 110 minutes." A two-reeler is about 20 minutes long. Most contemporary features (see FEATURE LENGTH) run between nine to twelve reels, although new projection techniques with FLANGE or open-reel feedout allow entire features to be put onto one extra large reel in a single film roll.

reel tension   Resistance on the take-up and feedout projector reels to eliminate slack in the film.

reel-to-reel   Recording ¼″ tape using a machine with feedout and take-up reels. In sound transfer terminology meaning making a copy from one format to the same format. For example, going from ¼″ sound recording tape to ¼″ tape for the copy/copies. Or going from a ¾″ VIDEOTAPE to a ¾″ copy.

re-establishing shot   A shot in a dramatic sequence that repeats the visual location of the action. Used conventionally to show passage of time, even changes of seasons.

reference burst   See COLOR BURST.

reflectance   Reflected   brightness bounced back from a surface, such as a reflector or a motion picture screen.

reflected light meter   Meter that "reads" light reflected from any person or thing within the scene frame.

reflector   A reflecting surface, frequently silver in color, used to bounce light to where it is needed. For exteriors, reflectors are often used to direct sunlight onto the actors or some other part of the scene. For interior lighting, they are used to bounce light from source to action area. Types of reflectors: A hand reflector is a lightweight reflector, small enough to be worked manually. A hard reflector is a highly-polished silver or aluminum foil surface, giving a mirrorlike reflection. A soft reflector is one that is coated with silver or gold reflection paper. It is softer in color than a hard reflector, and is pebbled to diffuse the reflected light.

reflector stand A special holder for the reflector. Usually metal, it comes in two basic sections; the YOKE, which holds the reflector, and the stand, which supports the yoke.

reflex camera One that reflects the light from a lens into the VIEWFINDER. This is done with an optical mirror configuration. Its advantage is that it lets the cameraman see the scene as it is to be, or is being, shot.

reflex viewfinder See VIEWFINDER.

regional A geographically limited TV transmission or reception area. Sponsors of regional programs are usually those who have their primary sales in local or regional markets covered by the particular TV station.

regional channel Radio broadcasting channel on which various stations can operate at 5 kilowatts or less.

regionalism A speech matrix of pitch, rhythm and pronunciation that is peculiar to a given geographical area, i.e., a southwestern accent, a New England accent, or one of the various accents of the boroughs of New York City. Regional sounds from other English-speaking countries, or countries where the native language is other than English, are referred to as "dialects." These regional accents are usually a liability for those looking for a position as a staff newscaster or announcer.

register Precision-matching of two or more patterns, such as an accurate image in a three-color TV picture.

registering The reaction, physical and facial, to the dialogue, action or general situation of the scene. A common complaint from director to actor is: "You're listening, but nothing's registering."

registration Proper alignment of film in a rigid position. In ANIMATION, the precision placement of layers or cels.

reissue To put a film back into distribution.

relay Forwarding transmitting device; and to forward such transmissions.

relay center Core locale where switching of messages takes place.

release A generic term used to designate a completed film going into distribution and exhibition.
A talent release is also called release form and personal release. A signed agreement by an on-camera person, professional or otherwise, giving the producer the right to reproduce that person's likeness and use it in any reasonable manner, relating only to the named production. See RELEASE FORMS in the Appendix.

release negative A complete NEGATIVE prepared specifically for printing RELEASE PRINTS.

release print A COMPOSITE PRINT made for general distribution. The release print is made after the final trial composite or SAMPLE PRINT has been approved. See ANSWER PRINT.

relief A slacking off of dramatic or rhythmic intensity. A markedly quieter, slower section than the scenes preceding or following. Comedy relief, if appropriate—and sometimes when it's not appropriate—is often used in lighter dramatic fare.

remake A full new production and release of a film made in earlier years. Examples: *A Star Is Born, Stagecoach, Beau Geste, King Kong,* etc.

Rembrandt lighting Overall "painting with light," characterized by rim-lighting, contrasting light-and-dark areas, and a general sense of what filmmakers refer

to as "mood," and PRODUCTION MAN-
AGERS as "expensive." Rembrandt lighting can be effectively used to delineate
the nature of the characters in a scene.

remote   A radio or TV broadcast from
a location outside the studio. Conventions, sporting events, on-the-spot news
are all examples of remotes. Also called
a FIELD PICKUP.

remote control   Controls initiated and
regulated from a distance—by wires, ul-
trasonics, radio signals or light.

renewal   A reissuing and time extension of a permit to broadcast, given at
the discretion of the Federal Communications Commission.

rental film   One rented for a fee to
the distributor or filmmaker for a limited
showing-time.

repeat   A rebroadcast of a program
aired at an earlier time or day.

replay   The immediate playback of a
videotape or audiotape, to check it for
use or exclusion in the final edited edi-
tion, by viewing it on a monitor or listening to it over a playback system

reprint   To make additional film prints.
from original or intermediate matrix.

reports   These daily records are written in production ledgers or on special
production sheets. Sound and camera
reports, for example, which indicate acceptable and non-acceptable TAKES and
additional relevant materials, are made
out of special long, rectangular pads with
multiple carbons; they are for annotating
each take separately. Production reports
are prepared by line producers and unit
managers. They contain the hours-worked
for each member of the cast and crew,
the amount of film stock shot, costs of
the shooting day, number of PAGES filmed,
balance of pages yet to shoot, location
and scouting data—in brief, everything
essential to the logistics of a shoot. The

SCRIPT CLERK'S notes can also be classified under the heading "production reports."

reproduction   *Contrasty reproduction*
is pictorial reproduction where the contrast of the observed image is overdone,
either accidentally or for a particular effect. When accidental, it tends to be excessive and objectionable.

Flat reproduction is pictorial reproduction that departs from normal reproduction in such a way that the CONTRAST of
the observed image is insufficient, and
also objectionable.

Normal reproduction is balanced, with
dark and light proportionate to one another.

re-recording   Electrical   process   of
transferring sound recordings from one
or more audio sources to other discs,
tapes or tracks. Also the combination of
all tracks (SOUND EFFECTS, DIALOGUE, music, etc.) onto one final release track.

re-recording system   A combination
of mixers, reproducers, microphones,
amplifiers, feed-in channels, recorders and
related devices that can be assembled in
precise configurations, as required. To be
mixed into the final sound(s), whether
speech, music or sound effects.

re-release   A new release cycle for a
film that has been released at an earlier
time. Putting back into circulation a film
that has been pulled from distribution.

rerun   A TV series put back on the air
in syndication, cable or network release
or into auxiliary markets—home videocassettes, videodisc, archival, etc. The
auxiliary markets are more often described as "reissues" than as "reruns."

residuals   Payments   to   performers,
writers, directors, composers and others,
for replays of TV programs aired after
their first showing or cycle. Residuals are
based on, but are over and above, the
original salary of the payee.

resolution, resolution power Ability of a LENS or emulsion to render fine detail in a photographic image.

In TV, resolution is the maximum number of discernible lines of a TV image.

résumé Crew member's or actor's summary or personal credits relating directly to his/her work in media. Used in seeking employment or in giving biographical information for a news release. Also called a CREDIT SHEET.

retained image An unwanted image that is burned in so that it does not fade immediately after it leaves the screen, but leaves a lingering trace-image.

retake A shooting of a SCENE after the main production has finished filming/videotaping. It is an expensive process and is avoided when possible. On many assignments video replays often avoid the problem of retakes, since any selected TAKE can be played back immediately and be evaluated on the spot.

reticle Lines on a camera viewfinder plate—etched in or printed on—that indicate TV-CUTOFF, general SAFE AREA, and the center of the frame.

retrospective A showing of films or videotapes highlighting the work of a particular producer, director, star, and—sometimes—writer.

reveal shot A SHOT that widens out and opens up by pulling back or zooming back to show where we are; often involving an element of surprise. Also called a discovery shot.

reversal film Film stock that, after EXPOSURE of the ORIGINAL, is processed to produce a POSITIVE image of the film, rather than the customary NEGATIVE image.

reversal optical A method of reversing the direction of motion of a SHOT by turning it over (tails-to-head, and vice versa) and rephotographing it in an optical printer in such a way that the emulsion side becomes the base side, and the base the emulsion side.

reverse The opposite angle of a single- or group-angled shot. If the camera is filming from the POINT OF VIEW of A, and looking at B, the reverse would be from the POV of B looking at A.

reverse action Action that goes backward, on a TV or movie screen. In filming, this is done by shooting with the camera upside down, then turning the processed film end-over-end. In TV, it is simply a matter of putting it in reverse mode.

revolving stage A playing-area stage that turns on a heavy pivot or axle, moving the entire scene so that it disappears behind theatrical curtains, or into darkness. Used initially in live theatre and then movie musicals, it is now also used in TV and MIXED MEDIA.

rewinds Geared devices for taking up or reeling off film. Used in conjunction with REELS or FLANGES, the rewinds may be activated manually or driven by an electric motor. Used mainly in CUTTING ROOMS, EDITING ROOMS, and projection booths.

rewrite A script that has been restructured and written again.

rf See RADIO FREQUENCY.

RGB The abbreviation for red-green-blue, the three basic colors and electronic guns that give color TV its full color spectrum.

ribbon mike A name for a high-sensitivity microphone developed in the late 1930s and early 1940s for radio. Still used for special recording sessions, especially for voice-over, where the sound of the actor must be resonant, close and intimate.

ride   To stay on top of and modulate the drop or gain in sound, as in "ride the gain" or "ride the meter."

rigging   1. Placing and linking power lines to studio lights, often set to a LIGHT PLOT. 2. Setting up special camera mounts, mechanical SPECIAL EFFECTS, sound baffles, PRACTICAL props, supports and platforms.

rip and read   Newscasting term meaning ripping the news directly from the teletype or printout machine and reading it, unedited, over the airways. Used literally and metaphorically. As a metaphor, it means not evaluating, not researching further, and not rewriting.

riser   A low platform a few inches in height, for raising a light, a prop, a singing ensemble, an actor or a cameraman above the studio floor.

RKO   See RADIO KEITH-ORPHEUM.

role   Part played by an actor.

roll   Roll can mean any of the following: a package of motion picture film, as it is ordered and comes from the manufacturer; a designation on a SLATE and corresponding production reports that indicates the film rolls as marked and the sequence in which they are used; the exposed film to be developed as it goes into and comes out of the lab; a command to start the cameras, followed by "SPEED!" and "ACTION!"; and the upward or downward drift of a TV picture, from an error in vertical synchronization.

roller stand   A century reflector mounted on a CENTURY STAND or on a general-utility stand, and on rollers, to give it easier mobility in a studio situation or a location site.

roll-up titles   See CRAWL TITLES.

room tone   A recording of sound presence, particularly in an INTERIOR setting or recording studio, where each environment has its own distinctive ambient sound. One form of PRESENCE.

rotoscope   A mechanism for projecting single FRAMES of FILM. This allows them to be rephotographed for SPECIAL EFFECTS, or for ANIMATION tracing.

rough cut   The version of an assembled WORKPRINT that immediately follows the STRING-OUT or FIRST ASSEMBLY. A stage in the film's completion, prior to FINE CUT.

R-rated   MPAA rating for films deemed not suitable for anyone under the age of 17 unless accompanied by an adult.

rumble   Low-pitched noises sometimes picked up on the recorded sound elements. They emanate from imperfect machine operations of a recorder, player or turntable.

runaway productions   Productions shooting all or most of their scenes out of a union's jurisdictional area—in other states or out of the country. The reason for this is to reduce required crew sizes and other union demands, and to reduce the overall costs of production. It can also circumvent performers' unions.

rushes   Prints rushed through the LAB, often on the same day the NEGATIVE is exposed. Rushes may be picture, sound or COMPOSITE.

S

safe-action area   Safety margin on the edges of the film, indicating how far into the FRAME the cameraman must be in order to compose properly for TV-CUTOFF. To secure accuracy in framing for film or TV, most professional cameras have a built-in grid on the internal clear glass plate. This is matched by a corresponding plate in projection facilities.

Projection plates include TV cutoff, ACAD-EMY, WIDESCREEN (in varying SCREEN RA-TIOS).

safety base The film BASE now used exclusively in professional motion picture houses. It is slow-burning, with an ACE-TATE BASE.

safelight The low-wattage bulb used in darkrooms. Usually yellow, it emits only enough light to work by without harming the effects of proper photographic exposure.

safety film Film stock using a SAFETY BASE.

SAG See SCREEN ACTORS GUILD.

sample print A COMPOSITE PRINT approved for release, in which all corrections found necessary in previous trial composites have been incorporated. Also known as final trial composite.

sandbags Standard working tool in film and TV. Its use developed out of live theater, where it served as a curtain-pull counterweight, and as support for augmenting the weight of stage legs and braces to help hold up the scenery. To these uses, film and TV added the functions of weighing down REFLECTOR or light stands, especially on exterior shoots, even more particularly on windy days. Sandbags also serve as ballast on the DOLLY, to help achieve smooth moves, and as an improvised ground-level camera mount. They are also useful as barriers for actors who might otherwise overshoot their marks.

satellite Relaying orbiting space station for international beaming of transmissions to receiving stations on earth, picked up by satellite-network-DISHes. Relay-transmission delay is approximately a quarter of a second. This information system has been powerfully effective in bringing us live events from all over the world.

saturated When the collector-current is "full," and cannot increase its power, despite additional supply from the base current.

saturation The measurement of the purity and vividness of a color. Also the clarity of the hue. Vibrant, glowing color with optimum distinctness can be described as "fully saturated." The color decreases in saturation as it moves nearer to a neutral gray.

In advertising, saturation is the heavy use of spot advertising to push a product or event on radio or TV (and possibly in print), over one or more stations for a necessary amount of time.

saturation booking Booking a film in numerous theaters in a given area, and simultaneously launching a heavy ad campaign.

saturation current Maximum current achieved when an increased voltage is applied.

save A command to hold, retain or cut power to conserve electricity or bulb-life.

Or to hold a take for printing, or on tape to mark it for nonerasure.

save the scene To figure out a way to salvage a seemingly-irredeemable scene or sequence. This can be done in a variety of ways: redoing the voice tracks (ADR), or re-editing it, with heavy use of CUTAWAY shots, deleting the problem area by finding another point to cut to within the scene that won't result in a jump in continuity. If it is a technical problem, there are also appropriate sound and picture techniques that can help: color-correcting, sound re-recording, reframing-reprinting, etc.

sawed-offs See BABY TRIPOD.

scale Formal meaning of the word is a manual of minimum payments for a union performer's function and time. Within the media trade it is more commonly used to mean "only scale," i.e., the bare minimum. Also heard is the phrase, "Scale plus ten." This means scale payments to the performer, plus 10% commission on the gross amount for the agent who secures the job.

scallop   Undulating distortion in a TV picture.

scanning   Horizontal beam sweep moving over the camera pickup tube. In film, reading the optical sound track and converting it to audible signals.

scanning beam   Collimated narrow ray of light which scans the optical sound track of a film print.

scanning line   Horizontal TV line across a TV tube generated electronically within the set.

scanning speed   Inches per second covered by the scanning beam, or applicable energizing source, for TV, fax machines, laser printers, etc.

scenario   See SCREENPLAY.

scene   A subdivision of an act in live theater. In film, a scene is synonymous with a SHOT; or, a filmed scene may be made using one basic number from end to end, then slated for coverage into subslates, i.e., Scene #27-a, 27-aa, 27-b, 27-c, etc. Another example: a full dramatic sequence (a "scene" in the sense of live theater) might be slated as Scenes #36-39, and marked/filmed as such in the master. After that, Scenes 36, 37, 38 and 39 are filmed separately. Even then, if a director decides to add a new camera angle to a section of dialogue, or add or delete some dialogue, he/she will do this by having the SCRIPT CLERK assign a new scene number to the SHOT, e.g., #37-a. In film and videotape shooting, scene number and slate number are the same.

scene dock   Scenery storage area for scenic props, flats and backdrops.

scenery   Scenic props, flats and backdrops, plus drapes, furniture and sometimes hand-props.

scenic designer   In TV, the person who creates settings and indicates scenic props. Roughly analogous to the ART DIRECTOR in film.

sci-fi   Short for science fiction, now established as a full-fledged, omnipresent media genre with its own cadre of fans. It has become popular in part due to the emergence of excellent special effects that can create the sci-fi fantasies dreamed up by their authors.

science fiction   See SCI-FI.

scoop   A semicircular-shaped light trough, powered by 500- to 1500-watt globes. A soft light.

score   Music for a film or videotape.

scoring   Composing, arranging, orchestrating, copying and recording the music. With the great potential and range of electronic music, all these functions can be handled by one person. Library scoring is essentially a job of selecting and laying in CUES.

scoring sessions   A live-performance session for recording the musical score.

scouting   Verb to accompany activities, i.e., the hunt for workable filming locales, of the LOCATION SCOUT or LOCATION MANAGER.

scraper   SPLICER part that scrapes off film emulsion in order to make a clean cement-splice.

scratch track   A roughly-recorded SOUND TRACK made in SYNCH to the picture, to be used as a guide in editorial synchronization or for FOLEYING and SCORING SESSIONS, and particularly for ADR sessions.

scratch print   A print that has been deliberately scratched, usually in a mutilator, to prevent its unauthorized duplication. Scratch-prints are provided by stock-shot libraries and are used by producers and directors for viewing purposes to locate and select shots to be duplicated from the library's vaulted masters.

screen   In film, the projected photographic image is formed on a whitish screen, which may have matte, beaded, metallic, perforated or nonperforated surfaces. The perforated screen allows more sound to reach the theater audience when loudspeakers are mounted behind the screen. Informally, in TV, the viewing surface of a master TV tube. In multiple theaters in malls or elsewhere, the basic unit indicating the polyscreen complex, i.e., "It's a ten-screen theater!"

Screen Actors Guild (SAG)   Union for on-camera actors in comedy, musical or dramatic roles; it sets pay-scales and working standards. It has United States membership only and is based in key American cities that are strong in media, such as New York, Chicago, Hollywood and Miami.

screen brightness   Full range of luminance emitted by a SCREEN, measured in candles per square foot.

screen credits   See CREDITS.

screen direction   The particular direction, left or right, as seen by the audience, in which the ACTOR is moving. This is also referred to as frame direction and camera direction. MASTER SCENES and COVERAGE should all be congruent in screen direction.

Screen Extras Guild (SEG)   Union for film supernumeraries who are also known as the atmosphere. On-camera performers without dialogue or specified roles, who form the human background of a scene. Now under SAG jurisdiction.

screening   The showing of a film on a motion picture screen; a presentation of dailies or completed film, or any intermediate stage, for a selected audience; a previewing of the film for a test audience.

screening room   Projection area that is equipped with state-of-the-art projectors and sound channels, in appropriate gauges and speeds, and with necessary aperture plates (Academy, TV-CUTOFF, WIDE-SCREEN, etc.). The screening room can be part of the lab's facility for viewing film, or a privately-owned room for private rentals, professional or otherwise.

screen left/screen right   See CAMERA LEFT/CAMERA RIGHT.

screenplay   Working SCRIPT for the film, evolving from concept to outline to treatment to SHOOTING SCRIPT. For Academy consideration, screenplays are divided into two basic categories, i.e., those adapted from another medium and those written directly for the screen.

screen ratio   See ASPECT RATIO.

screen test   Originally, a test made of an ACTOR or actors doing a specially selected scene; an on-film audition. The scene could be chosen specifically to see how the actor performed in a segment from an upcoming production; or it could be a general scene, even one chosen by the actor(s) if the test was mainly to determine whether or not the studio saw potential capabilities in the actor to warrant signing him/her to a salaried contract. As the studio system began breaking up in the 1950s, most contract players were dropped. Screen tests became less frequent and more expensive. Finally, the filming of such tests came to an end with only rare exceptions. Today, tests are made on tape. Auditions for TV shows, and especially TV commercials, are also taped to show to the client and/or director at another time, or to send to a different city for client viewing.

screenwriter   Author of works for the screen in any or all stages: idea, concept, outline, treatment, first working draft, shooting script. The true auteurs of films. Also called scenarist, script-writer and, simply, "writer."

scribe   Tool used by editors to scratch the emulsion of a print. This is done with the sharply-pointed scribe in order to conform and mark the original footage for SPLICING, and to indicate fades, disolves and other lab requirements.

scrim Light diffuser set in front of a lighting source to soften, or "thin out," the light. A scrim can be a wire-mesh diffuser set in a metal frame, or spun glass that is hand-held or mounted, parachute material, translucent materials, etc. A wire-mesh scrim is dropped in as a single, that is, one scrim. When a second one is added, it is referred to as a double. These terms apply to all basic materials, by extension. If a FLAG is made of translucent material, it, too, is called a scrim. Its effect is partly to cut off, partly to diffuse, the source of light near which it is placed. Thus, it is midway between a GOBO and a DIFFUSER. In FILM and VIDEOTAPE lighting, the scrim is placed in front of the lights to soften the glare and/or reduce the overall light level. On the legitimate stage, and sometimes used similarly in film or videotape, the scrim is a diaphanous gauze-like material that can be front-lit to be opaque or back-lit to give diffuse lighting and lend a sense of fantasy or unreality to the performers onstage.

script A written form to be used in the making of any film. In its early stages it is often designated as a TREATMENT; in its final stages, as a SHOOTING SCRIPT. See SCREENPLAY, SCRIPT FORMS in Appendix.

script clerk Crew or staff member, on a SET or on LOCATION, responsible for keeping full records of the shooting of all scenes. This means keeping track of the shots: full scenes, pickups, cutaways, inserts and variations, and indicating them all with full slate information, including TAKE number, shooting date, director's name, cameraman's name, and above all, the name and production number of the project. The script clerk must type out the handwritten on-the-spot notes, making them as clear as possible, for use by the DIRECTOR and EDITOR. Also called SCRIPT SUPERVISOR.

script form (educational/industrial and theatrical) See Appendix.

script supervisor See SCRIPT CLERK.

scriptwriter See SCREENWRITER.

search and seizure Under the Constitution and some state guarantees, reporters, newsgatherers, documentary filmmakers and journalists, in general, have the basic right not to have their notes, tape, films and augmenting materials seized, even in a court-authorized search. This right was set back by the Supreme Court in the *Zurcher v. Stanford Daily* case in 1979, after the high court ruled that a police search under the Fourth Amendment was legal because it would produce evidence necessary to a case. This led to a series of similar raids on the local, state and federal levels in the 1980s.

SECAM Abbreviation for Système Electronique Couleur avec Mémoire. Color TV system used in France, Eastern Europe, USSR, Haiti and French Guiana. With the PAL system, it shares the nations in Africa, the Levant and the Arabian Peninsula. Like PAL, it is a 625 line, 25 frames per second system.

second assistant cameraman See CAMERAMAN.

second cameraman See CAMERAMAN.

second unit A sub-unit of the production team, also known as the "B" team. Assigned to do pickup shots, overseas location shots to establish locale, stunt shots and backup shots in conjunction with the main crew, i.e., the "A" team.

SEG See SCREEN EXTRAS GUILD.

segue Used in radio as a script direction, indicating a piece of transition music from one scene to another. Sometimes used in TV scripts; rarely in screenplays. See also BRIDGE, STING.

selector relay   One that automatically indicates and activates one or more circuits.

self-balancing recorders   Recorder working in conjunction with a speed-averaging servomechanism.

self-blimped   Denoting sound cameras with built in sound-deadeners incorporated into the camera housing, to emit minimal or nondiscernible camera noise, so that camera sounds will not be picked up in sound takes.

self-powered   Equipment powered by itself. The power unit may be wet or dry cells, often with rechargeable batteries.

self-threading reel   Spool for storing tapes, which doesn't require external assistance to start the feedin/takeup process.

selsyn motor   Rotor-driven synchronous motor connected to a SYNCHRONIZING GENERATOR.

semiconductor   Electronic part made mostly of silicon, or specialized semiconductivity material; heat-efficient substances, operating well at high temperatures, used for the manufacture of transistors. Silicon and germanium are typical semiconductor substances.

senior   This is a large, focusable LAMP, with a mounted FRESNEL LENS and powered by a 5000-watt globe. It is midway between a JUNIOR and a 10K. Also called a 5K.

sensitivity   Calibrated range indicating the measure to which film emulsions respond to a given amount of light.

sensitometry   The applied science and technology of accurately measuring exposure and development criteria.

sensor   A triggering element that activates functions of start, stop or change in a circuit or mechanical system. In film projection, the sensor is applied to make automatic changeovers, shutdowns, etc.

sequel   A follow-up film based on previously established characters, like Rocky, Indiana Jones or the Karate Kid.

sequence   A section of a film that is a discrete segment by itself. It is sometimes set off by a fade-in and fade-out on either end. More frequently, however, it ends with a DISSOLVE, or even a CUT. The last-named two options tend to give the overall section in which the sequence works, a faster flow. FADEs tend to slow a film down, and should be used accordingly. Using literary writing as an analogy, the SHOT may be taken as a sentence; a scene, a paragraph; a sequence, a chapter.

serial   A long motion picture, broken up into chapters or episodes. In the 1920s, 1930s and 1940s they were the staple of the Saturday matinee at the neighborhood theatre. The feature became secondary in importance to the serial. These high-action melodramas were turned out rapidly for immediate audience consumption. Famous serials were *The Perils of Pauline,* a Gene Autry serial, *Flash Gordon, Captain Marvel, Batman,* and many others. Each episode ended with the hero or heroine—or both—in extreme peril. These "cliffhangers" were not resolved until the following Saturday, often with strained explanations that pushed credulity to the limit. Television and the expanding length of the double-feature programs in the picture houses finally gave the serials the *coup de grace.*

series   Film features or shorts in which there are repeating key characters, popular in the 1930s and 1940s. Examples: the Ma and Pa Kettle series, the Andy Hardy series, the Joe Doakes series (this last being a series of shorts). Akin to this were the short Pete Smith specials, the Robert Benchley shorts and the Fitzpatrick Travelogue films.
   In TV, series are comedies (sitcoms) or dramas that appear weekly, with a core

cast in nearly every show, and also recurring "regulars" who appear in appropriate segments.

service area Area surrounding a broadcasting station that determines its transmission range based on the dropout perimeters of its signal, and the quality of that signal. In brief, the broadcast area that can be efficiently serviced.

servomechanism A unit or system of feedback control, electromechanical in its operation.

set Scenic construction that forms the playing area of a film or videotape for a specific scene or body of the production.

set designer Person who makes the sketches and schematics for the construction of the set.

set dresser One responsible for positioning furniture, hanging drapes and arranging scenic props.

setting Time and place ambience. Whether Rome, circa 50 B.C., or London, 1770, the "setting" is what is created scenically by the ART DIRECTOR and SET DESIGNER, and detailed by the DRESSER to match locale and period. In the screenplay, "setting" is part of the description in the GENERAL DIRECTION. If the setting is a PRACTICAL one, such as seashore, or downtown in a contemporary big city, this is also indicated.

setup Physical placement of a camera in a specific spot, set or locale as well as the spot itself.

SHF See SUPERHIGH FREQUENCY.

sharp tuning Tuning-operation control over a narrow range of frequencies.

shift To move computer information from one location to another.

shoot To photograph with still or motion picture film. Now also used for videotaping, to refer to the actual visual and sound recording. "Okay, let's shoot our next video sequence!" Shoot also refers to the filming session itself. "We're going out on a shoot."

shooting call See CALL and CALL SHEET in Appendix.

shooting date The date specified for services of cast members and crew, personal denotation, plus indication of scenes that are scheduled.

shooting ratio Factor of film shot in relation to film actually used in the final cut. "They shot about ten to one," i.e., 10″ to get 1″ of eventual running length.

shooting schedule Logistical outline that is prepared at the end of the day by PRODUCTION MANAGER, ASSISTANT DIRECTOR, DIRECTOR and—sometimes—PRODUCER. It lists the location of the shoot and includes an attached map, if necessary, as well as contact names and numbers, the crew and actors needed, and their call times. It stresses any changes of venue, scenes-to-be, or cast and crew substitutions or replacements. It also gives the projected start and wrap times for each member of the cast and crew.

shooting script The final, scene-numbered working SCRIPT of a film. It details the shots one by one, in relation to their accompanying dialogue or other sound.

short subject A film that is under half an hour in running time. Includes short documentaries, animation films and live action films.

short wave Frequencies 1.6 to 30 MHz. These frequencies, being above the commercial broadcasting band, are for sky-wave transmissions over great distances.

shot An elemental division of a film. In professional practice, a shot is more often called a SCENE, and slated accordingly, basing its numbering upon those given in the final SHOOTING SCRIPT. The common descriptions of shots are necessarily relative to the basic composition of which they form a part. A *close shot* or *close-up* is one taken with the camera near to, or apparently near to, the subject, which can be an object or the human face. This image fills most of the action area. Abbreviated CS or CU. A *dolly shot* is one that is propelled along in obvious movement by a professional or improvised DOLLY or by using a BOOM on a dolly, as the dolly is in motion. If not in motion it becomes a BOOM SHOT, i.e., one made from the end of a boom, either locked down or mobile. An *establishing shot* is any shot that establishes the whereabouts of a scene, and possibly the historical era at the same time. It is a long, full shot, containing as much information as will be relevant to the scene that follows. A *high shot* is one that looks down on the subject from a height. An *insert shot* is of objects relating to the scene, which is CUT into a scene to further explain or to intensify the action. A *long shot* is one where the object(s) of principal interest—buildings, a herd of cattle, traffic—are, or appear to be, a goodly distance from the camera. Abbreviated LS. A *low shot* looks up at the subject from a lower position, often from ground level. A *medium-close shot* is intermediate in distance between a medium shot and a long shot. Abbreviated MCS. A *medium-long shot* is intermediate in distance between a medium shot and a long shot. Abbreviated MLS. A *medium shot* (mid shot) is one that shows a person at full height or looks at a scene from normal viewing distance. Abbreviated MS. A *moving shot* is one in motion, shot from a plane, boat, helicopter, train, automobile, snowmobile, bobsled, surfboard, etc. A *pan shot* is one that moves horizontally across the people, scenery or objects being filmed/videotaped. A *reaction shot* is one inserted in a DIALOGUE sequence to show the effect of an actor's words or reactions on the others in the scene, usually in close-up. In more general usage, it refers to any shot focusing or reactions. A *two-shot* is one showing two characters on camera. The terms *three-shot, four-shot,* etc., have corresponding meanings, though often after three or four in number, the term "group shot" is used. A *zoom shot* is one taken with a ZOOM LENS. Verb: "The cameraman *shot* the last scene this morning." "How many films has the D.P. *shot?*"

shot analysis   Shot-by-shot investigation of a film. It is often made by producers trying to figure out where the money went, or by film students studying cinema critically. In both cases these analyses are, at best, conjectural and extrapolative. However, for film students, such analysis can be extremely helpful in understanding the architectonics of a film and the efficacy—or lack of it—in the editing.

shotgun mic   One that can be handheld to record sound at more than the standard distances from the mike. Since it can pick up sound at a considerable distance, it also picks up a high level of ambience, and must be used accordingly. Not to be used for a critical sound recording.

shot list   A list of shots for the director or cameraman in newsgathering and documentary situations as a reminder or checklist. To augment and annotate the script, or to use where there can be no script until after the filming. It is also used in TV as a list of sequence of shots for the newscaster and broadcasting crew.

shrinkage   Gradual reduction of the film size due to the weakening of the support chemicals that plasticize the base, the chemical contraction of the emulsion and the general loss of moisture, all of these compounded by the age of the film, its handling, and its storage temperature. Today's acetate films are designed to allow for and seldom exceed a shrinkage rate of 0.5%, which lets the film continue to be used effectively for all normal projection purposes.

shutter   Device that momentarily covers the camera's aperture during the fraction of a second in which the film is moved between EXPOSURES. Also protects light-sensitive surfaces in a TV camera.

shutter speed   The amount of time the shutter is open that determines the exposure time of the FRAME.

sibilant   Hissing speech sound usually caused by breath escaping and resonating against the teeth or between the lips. A sound that should be minimized in professional speech, especially when speaking into a microphone as the mic tends to bring out sibilance.

sight gag   An action joke, fully or primarily visual and not relying heavily upon verbal elements. Also, a silent-comedy bit.

signal   The visual or audible electronically transmitted communication.

signal lamp   A lamp in a specific circuit which indicates operational conditions depending on its "on" or "off" state.

signal strength   The generated-transmitted strength of a signal.

signal-to-noise-ratio   Ratio, at any circuit point, of signal power at total strength in relation to noise power.

silent films   Phased out by the advent of "talking pictures," they set up the story-telling style and imagery and wrote the grammar of film movement. Actually, the silent films were never that silent. There was an orchestra in the pits of the big theaters and a piano player in the neighborhood houses who played background and mood music to accompany the film. The piano player often provided some sound effects: horses hooves, shots, sirens, etc. In houses with full orchestras, the sound effects were often handled by the percussionist. The "story" was told partly by the subtitles, but in the best silent films, the story was told primarily by the strength and continuity of the visual images.

silhouette   Image created by using mostly, or exclusively, back-lighting.

silicon   Non-metallic element used in its pure state as the basic semiconductor material.

silicon transistor   Transistor using SILICON as the semiconductive material.

silk   Once made of framed-silk, today's "silks" are diffusers of framed gauze, translucent fireproof plastic, fiberglas or various materials that are white. They are used to give a soft light when photographing food products, women's skin in cosmetic ads, "romantic" settings in a studio situation, automobiles, fine jewelry and products where quality needs to be stressed.

silver reflector   Made of space-suit material. A soft reflector that can be folded like a cloth and unfolded for use as a reflector. Also called a space blanket.

simple tone   Sound with a singleness of pitch. Also called a pure tone.

simplex   Satellite operation utilizing communications in one direction at a time: TV, fax machines, data transmission.

simulcast   Broadcasting the same program simultaneously over different media channels, i.e. an opera on TV, with sound augmented by an FM station broadcasting it at the same time; or the same radio program on FM and AM at the same moment.

singing sprocket   A highly irritating noise caused by film under great tension as it leaves the teeth of a sprocket. The usual offender is the holdback sprocket of the projector.

single A SHOT of one person. Also called a one-shot. See SCRIM.

single card An unshared screen credit, the only one in the FRAME. Photographed on a single titling card.

single system A method of sound recording in which the sound is originally recorded on the same strip of film as the picture image. Owing to the difficulties in film-cutting, caused by the difference between camera and editorial SYNCHRONISM and to film-sensitivity disadvantages, single-system sound recording (except for news coverage and on-the-spot interviews) has been abandoned in favor of DOUBLE SYSTEM SOUND RECORDING.

single track recorder Tape recorder that plays or records only one track at a time.

sitcom (situation comedy) A series in which the main characters are pre-established and plots are developed to involve these characters in an almost-believable situation; one that creates a problem that must be resolved in about 22 minutes (the TV "half-hour").

situation comedy See SITCOM.

sixteen mm (16mm) Film used primarily for filming documentaries; videotape has replaced film in most news departments. 16mm is also used for filming low-budget commercials, or even low-budget FEATURES. The features are then blown up to 35mm.

skipping effects Jerkiness of the movement of an image. A strobing effect in panning, for example. Unless desired for effect, the jumping images are totally distracting. See STROBE and STROBO-SCOPE.

skip distance Distance between two points on our planet, where radiowave connection is effected by bouncing a transmission from the ionosphere's layers.

skivings "Threads" of film-print stock coming from a projector, caused by film scraping against a metallic burr or a mis-aligned element in the system. One of many things a projectionist doesn't want to see on the projection room floor. Also called angel hair.

slapstick Comedy based on broad, rough physical action. Silent films were an ideal vehicle for slapstick, as it was international in its language and needed no sound, except musical punctuation by a pit orchestra or the theater's piano player. Originating as clown humor, it was first presented on the stages of Greece and the stages and streets of Rome. The "slapstick" itself was a lethal-sounding but virtually harmless instrument of two long sticks, joined together, that cracked loudly when struck against the body of a fellow clown. Slapstick is still full of hitting, buffeting and general physical abuse.

slate The identification of production scenes and take numbers. Can be done vocally, or by electronic flashing light, and most commonly by the SLATE BOARD. Slates are numbered according to the sequentially numbered scenes. A, B and C letters that follow a scene number indicate a variation of the basic shot of the scene (like "Scene 27-A"). X, Y and Z letters indicate an INSERT SHOT, one that can be used anywhere in that scene or even in another scene (like 27-X).

slate board A board placed in front of the camera at the start of each SCENE or TAKE, that identifies each, as well as showing the name of the picture, DIRECTOR and CAMERAMAN. See also CLAPPER BOARDS.

sleeper A motion picture with unpretentious expectations that suddenly becomes a box office success.

slide film A filmstrip made up of 35mm slides, shown in sequence to match either accompanying live commentary by a teacher or speaker, or with an attached synchronous sound track, that moves the filmstrip ahead frame-by-frame with electronic impulses.

slop-test Immediate processing in a portable lab, or rushing the film through a regular lab, with minimal quality control, in order to check out image.

slow motion The effect of objects moving much more slowly than at their standard rate of speed. This is done by shooting at speeds exceeding normal and projecting at the regular running rate.

slug A piece of LEADER inserted into a picture or sound WORKPRINT, to replace damaged, missing or unavailable footage.

slug in To put in the LEADER.

smear TV-image distortion that makes the picture stretch out horizontally and blur.

SMPTE See SOCIETY OF MOTION PICTURE AND TELEVISION ENGINEERS.

sneak preview Unannounced showing of a feature film not yet released to the public. This is done to test audience response, and is sometimes augmented by audience-reaction cards that are filled out by the viewers immediately after the showing.

snoot Metallic tubelike extension in front of a light, to narrow its beam, giving it more of a spotlight effect.

snow Imperfect TV reception, with a weak signal causing the picture to break up into dancing grains.
   As a film effect, snow can be made from many things: soapflakes, whitened cornflakes, small chips of balsa wood, sawdust, shredded white plastic sheets, crumpled styrofoam, diced feathers, etc.

soap opera Originally referred to in the 1930s to describe the daytime serials that sprang up in Chicago and New York. As many of these radio dramas were sponsored by soap companies, they came to be known as soap operas. The name stuck when the daytime serials re-emerged on TV, and even when they moved to prime time.

Society of Motion Picture and Television Engineers (SMPTE) State-of-the-art arbiters in the film and television fields. Their national conventions and trade-oriented shows often introduce the newest technological innovations and breakthroughs in media hardware.

sodium process One way of making a traveling MATTE. The action is filmed in front of a yellow screen, lit by sodium-vapor lamps. These lamps produce a color tonality that cannot be photographed, making them ideal for special effects lay-ins.

soft cut A quick DISSOLVE lasting only a few frames.

soft-edge wipe A kind of WIPE in which the boundary line between the two SHOTS is softened or blurred, often by shooting the wipe-masks out of focus. The degree of softness can be controlled.

soft focus Diffused focus using fog filters or scrimming materials in front of the lens. For filming with a "romantic," "otherworldly" or "other-time" look or to erase facial lines.

soft news News that is not happening at the moment; stories that are not usually ongoing. Features and human interest stories are examples of soft news.

soft porn Sexual situations and nudity, but no details of sex acts; relying on simulated sex. See PORNOGRAPHY.

solid flags/gobos Opaque light-cutters—no gauze or scrimming.

solid-state circuit A circuit that is complete unto itself, and is manufactured from one discrete unit of calibrated semiconductor material.

sonant   A voiced sound.

sone   A unit of sound as heard. This loudness measurement is based on a frequency of 1000 hertz. 1000 hertz is 40 decibels beyond a human listener's threshold.

sonic   Pertaining to what is produced by sound waves. Relating to the science of, and the general use of, sound. As an adjective, relating to the speed of sound.

sound   Total AUDIO components of a videotape or film, informally or technically: sound, dialogue, music, narration, etc.

sound bite   See ACTUALITY.

sound camera   Camera designed for sound shooting, i.e., picture and sound at the same time. It is silenced internally by either a supersilent film-driving mechanism or a self-blimped element inside the camera. The aim in both cases is to achieve minimal audible camera noise. The term is also applied to the recording camera in which the sound image is transferred to film via a modulator and a modulated beam of light, or its magnetic equivalent.

sound crew   Subdivision of CREW; their job is to record all production sound. In a recording studio situation, it refers to the paid staff handling the recording session.

sound dissolve   Analogous to picture DISSOLVE. A brief overlapping of two SOUND TRACKS.

sound effects (SFX)   All sounds, other than synchronized voices, NARRATION and music, which may be recorded on the SOUND TRACK of a film. Prior to RE-RE-CORDING, these effects usually occupy separate tracks called, appropriately, sound effects tracks.

sound effects library   An index or catalogued collection of the most com-monly used SOUND EFFECTS that are on hand at a production house or recording studio. Sound effects are most conveniently recorded on film, but are often re-recorded from discs and from unperforated magnetic tape. Sounds can now be digitally "sampled" and stored, to be used as is, or with digital restructuring and extension or layered augmentation, in order to create highly creative and imaginative sound effects. Some sound effects categories are: gun shots, car crashes, small crowd, large crowd roar, jet engines, train crossing bell and glass breaking. These effects can be used by themselves or in conjunction with "real sound."

sound head   Unit in a motion picture projector that converts photographic or magnetic sound tracks on the film into audible signals, amplified and sent out over the speakers.

sound-on-sound recording   Where previously recorded material from track is overlaid with a track or tracks from another sound source.

sound reader   Instrument for SOUND TRACK playbacks, used in editing.

sound speed   Standardized speed of 24 frames (in some countries, 25) per second for cameras and projectors for synchronous picture and sound.

sound stripe   A thin band of iron oxide applied to the edge of a strip of film.

sound track   A narrow band, along one side of a sound film, which carries the sound. In some cases, like stereophonic recording, several such bands may be used.

sound truck   A mobile conveyance fitted with a sound-recording channel. It usually carries drums on which microphones and other cables are wound. Still used in location televising by TV crews, but virtually phased out in motion picture use because of the new lightweight recording equipment.

soup Film developing lab argot for chemical developing solutions.

sources In news and documentary fact-gathering, the places from which data is derived directly or extrapolated. Whenever possible and applicable, the source-person or the source-document should be named. Such source acknowledgement is known as "attribution." Facts must be cross-checked, using more than one reference source.

south Lower area on animation field chart.

space blanket See SILVER REFLECTOR.

spacing Setting appropriate distances between microphones and speakers.

spaghetti western Popular in the late 1960s and well into the 1970s, these Italian-made westerns usually featured an American star, with the other Italian actors mouthing words or numbers that were replaced later by English-speaking actors in ADR sessions.

sparks The nickname for a crew electrician; commonly used in the United Kingdom.

special effects A generic term for trick photography. These artificially achieved effects are created and filmed on specially designed stages. Special effects include split-screens, matting, models (ships, trains, villages), and combination FOREGROUNDS and BACKGROUNDS. Special effects also employ such techniques as microphotography, split-screen process, multiple-image sequences, laser-scan techniques, as well as special instructions to the lab on development and printing. Differentiation should be made between optical special effects, such as listed immediately above, and mechanical special effects. Examples of mechanical special effects: a bridge collapsing as a car drives across it, a house bursting into flames, simulated motions of movement inside an auto-mobile, train, ship, passenger section of a stagecoach, airplane, etc.

special events Nonrepeatable occurrences of great public interest with set dates: a high-level NATO meeting with numerous world leaders present; coronation of a British monarch, or royal wedding in full regal panoply; an American political convention, nominating the party's presidential candidate; space-rocket (particularly a manned space unit) launching; and others.

speed Generic term for the magnitude of light transmission of some part of a photographic system, usually an emulsion or LENS. Emulsion speed is the sensitivity of a photographic emulsion to light: The higher the speed, the greater the sensitivity. Lens speed is the light-admitting index of a lens, measured by its F NUMBER or T-STOP.

Also, the correct rate at which a film mechanism is designed to run. The cry "Speed!" means that a sound or picture camera has reached synchronous speed, and that the scene is ready to be filmed. This is the cue for the director or his assistant to call "Action!"

speed of sound Speed sound travels through the air at sea level: 750 mph or 1080 feet per second. Or the differing rate at which it travels through another medium: salt water, the earth's mantle, etc.

spider A device of three pieces of metal, spreading out approximately 120° each from a central core. There is a cuplike indentation at the end of these metal pieces, as well as clamping devices. This allows tripod legs to be positioned and secured. The pieces are adjustable so that they can be spread, by extending them. Hence the spider is also referred to as a spreader. The function of the spider is to stop the TRIPOD legs from slipping on smooth surfaces, and to keep tripod-leg points from gouging wood, marble or carpeting.

spill light   Unwanted loss of light that is diffusing itself in a wider beam pattern than necessary for the proper illumination of a scene. It is a condition to be corrected before filming begins.

spill tank   See DUMP TANKS.

spin   Optical special effect in which an object is whirling in the frame. Many movies in the late 1930s and early 1940s had newspapers spinning rapidly into frame then coming to an abrupt stop, with the headline story coming boldly into focus. Another example would be to show dizziness evolving into a faint, or a person falling (stylistically).

spindle   Vertical rod on a phonograph turntable, which fits the center hole of the record. It centers the record into its proper playing position on the turntable.

splice, splicing   The joining of two pieces of film end-to-end, so that they form one continuous piece of film is called splicing, and the joint is called a splice. Splices are of two basic kinds, butt splices and lap splices. A butt splice is created when the ends of two pieces of film are made to abut directly to one another, one end against the other. This technique is seldom used except for the cutting of picture-release negatives, at which time it is important to retain frames that would be lost in a lap splice. A lap splice occurs when the ends of two pieces of film are made to overlap. They may be united by applying film cement to the overlapped area, after removing any emulsion present. This is the standard editing splice when working with film print. A negative splice is a narrower type of lap splice, used for both NEGATIVE and POSITIVE original picture material. This splice results in making the printed-through image of the splice itself invisible (or, in 16mm, as invisible as possible) under normal projection conditions. A positive splice is a wider type of lap splice, often used by film exchanges in the repair of RELEASE PRINTS.

splicer   A machine needed to SPLICE two lengths of film together. Splicers are often classified as hot or cold, according to whether heat is applied to the film joint to hasten the drying of the liquid cement. See EDITING BLOCK.
Also, the person doing the splicing.

splicing tape   Nonmagnetic tape for splicing two sections of magnetic tape together.

split-field lens   One that bifurcates focal planes and holds both in focus at the same time, or racks focus from one plane to another.

split-focus shot   Shot made with the SPLIT-FIELD LENS.

split reels   Standard REELS having one removable side, so that a film CORE can be mounted on the spindle, and wound film taken off at will and transferred to a FLANGE or a can without having to undergo rewinding.

split screen   A frame of film divided into two or more parts (viewed simultaneously), as separate, discrete elements, or repeat shots of the same image in each of the frame areas, the latter use employed for graphic impact and emphasis.

sponsor   Advertiser of a particular program or series, whose commercials are seen before, during and sometimes immediately after the program.

spool   See FEED SPOOL.

sports   Because of the viewers' demands for sports events, it is a field that has the most technically sophisticated coverage. Sports coverage by multiple-camera systems is always state-of-the-art, and has brought the instant-replay into prominence. There is not only play-by-play coverage of sporting events, but also during-the-game and after-the-game analyses, interviews with athletes as well as detailed discussions of sports issues and sports scandals.

spot   A commercial. Also, a spotlight.

spotlight   See FOLLOW SPOTLIGHT.

spot sheet   Sequential sheet prepared by the news copywriter for the video editor, indicating the types of shots to match the various segments of the story, with notations of running times of each shot.

spotting   The process whereby a location of individuals, words or modulations on a SOUND TRACK can be accurately determined. This is accomplished with a MOVIOLA sound-head.

spreader   See SPIDER.

spring-drive camera   One powered by a spring-wound motor, that is speed-controlled by a governor.

sprocket   A wheel carrying regularly spaced teeth of the correct pitch and separation to engage with film perforations and to move the film forward or in reverse, while maintaining SYNCHRONISM and REGISTRATION. See also FEED SPROCKET.

spurious   emanations   Unwanted emissions from a transmitting circuit.

spurious signal   An interfering signal that reads as noise. Either external or internal, in relation to the equipment.

spurt tone   An audio-tone lasting only a moment, used for dialing or signaling selection.

squawker   In a three-way system, the midrange speaker. Between the TWEETER and the WOOFER.

squeeze ratio   Horizontal compression in an anamorphic image, relative to its height.

squibs   Explosive caps used to give the effect of exploding bullets. When used on actors, in conjunction with blood capsules (makeup "blood" in plastic minibags), the performers are protected by a metal plate under their clothing, to which the squib is attached.

stabilization   The use of magnetic flux to steady the flow of electrons in a carbon arc. Important in projection, the term is also used relative to projectors to indicate the evened-out action produced by a damping roller or similar projector element that reduces wow and flutter in a soundhead.

stabilizer   A camera mount of any kind that is designed to minimize camera vibration. See DYNALENS, STEADICAM.

staff   For purposes of BUDGET and logistical planning, the staff is regarded as everyone but the performers. The CREW is the operational staff; all others, PRODUCTION STAFF. An example of production staff would be all those working on a given shooting assignment who work directly for the studio or production company: PRODUCER, line producer, PRODUCTION MANAGER, production associate, DIRECTOR (in some cases), production secretary and others. Those hired by their function are considered operational staff: CAMERAMAN, GRIP, soundman, STUNTPERSON, driver and others. Sometimes these categories are simply referred to as production staff or CREW.

stage   A filming room in which the sets are constructed and ACTION is filmed. Also called SOUNDSTAGE in films, and studio area in TV.

stage rental   Wall-to-wall rental of a soundstage for filming purposes. Sometimes basic lighting is included in the rental. It is important when renting to know: exactly what is included and what is not, i.e., whether or not there is a charge over-and-above the flat rate for the use of electrical current, or additional charges for office space, makeup rooms, dressing rooms, local phone calls, etc.

stag film   A pornographic film concentrating on explicit sex that is geared for male audiences.

staging   Full coordination and blending of settings, wardrobe, LIGHTING, costumes, CAST and action for filming.

stamper   Negative mold from which finished records are pressed.

Standard English   A paradigm of English usage based on the speech and writing of an "educated" person. More recently, American speech is referred to as Standard American English.

standard microphone   The most effective microphone for the special conditions under which it is to be used.

standard pitch   The note A. This tone is set at 440 hertz.

standard television signal   A TV signal that meets the technical and electronic requirements for an acceptable level of signal-propagation.

standby   A direction or signal to alert CREW and performers to be ready to start the next SCENE or SHOT immediately. Also, a person, such as a standby announcer, who can step in to fill in time if there are production holes or breakdowns, or if the program runs short, such as might happen in a special event. A standby is also a performer who can go on for another if the originally scheduled performer cannot, or does not, appear.

standby equipment   Backup equipment ready to expedite the resumption of operations as quickly as possible. Sometimes, this is a duplicate array of gear to fill in for any breakdown or malfuction in the primary unit.

standby light   A light, usually red or orange, alerting an actor or announcer that the next CUE is immediately upcoming. A radio term that is sometimes used in TV and film.

stand-in   Performer who is assigned to be a "substitute" for a star or featured player. The stand-in is usually the same sex, basic height and body build of the star, so that he or she can be used when the star's acting area needs to be lighted, or when there is a LONG SHOT on the back of the star riding away in a car, or when a given action by the star verges on stuntwork. Sometimes a stand-in is also a STUNTPERSON. See CAST.

standing set   A "permanent" set, i.e., one that will be used more than once, for a TV soap or game show, or for multiple-camera filming or taping of a TV series, usually a sitcom.

stand-up   An on-the-spot, present tense newscast in which the reporter is on-the-scene and standing up.

Stanislavsky method   See ACTOR'S STUDIO.

star   Leading player who is well-known and constantly publicized. The star has billing above the FEATURE PLAYERS, often with his or her name in larger lettering than either PRODUCER or DIRECTOR. All this, of course, depends upon the status of the star at the time of production.

star filter   Special FILTER that creates star-shaped HIGHLIGHT reflections. Used for visual emphasis, often to glamorize or romanticize a SCENE or product. It flourished in the late 1960s to mid-1970s and is still used today, but more sparingly.

starlet   Originally meaning "little star," and used to designate young female contract players or rising INGENUES. Today it refers to new female faces who have become TV or film regulars.

start mark   A synch mark on one or more film tracks, designating the point from which an operation such as printing, projection or synchronizing is to begin. Academy leaders incorporate two start marks, one for picture and one for sound.

stat   A reverse-printing card: black for white, white for black, used for titling and CREDITS.

state   Condition of a circuit, system, unit or component-element.

static electricity   An electrical field created from the electrical charge on various materials. A static charge on film may result in electric sparks. To be avoided or minimized during filming, editing or projection.

static interference   See ATMO-SPHERIC INTERFERENCE.

station break   A cue from the originating station to its affiliates to notify them of an upcoming interval between program segments, to be used for station identification, commercials, announcements, promos, etc. Also refers to the interval itself.

Steadicam   Trade name for a body-braced, self-balancing rig on which a camera can be mounted. Its gyro-balanced elements allow the cameraman to walk smoothly through crowds, into an elevator and out again, upstairs or downstairs, whatever is required. All of these actions can be filmed with maximum fluidity and minimal jolt. Panaglide is Panavision's counterpart to the Steadicam.

step-optical printer   LAB printer that exposes a specified film segment one FRAME at a time.

stereo   See STEREOPHONIC SOUND.

stereophonic   Multichannel sound. The more channels and diversity of placement, the more heightened the effect of being surrounded by the sound.

stereophonic sound   Sound recording, which can be divided into discrete playback channels, creating a third-dimensional audio ambience. Known informally as "stereo."

stereotypes   Standard "set" characters: the prostitute with a heart of gold; the gruff city editor with soft, sentimental core; the sensitive, young man who "finds himself" through love; the crackerbarrel philosopher. They become stereotypes through overuse.

stereotyping   Putting groups of people, by race, nationality, religion, occupation, or social class into a rigid conceptual mold. This stereotyping process is responsible for giving such unenviable concepts as the "lazy Mexican," "acquisitive Jew," "shiftless black," "ambitionless poor," "ruthless rich," "sophisticated French," "humorless British," "warmongering Germans," "crude blue collar workers," "effete homosexuals," etc. Fortunately, most of the racial stereotypes are disappearing.

Mass media has done more than its share in helping to disseminate and perpetuate these images, as well as some obnoxiously "affirmative" images: the always-smiling mom-dad-and-the-kids of the 1950s. Stereotyping can also be seen in type casting. Stereotypes dilute good characterization, dull the edges of an otherwise sharply drawn personality or event, present half-truths or nontruths as actuality and even pave the way for racial and religious persecution.

stet   Term taken from journalism and typesetting. From the Latin, it means, "Let it stand!" For example, a half-page of dialogue may be crossed out, then reinstated. To indicate this reinstatement, "stet" is written alongside the previously deleted material.

sticks   Nickname for a slate board.

still   A photograph taken with a still camera or a still shot blown up from a motion picture frame.

still cameraman   See CAMERAMAN.

sting   A musical chord, usually loud and staccato, within a SCENE, that gives dramatic punctuation to the action or serves as a SEGUE to the next scene.

stock footage   The material in a FILM LIBRARY that consists of SHOTS such as geographical or urban ESTABLISHING SHOTS, historical material and footage of other general application that is likely to be used on many productions over a period of time and is consequently kept in stock, catalogued and ready to use. These shots are of important events, famous places, and whatever it would be impracticable to shoot for each production.

stop   A fixed APERTURE designed to limit the amount of light passing through a LENS. Also applied to any specific setting of a movable lens diaphragm, which designates the effective speed of a lens working at other than its full aperture. See LENS, APERTURE, and LENS DIAPHRAGM.

stop frame   See FREEZE FRAME.

stop motion   See TIME LAPSE.

stopping down   The process of reducing the APERTURE of a LENS by means of a STOP or diaphragm.

stopwatch   The stopwatch used in media work is one specially calibrated into fractions of sections, sometimes with footage indications marked alongside its time-count indicating mark. It is used to time scenes, segments of film, narration and for marking time segments in a log book.

story   The once-upon-a-time plotline of the film or videotape. A skeleton on which the body of the screenplay can be built upon.

story board   Sketches of key plot incidents that can be easily visualized. These are placed in the action sequence of the film-to-be, numbered and captioned. It serves as a quick visual reference or explication of the screenplay. See STORY BOARD in Appendix.

story conference   A huddle for writers and top creative personnel, directors, producers, art directors, etc. The story is discussed and suggestions made for improvements.

story editor   Story-reader who evaluates scripts, treatments or story outlines submitted to the producer, director, film studio or production company. Story-reader weeds out the scripts and forwards only those that may have merit to the producer or director.

straight cut   Two contiguous shots, going immediately from one to another, with no intervening frames.

straight man   The performer who feeds the straight lines to the comic, so that the comic can deliver the gag line or punch line.

stray light   Any projected, unwanted light that does not produce screen-image.

strike   After filming, to take down all the SETS, electrical gear or special scenic or technical devices that have been specially rigged for a shooting session.

strip   A TV show running five days a week at the same time and on the same station each day.

stripe, magnetic   Narrow bands of sound-striping of magnetic oxide for recording sound; less frequently used as sound married to picture.

strip light   See BOARDER LIGHT.

strobe   Digital slow-motion that fractionates the action on the videotape into a sequence of freeze-frame images. Can be speed-controlled to create varying degrees of jerkiness or smoothness of movement.

strobing   A SCREEN image that moves in a jerking, fractionated way. This is especially distracting when perpendicular lines are moving quickly past the camera, e.g., panning a white picket fence, or a group of closely set architectural columns. Also, the deliberately produced effect of this movement, with a ghosting, trailing pattern following the direction of the action.

stroboscope Light that has a flashing frequency that can be set to work in the same rhythm pattern as a repeating motion, or fractionate movement into short consecutive bursts. When synchronous to the rhythm pattern, the moving object can be made to appear to be stationary, or at rest. If set at a rate not quite in synch with the moving device, it makes it appear to be moving in slow motion. Used for special TV and film effects, and for scientific analysis of movement or operational efficiency of a working object or animal, including the human animal.

strobotron Glow lamp used with electronic stroboscopes. It emits flashes of intense light with timed pulses.

student film One made under the aegis of a school (grade school, high school, college, trade school or university) and with undefined ownership. The minimal rates for the student filmmaker should be a shared copyright with the institution or its representatives.

studio Originally the production complex of a film company. Later it also meant a soundstage with attached offices, as in common current usage. Then, too, for the TV facilities of broadcasting stations: "We're going to videotape it at the NBC studios!"

studio camera See CAMERA, MOTION PICTURE TYPES.

stuntperson Originally differentiated as "stunt man" and "stunt woman." The performer who does the dangerous falls, leaps, trick horseback riding, fights, or whatever other potentially lethal actions are required, for the STARS or principal ACTORS. A stuntperson is often chosen

for a physical resemblance (at least, at a distance) to the actor being doubled.

stylus Cutting device, also known as a "needle," for making recorded discs. It is made of sapphire, steel or stellite.

subbing layer An adhesive coating that holds the film emulsion to its base.

subjective camera The viewpoint of camera-as-actor: You are now seeing this scene through the eyes of one of the principal actors. An example would be that of a hand-held POINT OF VIEW shot moving through a crowd. Used to intensify mood or given a sense of freneticism, violence or personal involvement in a scene, as well as to hold an audience. Attempts to carry a full-length feature entirely with subjective camera have not been successful; for example, *Lady in the Lake* (1946), directed by Robert Montgomery.

subject-to-camera Distance of the leading person or object in the scene to the camera lens itself. This point is often measured to the spot where the film is exposed as it goes through the camera.

subliminal cut A cut of a few frames; a miniscene lasting a fraction of a second used for intensification or foreshadowing.

submaster A secondary master that is often used to run off copies of a film print or videotape. It is often one immediate generation from the MASTER.

subplot A contrapuntal augmenting plot that follows the thrust of the primary plot. Used frequently to create tension by cutting back and forth between the two.

substandard A term used to describe all gauges or widths of film smaller than the theater standard of 35mm, the most important being 16mm.

subtext The real "message" beneath the veneer of words. The nonverbal ma-

trix of what a scene is all about. The
good actor and director use text as a
guide to the root of the scene—the subtext.

subtitles A translation of the DIA-
LOGUE into lettering, usually placed in the
lower third of the screen. Subtitles are
also used for closed-caption programs for
the hearing impaired.

subvoice-grade channel One of an
insufficient band width to function properly as a voice-grade channel. Often used
as a subchannel to a voice-grade primary
channel.

sungun A small, intense, hand-held,
battery-powered light. This hot portable
unit throws strong light in its immediate
area, and is used often in TV news coverage and DOCUMENTARY filmings.

superconductivity The decrease in
resistance and increase in conductivity in
tin, lead, thallium; etc., as the temperature moves downward toward absolute
zero. When the transition temperature is
reached for whatever materials are being
prepared for superconduction, resistance
will be nearly at a zero level. This allows
the manufacture of electronic equipment
with minimum dissipation of energy and
maximum operational efficiency.

supered titles (superimposed titles)
TITLES placed over stationary or moving
backgrounds.

superhigh frequency (SHF) A band
going from 3 to 30 GHz.

super Panavision Filmed in 65mm,
printed on 70mm, with an aspect ratio of
2.25 : 1 with 4-channel sound, or ratio
of 2 : 1 with 6-channel sound.

super-16 16mm film in which the
SOUND TRACK area is used to add extended width to the FRAME ratio. This
gives a larger image, and one that is in
wide-screen ratio. Used for low-budget
features, DOCUMENTARIES and short films.

Often blown up to 35mm master for
theatrical use.

supersonic Faster than the SPEED OF
SOUND. Frequencies above the normal
hearing range.

supersync signal Horizontal/vertical
sync signal used in commercial television;
at the end of each scanning line.

surface asperities Uneven surface
coatings on tape that cause imperfect
contacts between tape and record/play
heads.

surface noise Noise from a record
surface caused by uneven contacts of the
needle in the groove. Also called needle
scratch.

surface wave Ground wave traveling
along the earth's surface.

surge Abrupt changes in voltage level(s)
in a circuit.

surround channel Channels in a
sound system transmitting audio signals
to speakers deployed in various spots
within the theater to give the feeling of
"three dimensional" sound.

surround sound The sound produced by the various surround channels
that function simultaneously.

suspense An intensification of anxiety, danger or the "unknown" in an
already tense situation. Creates imbal-
ance in the audience's perceptions, throws
them off-track and shocks them suddenly
with the unexpected.

suspension of disbelief Dramaturgical term meaning to bring the audience
to a point of accepting whatever dramatic
premise must be acknowledged for the
entire story to have credulity. In films of
fantasy and strained story-points, this
suspension is often achieved by starting
the film realistically, then moving slowly
into the realm of fantasy; e.g., *The Ghost*

and Mrs. Muir, Frankenstein, Close En-
counters of the Third Kind, E.T. and
others.

sustaining A program without commercial sponsorship.

sweeps Overview ratings of all time
periods for every station in the United
States. Used to determine rates that can
be charged for time-selling, predicated
on a numerical head-count of viewership.

sweetening The addition of extra instruments to a music track that has already been recorded, either live or by
RE-RECORDING two recordings into one
COMPOSITE.

swing gang Crew on the night shift.

swish pan A type of panning SHOT
where the camera is swung rapidly on its
vertical axis, producing a deliberately
blurred, frenetic image. Also known as
whip pan, blur pan, zip pan.

switcher In TV, the control room
technician in charge of electronically
SWITCHING from one camera to another.

switching Altering the currents by
changing, making or breaking them in an
electrical circuit.

synch mark An editor's scratch mark,
greased-pencil indication or punched hole
to indicate the start frame of the picture
or SOUND TRACK.

synch pop Sound signal of one FRAME
at the front end of SOUND TRACKS, to
ensure alignment with the picture.

synch pulse Electrical pulsation added
to sound track by a synch-pulse generator to insure recorded speed synchronism.

synch-pulse generator The unit that
creates the synch pulse. It is inside the
camera, and sends the electrical pulsation
to the working tape recorder.

synchronism The relation between
picture and sound elements operating
with exact simultaneity. One speaks of
picture and sound as being in SYNCH.

synchronizer A device in CUTTING
ROOMS for maintaining SYNCHRONISM between picture and sound elements. It
consists of two or more SPROCKETs rigidly
mounted on a revolving shaft or drum.
The tracks are placed on the sprockets
and accurately positioned by their perforations, so that they can be wound
along by REWINDS while maintaining a
proper synchronous interlocking.

synchronizing generator Electronic
generator providing sync pulses to a TV
studio and its transmitter equipment.

synchronous   computer Digital
computer where all standard operations
are regulated by spaced signals from a
master clock.

synch-signal A voltage pulsation that
determines scanning synchronization.

synch sound Sound that matches
FRAME-to-frame with the picture; especially critical in lip movements as actors
speak dialogue in CLOSE SHOTS. The
frame-to-frame marriage of sound and
picture.

syndication Distribution of a program
or programs in the independently-owned-
stations market. Programs can be syndicated nationally, regionally or on a sta-
tion-by-station basis.

synopsis A short or preliminary version of the SCRIPT of a film. Also, a summary of a complete film, often intended
to be catalogued for future reference.

synthesizer Electronic unit that can
create multiple frequencies and produce
tones for musical notes or sound effects.

synthetic   stereo Using monaural
material and extending and reprocessing
it to create a "stereo sound."

system noise System output without any signal in operation.

T

T See TRANSFORMER.

tabletop photography Still or motion picture photography (sometimes used in videotape shooting) of objects shot at extremely close range with special lenses or with standard closeup hard lenses. Many shots where the camera moves over and around a bar of soap or a sponsor's package, picking out extreme close-up details are examples of tabletop photography.

tag Closing announcement at the end of a commercial or the closing word after the program material comes to a close.

tail End of a film strip of any length. When wound with the end on the outside of the film roll, it is often marked tails or tails out. See FOOT.

tailing Elongated, luminous spotting on the TV screen. These spots are also referred to as hangover.

tail-out See HEAD-OUT.

tail-slate A slate marking a scene at the tail end instead of the beginning of a scene. Sometimes, to compensate for possible synch drift, a slate is put onto both ends of a take.

take Each performance of a piece of action in front of a live camera is called a TAKE. Unless there is a special marking for scenes, takes are matched to scene number in the shooting script. For example, "Scene #1, Take #1" would be the slate for the opening scene of the film. The scene number would be shot as many times as necessary, with each filming having a separate take number. These take numbers are photographed on the scene I.D. section of the slate board, called out vocally for audio recording, and noted by the SCRIPT CLERK, as well as set down in camera and sound reports.

take-up reel The REEL on which film is wound after being run through film machinery such as projectors, cameras or printers.

take-up spool A plastic notched spool used in filming to take up film fed through the camera mechanism. A spool also acts as a CORE for the film ROLL itself. These spools are also used, in conjunction with FLANGES and split REELs in editing the film.

talent Any person or animal working as an on-camera, radio or microphone performer.

talent fees Costs in a commercial for those providing "creative services": actors, writers, composers, arrangers, announcers, etc.

talent union A guild representing and protecting performers: SCREEN ACTORS GUILD, AMERICAN FEDERATION OF TELEVISION AND RADIO ARTISTS, and SCREEN EXTRAS GUILD, among others. See UNIONS.

talkback A mic-and-speaker direct communications circuit between the TV control booth and the TV studio.

talkie Colloquial name from the late 1920s for a "talking motion picture," a picture with sound.

talking head A description of a style of reportage or DOCUMENTARY filming or videotaping in which the main themes are carried by the on-camera interviewees talking straight into the camera, as opposed to recreated events, CINEMA VERITÉ, or cutting away to those things the voice-over extended interview or narration are talking about.

talk show An informal interview/discussion program, starring a host/hostess, and featuring talks with celebrities, name performers, newsmakers, sports stars and others. It is taped before a live audience, in most cases, with a later release time, or in some cases sent out directly as it is being simultaneously taped for future use. Current examples: "Larry King Live," "Donahue," "The Tonight Show" and "Late Night with David Letterman."

tally lights Lights that go on to let the on-camera performer or crew know that a camera is live or on-the-air.

tank A pool of water on a studio lot, used for shooting aquatic scenes, the pool being used by itself or in conjunction with mechanical effects to simulate lakes and rivers, as well as the ocean. The Red Sea was parted in De Mille's *The Ten Commandments* by mixing footage shot in Egypt in the desert with special matting, augmented by close-up and medium shots filmed in the tank on the Paramount lot. Tank shots also include ship models at sea, plane models crashing into water, submarines or scale models submerging and re-emerging, heavy storms at sea, with the ship(s) cutting through the turbulence of wind and wave. The film *Das Boot* used a full-scale submarine conning tower, on which the actors stood amidst their simulated storm, as well as model shots of the "full" submarine.

tape Plastic-base audio or videotape (sometimes they are interchangeable) for electronic sound or picture—recording, transfer, mixing, multiple reproduction. The reproductive and recording coating is metallic oxide. Used as a verb, to record action, sound or picture on tape.

The measuring tape used by the assistant cameraman to establish the distance between the camera's focal plane and the subject to be filmed or videotaped. The accurate measurement between these two basic points allows for correct focus and PARALLAX adjustment.

tape cartridge Magnetic tape cassette or holder, prethreaded for immediate play upon insertion into its compatible playing deck.

tape deck Playing and recording unit that moves tape through the mechanism for either play or record.

tape drive The unit in a tape machine moves the fed-in, pulled-up tape past the sound heads.

tape player A play-only tape deck.

tape recorder Mechanical-electronic unit for recording sound: speech, music, effects, etc.

tape speed Rate of movement of tape past sound head(s) when playing or recording. 7½ inches per second (ips) for home and sometimes professional use. 15 ips is for professional use only, particularly for music.

tape splice Film SPLICE made with a butt splicer and a short bit of splicing tape.

tape splicer Piece of equipment designed to join film with professional splicing tape, either prepunched or punched on the splicer itself.

target audience An audience for whom a film or TV program is slanted or custom-made, and for which there has been a proven, active audience response in the past for a film in the particular genre. Defined, demographic portion of an audience that the client and station wishes to reach.

TBA See TO BE ANNOUNCED.

TBD See TO BE DETERMINED.

TD See TECHNICAL DIRECTOR.

teaser An introduction to an episode or special program (radio or TV) that catches the attention of the audience, in order to hold it through the COMMERCIAL BREAK and on through the entire program.

tea wagon Common term in film and TV for a small, wheeled console that is sometimes used by MIXERS when controlling audio on a soundstage.

tearjerker A dramatic (more often melodramatic) film or videotape relying heavily on pathos. Satirically rated by the number of tear-stained handkerchiefs it will take to get through the drama: one-hankie, two-hankies, etc.

technical adviser Person hired to give historical, technical or biographical information regarding the subject of a film or TV program. This information can be personal or general. For example, a retired star might act as a technical adviser on a biographical film. In more general approach, an expert on American history might advise on a film or TV program about the Civil War.

technical director (TD) In TV this is often the floorman. He or she cues actors and sometimes cameras, and ensures that all equipment is functioning properly, the last check-up being DRESS REHEARSAL or tech rehearsal. In film the TD coordinates the efforts of the various tech crews, i.e., sound with camera, SPECIAL EFFECTS with GRIPS, etc.

Technicolor One of the major world-class film laboratories, and one of the leading pioneers in color cinematography. The Technicolor three-strip process is considered by many to have been the ultimate in achieving beauty of color, and in separation and delineation. It was abandoned by the studios because it was too expensive to use for FEATURE-LENGTH productions. Replaced by updated 35mm and 65/70mm stock. The process is now being used in Asia, however, notably in mainland China.

techniscope An anamorphic system using 35mm film with half the frame height. This was blown up to full size, then squeezed down to an anamorphic image that was projected at a ratio of 2.35 : 1. The system was devised to save basic raw stock in filming for a wide screen.

telecast A TV broadcast; to transmit a television program.

Telecine Device used originally, and still used, for sending out motion pictures over the TV channel(s). Now it is also used to convert original film to video "prints."

telephoto lens A LENS, usually of greater than normal FOCAL LENGTH, so constructed that the back focus is different from the effective focal length of the lens: usually less, in order to increase compactness; sometimes more, to allow for the use of a WIDE-ANGLE LENS in a camera where a prism must be interposed between lens and film. More generally, this term is mistakenly used to mean a long-focus lens. See also LONG-FOCUS LENS under LENS.

teleplay A script for television. It is analogous to SCREENPLAY for film.

teleprocessing Transmission, reception, storage and retrieval. It is a system where data-processing is tied into a communications facility or electronic network. Initially an IBM trademark.

teleprompter Electro-mechanical cueing machine that projects the idiot board on a slanted glass plate in front of the camera lens. Because of the angle of the slant, the on-camera talent can see the text but the camera doesn't pick it up. This way it remains invisible to the audience.

telethon A portmanteau word combining television and marathon. A multihour TV special for the purpose of raising money for various charity groups, or through nonprofit organizations for immediate relief of a stricken country or area. The drawing-card attraction of these programs are the name stars who appear.

teletypewriter One of the basic units in a news room for receiving news stories from various press services: Reuters, Associated Press, etc. It types out the transmitted story onto a roll of paper, and is detached when the story is completed. See RIP AND READ.

televise   Transmission of a scene or image for reception on a TV monitor.

television (TV)   The full electrical/mechanical system for transmitting broadcast of picture and sound to receivers (TV sets). The transmitted broadcasts. Also, as a general term for the TV industry.

television screen   The wide and fluorescent end of the picture tube; its "screen."

television signal   Audio and video signals broadcast at the same time and transmitted through intermediate stages to a TV receiver.

telly   What the British call their TV set, i.e., "Let's see what's on the telly!"

Telstar   The first international TV satellite, using a microwave communications system, to receive and retransmit broadcasts from all over the world as they are happening.

test   A runoff and exposure of a few feet of film at the head of an undeveloped film roll, to see if there is printable and acceptable image before developing the entire roll or rolls.

test pattern   A chart filmed to check out the accuracy of lenses and the resolution of image. These patterned cards are designed to determine sharpness over the entire lens surface and within the camera's optical system.

that's a buy   Meaning, in TV, "That's an acceptable TAKE. Mark it O.K., and save it. In film, it means "That's a print."

theatrical film   One that is designed for use in motion picture houses in general or specialized distribution.

theme music   Music with a recurring motif or extended melody that identifies

a leading character, or a mood—romance, danger, violence. Sometimes the same theme is used for all situations in a theme-and-variations structure.

theme song   The identification to the ear of a weekly or daily TV show. Examples: "Sesame Street," "Mister Ed," "All in the Family," "The Golden Girls," etc. At times the theme song is a well-known standard; in other instances, it's written specifically for the program. Being the audio "logo" for the program, the name of the show is often carried in the lyrics.

thermal microphone   Microphone operating on variations in temperature in a heated conductor, a temperature that rises or falls as the sound waves strike the microphone.

thin   Describing a photographic image, the term refers to a picture with low density, overexposed, watery-looking, or diffuse. In film stock it refers to film thickness. The thinner the film stock the more footage that can be put onto a roll's diameter.

thirty-five mm (35mm)   For years, the standard motion picture FILM-STOCK size. It is still the working stock for FEATURE-LENGTH films and high-budget commercials. For features, however, it is sometimes replaced by wide-gauge film (65 or 70mm), or by 16mm, which is then blown up to 35mm.

threading   The act of placing film on the proper SPROCKETs and rollers, aligning it in the GATEs, forming LOOPs, and doing whatever else is necessary to ensure its proper passage through a camera, PROJECTOR, VIEWER or printer.

three-dimensional   Film system that produces the effect of real and tangible objects or persons in third-dimensional space. Usually requires special glasses for viewing. More commonly referred to as "3D," it has now not only been shown in theaters, but over TV as well. In 1935 MGM tried it, then let it subside. This used the red and green 3D glasses. 3D was resuscitated in 1952, in a desperate attempt to find something that could be shown in theaters and not on TV. The first 3D film of the television era was a badly written and minimally directed and acted opus called *Bwana Devil*. A few dozen 3D films followed, and more were in development, but the logistical problems of monitoring the special Polaroid viewing glasses, and getting them returned and redistributed, was too unwieldy. Then too, new widescreen processes were coming in, and the public preferred these to the awkward, and often headache-producing, 3D screening.

three-gun color picture tube Trigun picture tube with RGB elements, each gun controlled separately but the three brought into concord for color reception.

three-sixty A pan shot of 360°. This full-circle movement is also known as a 360 pan and a circle shot.

throat microphone One that fits snug against the larynx for audio in situations of a high noise level, where the ambient sound would otherwise drown out all else, i.e., inside a canning factory, the interior of a helicopter, next to a jackhammer at a construction site, etc.

throw Effective distance for holding a projected image clearly on the screen. Numerically bracketed to give suggested minimum/maximum distances. Ultimately, however, the efficiency of the throw can be no better than projector and film image.

throwaway line A line, delivered quietly in the course of dialogue, particularly in comedy, that stands out by the fact that is underplayed, not punched, "thrown away."

tight shot A shot in which the person or object takes up the entire frame. For people, it is called an EXTREME CLOSE-UP. Director's command: "Okay, you've got the close-up; now move in tight."

tilting Pivotal vertical movement, up or down, of the camera head. Contrast with panning.

timbre The specific differences in tonal color or musical sound between acoustical or electronic musical instruments; The individuality of each instrument as it plays the same note; the "character" of the instrument. The disparity of tones amidst the instruments is referred to as "differences of timbre." Pronounced TAHM-BER, with a soft "r" at the end.

time buyer Ad agency person who purchases open commercial broadcast time segments—for programming and commercials—for clients.

time coding The numerical synchronization of sound and film elements, encoded with matching numbers (frame to frame) to ensure synchronicity. See TIME-CODE SHEET in Appendix.

timed Evaluation of proper printer-light setting appropriate to a specific SHOT.

timed workprint One that has been color corrected scene-by-scene with appropriate printer-light levels for each shot. As opposed to ONE-LIGHT PRINT.

time-footage computer A footage-to-time card, consisting of a converting wheel (footage-to-time, 35 to 16mm differentials, and time-to-footage) and an accompanying columnized chart. Copyrighted by Alan Stensvold in 1944. See the Appendix.

time lapse A specific length of extended time between the exposure of each individual frame. Achieved by shooting, on a locked-down camera, one FRAME every few seconds, minutes, or other pre-set time frame. By using this technique, flowers grow rapidly before the eyes of film or TV audiences, clouds rush by at an incredible speed and traffic passes in a hectic, accelerated blur.

timer Person who makes the timing evaluations of each SHOT and decides how much, if any, color correction is needed.

timing   Sense of rhythm employed by an actor within lines and between lines. The sense of when to come in with one's dialogue. Important in drama, critical in comedy.

timing card   A punch-card or punched-tape, or computerized tape readout, that sends information to the film printing machine, so that it makes the proper color corrections. It is a guide list that gives printer-light numbers for making prints from the original film. The card is held for reference in making additional prints.

title   The registered name of the SCREENPLAY or teleplay. Also, the person in whose name it is registered, or to whom it is transferred by sale, lease or power of attorney, is said to "have title" to the script.

Title credits list the actors in a film and the technicians and staff who made it. Crawl titles are often used to carry closing credits of cast and crew. They "crawl" slowly upward on a large, unseen drum in front of the camera. Also called roll-up titles.

title changes   Changes made for marketing or legal reasons. Tennessee Williams' play *Orpheus Descending* was changed to *The Fugitive Kind, Sobbin' Women* to *Seven Brides for Seven Brothers, Eight Arms to Hold You* to *Help!* When D. W. Griffith made the novel *The Clansman* into a motion picture, he re-titled it *The Birth of a Nation.*

to be announced (TBA)   Indicates that a specific program or information will soon be available.

to be determined (TBD)   Usually found in scripts, TBD indicates that certain decisions have not been made yet. TBD would appear in the picture column of a script to indicate that an image has not been selected yet for a particular scene.

TODD-AO   70mm print system, in which prints are made from 65mm exposed negative, that was filmed with a customized camera. The added width of the film print allowed room for six magnetic sound tracks.

tone   Sound wave (transmitted) or sensation (received) having pitch; an auditory wave.

tone arm   Playing arm on a pivot of a record player. It contains the pick-up cartridge and "reader," i.e., electronic beam or needle.

tone control   A knob, level or handle that can be manipulated to vary the frequency response of an amplifier to the desired auditory result. The control intensifies or thins out the bass or treble part of the audio-frequency range.

top lighting   Lighting that is rigged directly above the action area.

total distortion   Entire complement of all varieties of signal distortions regarded as a full entity.

track   Film with audio-striping or magnetic metallic oxide professional recording tape, in whatever gauge, to work with the film print or videotape picture.

Also, grooved or speed rails on which a camera dolly makes a tracking shot. Sometimes on-the-spot improvised tracks are plain, long wooden boards.

tracking   Having precisely tuned circuits follow a frequency indicated by the tuning dial across the full tuning range.

Also, the stylus of a disc recorder as it records, or a pickup arm as it plays, moving along the record grooves.

Tracking is also used as a synonym for DOLLYING.

traffic   TV broadcasting department that handles programming and scheduling for the station.

tragedy   Dramatic work in which the leading characters go through painful or lethal experiences. This ambience of suffering and internal conflicts eventuates in dire calamity at best, and death at worst.

trailer Film at the end of a release print, on which is indicated the film title, the reel number and some film leader.

A trailer is also a short ad for upcoming films; a preview of COMING ATTRACTIONS.

training film An in-house "how-to" film, showing techniques and procedures to employees. Training films are often half instructional and half propaganda in order to educate and indoctrinate. The films are used in conjunction with live lectures, demonstrations and other media as part of an overall injection of information.

transceiver Two-way radio, transmitting and receiving. Used often on location for production coordination. Basically, for portable and mobile use.

transduction The conversion of energy in one form into another. For example, a microphone converts acoustical energy into electrical energy.

transfer To copy picture or sound being transmitted by one recorder onto another. Or, to make a tape copy from film.

transformer (T) Electromagnetic induction device that transforms voltage to a higher or lower magnitude, or to a different type of voltage; e.g., AC to DC, or vice versa.

transistor Semiconductor made from silicon or germanium. It has three basic electrodes: emitter, base and collector. It has almost fully replaced the electron tube.

transition Something that joins two scenes together, taking you from one to the other: a dissolve; a musical theme; a sound effect; an outgoing image matched by the incoming shot: a segue.

translucent Diffusion-material quality of soft light being transmitted in a lower intensity and more scattered pattern.

transmission Electronically transferring forms of intelligence, signals, messages, etc., from one point to another.

transmission system Interlinked elements designed to function as a transmitter of signal waves.

transmission time Measurable interval between transmission and reception.

transmitter Full complement of equipment for generating or amplifying a signal in radio or TV and sending it on to the transmitting antenna.

transparency process See PROCESS PROJECTION.

travel ghost Projectionist's term describing the "ghosts" that are created when the projector shutter is not calibrated properly. The "ghosts" make their appearance above or below dark areas, determined by whether the shutter is "ahead" or lagging behind.

traveling matte Two action shots, optically overlapped and filmed simultaneously on a special camera. This can put the performer in any setting required by the script, as long as the performer's action can be made to conform with the background action, or vice versa. This technique has been especially effective for performers playing dual roles and having to appear opposite themselves on the screen at the same time.

traveling shot One in which the camera moves bodily in relation to its object. The camera can be mounted on a car, crane, dolly, Steadicam mount, body-brace or whatever is required by the production demands.

treatment A more detailed form of a script concept than a synopsis or initial outline. It sets forth story and theme sequentially in a motion picture approach, without going into SCRIPT form.

treble   In harmonic music, vocal or instrumental, the higher part. The control unit on a recorder or mixing unit that can accentuate or minimize this range: 256 hertz, i.e., middle C, and higher. Also known as treble boost.

treble boost   See TREBLE.

tremolo   A wavering effect, where the tone fluctuations vary in intensity but not in pitch.

trespassing   To go on to another's land or property without permission or right. In media work it is considered trespassing to film or videotape while on another person's property unless permission has been granted by that person or his/her delegate. In news and documentary coverage, it is best not to trespass, even in an important story, as you can be arrested for it, particularly if you break-and-enter. Breaking-and-entering is only "heroic" in the movies. In real life it's more likely to be regarded as a felony.

triad   The three dots, a phosphor of each red-green-blue color-transmitting elements on the screen of the TV picture tube.

triangle   A device that is triangular or shaped like a three-pointed star, and which receives the three legs of a TRIPOD in order to prevent the legs from slipping apart. See SPIDER.

trim   The two carbons used in carbon-arc luminaires and projectors to create luminance.

In editing, to snip the film into lengths that are to be integrated into the assembly or to bring it down in length.

trim bin   A traveling, wheeled bin with a loose cloth inner liner (to protect the film from dirt and dust) in which the physical film trims are stored.

trims   Film segments that have been removed and are put on hold in the TRIM BIN.

tripod   A simple three-legged support, often used to hold FIELD CAMERAS as well as studio cameras. Also called LEGS.

tripod head   Interlocking, rotating device that connects the camera to the tripod.

trucking   See DOLLYING.

trunk circuit   Circuit connecting switching centers.

T-stop   Amount of light, minus absorption and reflection, that reaches the LENS. This is in contrast to an f-stop reading, which gives an overall indication of the transmitted light. See F NUMBER.

tubby   See BOOMY.

tuned   Set to function and resonate at a given frequency.

tuner   Electromechanical unit for tunning, particularly an audio/video recorder or receiver.

tuning   Adjusting input of a circuit's frequency to achieve maximum operation efficiency.

tuning control   Control knob, button or lever that adjusts tune circuits.

turntable   Revolving plate for playing or recording records.

turret   A revolving mount attached to the front end of a camera, carrying three or more LENSes and enabling them to be swung quickly into position in front of the photographing APERTURE.

TV   See TELEVISION.

TV-cutoff   Grid in a film camera viewer showing the TV-cutoff area and indicating SAFE-ACTION AREA. Also, the cropping of a film frame in TV transmission.

TV-Q   Audiences awareness rating of TV stars that is used to gauge their popularity. This is accomplished by demographic referencing from other sources, and by direct phone surveys, augmented by one-to-one live queries by field interviewers.

tweeter A loudspeaker that reproduces and emits only the high frequencies of the audible sound spectrum.

two-track recording Splitting ¼″ tape into two tracks/channels, allowing for using the tracks as a stereo pair, or as separate monophonic tracks.

two-way communication Communication equipment or system for sending and receiving.

Tyler mount A vibration-eliminating camera mount, developed by Nelson Tyler, and developed first for aerial use, primarily helicopter. Now it is also used for hood mounts, boat deck mounts, etc.

type-casting Casting for appearance first, talent second. Filling roles with actors who have played a similar role in the past or who are of the exact appearance described in the script. Also, a DI-RECTOR or PRODUCER will say, "Get me a Marlboro, outdoors type," or "Get me a Kevin Costner type!"

U

Uher Workhorse portable audio recorder, replaced by the Nagra. Still used in studio-recording situations.

UHF See ULTRAHIGH FREQUENCY.

ultrahigh frequency (UHF) Has the frequency designation and specified range of 300–3,000 megahertz.

ultrasonic cleaner A combined use of cleaning liquid activated by ultrasonic waves. Used to remove dirt or excess material on the film surface.

umbrella and stand A silverized photographer's reflection umbrella for bouncing light directly into the scene and indirectly onto the actors or set pieces. Often used in commercials for photographing the sponsor's product, it originated with still photography.

unaffiliated An independent broadcasting station not contractually associated, or directly part of, a major network.

unauthorized use Unethical and sometimes illegal use of films, video and audio tapes. People have been running off unauthorized film prints from the earliest days of motion pictures to the present. Today, however, more tape copies are printed than films, for the simple reason that it is much easier and far cheaper to make tape instead of film copies. Depending upon the utilization of the copy, a substantiated case of unauthorized use can be regarded as either a misdemeanor or a felony.

undercrank The term originated in the silent film days, when cameras were hand-cranked. To run the camera slower than sound speed (24 fps), resulting in speeded-up action when the developed image is projected.

underexposed Film that has not gotten enough light within the camera, resulting in dark, flat images without sharpness. Underexposed film, especially when black and white, is often unusable because the images cannot be distinguished. It is the opposite of OVEREX-POSED.

underground film A term popularized in the late 1960s and early 1970s, denoting a film that is too volatile in its subject matter or experimental in the treatment of that subject matter to be commercial. They are usually independently produced and generally underfinanced. Many film buffs described Stanley Kubrick's 2001: A Space Odyssey as a multi-million-dollar underground film.

underplay To perform a role in a low-key, restrained manner.

understudy One who is rehearsed in the star's role and ready to appear if there is any problem that prohibits the star from performing. More common on stage than in film or television.

underwater housing A waterproof casing in which a camera can be inserted and totally enclosed but still be operated outside this casing; for underwater filming.

undeveloped Film that has been shot but not yet put through the LAB for development.

unexposed Raw stock not yet exposed to light; virgin, unused stock.

unidirectional Moving solely in one direction, i.e., DIRECT CURRENT.

unidirectional microphone One that picks up sound from its front side—the live side. But the back side is "dead," and picks up no sound, being inactive.

uniformity For tape to maintain a consistency of output of a level functionally equivalent to the recorded input.

union A working person's organization. The craftsmen and artists working at the major studios are almost all union members. In independent, off-the-lot film and tape productions, the employees are often a mix of union and nonunion. The unions are supported primarily or solely by membership dues. The function of these unions and guilds is to set up working rules, adjust base rates, arrange for membership meetings and social functions, negotiate with management, call strikes, issue bulletins, and, in some unions, offer legal advice and intern openings for those starting out in the particular discipline of the union.

union card A card that is issued to UNION members to show their active status. It is supposed to be on the person of any union member who is working on a production, or on salary at a studio or production company.

union list A list put out by the UNION to its membership of signatory and fair-practice production companies. Union list also means a roster of those who are on active status and available for employment. Also, a list of nonsignatories or companies whose labor practices the union deems unfair.

unit manager The person in control of the business aspects of a production unit on LOCATION.

unit production manager (UPM) PRODUCTION MANAGER assigned to a specific filming group or production. A LOCATION MANAGER.

United Press International (UPI) A major news-wire printout service.

Universal Studios A major motion picture studio, turning out products for theatrical and television distribution. Also, the location of MCA's "black tower" world headquarters. Known internationally as the home of the studio tour, which is its greatest net-dollar-producer.

unpublished motion picture In copyright law an unpublished motion picture is a film (or tape) that has no copies for sale or distribution. Copyright can be obtained for such film/tape by sending a title, description and copyright form to the Copyright Office in Washington, D.C., along with the current registration fee.

unsteadiness Unwanted and totally distracting amount of vertical movement on the screen, emanating from the projector.

untuned Not resonant in any immediately available frequency.

up If an actor or actress has the lines down cold and comes in quickly on CUE, that person is "up in his/her lines." However, if the performer begins a TAKE, suddenly goes blank, and with a glazed stare says, "Sorry, I'm up," he or she has momentarily forgotten the lines. To say that a performer is "really up in performance" means that the person is working with full technical and creative capacity, with high energy.

up and under A music or SOUND EFFECTS term that originated in radio and is randomly used in SCREENPLAYS and teleplays. It means that the music or sound has already been established as a presence behind the scene, and now should rise, then drop back under to a BACKGROUND presence, allowing other sound to have FOREGROUND prominence. For example: The scene is an office building. Both music-of-the-city scoring and traffic sounds are heard behind the DIALOGUE of the actors. The scene then switches to outside the office, in the busy street below. The music and street noises come up to full strength; the scene switches to back inside the office, and once again traffic sounds and music drop to a background presence.

UPI See UNITED PRESS INTERNATIONAL.

uplink Signal transmission from a ground station to a SATELLITE.

V

value Brightness measurement of color.

variable area recording Recording onto a soundtrack laterally divided into opaque and transparent areas.

variable density recording Recording by means of an OPTICAL-SOUND recorder, designed to produce a number of density gradations perpendicular to the edge of the sound track and extending across its full width. The distance between gradations is determined by the recorded frequency.

variable-speed control A mechanism that varies the speed (fps rate) at which a camera runs.

variable speed motor The driving device of the VARIABLE SPEED CONTROL.

vault Climate-proof, fireproof storage spaces for film or tape. Its temperature and humidity make it particularly appropriate for the storage of original materials.

VCR See VIDEOCASSETTE RECORDER.

velocitator A movable camera mount intermediate in size between a DOLLY and a BOOM. It will carry a heavy camera up to a height of about 6′, but it is not intended to be raised or lowered rapidly while the camera is running. The movement is ordinarily hand-operated.

velocity-lag error Gap between input and output of a device, directly proportional to variable rate-of-output.

velocity microphone Microphone which has an electrical output corresponding directly to incoming soundwaves. Basically bidirectional.

verification Checking and rechecking a news or documentary story for detailed accuracy, preferably from more than one source.

very high frequency (VHF) VHF was the original TV band; it has a frequency band of 30–300 megahertz and a wavelength of 10–1 meters. See UHF.

very low frequency A band below 30 kHz, with a wavelength of 10 to 1 meters. ·

VHF See VERY HIGH FREQUENCY.

VHM A ¼″ home tape-recording format; the Beta system.

video A common name for television, in general; the TV sets were first called "videos." A prefix meaning "television," as in videocast, videomasking.

In script forms, a designation on a two-column script, to indicate the picture (video) as opposed to the column that connotes SOUND. See also MUSIC TELEVISION.

video amplifier Part in a TV circuit that amplifies video frequencies once they are demodulated.

video assist A small videotaping camera, recorder and PLAYBACK system that records filmed TAKES directly through the film-camera and sound units, with the capability of playing back any take immediately after it is completed. This allows the DIRECTOR, PRODUCER (if it is a commercial, the client and ad agency producer or account executive) to view and evaluate the take before deciding whether to move on to the next scene or first to go for another take. Also called video playback.

video carrier The signal that carries information regarding sound, picture and nonaudible/nonvisible technical information.

videocassette recorder (VCR) Any VIDEOTAPE recorder that records and plays back a tape in any of the formats: ½", ¾" or 1". The ½" system most common in America is the VHS; the ¾" is the U-Matic system. The 1" system is used almost exclusively for professional VIDEO recording, replacing the standard 2" tapes used originally for television broadcasting. The 1" tape does not operate with self-contained cassettes, but with recording tape moving from feed roll to take-up roll. Reel-to-reel 2" tape is now used for multi-track sound-recording.

video data digital processing The enhancement and equalization of video signals using a digital computer system.

videodisc A disc or "recorder" that stores images to be electronically reassembled for VIDEO transmission. A CD is its audio counterpart.

video enhancer Special circuit to enhance the picture, by improving detail and color intensity. Used often to sharpen low-quality images, in dubbing.

video format There are three fundamental VIDEO-broadcasting formats in the world. In the United States and Japan, NTSC; in the rest of the world, the PAL or SECAM system.

video frequency Signal-voltage frequency derived from the TV scanning process that carries the picture information.

video integrator Device utilizing signal redundancy to minimize noise in the signal-to-noise ratio.

video leader Professional heads/tails LEADER, SMPTE-approved, for video film.

video mixer Electronic unit that combines signals from two or more TV cameras.

video playback See VIDEO ASSIST.

video processing Electronic adjustment of a video signal for specific purposes, such as increasing brightness, varying color quality, etc.

video signal Image-carrying signal for TV. Zero to about 4 megahertz. The signal also contains necessary equalizing and synchronizing pulses.

videotape Tape for recording and playing back a VIDEO scene. TAPE can refer to either AUDIO tape or videotape, the specific meaning to be determined by context.

videotape recorder A unit that records TV sounds and picture signals on a tape that can be played at another time.

viewer Film-editing apparatus that presents images from the film that is being edited. These images are enlarged to various sizes and can be shown at any speed required, or stopped on a particular frame for evaluation.

Also, a single member of the TV audience, regarded as the basic unit in most demographic surveys for television.

viewfinder An optical device forming part of a camera or attached to it, which provides an image (usually magnified) closely approximating that which is formed by the LENS, and that strikes the film. The direct viewfinder is one that usually incorporates a FOCUSING MICROSCOPE which enables the cameraman to scrutinize the image which the lens is actually transmitting to the film. It therefore requires no correction for PARALLAX. The monitoring viewfinder is one that is external to the camera. It enables the cameraman to watch the scene while the camera is turning. It is ordinarily equipped with accurate compensation for parallax, and in some designs gearing is provided to couple the finder to the lens-focusing mount. The reflex viewfinder is one that sees through the lens while the picture is being taken. It is constructed with a silvered mirror on the back of the SHUTTER, which allows a continuous image to be formed for the eye (while the same is happening to the film) through the PERSISTENCE OF VISION. The brightness varies with the lens APERTURE.

viewing filter The classic lorgnette-like glass filter that the cameraman or director holds up to the light to evaluate it. It gives him an estimate, either for INTERIORS or EXTERIORS, of how much light and what quality will be needed for the scene.

vignette A short dramatic sketch. Some programs or films are made up of thematic vignettes: "Saturday Night Live," *Twilight Zone* (the movie), *New York Stories.* A variety show is made up of vignettes of music, dance, drama and comedy.

vignetting A camera term meaning that something outside the LENS is cutting into the field of vision, e.g., a LENS HOOD, a MATTE BOX, a lighting GOBO, or when the lens is wider than the full APERTURE. Result: an extraneous image within the frame.

virgin tape Film stock not yet exposed, or videotape on which no audio and visual signal has been recorded. Also called RAW TAPE.

visual effects A broad term that includes, and is sometimes synonymous with, SPECIAL EFFECTS. In its wide application, it means not only special effects but also SETS designed for light absorbency, pushed-stop filming, and customized LAB instructions; as well as special LIGHTING and creative utilization of standard camera FILTERS, SPEEDS and LENSes.

visual primary A term meaning that the visual aspect of a film dominates the sound.

visual transmitter TV transmitter for picture only.

VO See VOICE OVER.

voice-grade channel Channel functional for transmission of speech. Frequency range: 300–3000 hertz.

voice-operated device A unit or system that can be activated and even controlled by the human voice.

voice over (VO) Voice of unseen speaker (narrator, commentator, actor, host/hostess, announcer, etc.) that is heard above a shot or scene. See OFF-SCREEN.

voice test Vocal analogue to a SCREEN TEST. Audition for an actor, announcer or narrator, to determine voice quality and interpretation of text.

voltage Electrical force creating the "pressure" to make the current flow through an electrical conductor.

volume Intensity measurement of a train of sound waves. Informally, the "loudness" or "softness" of a sound.

volume control Device for altering the loudness of a radio or TV receiver; a variable resistor.

volume range Maximum and minimum levels of VOLUME (measured in decibels) that a system can handle.

VTR See VIDEOTAPE RECORDER.

VU meter Volume-units meter used on many sound recorders and PLAYBACK units to register loud/soft gradations of amplitude.

W

W See WATT.

wafer A thin sheet of silicon or germanium serving as a semiconductor-base. Works with parallel faces of matrices and microunits.

walk-on A performance bit with no lines for the performer.

walk-through A marking rehearsal in which the performers give only cue lines relative to positioning, or use no dialogue at all. Usually, it is a rehearsal for the benefit of the crew, so that the camera sees where it has to be when, the sound crew determines how it will have to adjust to camera and to performers, and the lighting and grip bunch what, if any, adjustments have to be made during the shot.

Walla-Walla A radio term meaning a general background burble of conversation. It comes from the actors' off-mike sound, as though mumbling "Walla-Walla." Occasionally used in TV and film production.

walla plate Hunk of metal with an attaching bracket or slot that can be secured to a wall or heavy piece of timber and be used to support a scenic light.

Walt Disney Company See DISNEY STUDIOS.

wardrobe Clothes worn by performers, either self-supplied or provided by the studio. They are called "costumes" when other than contemporary standard street wear. Technically, a costume is anything that is designed and fabricated for a particular performer or group of performers.

wardrobe department All costumes, street wardrobe, materials and personnel responsible for wardrobing a film, including the special truck and the wardrobe master or mistress.

warm-up A welcoming and orientational introduction to relax and inform a live studio audience before taping a show. It relies heavily on topical humor and audience participation.

Warner Brothers Early film studio dating from the "silent" days. At that time it was on the verge of bankruptcy, and decided to gamble everything on a new sound process called Vitaphone. It supplied the SOUND TRACK for the first full-length "all-talking, all-singing" motion picture (a talkie). From this, Warners became one of the major studios, and remains so today.

warning bell In the projection room, a bell that rings a few moments before the end of a motion picture REEL to alert the projectionist that the next reel is coming up, and to standby the other projector to make the switchover.

On a soundstage, a loud bell or klaxon-horn that sounds off on the SET just before the TAKE begins. This alerts everyone to be quiet, and to ready themselves for the take. Two bells means that the take is over—an all-clear signal.

warning light Red blinking or rotating light outside a movie or TV stage that means the filming is underway; be quiet and do not enter the stage until the light is switched off.

watt Power expended as 1 ampere of direct current flow through a resistance of 1 ohm. In alternating current a watt is a multiple of effective volt-amperes by circuit power.

wave Physical undulations in an electrical current (rising/falling, advancing/retreating) as it moves through a medium.

wave band Band of frequencies considered as a single entity, assigned, for example, to a communications system or outlet.

wave-band switch Switch in a receiver or transmitter that can change frequency bands by physically moving to various positions.

wave length As used in media, it refers to broadcast frequencies.

wave machine Mechanically or manually driven apparatus that works in a studio tank to create waves for production shots, either for full-sized people and objects or for scale models.

wave trap A trap to beep out unwanted signals or interference. Wave-traps are control-tunable.

wax pencil A crayon-like "lead" in special "pencil" used for marking film.

weave Horizontal frame motion apparent on the screen; from bad print or loose feed and take-up system in the projector.

wedge Short piece of film that is optically darkened, frame-by-frame, which allows the calibrated gradation to be lab-evaluated.

west Left side of an animation field chart.

westerns A film genre that started with *The Great Train Robbery,* and has continued ever since. It is a drama (or comedy) that takes place in the American West, with wide-open scenic grandeur, grubby little frontier towns, and farms and ranches. These are the "classic" westerns, which take place from the end of the Civil War (1865) to the turn-of-the-century. There are also contemporary westerns: *Lonely Are the Brave, Electric Horseman, The Misfits.*

wet cell Liquid electrolyte cell allowing for free-flowing electrical output.

wet-gate printing A system that saturates the printing stock with a solution of tetrachlorethylene prior to its exposure to the master or original. It does away with most scratches by filling in gouged areas, and minimizes such effects to produce a cleaner, sharper image on the print.

WGA See WRITERS GUILD OF AMERICA.

whip A sudden, rapid movement of the camera. For example, a SWISH PAN.

white TV white is made up of a pre-calibrated mixture of R-G-B (red, green, blue). This is accomplished by simultaneous excitation of all three phosphors.

white balance An electronic camera evaluation and setting activated by a WHITE CARD that signals to the video camera, "This is your white reference." Using this referent, the camera adjusts its colors accordingly. This videocamera adjustment can be used with varying light sources: indoor or outdoor, fluorescent or incandescent, etc.

white camera tape To be differentiated from GAFFER'S TAPE or black/gray friction tape. Used mainly to put around the circumference of film cans, both to keep the cans together and to prevent light leaks. Also used as blank labels for marking the cans with production information particularly relating to lab instructions. Used for this same function of information-labeling on SLATES. Sometimes used on film magazines with light-leak problems.

white card Plain white smooth-finished cardboard or art-board used as the visual WHITE BALANCE referent.

white light Light producing a color analogous to sunlight at noon.

wide-angle lens A LENS allowing a framed view of 60° or more. Used to photograph the panoramic, or to include as much of a scene as possible that is shot in cramped quarters, like in a submarine film. In brief, to give a broader playing area to a given scene.

wide-band axis Color TV transmission band width.

widen To open a shot by DOLLYING or ZOOMing back, or physically walking the camera back with a Steadicam.

wide open The iris of the LENS opened to its fullest, allowing a shot to be made at the lowest possible f-stop.

"wild" recording Any sound recording that is not made synchronously with the picture. SOUND EFFECTS and random voices are usually recorded this way; also called non-synch.

wild sound bite Recorded sound segment, usually recorded on the spot, such as factory noise, sirens screeching and fire crackling or roaring. These sounds are used in the edited news videofilm.

wild spot A broadcast commercial not integrated into the body of a program, but one that is broadcast locally during a station break.

wild wall A wall of a set that can be moved so a camera can be placed in the spot that the wall occupied and the wall be refitted into the set for REVERSES. This allows for the shooting of all four walls of a set while not limiting camera moves.

wind machine A massive, electrically powered fan, from a regular wall outlet or generator, that simulates various degrees of wind from light breeze to tumultuous windstorm. In some action shooting, wind machines create their effects with power-driven airplane propellers.

winds FILM STOCK for loading into a camera is wound emulsion side in. This is called a B-wind. Double-perforated stock for filming is wound the same way. A-wind stock is rarely used in filming, but is wound in this manner: emulsion side up, and with the single sprocket on the opposite side of the film roll, ready for printing. In TV, A-wind is when the coated surface of the tape faces toward the hub; B-wind is when it faces away from the hub.

wind sleeve Protective device to keep wind away from microphone, made of a light porous plastic that slips over the live microphone. See ZEPPELIN WINDSCREEN.

wipe An optical transition effect between two succeeding SHOTS on the SCREEN, in which the second shot appears and "wipes" the first off the screen along a visible dividing line. Wipes may be from top to bottom, side to side, or in any one of a large number of patterns. See FLIPOVER WIPE.

wireless mike A minitransmitter and microphone combination that can be concealed in or on the performer's clothing, and is in "radio" contact with the receiving tape recorder.

wirephoto facsimile Photographic facsimile usually transmitted over a phone line or via a telegraph system.

woodshedding Originally a musical term meaning, "going to the woodshed and practicing on that instrument over and over until you get the sound you're after." It now applies to actors, announcers and other performers, and means to go off alone to a place and practice music or rehearse lines.

woofer Loudspeaker used to reproduce the low frequencies of the sound spectrum, in opposition to TWEETER.

working title One given temporarily to a media project. It may continue on through all phases of production and then be changed or allowed to stand in final release form of the film, videotape or recording.

workprint A LAB print from developed ORIGINAL, used by the EDITOR to first synch up the sound, and then to put into a first ASSEMBLY. The visual material used for the final editing.

Also, a sound print that contains original sound, DUBBED sound, SOUND EFFECTS, etc. The musical track is generally added later. Used for final assembly and fine cut of the film.

wow Sound-reproduction distortion from speed-drive variations of turntables or tape-drive mechanisms.

wrangler See ANIMAL HANDLER.

wrap To end a shooting day. As a noun: "That's a wrap!" As a verb: "Okay, let's wrap it!" At the end of filming: "That wraps the picture!"

wratten filter Camera filter for filtering out a specific band of light or intensifying that band by other filtration. Used originally in motion picture cinematography; now also on TV cameras.

Writers Guild of America (WGA) Screenwriters' union with bicoastal headquarters in Los Angeles and New York City.

X

xenon arc Short arc in quartz sheet (the "envelope") that uses DC current going from cathode to anode to make an electric arc in the xenon-gas atmosphere. The color spectrum and tonality of this light is similar to daylight.

xenon bulb Quartz bulb powered by the XENON ARC, by the two xenon-enclosed electrodes. Usually called a xenon tube.

xenon projector A motion picture theater PROJECTOR that replaces the arc projector. Its advantages are that it uses a bulb instead of a burning carboniferous element, allowing a longer use of the projector before the bulb is changed and not requiring a full venting system to carry off the extreme heat generated by an arc projector.

xenon tube See XENON BULB.

xmitter Short for TRANSMITTER.

X-rated One of the five ratings given to films in RELEASE. "X" means that the material is for "adults only," that is, those seventeen or over. Some states make this 18 or over, or even 21 and over. The "X" rating is theoretically for excessive violence or explicit sex, but few films have received an "X" rating for violence. After receiving an "X" rating and then going on to win an Academy Award for Best Picture, Midnight Cowboy brought about a reevaluation of the rating, especially considering the modest scene of non-explicit sexuality which gave it that rating. Pornographic films are automatically rated "X." In fact, "X-rated" has become synonymous with "porno films." The X rating has recently been replaced by the designation NC-17. See MOTION PICTURE ASSOCIATION OF AMERICA.

X-sheet Animation filming sheet with written exposure specifications.

X-wave One of two waves divided by Earth's ionosphere. The other is the "O" (for ordinary) wave.

Y

Y-cable See Y JOINT.

Y-connected circuit A yoked, three-phase circuit, allowing two sources of current to feed into one circuit, or one source to be bifurcated.

yellow Minus-blue color subtractive utilized in the three-color film process.

yellow filter group A series of FIL-TERS in the yellow range, used to intensify the yellow hues of a scene.

yig devices Solid-state filters for wideband tuning in microwave circuits.

Y joint An electrical connection of a main-trunk cable, branching off into two cables with connecting units at all three ends. Also called Y-cable.

yoke A holding frame for LAMPs and REFLECTORS, mounted on a special stand, plate or clamp; or safety-chained to an overhead grid support.

yo-yo A verb describing the movement of a mike or camera that PANS back and forth within a SCENE. Also called ping-ponging.

Y-signal Luminance transmission primary, used for color pictures, for detailing and brightness. This information is carried at 1.5–4.2 megahertz range.

Z

Zeppelin windscreen A long tube with perforations on its frame and cloth inner lining that works with the SHOTGUN mike, to cover and protect it from wind, thereby greatly reducing or totally eliminating wind noise. A type of WIND SLEEVE.

zero transmission-level reference point Preselected point in a circuit. Its level becomes a reference for subsequent transmission levels.

zip pan See SWISH PAN.

zone of silence A geographical area between two transmitting/receiving points where regular radio signals cannot be heard.

zoom The apparent motion of the camera toward or away from its object is known as zooming, either as a zoom in or zoom out. This is accomplished with a ZOOM LENS. See PULL BACK.

zoom lens A LENS of variable magnification that enables zooming effects to be easily achieved without moving the camera toward or away from its object. Parallactic effects, which usually accompany real movement, are absent from zoom lens shots, which are therefore most useful when the object is at a great distance, i.e., following the ball in motion on a football field. The lens has wide use in television, where cameras often cannot move with great speed or are even locked in to a given spot, i.e., at political conventions or an awards telecast.

APPENDIXES

Note on the Appendixes

All of the forms included in this Appendix can be used at any level of media status—tyro, apprentice, journeyman, master. They are professional tools that will prove to be invaluable in actual production situations.

They are listed in order of use, starting with the script, then moving to pre-production forms, to production sheets and post-production logging records.

CONTENTS

Appendix I: Script Form (Theatrical)

The theatrical script form is for feature films, usually fictional. The old-fashioned script with each shot indicated as to angle is now a dinosaur. It has taken about a century for studio heads to realize that directors pay little or no attention to specific shot angles and moves indicated by the writer. So today, scripts are simpler, written in "master scenes" similar to a stage play.

Immediately following the theatrical script form is a script in an educational/industrial form, used for educational films, some documentaries, motivational films, in-house training films, etc.

EXT.: HELGA'S DRIVEWAY. ABOUT A HALF HOUR LATER. A JEEP-TYPE TOP-DOWN VEHICLE COMES WHEELING IN RAPIDLY, NOISILY.

INT.: THE MAIN LIVING ROOM-DINING AREA OF HELGA'S HOME. THERE ARE A NUMBER OF WELL-GROOMED, EXPENSIVELY ALMOST-DRESSED WOMEN, AND FEWER MEN...MOSTLY YOUNGER. A HOUSE-COATED SERVANT WALKS OVER TO HELGA AND WHISPERS SOMETHING IN HER EAR. SHE NODS, AND EXCUSES HERSELF.

EXT.: HELGA'S DRIVEWAY. THREE YOUNG MEN AND A DRIVER SPRING OUT OF THE JEEP. THEY COMB THEIR WINDBLOWN HAIR. LO AND BEHOLD! WHO IS THE DRIVER BUT <u>DMITRI</u>.

HELGA COMES OUT OF THE HOUSE, SPOTS DMITRI.

HELGA

Ahh, Dmitri...I like your friends.

SHE GOES OVER TO DMITRI, TAKES HIS HAND, SLIPPING SOMETHING INTO HIS PALM AS SHE GREETS HIM.

HELGA

A little something for your efforts.

DMITRI

My pleasure.

INT.: LIVING-DINING ROOM.

INTO THE FESTIVITIES BARGE HELGA WITH DMITRI AND FRIENDS.

LORRAINE

Ohh, my God, it's Dmitri. (SIGHS) Ohh,

well---

MARTIN

Dmitri!? How did he get to---

LORRAINE

He <u>does</u> get around.

227

Appendix II: Script Form (Educational/Industrial)

The script form on the facing page is one that is used for corporate-image films, educational-informational structures, and commercials. Commercials, however, usually have a sketched image in the "picture" or "video" column, of each basic setup.

This particular form shown here is an educational-informational script on Galileo and his times.

NARRATOR:

War. 78–80

Famine. 82–84

Revolt. 86–89

Europe in the sixteenth century 91–92
was a world torn and bleeding.
The Spanish Inquisition had spread
throughout the Western world . . .
the Huguenots driven from France.

It takes great men to bring order 94–95
out of world chaos. In 1564,
two of the greatest men in the
history of the Western World were
born. One was born in England.

His name: William Shakespeare. 97–98

The other was Galileo Galilei 99
of Italy.

Galileo was born in the city 100–101
of Pisa.

His father had begun his own 103–104
career in science . . .

(CU: DRUMSTICKS DRUM-
MING A TAMBOUR)

(FULL SHOT: "FAMINE"
FROM HOLBEIN'S "TO-
DENTANZ")

(FULL SHOT: OPEN SKY. A
SPEAR MOVES IN; A
SWORD CROSSES THE
SPEAR)

(FULL SHOT: MAP OF 16th
CENTURY EUROPE)

(CAMERA MOVES IN TO
CU OF ENGLAND)

(CAMERA PANS ACROSS
MAP TO ITALY)

(FULL SHOT: PRINT OF
PISA)

(LIVE SHOT: BOILING
WATER IN ALEMBIC)

Appendix III: Budget Form

The budget form on the facing page is known as a Top sheet, Front sheet or Summary sheet. For each numbered category on the Top sheet, there is a fully detailed, 17-page breakdown of that category within the full budget.

For example, item #8, Production Staff Salaries, is broken down into subheadings such as PRODUCTION MANAGER, FIRST ASSISTANT DIRECTOR, CASTING DIRECTOR AND STAFF, LOCATION AUDITOR and other members of the PRODUCTION STAFF.

Note: Categories #1–#7 are *above-the-line* items; #8–#22, *below-the-line*.

PICTURE BUDGET DETAIL

TITLE _____   PICTURE NO. _____

DATE PREPARED _____ , 19 _____

ACCOUNT NUMBER	DESCRIPTION		TOTAL		TOTALS		TOTALS	
1	Story							
2	Continuity and Treatment							
3	Producer							
4	Director							
5	Cast							
6	Bits							
7	Extras							
	Sub Total							
8	Production Staff Salaries							
9	Production Operating Staff							
10	Set Designing							
11	Set Operation Expenses							
12	Cutting - Film - Laboratory							
13	Music							
14	Sound							
15	Transportation - Studio							
16	Location							
17	Studio Rental							
18	Tests and Retakes							
19	Publicity							
20	Miscellaneous							
21	Insurance - Taxes - Licenses and Fees							
22	General Overhead							
	Sub Total							
	Grand Total							

Approved _____   Producer

Prepared From _____ Page Script Dated _____

_____ Day Shooting Scheduled at _____   Studio

Director _____

Budget by _____

_____

ENTERPRISE STATIONERS 7401 SUNSET L. A. CA. 90046 (213) 876-3530

Appendix IV: Break-Down Sheet

The break-down (also "breakdown" and "break down") sheet on the facing page is a basic information sheet that is usually filled out by the assistant director or production manager.

It indicates the scenes and/or pages to be filmed/videotaped, gives the location of the set, whether it is a day or night shoot, names of cast and crew needed, etc. The headings are mostly self-explanatory, once it is understood that "EST" stands for *estimated*, "PGS" for *pages*, "D" or "N" for *day or night*, and "SC" for *scene*.

At the studio these sheets are handed out to cast and crew with required advance-notice times acceptable to the various unions and guilds.

This advance-notice sheet does not take the place of a call sheet.

BREAKDOWN PAGE NO.

D or N	SET OR LOCATION				TOTAL SC.
					TOTAL PGS.

SC #	PGS.	EST. # SET-UPS	EST. PROD. TIME	DESCRIPTION

CAST	SILENT BITS, ETC.	EXTRAS

WARDROBE		PROPS, ETC.	PRODUCTION NOTES
CAST #	CHNG. #		

ENTERPRISE STATIONERS 7401 SUNSET L. A. CA. 90046 (213) 876-3530   ⑦⑨

Appendix V: Storyboard

The facing page has a basic form for storyboards, which may be clustered together or printed in separate panels (larger than those pictured here) and pinned up on a work-board in order to study them.

The upper narrow box above the drawing-space is for scene number identification; the box below it allows for a few words to describe the image.

If more detailed dialogue is to be added, the caption-box can be enlarged. It can be at the top of the drawing-space or below it.

For commercials the captions are often typed in one vertical column, matching up to the sketched or photographed image in the vertical column alongside.

The storyboard reads like a comic strip, left to right, top to bottom. The first six boxes have been filled in as examples.

MUSIC: INTRO.	⟶	CAR CLEARS FRAME
[OPTICAL BLACK] FADE INTO:	[FULL TITLE-SUPERED OVER SHOT OF CAR ON HIWAY] DISS TO.:	
LANDSCAPE ONLY	⟶	INSERT: SPEEDOMETER
	[SUPER IN CREDITS AS LANDSCAPE GOES FROM COLOR TO SEPIA]	[AT 60 AND CLIMBING]

Appendix VI: Deal Memo

The deal memo on the facing page has all the key elements needed for such a notational agreement as to basic terms. Implementation of their terms, and extensions of specific and updated contractual points would be handled in a letter of agreement or a full contract.

In the items listed as "ACTOR'S *CORPORATION NAME*" and "ACTOR'S *CORPORATION I.D.#,*" these terms are applicable to the actor who has his own corporation and is running all payments through that corporation. He/she is being "loaned out" through the instrument of a personal corporation.

"PAYMENT FOR: (NATURE OF PAYMENT)" refers to whether the payment will be in cash, cashier's check, company check with all proper city, state and federal withholdings, or if the sum will be paid in a gross amount, letting the actor's corporation or DBA entity handle all taxes and deductions.

"AMOUNT" refers to gross or gross/net payment. This can be against the total amount due or, in brief assignments, the full total amount.

CORPORATION   DATE:

DEAL MEMO

PROJECT

JOB NUMBER

FROM:

TO:

RE.: (ACTOR'S NAME)   SOC. SEC.#:

ACTOR'S ROLE:

JOB CLASSIFICATION:

COMPANY NAME:

ACTOR'S CORPORATION NAME:

ACTOR'S CORPORATION I.D.#:

AGENT'S NAME:

ADDRESS:

PHONE NUMBER:

RECORDING DATE:

TIME:

PLACE:

PAYMENT FOR: (NATURE OF PAYMENT)

AMOUNT:

Appendix VII: Directorial Reminder Sheet

This is a good sheet for beginners, or for veterans who don't use storyboards.

An additional aid for quick scanning and instant orientation is to have anything relating to sound or picture color-coded for spotting. For example, let's say "red" is for picture, "blue" for sound. Not only would SOUND be marked with a *blue* marker and the category PICTURE with a *red*; but if a note under the heading "TIMING" related to *sound*, then a blue marker would be used. If under ACTORS a note referred only to *picture*, it would be marked in *red*, etc.

Also, should a special effect (under the heading CAMERA) need work in both *picture* and *sound*, a third color can be used.

"LAST MINUTE IDEAS/OTHER INFO. AND REMINDERS" can be either marked in corresponding colors, or done completely with a regular black-inked ballpoint pen, or pencil. The latter choice of pencil would be more useful if the notes are going to be typed up immediately by one of the production staff.

DIRECTORIAL REMINDERS   SEQUENCE(s)#: _____

ESSENCE OF SCENE/SEQUENCE or SHOTS: _____

CAMERA: (Special Effects & Pivotal Action underlined)*

SOUND: (O.S. Effects & Audio Emphasis underlined)*

TIMING:

ACTORS:

LAST MINUTE IDEAS/OTHER INFO. & REMINDERS:

239

Appendix VIII: Production Calendar

The production calendar (facing page) is a standard working-tool, particularly when a local/regional production house is working with either an out-of-town client or ad agency, or both. Copies of the calendar include the time allocated for the shooting of the industrial or commercial film that is to be made. In this case, it is a commercial, and there is only one *shooting day,* and ten *prep days.* These are active prep days in the pre-production period immediately prior to the shoot. This does not include the concept and development stages, or the drawing-of-contracts period.

Often, along with this sheet, there is a contact list of the staff and crew, with names, addresses, and all phone numbers—fax numbers too, if applicable.

Copies of these sheets are given to all clients who are going to be present at the shoot and all members of staff and crew.

These are all fictional company names, but the schedule is from an actual shoot.

CLIENT: Transcon Airlines

AGENCY: Sharp and Duro

AGENCY PRODUCER: Mercedes del Rosario

ART DIRECTOR: Marci Quayle

DIRECTOR: Ty Randt

PRODUCER: Wes Lake

(MONTH, YEAR)

SUNDAY	MONDAY	TUESDAY	WEDNESDAY	THURSDAY	FRIDAY	SATURDAY
	1 PREP CASTING	2 PREP LOCATION SCOUT	3 PREP CASTING LOCATION SCOUT	4	5	6
7	8	9	10	11	12	13
14	15 PREP CASTING	16 PREP LOCATION SCOUT	17 PREP CASTING LOCATION SCOUT	18 PREP LOCATION SCOUT	19 PREP SCOUT IN S.F.	20
21	22 PREP CLIENTS ARRIVE L.A.	23 PREP CASTING CALLBACKS	24 PREP CLIENTS TRAVEL TO SAN FRANCISCO	25 PREP	26 PREP TECH SCOUT STILL SHOOT	27 SHOOT
28	29 HOLIDAY	30 WRAP DAILIES CFI 11AM RM #5	31		31	

241

Appendix IX: Call Sheet

The call sheet is an information page given to crew and cast, notifying them of time, place and other relevant information regarding the next shooting day.

At the studio the call sheet is handed out to each staff, crew and cast member as the shooting day nears completion. On location the call sheet is usually slipped under the door of each room. It goes to all members of the production team: cast, crew and staff.

On the facing page is a typical call sheet.

As well as handing out the sheet itself, the "call" is also given by an assistant director, who states the call time-and-place while handing out the sheet.

PRODUCTION:_____

DATE:_____

CAST	CALL	CAMERA/SOUND/LIGHTING EQUIPMENT AND FILM STOCK

Appendix X: Release Forms

These personal release forms cover most on-camera, still camera or videotape/film camera situations.

The one on the facing page, the personal release form, is used with this or comparable wording in filming theatrical or news and documentary films or taping comparable videotapes. In documentary and news coverage, the open space that follows the words ". . . we agree to pay you the following amount . . ." is filled in with a simple disclaimer, i.e., "no payment," "payment waived," "reportage/no payment" or something similar. If payment *is* to be made, the agreed-upon amount is filled in in that space.

"Photographed by" is followed by the name of the production company or still photographer, and "film tentatively titled" with the working title and/or production number of the project.

On the page following the personal release form is a form with the heading "RELEASE—Authorization to Reproduce Physical Likeness." This is used mostly for models in still photography, but can be used for film and videotape as well. "For good and valuable consideration, the receipt of which from . . ." is followed by the name of the employer. "I hereby grant to said . . ." repeats the name of the employer or the specific representative in the form of an agency producer or production company executive, the still photographer himself, or his/her representative.

PERSONAL RELEASE FORM

THIS WILL CONFIRM that I have agreed to be photographed by

and its successors (hereinafter called PRODUCER) and that PRODUCER will own any and all rights in said photography of me on the film tentatively titled

This will permit PRODUCER to proceed with the said photography and I now waive, as to PRODUCER and its successors, assigns and licensees, all personal right and objections to any use to be made of me, my name or my personality in connection with the use of photography containing my photograph, for any and all motion picture, radio and television purposes, and performances thereof, accompanied by any narration and dialogue whatever, and the publicity in connection therewith, and/or for any other trade and advertising purposes. I understand that in proceeding with said photography PRODUCER will do so in full reliance on the foregoing permission.

In consideration of the above release, we agree to pay you the following

amount ....

Dated...

SIGNATURE:...

PRINT NAME HERE:...

ADDRESS:...

....

....

....
Witnessed by

ENTERPRISE PRINTERS & STATIONERS, HOLLYWOOD, CALIF. Telephone: 876-3530   99

RELEASE

AUTHORIZATION TO REPRODUCE PHYSICAL LIKENESS

For good and valuable consideration, the receipt of which from _____

is acknowledged, I hereby expressly grant to said_____
and to its employees, agents, and assigns, the right to photograph me and use my picture, silhouette and other
reproductions of my physical likeness (as the same may appear in any still camera photograph and/or motion
picture film), in and in connection with the exhibition, theatrically, on television or otherwise, of any motion
pictures in which the same may be used or incorporated, and also in the advertising, exploiting and/or publicizing
of any such motion picture, but not limited to television or theatrical motion pictures. I further give the said company the right to reproduce in any manner whatsoever any recordations made by said company of my voice and all
instrumental, musical, or other sound effects produced by me.

I hereby certify and represent that I have read the foregoing and fully understand the meaning and

effect thereof and, intending to be legally bound, I have hereunto set my hand this _____day of

_____ , 19_____.

WITNESS: _____

_____   _____

ENTERPRISE PRINTERS AND STATIONERS · PHONE 876-3530 86

246

Appendix XI: Time-Footage Computer

The Stensvold Time-Footage Computer was computing before the personal electronic computer appeared so suddenly and prominently upon the world scene, before the neologism "teleprocessing" was put into circulation.

Alan Stensvold was a professional, working cameraman, and a member of the American Society of Cinematographers, who found it a constant irritation having to stop and compute footage shot, footage remaining and/or running time remaining on a film roll. What was needed was something that would do that computing instantly. The result was the Time-Footage Computer.

There are similar graphs, wheels and charts in the American Cinematographer's Handbook and other trade publications, but the accuracy and convenience of the Stensvold Time-Footage Computer, with its time–to–footage concordance wheel on one side and the corresponding graph on the other, have made it a simple, workable at-hand tool—a basic one for professional and beginning cinematographers.

It is a great aid in computing, i.e., "figuring," "calculating," ratio of final running length/time of footage against whatever the projected ratio is of footage shot against footage used, 3-to-1, 20-to-1, 200-to-1, or whatever that ratio is.

On the next page is the conversion wheel. On the page following that, the graph.

THE
16-35 MM MM
PROFESSIONAL
TIME-FOOTAGE
COMPUTER

CONSOLIDATED FILM INDUSTRIES
959 Seward St. • Hollywood, Calif., 90038
HOllywood 9-1441
•
Copyright 1944
by
ALAN STENSVOLD, A.S.C.

35mm & 16mm

FILM

FOOTAGE

TABLE

16mm FOOTAGE EQUALS
4/10 x 35mm FOOTAGE

CONSOLIDATED

FILM

INDUSTRIES

•

959 Seward St.
Hollywood, Calif., 90038
HOllywood 9-1441

SEE OTHER SIDE FOR
16mm—35mm
TIME-FOOTAGE COMPUTER

SECONDS	35MM FOOTAGE	16MM FOOTAGE	MINUTES	35MM FOOTAGE	16MM FOOTAGE
1	1½	⅗	1	90	36
2	3	1⅕	2	180	72
3	4½	1⅘	3	270	108
4	6	2⅖	4	360	144
5	7½	3	5	450	180
6	9	3⅗	6	540	216
7	10½	4⅕	7	630	252
8	12	4⅘	8	720	288
9	13½	5⅖	9	810	324
10	15	6	10	900	360
11	16½	6⅗	11	990	396
12	18	7⅕	12	1080	432
13	19½	7⅘	13	1170	468
14	21	8⅖	14	1260	504
15	22½	9	15	1350	540
16	24	9⅗	16	1440	576
17	25½	10⅕	17	1530	612
18	27	10⅘	18	1620	648
19	28½	11⅖	19	1710	684
20	30	12	20	1800	720
21	31½	12⅗	21	1890	756
22	33	13⅕	22	1980	792
23	34½	13⅘	23	2070	828
24	36	14⅖	24	2160	864
25	37½	15	25	2250	900
26	39	15⅗	26	2340	936
27	40½	16⅕	27	2430	972
28	42	16⅘	28	2520	1008
29	43½	17⅖	29	2610	1044
30	45	18	30	2700	1080
31	46½	18⅗	31	2790	1116
32	48	19⅕	32	2880	1152
33	49½	19⅘	33	2970	1188
34	51	20⅖	34	3060	1224
35	52½	21	35	3150	1260
36	54	21⅗	36	3240	1296
37	55½	22⅕	37	3330	1332
38	57	22⅘	38	3420	1368
39	58½	23⅖	39	3510	1404
40	60	24	40	3600	1440
41	61½	24⅗	41	3690	1476
42	63	25⅕	42	3780	1512
43	64½	25⅘	43	3870	1548
44	66	26⅖	44	3960	1584
45	67½	27	45	4050	1620
46	69	27⅗	46	4140	1656
47	70½	28⅕	47	4230	1692
48	72	28⅘	48	4320	1728
49	73½	29⅖	49	4410	1764
50	75	30	50	4500	1800
51	76½	30⅗	51	4590	1836
52	78	31⅕	52	4680	1872
53	79½	31⅘	53	4770	1908
54	81	32⅖	54	4860	1944
55	82½	33	55	4950	1980
56	84	33⅗	56	5040	2016
57	85½	34⅕	57	5130	2052
58	87	34⅘	58	5220	2088
59	88½	35⅖	59	5310	2124
60	90	36	60	5400	2160

Appendix XII: Time-Code Sheet

Time-code in videotape is analagous to edge numbers in film. Some videotape, however, that is transferred from film, but to be edited on tape, will use both the time-code and edge numbers. This sheet is primarily for tape, so the term "REEL" is sometimes referred to as "ROLL" instead.

The "SCENE" designation is the slated scene. "TAKE" is the same as in film, also. "TIME CODE IN" indicates the footage count to the frame at which the desired shot comes in, so that "TIME CODE OUT" means the last frame of the scene, at which point that frame goes *out* and the new frame of the next shot comes *in*. "NOTES" are reminders to the editor and/or director. They can be about color corrections within a scene, or sound, or denote a word-cue for a cut or dissolve, or any required operation.

The cues are run in sequence, each cue going straight across the page in a direct left-to-right horizontal reading. Each cue follows its preceding one directly above it. Sometimes a space is left between cues, so that additional shots can be denoted later.

This is a basic form, but each production company should work with whatever form is best for them, as long as it has areas for all the pertinent information and is easily readable. This sheet is used both in off-line and on-line, although some on-line forms may also have TIME CODE IN/TIME CODE OUT columns for sound only.

	SCENE	TAKE	REEL	TIME CODE IN	TIME CODE OUT	NOTES